SABOTAGE

SABOTAGE

A Study in Industrial Conflict

Geoff Brown

SPOKESMAN BOOKS

First published in 1977 by:
The Bertrand Russell Peace Foundation Ltd.
Bertrand Russell House
Gamble Street
Nottingham
for *Spokesman Books*

Printed in Great Britain by
Bristol Typesetting Co. Ltd.
Barton Manor
Bristol

ISBN 0 85124 158 1

To Sue and Noah

'Sabotage does not necessarily mean destruction of machinery or other property, although that method has always been indulged in and will continue to be indulged in as long as there is a class struggle. More often it is used in a quieter way. Excessive limitation of output is sabotage. So is any obstruction of the regular conduct of industry.'
Frank Bohn, 'Some Definitions : Direct Action—Sabotage' in *Solidarity* (USA) May 18, 1912

'. . . deliberate violence is, no doubt, a relatively minor fact in the case, as compared with deliberate malingering, confusion, and misdirection of work that makes up the bulk of what the expert practitioners would recognise as deliberate sabotage.'
Thorstein Veblen *On the Nature and Uses of Sabotage* (1919)

'There is no need to smash machinery if one's ends can be served by less destructive methods, and there are forms of sabotage, . . . much more capable of clogging the wheels of capitalism than the outright smashing of the machine itself.'
William Mellor *Direct Action* (1920)

'Sabotage consists of the workers putting every obstacle in the way of the ordinary modes of work. . . . The term itself is derived from the French word, *sabot*, wooden shoe, and means *to work clumsily as if by sabot blows*. The whole import of sabotage is actually exhausted in the motto, for bad wages, bad work.'
Rudolf Rocker *Anarcho-Syndicalism* (Indore, n.d.)

'. . . the productivity of capital is itself partly determined in the class struggle. It is part of what labour and capital are bargaining about when they debate manning, productivity, the speed of the line, the introduction of new equipment and so on.'
Andrew Glyn and Bob Sutcliffe *British Capitalism, Workers and the Profit Squeeze* (1972)

Acknowledgements

This book started life as a talk given to a group of people at Ruskin College, Oxford, in 1972 at the request of Raphael Samuel. Since then it has been much added to and revised, though I remain grateful to the people at Ruskin, and especially to Raphael, for the warm response they gave it and for the many new lines of enquiry they suggested. The book would never have seen the light of day had it not been for the enthusiasm and encouragement of Ken Coates; and nor could I have done without the pertinacity of Ken Fleet in demanding the manuscript. Tony Topham was kind enough to give the book a thorough reading and to suggest a number of improvements—some of which, I regret to say, I have been too stubborn to adopt. John Parrott gave me invaluable help with the chapter on the car industry, both in the form of material and stimulating conversation during the few months in which I was supervisor for his Diploma thesis at Ruskin College. Over the last few years I have learnt much from conversations with Sigurd Zienau, and I am grateful for the suggestions for further reading that he has given me in connection with this and many other subjects. I wish also to thank Keith Bradshaw and George Johnston, not only for the help they have given me on specific points, but also for their comradeship in the normal course of our joint endeavours in the promotion of working class adult education. Mrs. Sheila Oscroft was kind enough to help with the typing, and for this I am most grateful.

None of these people should, of course, be blamed for the book's many theoretical and analytical inadequacies, nor are they responsible for any of the judgements made in it. People in Workers' Educational Association and university extra-mural classes in Nottinghamshire and Derbyshire—especially the miners in Sutton-in-Ashfield and engineering and foundry workers in

Derby—who have been subjected, unwittingly, to parts of it are also to be thanked for their ideas and criticisms. Above all, I wish to thank Sue and Noah Brown for their companionship and support.

Contents

Introduction

I hope that readers will not feel disappointed because this book does not deal exclusively or even primarily with industrial sabotage in its sense of deliberate destruction or disablement of machinery. I do not here follow the allegedly 'broad definition' of industrial sabotage employed by Laurie Taylor and Paul Walton in their pioneering, but not always satisfactory, essay on the subject : 'that rule-breaking which takes the form of conscious action or inaction directed towards the mutilation or destruction of the work environment (this includes the machinery of production and the commodity itself).' ('Industrial Sabotage : Motives and Meanings' in S. Cohen, ed., *Images of Deviance*, Harmondsworth 1971, p. 219). In this book I have instead adopted the considerably broader definition of sabotage that was developed by revolutionary syndicalists and industrial unionists around the turn of the century. This definition was admirably summarised by the young Guild Communist, William Mellor, in his book of 1920, *Direct Action*. Mellor explained that :

> 'Sabotage means the clogging of the machine of capitalist industry by the use of certain forms of action, not necessarily violent and not necessarily destructive. It is commonly supposed to mean, purely and simply, the smashing of machinery, either by the direct breaking-up of or by rendering them useless by methods involving a deterioration of their value and efficiency. This idea of sabotage is very partial and unfair. The machinery of capitalism can be clogged quite effectively without the employment of that form of sabotage which expresses itself in destruction.'

Walton and Taylor are, however, to be thanked for giving attention to a much neglected phenomenon—one, indeed, that

xi

seems to be protected from discussion and exploration by the existence of a powerful taboo. It is greatly to be regretted, however, that they perpetuate the view of sabotage as exclusively involving the destruction or disablement of the means of production, and also that they give further circulation to the hoary old myth that the word 'sabotage' itself derives from the fact that clogs were thrown by French speaking workers into their machines in order to damage them. This may well have happened, but in fact the word *sabotage* derives from the older French usage involving the word *sabot* : such as 'dormir comme un sabot' (to sleep extremely deeply or heavily) and 'travailler comme un sabot' (to work slowly, clumsily, and over-deliberately).

Only rarely in recent years has sabotage been discussed as a labour movement tactic in the sense that it was thought of by the syndicalists in the past. Very little has been said about it since the turn of the century when it was brought to the forefront of discussion by Emile Pouget and his comrades in the C.G.T. in France—our starting point in this book. In more recent years the writings of the *Solidarity* group on sabotage have been a notable exception to the general neglect of the subject. Academic writers have, by and large, ignored it altogether. The three page discussion of sabotage in the sense that it was used by the syndicalists in K. G. J. C. Knowles' book *Strikes* (1952), where it is included in a section headed 'By-forms of industrial warfare', remains one of the best and most accurate accounts of the subject. The only other academic paper of any substance is that by Richard S. Hammett, Joel Seidman and Jack London called 'The Slow-Down as a Union Tactic' (in the *Journal of Political Economy* of April 1957). As those authors point out, the 'slowdown' is one of the least written about 'types of pressure employed in union-management relations.' They define the 'slowdown' in a way that would have struck a chord with many of the original advocates of sabotage :

> 'a form of on-the-job activity in which workers, while appearing to be engaged in their usual routines, deliberately limit their output in order to exert pressure upon management to make some desired change.'

The authors observed that the 'slowdown' was 'fairly common' in American industry and to make their point they argue that 'Few would disagree with the worker who said : "You can always put out more work. No man puts out all he can." ' They also note that sabotage of this sort to be effective needed to be highly organised, but that did not mean that workers needed to be highly union-minded or even unionised. The 'slowdown' or sabotage, in fact, often involves workers in by-passing official union structures and procedures. Unions have not often openly advocated sabotage—even in the form of deliberate output restriction (or 'ca'canny' as it has been called in the British labour movement) let alone in its sense of machine-breaking. The case involving the National Union of Dock Labourers in the late 1880s and early 1890s with which this book starts represents one of the few occasions when the tactic has been given official union blessing. But there has, in fact, been plenty of sabotage in British industry since the days of the National Union of Dock Labourers. And it has been both cause and consequence of much of the development of management thought and practice. The literature of the conflict between capital and labour is, as I hope to show, littered with frequent references to sabotage. The disjunction between capital's view of what constitutes a 'fair day's work' from labour, and labour's own views on that subject have been and still are central to 'industrial relations'. Restriction of output has been one of the most abiding complaints by managers about workers—and much managerial effort has been devoted to attempts to eradicate it. I hope that those against whom these complaints and efforts have been directed will find this book helpful.

Geoff Brown

Part One

SABOTAGE AND THE SYNDICALISTS

I

EMILE POUGET AND THE C.G.T.

In June 1889, Havelock Wilson's young but rapidly growing National Amalgamated Sailors' and Firemen's Union was organising strikes in various ports throughout Britain. In many places the dock labourers came out too. This is what happened in Glasgow. On June 11th Edward McHugh, a former commercial traveller and friend of Henry George, brought the union he had formed in February 1889, the National Union of Dock Labourers, out on strike in Glasgow.[1] The strike met with a quick response from the port employers in Glasgow. Very quickly blacklegs were brought into Glasgow in considerable numbers from Dundee. The men from Dundee got the police protection they had been promised, and quickly set to work. But they soon left work in a body after the strikers managed to make contact with them and to explain their case. Sixty labourers from Tilbury, brought in by the employers to replace the strikers, turned back for London once they found that the labour shortage they had been going to fill had arisen because of the strike.[2] Similarly, men from Leeds turned back when they discovered the real reason for their being needed.[3] But these small victories for the strikers were not enough. Blacklegs were coming in from all over Britain, and the promise on the company posters that police protection would be guaranteed was being honoured. Edward McHugh and Richard McGhee could do little more than to call for increased picketing.[4]

There were a number of serious scuffles between strikers and blacklegs. At one point McHugh told some blacklegs that he feared for their lives, since some of his men had revolvers.[5] But all this was to no avail. The employers were clearly determined to break the strike. They had imported hundreds of blacklegs from Scotland, and especially from England.

3

In this way they were more or less able to keep up the regular hours of sailing, and to deal with the cargoes. They told the press that they were 'not unwilling to fairly remunerate their employees; but they have resolved at all costs to reduce the influence of the union, observing that the shipowners all over the country are determined to be the masters, and not a few strangers, who, as a committee, . . . interfere with the shipping commerce of the country.'⁶

On June 23rd the strikers held a meeting at which the whole situation was considered. At this meeting such points as 'their severance from the union, the rate at which the Englishmen can work, the rates of wages, and so on . . .' were discussed. The *North British Daily Mail* reported that:

> 'None favour the idea of renouncing their combination as a union; indeed that seems to be the last right they would forego, maintaining they have equal rights with tradesmen in having a society of their own. Trades, they say, have less need of unions than bodies of men numbering thousands, and whose work is more irregular. Again, they flatter themselves of being able not only to discharge or load a ship in less than quarter the time taken by inexperienced hands, but they rejoice in being able to deal with cargo with far more caution.'⁷

It is highly likely that amongst the points raised in this discussion between the strikers about the inefficiency of the blacklegs is the fact that one of the 'scabs' was drowned after falling into the river while wheeling a truck along a plank.⁸ This dramatic illustration that dock labour was not an 'unskilled' occupation, was constantly borne out by the performance of the 'scabs'. Their speed of work was much slower than that of regular dock labourers; it took more of them to load and unload cargoes than it did the dockers. Although this fact was not openly admitted by the shipping companies there is some evidence that they would very much like to have seen the dockers return to work. A small incident bears this out. As the strike continued into July, a rumour arose that the Allan Line offices were so dissatisfied with the work of the blacklegs that they wanted to re-employ the dockers. Although this had been denied officially by the Allan Line, one of the foremen at the Allan Line sheds had pleaded with the strikers to go to the boss, 'as they were sick of the men they had at present, and could not get on with their vessels at all.'[9]

Shortly after this the National Union of Dock Labourers made a final effort to settle the strike. Deputations were sent to the various firms asking if they were willing to grant the union's demands. When this last-ditch attempt failed, the Union decided to call the strike off in order not to exhaust all its funds. At a meeting of the dock labourers on Friday, July 5th it was resolved to return to work at the old rate on the following Monday.[10] On Monday morning before the dock labourers went back to work they were addressed by Edward McHugh. He told them :

'You are going to return to work today at the old rate. The employers have repeatedly said that they were delighted with the services of the farm workers who have replaced us over the past few weeks. We have seen them; we have seen that they don't know how to walk on a boat, that they have dropped half the stuff they carried; in short that two of them can't do the work of one of us. However the employers have said that they are delighted with the services of these people; let us therefore do the same and practice ca'canny. Work like the farm workers worked. Only it happened that several times they fell into the water; it is useless for you to do the same.'[11]

The Glasgow dockers returned to work, and for two or three days went 'canny', and worked as slowly and inefficiently as the blacklegs had worked. It was not long before the employers called for McHugh and pleaded with him to ask his members to work how they used to work. If they did the dockers would get the ½d. an hour rise they had failed to get by striking.[12] The success of the ca'canny tactic at Glasgow led McHugh and McGhee to make it the distinctive policy of the union. Reviewing the first full year of the N.U.D.L's activities and looking back to the Glasgow strike, they wrote :

'The distinctive policy of the Union was inaugurated in Glasgow during the great strike of June, 1889, and was the logical outcome of the publicly proclaimed satisfaction on the part of the employers with the work—small in quantity and wretchedly bad in quality—done by scabs. Then as now we were advised in the organs of the shipowners "to take a few lessons in political economy" . . .'

The N.U.D.L. took its lessons, and reported that :

'Having mastered all the mysteries of the doctrine of value and the distinction between "value" and "price", we were made familiar with the multitudinous forms of orthodox adulteration from jerry buildings and coffin ships to watered milk and shoddy clothes. With only one exception we found the all-prevailing practice to be this, that the "QUALITY" of each commodity, whether it be a dwelling-house, a suit of clothes, or a Sunday's dinner, is regulated according to the price which the purchaser is willing to pay—the one exception being labour.

'We began to ask ourselves and our fellow-members why the "quality" and "quantity" of labour should not be subject to the same law as other marketable commodities. We were witnesses of the fact that a trifling increase in wages was scornfully and insultingly refused to Union men, whilst at the same time inexperienced and consequently inefficient scab labour was imported at enormous cost and trouble, and paid at higher rates than were asked by Union men, and, in addition to higher wages, we saw the scabs delicately entertained and provided with free food and lodging, tobacco, and beer,—the ability to do these things demonstrating beyond the possibility of doubt that the demand made by Union men was a very modest one indeed, and one which the employers could easily have afforded to grant.

'We had the most convincing proof of the *limited quantity* of work done by scabs in the detention of vessels, and of the *inferior quality* in the fact that the ships when stowed were pronounced unseaworthy. For these unsatisfactory results the employers paid generously.

'There is no ground for doubting that the real relation of the employer to the workman is simply this—to secure the largest amount of work for the smallest wages; and, undesirable as this relationship may be to the workman, there is no escape from it except to adopt the situation and apply to it the commonsense commercial rule which *provides a commodity in accordance with the price.*'

All this could be supported by chapter and verse from the economists. W. S. Jevons was singled out, having stated that :

'If those who want goods at a certain price cannot get them, they will have to offer a higher price, so that they may induce other people to sell. The higher the price the greater the supply.'

The N.U.D.L. commented :

'This is precisely what we affirm with regard to labour. If those who want dock labourers at a certain amount of wages cannot get them, they will have to offer higher wages. The higher the wages the greater the quantity and the better the quality of work, and *vice-versa*. . . . The employer insists upon fixing the amount he will give for an hour's labour without the slightest consideration for the labour; there is surely, therefore, nothing wrong in the labourer on the other hand, fixing the amount and the quality of the labour he will give in an hour for the price fixed by the employer. *If employers of labour or purchasers of goods refuse to pay for the genuine article they must be content with veneer and shoddy.*'[13]

The N.U.D.L., whose claim to be 'the pioneer organisation of what is called the New Unionism'[14] is well founded, made a special effort to inculcate its members with the theory and practice of the tactic which had worked so well in Glasgow in 1889. The tactic seems to have spread to the London dockers not long after their success in the famous strike of the summer of 1889. The consequent increase in the dockers' bargaining power led to widespread rank and file sentiment for the manning ratio on gangs to be increased. This aspiration led to a serious slowing down in the tempo of work. Since, as the historian of trade unionism in the Port of London records, 'Such "ca'canny" practices were bound to generate among the workers a most determined resistance to union monopoly', the London based Dockers' Union officials found themselves encountering difficulties in dealing with the port employers.[15] Tom Mann, the union president, signed several appeals intended to get the men to work more energetically,[16] and he even went so far as to suggest in 1892 in evidence to the Royal Commission on Labour (of which he was a member) a new system of 'co-operative' working, 'by which the minimum time rates would be abolished and the men left to stand or fall by their earnings on a piece-work basis.[17] A similar appeal had, indeed, been issued by the Executive of the union immediately after the conclusion of the strike. In a 'Manifesto Urging Members of the Union to Work Energetically it was stated that

'Complaints have been made by the Dock Directors that the men are not working as energetically and heartily as in times past, and in consequence they are not only put to a very considerable expense, but very serious delays are brought about in the departure of vessels.

'The Union will, of course, at all times and places protect its members against anything in the nature of nigger-driving, but we regret to know that at some of the docks the men are not working with that hearty goodwill and efficiency that is necessary to make our position strong. . . . We therefore most earnestly appeal to all our members, now that they are secure from many of the former indignities they formerly had to battle against, to work in a smart and workman-like manner.'[18]

Although the London dockers' leaders clearly disapproved of the 'ca'canny' policy, the Glasgow dockers' leaders made extravagant claims for its efficacy. 'A strike of workmen may be defeated,' wrote McGhee and McHugh, 'but this strictly economic and commercial policy is invincible.'[19] Sidney and Beatrice Webb read the report in which those words appeared. They were neither amused nor impressed. In 1897 they recorded that the N.U.D.L.'s advocacy of 'ca'canny' earlier in the same decade was the only case they knew of where a trade union had advocated what they called 'an insidious diminution of their energy without notice to the employer.'[20] They were worried, it seems, not only for the employer, but also for the workmen who practised such a policy. They commented :

'To the unskilled labourers of a great city, already demoralised by irregularity of employment and reduced below the average in capacity for persistent work, the doctrine of "go'canny" may easily bring about the final ruin of personal character.'[21]

The original Glasgow story was re-told many times. The person largely responsible for its repeated re-telling was the French anarcho-syndicalist, Emile Pouget (1860–1931). Between 1889 and 1894 Pouget edited and master-minded the production of the 'most famous, the most violent and the best written of all the anarchist papers published in Paris,'[22] *Le Père Peinard*. The early 1890s in France were the high point of anarchist propaganda by the deed with the bombplantings of Ravachol in particular attracting great notoriety for the anarchist movement. An assassination attempt on the French president, Carnot, in 1894 was followed by a massive attempt by the French Government to repress the anarchist movement by restrictive press laws and by putting many leading anarchists on trial. *Le Père Peinard* was forced to close down, but Pouget quickly came over to England where he spent part of 1894 and 1895 in exile in London. From his Islington address of 23 King Edward Street, Pouget published eight further issues of *Le Père Peinard*. By October 1896, when the heat had gone out of the situation in France, Pouget had returned to Paris and resumed publication of his paper there.[23] His period of exile in London had an important effect on his thinking, and this was in turn crucial for the future development of French anarchism. Pouget, like many other French anarchists, realised that the period of the assassination attempts (*'attentats'*) had been counter-productive. He was clearly impressed by the effectiveness of British socialist initiatives in the trade union movement, and by the 'New' unionism generally. In an article in the London published *Le Père Peinard* of October 1894 he called on the French anarchists to enter and revolutionise the French trade unions, *les syndicats*. The traditional sectarian isolationism of French anarchism took a fair degree of overcoming. But Pouget kept at it, arguing for instance in 1897 that : 'If there is one place where the anarchists must get themselves into, it is clearly the trade union movement.'[24]

Not long after, other anarchists re-iterated his call. An important pamphlet, *Les Anarchistes et les Syndicats* (1898) criticised 'the repugnance of certain anarchists for entering the trade unions.' It was in these initiatives that the subsequent anarchist near domination of the French syndicalist movement had its origins. In the words of Georges Sorel (a close observer of the French syndicalist movement, but by no means an influential theorist in it) :

'Historians will see, one day, in this entry of the anarchists into the trade unions, one of the greatest events which took place in our times.'[25]

Pouget kept his eye on developments in British trade unionism in the 1890s. And so did a French institution, *le Musée Social*, which was particularly interested in labour questions. In September 1895 *le Musée Social* sent a team of investigators, including Octave Festy and Paul de Rousiers over to England to study the trade union movement. The result was a book, published in 1896, under the title of *Le Trade-Unionisme en Angleterre*. *Le Musée Social* kept up its interest in British developments, and printed in 1896 in one of its circulars, the story of the 1889 Glasgow ca'canny incident.[26] Pouget incorporated material from the circular into his pioneering pamphlet, *Le Sabotage*. Here he referred to the Glasgow incident as one of the landmarks in the development of sabotage. It was, to translate his words, 'the practice'. He continued by dealing with the theory, taking his text from an English pamphlet published in the mid-1890s. The pamphlet he quoted from was published by the International Federation of Ship, Dock, and River Workers.[27]

This organisation—which in 1898 assumed its present name of the International Transport Workers' Federation—was founded in 1896 by a group of the leading figures in the British dockers' and seamen's unions. The great gains that had been made by these unions in the late 1880s and early 1890s had been seriously eroded by a vigorous employers' counter-offensive. The Shipping Federation had been formed, and it had developed sophisticated strike-breaking machinery and had encouraged the growth of the National Free Labour Association. Throughout the 1890s the transport workers' unions had been looking for a chance to re-establish themselves. One organisation had been tried, and had failed. In 1896, Havelock Wilson, Ben Tillett, Tom Mann, L. M. Johnson, Richard McGhee, Edward McHugh, James Sexton and others decided to try again by launching a national organisation that would co-ordinate the work of their unions and stimulate them to a new strength. The National Sailors' and Firemen's Union already had some branches in the Continental ports, and were concerned, following the nature of their trade, to operate on an international basis. This desire became a reality at the time of a strike in the port of Rotterdam. L. M. Johnson, the editor of the *Seamen's Chronicle*, the organ of the N.S.F.U., explained the origins of the International Federation in the following way :

'It arose from an almost fortuitous meeting on the terrace of the House of Commons of Mr. Havelock Wilson, M.P., Mr. R. McGee, M.P., Mr. Tom Mann, and myself. As a result of a conversation there a meeting of delegates of the unions connected with the shipping and carrying trades was held in Anderton's Hotel, London, and it was decided to form a national Federation of the whole of the unions of the trade. Whilst this was being carried out, a strike occurred at Rotterdam. . . . Mr. Wilson . . . on going over, was struck with the idea of making the movement international.'[28]

The Rotterdam Strike, which began in May 1896, thoroughly internationalised the newly formed federation. Strenuous efforts had to be made by Wilson, Johnson, and McHugh to prevent British sailors from working the cargoes on their ships that the Dutch dockers would not handle, and to prevent the importation of blacklegs from Amsterdam. An 'Appeal to British Dock Labourers' was issued. Part of it read as follows :

'. . . we desire you to bear in mind that the same class of employers who are endeavouring to crush the workers in Rotterdam will, if they succeed, make further reductions of your own wages in England, with endeavour to use the labourers of Rotterdam, in the event of your resisting such reductions, to bring about your defeat.'

Tillett, Sexton and other leaders of British transport workers' unions sent letters and telegrams of support to the Dutch dockers, and promised that they would do all they could to prevent blacklegs leaving England for Rotterdam. The Dutch strikers, after making some concessions, settled the strike. The settlement was sufficiently in their favour for them to claim victory. The *Seamen's Chronicle* commented :

'So ends, and ends happily, an eventful industrial dispute, and one which has done more, probably, than is fully realised to bring about international unity amongst the workers than anything that has taken place for years.'[29]

Encouraged by this success, a letter was sent to the press announcing the formation of the International Federation. Tom Mann and L. M. Johnson, after detailing the reductions in wages that had been made in the transport industries since 1889, concluded with the following statement: 'The demands will be made shortly, and if they result in a cessation of labour, every port in the three Kingdoms, on the Continent, and the principal ports of America, will be simultaneously affected.[30] During the weeks that followed the activities of the Federation were surrounded by rumours of an international strike if the demands drawn up were not granted. After a spell of initial audacity, the Federation's leaders realised that they did not yet have the depth of organisation necessary to call a successful international strike. Tom Mann's views were reported in August to be as follows :

'He did not pretend that they were arranging for a big strike. They were not seeking a strike. They held it their duty to avoid a stoppage of labour, but they were determined that their grievance should be redressed by hook or by crook.'[31]

But, in spite of the denials, rumours did appear in the press that the Federation was planning a strike. And these rumours became more widespread after the Federation submitted its demands to the Shipping Federation. The latter was given until September 21st, 1896, to grant the demands. Much of this was clearly bluff on the part of the International Federation. It was not very long before the ultimatum was extended until September 28th.[32] The *Seamen's Chronicle*, the newspaper of the Sailor's and Firemen's Union and the chief organ of the International Federation, was itself strangely contradictory about whether or not strike action would follow if the demands were not met. In the August 29th issue an unsigned article promised a strike. Yet in the same issue an interview that Tom Mann, the Federation's President, had given to the *Weekly Sun*, was reprinted giving the opposite view. When asked about the threatened strike, Mann replied forcefully :

'Strike! We are certainly not going to strike. . . . We are not organising a strike.'

Before long, the *Seamen's Chronicle* did some thinking out loud about strikes. It was concluded, realistically, that organisation was the priority for the Federation, and also that effective organisation would make strikes largely unnecessary.[33] The next week it became more clear what the Federation had in mind if the Shipping Federation rejected the demands—and it seemed highly likely that it would. The *Seamen's Chronicle*, in an article called 'Value for Value', stated that :

'if, after the 28th September, the employers refuse to accede to the moderate demands of the men, then the weapon is to use the famous "Ca'canny".'

If the employers decided to ignore the demands :

'they will find it the most costly and expensive luxury they ever indulged in. Value for Value will be put into operation. Pay £4.10s. a month to a seaman and he will give them £4.10s. worth of seamanship or firing. Pay them £3.10s. and they will give £3.10s. worth of work. The same simple commercial rule will be religiously observed by the dock and river workers, and they can and will reduce this system to a positive fine art. . . . There will be no strike—not a bit of it! Men will remain peacefully at work, but they will hurry up or ease down according to the pay received.'[34]

This is the first of many statements on 'value for value', or 'ca'canny', by the International Federation. It was clear that the employers were not going to be frightened by the Federation's threat of strike action. The International Federation had neither the organisational strength nor the financial resources to conduct an international strike. It is, of course, more than a coincidence that McHugh and McGhee, the National Union of Dock Labourers' leaders in Glasgow in 1889, were active members of the Central Council of the International Federation.[35] In an interesting editorial in the same issue of the *Seamen's Chronicle* mention was made of the successful use of ca'canny in Glasgow seven years earlier. There was nothing but enthusiasm for the new tactic. Strikes were now called 'old, effete, barbarous weapons—and they are only fit for museums! . . . Strikes are as effete as the ancient modes of agriculture, locomotion, and communication; they must give way to modern methods— value for value!'

When, at the end of September 1896, the employers had still not met the International Federation's demands, the International Federation balloted its members on what action should be taken. These were the three questions asked in the ballot paper: '1) Are you favourable to an immediate International Strike to enforce the demands sent in to the employers, as per accompanying statement? 2) Are you favourable to a further period of organisation prior to definite action being taken? 3) Are you in favour of resorting to "Ca'canny", i.e. value for value, as explained in the accompanying leaflet, until such time as the employers agree to meet your Representatives in conference?' The questions were loaded. It was pointed out with the ballot papers that 'in the event of a strike this year, no Strike Pay will be given'. The Federation leadership had settled in its own mind for ca'canny. This is abundantly clear from the number of articles on the subject in the *Seaman's Chronicle*. It can further be seen from the fact that the results of the ballot were never made known to the Federation membership. As was revealed some years later by the Swedish transport workers' leader, Charles Lindley, the ballot showed strongly in favour of a further period of organisation.[36] But, in spite of this set-back the Federation leadership continued to try to convert the membership to 'ca'canny'. In fact, it erected a distinct theory around the tactic— what E. J. Hobsbawm has called 'free market bargaining'.[37] A special leaflet, 'What is Ca'Canny' was issued on October 22nd, 1896. Part of it read:

'If labour and skill are 'marketable commodities' then the possessors of such commodities are justified in selling their labour and skill in like manner as a butcher sells beef . . . [if the housewife] . . . will only pay two shillings, she will have to be content with an inferior quality of beef or a lesser quantity.'[38]

The ca'canny leaflet aroused much interest. It was quoted at length in *The Times* of October 10th, 1896, and a number of shipping trade journals reprinted it. What it was recommending seems to have struck a responsive chord amongst dockers in London. In 1897 Charles Booth and a collaborator noted that:

'An attempt on his [the employer's] part to reduce wages, or the refusal to raise them, is not met by seeking to increase the value of the services offered, but always and solely by the refusal to render them at all, or the threat of this; or occasionally (if a strike is inconvenient) even by the opposite and really suicidal plan of giving as little value as possible in exchange for the wages earned—known as the "ca'canny" policy—that is, by the fatal recourse of giving inferior work to match inadequate pay.'[39]

The leaflet on ca'canny that was published by the International Federation of Ship, Dock, and River Workers was translated by the *Musée Social* in Paris, and published by it in French in October 1896. It was from this translation, as we saw, that Emile Pouget derived much support for the development of his ideas on sabotage. The translation of the ca'canny leaflet, and an instance of sabotage on the French railways the year before, were extremely important starting points for the infiltration of sabotage into the canon of French revolutionary syndicalist theory and practice.[40] But, as Pouget himself was the first to admit, it must not be thought that these events or his own championing of sabotage, meant that sabotage only made its appearance in France from around that time. By its very nature, sabotage had a much longer history than that. But it was previously only practised 'unconsciously' and instinctively by the workers. Only after the mid-1890s, did sabotage, to translate Pouget's words, 'receive its theoretical consecration and take its place among the established, approved, recognised and advocated means of struggle of the syndicalist organisations in France.'[41]

It was at the Toulouse 1897 Congress of the Confédération Générale du Travail that sabotage received this 'bapteme syndicale.'[42] The Prefect of the Seine had refused leave to the delegates of the municipal workers who were meant to attend the Congress. This decision was regarded as being extremely high-handed, and so at the first session of the Congress a resolution condemning the Prefect's actions was passed. One of the delegates—Pouget himself—then rose to point out how little the Prefect would be worried by the criticisms of a workers' congress. It was his advice that the Congress, instead of bothering about making protests and denunciations, should rather take action. Pouget then reminded the Congress that action of the sort he was talking about was due to be discussed at a later session of the Congress, so he concluded by putting forward the following resolution :

'The Congress, recognising that it is superfluous to blame the Government—which is carrying out its role of tightening the reins on the workers—calls on the municipal workers to do a hundred thousand francs worth of damage in the city of Paris services, to recompense M. de Selves [the Prefect] for his veto.'

This proposal immediately caused a storm; and eventually the resolution was ruled out of order. But, as far as Pouget was concerned, it had had the desired effect. It had opened up the question for discussion at the later session of the Congress.

Several days later, the Congress commission on boycott and sabotage, through Paul Delesalle, made its report to the Congress.[48] The idea of sabotage then met with widespread sympathy. The burden of the report was that up till then the workers had affirmed themselves as revolutionaries. But for the most part this revolutionism had remained a theoretical and not a practical thing. A great deal of theoretical and educational work had to be done, but, important as this was, there had been a failure on the practical level to resist the encroachments of the capitalists. The report pointed out that meetings of the C.G.T. always dispersed with shouts of 'Long Live the Social Revolution', but no really practical steps were taken to bring it about. The strike was regarded as the sole tactic. But, the report continued, there were other methods which could be used in a certain measure to hold the capitalists in check. One of these means was the boycott. The other was sabotage. The report then proceeded to detail the use of ca'canny in Britain, and outlined, using the International Federation of Ship, Dock, and River Workers' leaflet, the value for value, labour as a commodity theory. It concluded by using the catch phrase of ca'canny, of sabotage : 'For Bad Pay, Bad Work.'[44]

The resolution on sabotage was re-adopted by the 1898 and 1900 Congresses of the C.G.T. The particularly large vote in favour of the tactic at the 1900 Congress, according to Pouget, closed the period of the theoretical gestation of sabotage and its infiltration into the French syndicalist movement. From then on, sabotage became an important part of syndicalist theory and practice, so much so that in an anti-strike law put through by the Briand administration, it was deliberately singled out. The law defined sabotage as 'the wilful destruction, deterioration, or rendering useless, of instruments or other objects, with a view to stopping or hampering work, industry or commerce.'[45] Sabotage had become an integral part of syndicalist thought. In Victor Griffuelhes' *Le Syndicalisme Révolutionnaire*, a classic statement, sabotage takes its place alongside the strike, and the general strike as the main means of direct action. Griffuelhes wrote that the strike was 'for us the weapon par excellence that present society puts into the hands of the working class.'[46] Sabotage was 'a form of workers' struggle which is the contrary to the strike. The strike is the workers' struggle carried on outside the place of work that is stopped, sabotage is the struggle being carried out at work.'[47] So much stress seems to have been put on sabotage by certain leading figures in the C.G.T., that Leon Jouhaux, the General Secretary of the C.G.T. from 1909, felt it necessary just before the First World War to explain that sabotage might not always be the best tactic to adopt, and suggested that it was an 'incidental' rather than a central tactic in the workers' struggle.[48] Some historians have, indeed, concluded that the French syndicalist predilection for sabotage was a sign of weakness rather than of strength and that it indicated an inability to organise effective strikes. The most recent historian of French syndicalism has gone much further and has argued that in general French workers were moderate in their aims and actions and that they were largely uninfluenced by the rhetoric of syndicalist leaders. One of the major exceptions he finds to this pattern is in the conduct of the French railway strike of 1910. He notes that before the strike syndicalist leaders paid a fair amount of attention to the advocacy of sabotage, and that during the strike, 'significant acts of sabotage occurred. . . . Between October 8th and 21st, 1,411 acts of sabotage were reported,

1,035 of them on the Nord line, where the excitement had been highest. In the next three months there were 912 sabotage efforts, and for some time thereafter strikes by ditchdiggers and other labourers included some wire cutting. This sabotage undeniably shows syndicalist influence as well as worker frustration.' But, he adds, most of the acts were quite minor and did not involve the vast majority of railway strikers.[49]

Similarly, Georges Sorel had been stating as early as 1905 that sabotage 'does not at all tend to direct the workers in the path of emancipation.'[50] Remarks of this sort must be set against the continuing advocacy of it by Pouget, and others like Sébastien Faure. In 1913 both of these delivered speeches on the subject of 'technical instruction as revolution's hand-maid'—in which they stressed the importance of the electrical and other industries, and pointed out ways in which the power might be cut off during industrial disputes.[51]

The theory of sabotage migrated round the world along with the rest of syndicalist theory. Britain did not escape this influence. But before dealing with this migration of sabotage to English speaking countries, and its 'return' to Britain, it is useful to go into further detail about what forms sabotage might take. Pouget's *Le Sabotage* is again the best source for this information. Apart from outlining the all-important ca'canny, value for value, policy, Pouget had some other suggestions. He refused to be dogmatic about what forms sabotage might take, but he did indicate a number of main types. For him 'the primary and instinctive form of sabotage' was slowing down on the job. This tactic, he felt, was unlikely to be widely adopted by workers on piecework.[52] For such workers other methods presented themselves. Not long after the 1900 Congress of the C.G.T., the *Bulletin de la Bourse du Travail de Montpellier* gave the following suggestions, amongst many others :

'If you are a mechanic, it's very easy for you with two pence worth of ordinary powder, or even just sand, to stop your machine, to bring about a loss of time and a costly repair for your employer. If you are a joiner or cabinet-maker, what is more easy than to spoil a piece of furniture without the employer knowing it and making him lose customers?'[53]

The list was a long one. It showed that in any trade or occupation, and under any payment system, sabotage could be practised in one form or another. Apart from the two main methods discused so far—slowing down on the job, and deteriorating the quality of work—Pouget had some other variants. There was sabotage by 'la méthode de la bouche ouverte"—open mouth sabotage. This involved workers divulging the industrial or commercial secrets of their employers, or making public instances of adulterated or shoddy products. Possibly a more important tactic, to which Pouget devoted a separate chapter, was 'l'obstructionnisme', or what has become known in Britain as working to rule. Pouget defined 'l'obstructionnisme' as sabotage in reverse—applying the rules with a meticulous and exaggerated care.[54]

NOTES

1. *North British Daily Mail*, June 12th, 1889. On McHugh and his close associate, Richard McGhee, see *Sir James Sexton, Agitator* (London 1936) p. 93. McHugh resigned as General Secretary of the N.U.D.L., which by then had transferred the main base of its activities from Glasgow to Liverpool, in 1893—when James Sexton took over (p. 107).

2. *North British Daily Mail*, June 13th, 1889.

3. *N.B.D.M.* June 14th, 1889.

4. *N.B.D.M.* June 13th, 1889.

5. *N.B.D.M.* June 17th, 1889.

6. *N.B.D.M.* June 20th, 1889.

7. *N.B.D.M.* June 24th, 1889.

8. *N.B.D.M.* June 22nd, 1889.

9. *N.B.D.M.* July 4th, 1889.

10. *N.B.D.M.* July 6th, 1889 and *The Evening Citizen* (Glasgow) July 6th, 1889.

11. Quoted in Emile Pouget *Le Sabotage* (Paris n.d. ? 1909) p. 6.

12. E. Pouget *Le Sabotage*, pp. 6-7.

13. National Union of Dock Labourers, *Report of Executive* for year ending 30.6.1891 (Glasgow 1891), report signed by Richard McGhee (President) and Edward McHugh (General Secretary), pp. 13-15.

14. N.U.D.L., *Report of Executive* for half-year ending 31st December 1892 (Glasgow 1893) p. 19.

15. John Lovell *Stevedores and Dockers* (London 1969) p. 125.

16. See the *Labour Elector* 30th November and 7th December 1889.

17. John Lovell *Stevedores and Dockers* pp. 125-126.

18. See H. Llewellyn Smith and Vaughan Nash *The Story of the Dockers' Strike* (London 1889), Appendix F, p. 190.

19. N.U.D.L., *Report of Executive* for year ending 30.6.1891 (Glasgow 1891) p. 15.

20. Sidney and Beatrice Webb *Industrial Democracy* Volume 1, (London 1897), p. 307.

21. Sidney and Beatrice Webb *Industrial Democracy* Volume 1, pp. 307-308. They also added (not entirely accurately) a footnote on p. 309: 'It is only fair to Trade Union officials to say that the two enthusiasts who, in despair of otherwise benefiting the unfortunate labourers, initiated this policy, did not belong to the ranks of the workmen—a fact which the reader of their able and ingenious argument will already have perceived. They were shortly afterwards formally excluded, as middle-class men, from the Trade Union Congress at Glasgow in 1892. When, in 1896, it was suggested that a similar policy should be adopted by the International Federation of Ship, Dock, and River Workers, it was opposed by such leaders as Ben Tillett, and rejected by the members' vote.'

22. Raymond Rudorff, 'Extremists in an age of affluence', in *Observer Magazine*, 15th October, 1972.

23. See the entry on *Le Père Peinard* in Robert Brécy *Le Mouvement Syndical en France, 1871-1921* (Paris 1963) pp. 134-135, and for details on Pouget see Paul Delesalle 'La Vie Militante d'Emile Pouget' (originally published in *Le Cri du Peuple* 29th July and 5th August 1931) in Daniel Guérin (ed.) *Ni Dieu, Ni Maitre: anthologie historique du mouvement anarchiste* (Lausanne n.d.) pp. 424-429.

24. Quoted in Robert Brécy *Le Mouvement Syndical en France, 1871-1921* p. xii—on which this account is based. Pouget was secretary of the C.G.T. between 1901 and 1908.

25. Georges Sorel, quoted at head of Chapter VIII, 'Anarchists and Syndicalists' in James Joll *The Anarchists* (London 1964). See the whole of Joll's chapter for an account of these developments, and also Daniel Guérin *L'Anarchisme* (Paris 1965), Part 3, Chapter 1, 'De 1880 à 1914'.

26. See Circulaire No. 9 of *Le Musée Social* (Paris 1896).

27. Emile Pouget *La Sabotage* (Paris n.d., ? 1909) pp. 6-7.

28. Quoted in K. A. Golding, 'How it all began . . .' in *I.T.F. Journal*, June-July 1956—which is a convenient brief account of the origins of the International Federation.

29. *Seamen's Chronicle*, May 23rd 1896: on which this account of the strike is based.

30. Letter signed for the Central Council of the International Federation of Ship, Dock, and River Workers, by Tom Mann and L. M. Johnson, July 11th, 1896.

31. *Seamen's Chronicle* August 15th, 1896.

32. *Seamen's Chronicle* August 29th, 1896.

33. *Seamen's Chronicle* September 12th, 1896.

34. *Seamen's Chronicle* September 19th, 1896.

35. Edward McHugh was, in fact, sent by the I.F.S.D.R.W. to organise transport workers in the U.S.A.—where he set up the American Longshoremen's Union ('the McHugh organisation') on which see

Charles H. Barnes *The Longshoremen,* and reports in several issues of the *Seamen's Chronicle,* for instance that of November 7th, 1896 where McHugh reports that he had been explaining the International Federation's policy to East coast longshoremen. He said then that the 'ca'canny' leaflet was getting a good reception amongst them, and added that it had been translated into Italian. It is also interesting to note that the U.S. Commissioner of Labor in *Eleventh Special Report: Regulation and Restriction of Output* (1904), p. 725 reprinted the I.F.S.D.R.W. 'ca'canny' circular of October 1896, though it commented on p. 735 that by 1904 no respectable English union would publicly advocate 'underworking': information from Steven Sapolsky's very valuable paper, 'Puttin' on the Boss: Alienation and Sabotage in Rationalized Industry', paper given at the Department of History, University of Pittsburgh, July 1971, p. 24.

36. See K. A. Golding, 'How it all began . . .' in *I.T.F. Journal* June-July 1956.
37. E. J. Hobsbawm, 'Custom, Wages and Work-load' in *Essays in Labour History* eds. A. Briggs and J. Saville (London 1967 edn.) p. 122.
38. Quoted in E. J. Hobsbawm, 'Custom, Wages, and Work-load', p. 122, note 4; see also E. H. Phelps Brown *The Growth of British Industrial Relations* (London 1965 edn.) p. 290.
39. *Life and Labour of the People in London,* edited by Charles Booth, Vol. IX (London 1897), Chapter XII, 'On Industrial Remedies' by Booth and Ernest Aves, p. 415. See also David F. Wilson *Dockers: the impact of industrial change* (London 1972) p. 55.
40. A recent general account of French revolutionary syndicalism in theory and practice is F. F. Ridley *Revolutionary Syndicalism in France* (Cambridge 1970), see especially pp. 120-123 on sabotage.
41. Emile Pouget *Le Sabotage,* p. 10.
42. Emile Pouget *Le Sabotage,* p. 3.
43. See F. F. Ridley, *Revolutionary Syndicalism in France* (Cambridge 1970) pp. 120-121.
44. This section has been based on Emile Pouget *Le Sabotage* pp. 10-14. The Commission's report was later published separately as *Boycottage et Sabotage, Rapport discute au 9e Congres corporatif de Toulouse, septembre 1897.* (Paris n.d. and 2nd. edn. 1908.)
45. Quoted by J. H. Harley *Syndicalism* (London n.d. ? 1913) pp. 37-38.
46. Victor Griffuelhes, 'Le Syndicalisme révolutionnaire' in V. Griffuelhes and L. Niel *Les Objectifs de nos Luttes de classes* (Paris n.d. ? 1910) p. 25.
47. Victor Griffuelhes, 'Le Syndicalisme révolutionnaire', p. 29.
48. See G. D. H. Cole *The World of Labour* (London 1920 edn.) p. 95.
49. Peter N. Stearns *Revolutionary Syndicalism and French Labor* (New Brunswick 1971) p. 70. See also *The Syndicalist,* January 1912, where it was reported that, between 30th October 1910 and 30th June 1911, 2,967 railway signal wires were cut. A contemporary work (which Stearns seems not to have consulted), Adrien Gérard's *La Violence dans Les Grèves Anglaises* (Rennes 1913) set out to compare labour violence in England with that in France, and in general concluded that the British scene was less violent, although the strikes were more momentous, than that in France.
50. Quoted in A. D. Lewis *Syndicalism and the General Strike* (London

1912) p. 63. See also Alexander Gray *The Socialist Tradition* (London 1963 imp.) p. 423.

51. André Tridon *The New Unionism* (New York 1913) pp. 47-48. Pouget, along with Pataud of the Electricians' Union, incorporated this sort of action in their account written in the form of a novel of how a syndicalist revolution might be brought about, *Comment Nous Ferons la Révolution*. The examples can be found on p. 32 of the English translation of this work: *Syndicalism and the Co-operative Commonwealth* (Oxford 1913), translated by Frederic and Charlotte Charles, with foreword by Tom Mann and preface by Peter Kropotkin.

52. E. Pouget *Le Sabotage* pp. 33-34.

53. Quoted in Pouget, op. cit., p. 34.

54. Pouget, op. cit., p. 55.

II

SYNDICALISM IN BRITAIN AND THE LABOUR UNREST, 1910–1914

The story of the introduction of syndicalist ideas into the British labour movement is well-known. The history of syndicalism in Britain is intimately connected with the activities of Tom Mann in the years just before the First World War. Mann is an outstanding figure in British labour history. In the 1880s he had been closely associated with the early development of the S.D.F.; in 1889 he came to national prominence as one of the leading figures in the London Dock strike of 1889. If his career in the labour movement had ended at that point he would have been sure of some recognition as a 'founding father' of the trade union movement. But Mann's contribution did not end there. In the 1890's he became the first general secretary of the Independent Labour Party, he sat on the Royal Commission on Labour, founded the Workers' Union, and dabbled temporarily in non-socialist radical movements. At the close of this period of his life, attracted by the progress of the Labour parties there and by the industrial conciliation and arbitration schemes being enacted, he emigrated to Australia. His enthusiasm for Labourism and for schemes of 'industrial peace' soon disintegrated in the face of the reality of working class life in Australia and New Zealand. Consequently he returned to his political roots and founded the Victorian Socialist Party, and generally did much to help the spread of Marxist socialism and trade unionism in Australia. His experience in the famous Broken Hill Strike of 1908 and 1909, in particular, led him to revise his political and industrial ideas. 'During the latter part of 1909,' he wrote, 'I devoted special attention to industrial unionism. As a result of the Broken Hill experiences, I realised more clearly the need for perfecting industrial organisation. It was plain to me that economic organisation was indispensable for the achievement of economic

23

freedom. The policy of the various Labour Parties gave no promise in this direction, nor did the superadding of political activities to the extant type of trade unionism seem any more hopeful.'[1]

From then on Mann concentrated his propaganda effort on the need for industrial unionism, which he proposed should be created by the amalgamation of existing trade unions. After returning to England in the Spring of 1910, Mann made a brief exploratory visit to France to study the revolutionary syndicalism of the *Confédération Générale du Travail*. Shortly afterwards he began to publish a series of pamphlets called the *Industrial Syndicalist*, and later in 1910 formed the Industrial Syndicalist Education League.[2] *The Industrial Syndicalist* and the Industrial Syndicalist Education League, although borrowing some ideas from the American tradition of industrial unionism, differed in one important respect from it. Mann and the other British syndicalists believed that the French revolutionary syndicalist tactic of 'boring from within', of working inside the existing trade union movement in order to transform and revolutionise it, was more appropriate to Britain than the tactic adopted by the Industrial Workers of the World in America of standing outside the existing trade unions and forming instead new *industrial* unions. The Industrial Syndicalist Education League therefore, put its main stress on the need for less sectional action in the trade union movement, and worked in the long term for the amalgamation of existing trade unions into industrial unions.[3]

In the early days of the campaign Mann used the words 'syndicalism' and 'industrial unionism' indiscriminately. His amalgam of the two 'labels' into 'industrial syndicalism' enabled Mann simultaneously to acknowledge the French and American components of his thinking, and also to differentiate what he was after from the policies of the existing Industrial Unionists in Britain, who favoured dual unionism. Mann's powerful and tireless oratory, his dynamic leadership in the 1911 transport workers' strike at Liverpool, his access to the ears of important trade union leaders like Havelock Wilson and Ben Tillett, the whole spate of strikes in this famous period of 'labour unrest', and perhaps most important of all, the prosecution in 1912 of the paper that Mann and his colleague Guy Bowman were then issuing, *The*

Syndicalist, all contributed to the notoriety of the syndicalist movement in the public eye, and made 'syndicalism' a household word in Britain. Syndicalism was unceasingly denounced in the national press, and even in much of the socialist and labour movement press. MacDonald and Snowden of the I.L.P. denounced it; Hyndman and Quelch of the S.D.P. disapproved of it. Indeed, in the Social Democratic Party a quite marked crisis arose over Syndicalism. Mann had rejoined the S.D.P. immediately after his return from Australia. Shortly afterwards he resigned, and others resigned or were expelled with him. An indication of the mainstream S.D.P. view on syndicalism can perhaps best be seen by the fact that a well-known member of the S.D.P., A. S. Headingley, was around this time giving a standard lecture with the title, 'Syndicalism indigenous to France; inappropriate to England.'[4] In the S.D.P.'s paper, *Justice* of July 29th, 1911, sabotage too was roundly condemned with the words : 'We have no sympathy with sabotage in any form.' A leading member of the Socialist Labour Party, George Harvey, agreed with the S.D.P. over syndicalism and sabotage if over nothing else. Harvey wrote :

'It ought to be plainly seen by any thinker that "Direct Action" and Sabotage are reactionary methods of warfare in advanced capitalist countries, and that their advocacy is a crime against the Labour Movement inasmuch as it spells—the running of the Labour Movement to disaster on the rocks of Anarchism.'[5]

Syndicalism, the word itself being foreign, was frequently picked out for its 'un-Englishness'. Sabotage was, perhaps, the part of the syndicalist doctrine that was considered to be most alien. The Industrial Syndicalist Education League, however, was prepared occasionally to give a fair amount of prominence to sabotage. It was often talked of at syndicalist meetings and in the syndicalist press, especially on those occasions when the whole panoply of syndicalist tactics was being recited. At a conference of the Industrial Syndicalist Education League, for instance, on November 12th, 1912 in Manchester (when Alfred Rosmer and Leon Jouhaux of the French C.G.T. were present) the fourth resolution on the agenda called on the workers 'to devise means of Direct Action against the State as well as against the capitalists—such as the Strike, the Irritation Strike, the Pearl Strike, Sabotage, the Boycott, and Anti-Militarism'. Tom Mann, who was moving the resolution, then proceeded (significantly) to explain what was involved in the irritation and pearl strikes and what sabotage was. 'Which explanation,' we are told, 'was followed by a very keen and energetic discussion.'[6] Otherwise however, Mann seems to have paid relatively little attention to sabotage. On one of the few occasions when he did deal with it, it was in a humorous fashion—for instance, at a large meeting on October 24th, 1912 of about 2,000 people at Canning Town Public Hall under the auspices of the Transport Workers' Amalgamation Committee. Here he used a 'parable' he was to use on several other occasions. 'Direct action must be used. In the time of the Israelites a man named Moses came along and said to them "Come, friends, are you willing to revolt against your terrible conditions?" "Revolt", said they, "what do you mean?" "Why," said Moses, "the strike. Use Direct Action", and he went from one to another of the twelve tribes and obtained their consent, and then they all said to Pharoah, "Let us go". But the capitalists hardened their hearts and would not let them go; then Jehovah applied "sabotage", the plagues of lice, darkness &c., and finally killed their eldest sons to punish them for their wickedness. He mentioned "sabotage" because he knew the finnicky minds of the men, their weak-kneedness, and he declared that the Israelites were never treated so terribly as the workers, the slaves of today, were by their Pharoahs—the capitalists—and so he advocated that the men should punish them, and they should sabot.'[7]

Mann's collaborator, Guy Bowman, seems on the other hand to have made much more of sabotage in his speeches and in his writings in *The Syndicalist*. When he was trying, unsuccessfully, to establish the paper as a weekly in the early part of 1913 he issued an appeal for funds to 'set up the WEEKLY SYNDICALIST as *the* journal of Direct Action, Sabotage, and Anti-Militarism.'[8] In an article, almost certainly written by him in *The Syndicalist* of February 1913, attacking the formation of the Civilian Force (a body set up to assist the 'community at large by preventing the disturbance or breakdown of any Service or

Public Utility') an appeal was made to the readers of the paper to 'fight the bosses whilst you work for them, sabot their material, exhaust their profits, sabot their plants whilst they are exploiting you, and when none can offer you personal violence or take your place. To the organised violence of the master-class we offer an individual warfare of sabotage.' And in the same issue Bowman recounted a conversation he had had with a telephone company linesman who complained that there seemed to be no way he and his fellow workers had of redressing their grievances, because the telephone operators would not come out on strike. Bowman became angry at this and asked why on earth the linesmen could not do anything about it themselves—were not the linesmen employed to 'repair broken wires, lay fresh lines, and make up new connections. . . . And if linesmen make connections, can't you make *dis*-connections?' He suggested that 'some stout cord could be substituted for wire, or that wires could be run to earth'. At a number of meetings at about the same time Bowman made sabotage a central theme. At a meeting of the Hammersmith Branch of the British Socialist Party on November 17, 1912, a doctor asked Bowman how the medical profession could practise sabotage. Bowman replied that doctors did not need to resort to such tactics since they were members of a highly organised profession—but for ordinary trade unionists the position was different and 'Sabotage was as much an instrument to prevent Trade Unionists being defeated by the un-class conscious majority as it is against the employers'. At a meeting of Knightsbridge Shop Assistants on November 20th Bowman used the French Railway Strike of 1911 as an example of an occasion when sabotage had been successfully used. 'By altering the destination labels, by obstructions, by cutting the telegraph wires, capitalist business was interrupted.' He used the same example to some comic effect at a big meeting at the Catford Clarion Club on December 8th. The report reads 'The much-abused and misrepresented weapon of sabotage was very capably dealt with, and did much to remove the prejudice towards this method employed during the recent unrest'. Bowman encountered an example of this prejudice against sabotage at a meeting of the Letchworth Debating Society, where the chairman, a banker, made slighting remarks about sabotage. But many in the audience came to Bowman's defence and 'arose and testified to the efficacy and prevalence of Sabotage in this country, and that Sabotage, at any rate, was not a French importation.'[9]

The London organiser of the League, F. J. Passmore, a railwayman, at meetings of Amalgamated Society of Railway Servants' branches in January 1913 also used the example of the French Railway Strike to some effect. At meetings of the Hornsey and Wood Green Branches, 'His illustrations of sabotage were splendid, and the shunters of the G.N.R. agreed that it would be far better to obey the company's rules and only shunt a couple of trains per shift of duty, whilst at the same time avoiding accidents and loss of life, than to court disaster by disobeying the company's rules, which we do for their benefit and not our own.' At two meetings of the West Central Electric A.S.R.S. Passmore argued that strikes were not always necessary : 'How foolish it is to go on strike, thus placing ourselves in the power of the companies, who can starve us into subjection, when, by a little intelligent use of sabotage, &c., on the job, we could obtain our ends.'[10] On other occasions, however, the syndicalists dealt with sabotage only in a very vague fashion. Thus, according to 'Remus', a member of the National Executive of the National Union of Clerks in *The Syndicalist* in 1914 :

'Sabotage is one of the chief weapons to be used in the attack on the capitalist state, and it has the advantage of not requiring the active co-operation of the whole of the workers in an industry to ensure its successful application.

'A militant minority in the Unions can, by adopting the various forms of Sabotage, demoralise an industry, and by so doing, compel the "timid" majority to share in the benefits obtained. . . . Another advantage of Sabotage is that it can be practised while the workers are drawing the sinews of war, in the shape of wages—thus hitting the enemy doubly, and not having to rely upon Trade Union funds.'

The general lack of specific proposals in the article was explained away by its author on the ground that it was not wise 'to divulge plans to the enemy.'[11]

One of the rare occasions when sabotage was fully and seriously discussed by the syndicalists in Britain was in an article

by E. J. B. Allen, the assistant general secretary of the Industrial Syndicalist Education League, under the title, 'Is Sabotage
Un-English?' Allen began his article by pointing out that syndicalism and sabotage were considered alien to Britain. But Allen
disagreed with this and pointed out that only the words, and not
the concepts behind them, were foreign importations. Writing of
sabotage he was quite explicit about this. 'But if the word "sabotage" is French,' he wrote, 'the practice is undoubtedly English. It
is as old as the Labour movement.' In saying this he was not
only referring to the 'unconscious' practice of sabotage, but also
to the conscious advocacy and practice of it. He explained :
'Our most common workshop phrase—"Bad pay, bad work"—
is a whole philosophy in miniature.' Beginning at Luddism and
Plug-drawing, going through 'rattening' and the Sheffield out-
rages and other incidents noted by the 1867 Royal Commission
on Trade Unions, he reached the dockers' strike at Glasgow of
1889. He then went on to say that although sabotage might not
be much talked of or written about in Britain, its practice was
in fact very widespread. He gave examples from *The Miners'
Next Step*, and from amongst railwaymen in Manchester in
1911. At Manchester, according to Allen, just before the 1911
railway strike, trucks for the same destination were shunted to
a dozen different sidings, with the consequent result that it took
longer than usual to get things back to normal after the strike
had ended. All this led him to conclude :

'So, after all, sabotage is English. Just as we have made Syndicalism a household word, so shall we also make the word
"sabotage" equally well known. . . . One can safely say that
there is as much sabotage practised habitually in England as
there is in any other country.'[12]

The Miner's Next Step, which Allen mentioned, and which was
published by the Unofficial Reform Committee of the South
Wales' Miners' Federation in 1912, is the most famous of all the
syndicalist texts. The ideas embodied in it were very much the
result of extensive rank and file industrial and educational
activity. It was the result of the collective efforts of a group
of young militants which was leading a vigorous fight against the

entrenched 'Lib-Lab' old guard on the S.W.M.F. Executive. Under pressure from the active minority the old style union leaders of the South Wales Miners produced a rather inadequate scheme for the re-organisation of the Federation, entailing merely a 'highly bureacratic scheme of centralisation' and an increase in union contributions. A new scheme was produced by the militants after many meetings throughout the coalfield. According to the foreword of the pamphlet: 'Hundreds of men (trade union officials, executive members, and workmen) have given up their time and money to do this work.'[13] Many of the leading group involved in the pamphlet's production, men like Noah Ablett, W. F. Hay, W. H. Mainwaring, Noah Rees, and George Dolling, were connected with the educational work of the Plebs League and the Central Labour College which had grown out of the Ruskin College strike of 1909.[14]

Most of *The Miners' Next Step* is devoted to a critique of non-militant unionism and in positive terms to a platform for far-reaching change in union strategy and objectives based on militant and co-ordinated struggle against the coal-owners. Sabotage is one of the tactics proposed. In a section under the heading, 'The Uses of the Irritation Strike', it is stated that a further pamphlet would soon be published dealing with 'different methods and ways of striking'. No such pamphlet ever appeared, but some preliminary remarks on the subject were included in *The Miners' Next Step*. The chief way, it was stated, in which the workers could bring pressure on the employer was by reducing the latter's profits. 'One way of doing this,' it was pointed out, 'is to decrease production, while continuing at work.' This tactic had already been used on a number of occasions by miners in South Wales. The following example was given:

'At a certain colliery some years ago, the management desired to introduce the use of screens for checking small coal. The men who were paid through and through for coal getting, e.g. for large and small coal in gross, objected as they saw in this, the thin edge of the wedge, of a move to reduce their earnings. The management persisted, and the men, instead of coming out on strike, reduced their output by half. Instead of sending four trams of coal from a stall, two only were filled and so on. The management thus saw its output cut in half, while its running expenses remained the same. A few days' experience of profitable industry turned into a losing one, ended in the men winning hands down. Plenty of other instances will occur to the reader, who will readily see, that production cannot be maintained at a high pressure without the willing co-operation of the workmen, so soon as they withdraw this willingness and show their discontent in a practical fashion, the wheels begin to creak.'[15]

One would imagine that in the case given there the coal owners could have out-manoeuvred the men by increasing the size of the labour force, (which would not have further increased running costs) and one suspects that the loss of earnings to the miners by their deliberate policy of restricting output could easily have been undermined by the workers not being able to maintain full solidarity in the face of demand for higher earnings which could only derive from increasing the output. Something like this clearly happened amongst the Scottish miners in the late 1870s. The miners organised by Alexander Macdonald faced with falling wage rates were urged by their leaders to overcome this by carrying out a policy of restriction of output, in the hope of keeping wages up by limiting the supply of coal and thus raising its selling price. But this policy, Fred Reid tells us, was beaten by the fact that a big pool of surplus labour (Irish immigrants and the Glasgow unemployed) was available to take the miners' jobs. As Reid puts it : 'Any collier who refused to "fill the master's darg"—as the daily output of a hewer was called—and who tried to produce only the union's "wee darg" was simply shown the way out of the workings, or disciplined in some other way by the company.'[16]

But the South Wales miners had other ways to get round the problem, and in the Cambrian Combine strike of 1910–1911 a combination of difficult working conditions ('abnormal places'— where a system of allowances or considerations was operated to offset the difficulties of a miner producing a good output and thus a good wage) and deliberate restriction of output by miners seems to have applied. When a new seam was opened— as was the case with the Upper Four Foot Seam at the Cambrian Combine's Ely Pit in 1909—a price list had to be fixed based on the general preliminary practice of getting about fifty colliers to work the seam on day wage rates of 6s. 9d. per ton. The output produced during this period of preliminary working formed the basis for the subsequent establishment of a piece work price list. At the Ely Pit during the discussion between the men and the management the latter contended that the output was not 'a reliable indication of what number of tons could be produced, as the colliers were not working to the best of their ability.'[17] It was out of the conflict between the owners' insistence on a cutting rate of 1s. 7d. per ton, and the men's insistence on a rate of 2s. 6d. per ton, that the long drawn out Cambrian dispute had its origins. The employers' historian of the dispute stated in 1911 that this practice of ca'canny was by no means uncommon. 'As is almost invariably the case,' he wrote, 'when a new seam is opened the men were working "ca'canny" in order to try and prove that the seam was a difficult one to work.'[18]

During the 1910 strike the engine house at the Ely Pit was stoned and the winding engine was brought to a standstill.[19] During the national coal strike in 1912 a French observer noted that on March 8th Staffordshire miners threatened the men who were manning the pumping station at Stow Heath Colliery near Wolverhampton, and that they were successful in inducing the men to leave their work.[20] J. E. B. Seely, who as Secretary of State for War at the time was responsible for sending troops into South Wales during the 1912 strike, recalled the situation in South Wales in the following words :

'A telephone was installed from the troubled area to the War Office, and constant reports were received. One morning I received a telephone message, saying that a mass attack on the pitheads was to be made that evening, that it was no secret that the intention was to burn the pitheads, wreck the machinery, and flood the mines. . . . The miners were completely out of hand, quite off their heads with excitement.'[21]

The ferment of ideas embodied in pamphlets like *The Miners' Next Step*, the publications of the Industrial Syndicalist Education League, and the I.W.W.-influenced papers of the Industrial Democracy League was a key feature of the British trade union movement in the years just before the First World War. These few years have ever since been labelled as the 'Labour Unrest'. The four years 1911–1914 showed a marked increase over previous years in the number of days lost due to industrial disputes; there were important national strikes amongst miners, railwaymen and transport workers, as well as a whole host of smaller local strikes; and there was a very considerable increase in membership of the trade union movement.[22]

The strikes were often marked by outbreaks of labour violence. During the Railway strike of 1911, for instance, a great many trains were stoned and signal boxes attacked and sometimes destroyed. The following things happened on the Great Western Line alone : 7 engines and 44 other vehicles damaged, 96 wagons looted, 6 signal boxes destroyed, and several warehouses burned or looted.[23] The violence and other vigorous crowd activity was more often than not an extension, by 'riot', of collective bargaining. Much of the violence was exacerbated by the frequent attempts by employers to introduce blackleg labour, and by the authorities' deployment of police and troops in the strike situations. Mass picketing was often extremely vigorous, in some places rioting broke out, and employers' offices and other places of work were attacked by strikers. A detailed analysis of the 1911 dock strikes in Hull and Manchester/Salford has revealed that although the advocacy of syndicalism by local and national leaders probably had the effect of encouraging solidarity actions on the part of initially uninvolved workers, it is unlikely that the violence and acts of destructive sabotage were the result of syndicalist influence. It has been concluded that, on the waterside in Hull and Manchester at least, the causes of the violence are more likely to be related 'to the character of an industry which employed a basically unskilled workforce who could easily be replaced by others'. The two other likely causes given, which probably have a general application to all the industries involved in the strikes, are, as was mentioned earlier, the use of blackleg labour by employers, and the reactions of the Government and its use of police and troops.[24]

Although it is not our purpose here to discuss how much influence the syndicalists and industrial unionists had on the industrial relations of this period, the emergence of the *Daily Herald*, a workers' daily paper embracing syndicalism, social-democracy, women's suffrage and most other advanced causes of the day in an admirably non-sectarian manner, must be noted. The *Daily Herald*, unlike the syndicalist texts, enjoyed a truly mass readership in working class circles.[25] The attention that the *Daily Herald*, therefore, gave to cases of sabotage is of considerable importance. One very interesting case to which it devoted a good deal of attention was that of Guard Richardson in early 1913. In February 1913, Richardson, a guard from Normanton, was dismissed by the Midland Railway Company for refusing to carry out an order. Richardson, an extremely faithful and conscientious railway servant, on January 17th, 1913 was working a goods train from Nottingham to Sheffield. He was ordered by a foreman at Chesterfield to add three extra wagons to his train. These were to be taken on to Sheffield. Richardson consulted Rule 253 of the Company, which read :

'The guard in charge of a train must satisfy himself before starting and during the journey that the train is properly loaded, marshalled, coupled, lamped, greased, and sheeted, and that the brakes are in good working order, and that the train is in a state of efficiency for working.'

He also consulted the Appendix to the Company's rules, which stated that goods trains of more than 18 wagons proceeding from Chesterfield to Sheffield via Dronfield had to have a 15 or 20 ton brake. Richardson's train with the three extra wagons had a load equivalent to 36 loaded wagons, and yet it was only provided with a 10 ton brake. He therefore refused to take the extra wagons. For this refusal to carry out a verbal order—in spite of the fact that the Company's rules were on his side— Richardson was sacked.[26]

Shortly afterwards, on February 17th, 1913, Richardson's scrupulous attention to the rules was fully vindicated. Another guard, this time of a train leaving Storries Hill, Cudworth, was instructed *en route* to add more wagons to his train, again in violation of the brake capacity requirements laid down in the railway company's Appendix to its Rules. This time the guard complied with the verbal order. Shortly afterwards the train broke off from the engine and the rear portion of the train was derailed.[27] It was, of course, because of the fear of accidents that such detailed rule books were introduced onto the railways. As early as 1839, the Select Committee on Railways had recommended that it was essential for public safety that railway companies 'should have more perfect control over their servants.' The companies sought to impose this control through extremely detailed rules on working practices. This was backed up by the adoption of regulations in 1840 and 1842 which made it possible for erring railway servants to be brought immediately before a magistrate and given either a £10 fine or 2 months imprisonment.[28] A recent writer has commented:

'On the operating side, the railway rule book has become a national institution. "Working to rule" is a railwayman's phrase that has passed into the language. The regulations that drivers and guards and signalmen are supposed to follow are so numerous and so precise that to observe them to the letter is to bring the railways almost to a standstill.'[29]

The *Daily Herald* not only reported the Guard Richardson case, it also commented extensively on it in an editorial. Richardson's case, the editorial argued, was 'an eloquent example of the new sabotage, and an impressive list of its possibilities. The new sabotage means a scrupulous regard for property and life, a thoroughgoing adherence to the rules framed by the railway companies themselves in accordance with Board of Trade regulations.' It added that the strict carrying out of the rules and regulations 'would mean chaos.' 'The new sabotage, legality in excelsis, the essentially law-abiding strike, would mean paralysis!'[30] In the same issue of the paper there was also an article under the title, 'Stopping in on Strike', which went into detail on some of the ideas outlined in the editorial. The following words were printed in heavy type:

'If the railwaymen desired a novel method of striking against the companies, with the hope of doing more to paralyse the railway traffic than could be done by a national strike, they could not devise a more ingenious method than deciding upon strict observance of the running regulations, framed in accordance with the conditions imposed on companies by the Board of Trade.'

It was noted that the Italian railwaymen had successfully and extensively used this working to rule tactic at the end of 1911; and that in Britain too there were railwaymen who didn't need the potentialities of working to rule spelt out to them. Only the previous month some shunters on the North Eastern Railway had used similar tactics 'as a protest against the infliction of fines as part of the recent strike settlement.' The general lesson was summed up by the *Daily Herald* :

'The policy of "Staying in on Strike ", instead of coming out to be starved, can be applied with deadly effect to the railway companies. . . . There must be no more breaking of the rules in the interests of the capitalists. The men must make up their minds that in future they will carry out the rules.'[31]

The *Daily Herald* at this time was being edited by the syndicalist sympathiser, Charles Lapworth. Lapworth greeted the manifestations of the 'Labour Unrest' with great enthusiasm.[32] At the end of 1913 the *Daily Herald*'s columns dealt with sabotage again. In November 1913 it was widely expected that there would soon be a Post Office strike. The *Daily Herald* pointed out that the French Post Office strike had some valuable lessons, and it asked :

'Why not wholesale *sabotage* as a preliminary? . . . Scabs must find an impossible task before them in trying to do the work; even outsiders know a little of the intricacies of the postal machine, so surely ways and means must suggest themselves to the experienced man.'[33]

Scarcely a month after this suggestion had been made, the *Daily Herald* was reporting a news agency item which suggested that this form of direct action in the postal service had become so widespread that it was 'a grave danger to the safe conduct of His Majesty's mails.' It was also reported that a secret committee of militants had decided to operate a policy of sabotage, or the 'stay in strike' as they preferred to call it, whether or not the National Joint Committee of the Postal Associations decided to hold a strike ballot. One of the secret committee said :

'If necessary we will send the Scotch mail to America and the Irish mail to France, and when it is returned we will repeat the performance. Telegrams will be transmitted nowhere without detection by the insertion of pieces of paper between the wires.'[34]

Also in 1913, one of the most notable strikes of that year was the Leeds Corporation Strike, a dispute which involved the vast majority of the employees of Leeds Corporation—from tramway men to paviors' labourers—and which sharply divided the city on class lines, even to the extent of disabusing the infant local branch of the Workers' Educational Association of the merits of its relationship with the University whose Vice-Chancellor (a long standing supporter of workers' education and the president of the branch) encouraged his undergraduates to act as blacklegs.[35] Just as during the hey-day of the 'New Unionism' the Leeds gas workers had led the Leeds labour movement, now again in what was in many respects the sequel to and culmination of that earlier expansion of trade unionism amongst less skilled workers, they took the lead once again. The British municipal gas industry was becoming increasingly capital intensive in the period 1873–1914, but it often took large incidents of labour militancy to speed the process of modernisation. Ironically, one of the consequences of the gas workers' withdrawal of their labour in late 1913 was to expose a situation which encouraged the Leeds Corporation to belatedly modernise and re-organise its gas production by introducing new capital equipment to replace older methods requiring a bigger labour force. A Special Committee of the Corporation, in an enquiry into the strike, made this recommendation after finding that just before the strike 947 experienced workmen were employed in gas production. Towards the end of the strike the same amount of gas was being produced by 708, largely inexperienced and volunteer, workers. The Special Committee commented (and their words probably hold good, suitably translated, for much of pre-First World War British industry):

'This clearly proves that the various gas works have been over-manned in the past and that the system of "go easy" has been in operation.[36]

37

As we shall see later the First World War—which was only a few months away—brought the problem of the widespread practice of 'go easy' to a sharp focus and greatly accelerated the attempt by the controllers of British industry to put what they regarded as their own house in order.

NOTES

1. *Tom Mann's Memoirs* (first published 1923, London 1967 edn.) p. 193.
2. For details on Mann's life see his memoirs, Dona Torr *Tom Mann and his times*, Vol. 1, 1856-1850 (London 1956), his career in Australia see Ian Turner *Industrial Labour and Politics* (Canberra/Cambridge 1965).
3. See *Tom Mann's Memoirs*, esp. Chapter XVIII, and Tom Mann *From Single Tax to Syndicalism* (Walthamstow 1913) and especially Guy Bowman's preface to the book.
4. *Justice*, March 16th, 1912.
5. George Harvey *Industrial Unionism and the Mining Industry* (Pelaw-on-Tyne 1917), p. 191.
6. Report of conference in *The Syndicalist* December 1912.
7. *The Syndicalist*, November 1912.
8. *The Syndicalist*, January 1913.
9. *The Syndicalist*, January 1913.
10. *The Syndicalist*, January 1913.
11. 'Syndicalism for Clerks' in *The Syndicalist* August 1914.
12. E. J. B. Allen 'Is Sabotage Un-English?' in *The Syndicalist* October 1912.
13. *The Miners' Next Step: Being a Suggested Scheme for the Reorganisation of the Federation*, issued by the Unofficial Reform Committee (Tonypandy 1912) pp. 3-4; see also Ness Edwards *History of the South Wales Miners' Federation* Vol. 1 (London 1938) pp. 67-70.
14. See W. W. Craik *The Central Labour College* (London 1964) and Brian Simon *Education and the Labour Movement 1890-1920* (London 1965) Chap. IX, for accounts of these developments. Statements as to the precise composition of the leading group involved in the writing of the *Miners' Next Step* vary—see for instance the sources mentioned above, and compare E. D. Lewis *The Rhondda Valleys* (London 1959) p. 179. The entry for A. J. Cook in *The Labour Who's Who 1924* (London 1924) credits him with part authorship.
15. *The Miners' Next Step* (Tonypandy 1912) pp. 27-28. See also David Douglass *Pit Life in County Durham* (History Workship Pamphlet No. 6, Oxford 1972) pp. 35-42 for an invaluable historical and contemporary account of restriction of output amongst miners.

16. Fred Reid, 'Keir Hardie's Conversion to Socialism' in *Essays in Labour History, 1886-1923* (London 1971) eds. A. Briggs and J. Saville, p. 25.

17. Ness Edwards *History of the South Wales Miners' Federation*, Vol. 1. (London 1938) pp. 34-35.

18. David Evans *Labour Strife in the South Wales Coalfield* (Cardiff 1911) p. 8.

19. See *The Tyranny of Trade Unions By One Who Resents It* (London 1912) p. 99.

20. Adrien Gérard *La Violence dans les Grèves Anglaises* (Rennes 1913) p. 113, note 51. Gérard also mentions several examples where strikers, for instance at Darlington, took action to prevent galleries from flooding and to keep ventilation going.

21. J. E. B. Seely *For Ever England* (London 1932) p. 107.

22. A recent critical analysis of the Labour Unrest (which starts with an examination of some of the basic facts and figures) is H. Pelling 'The Labour Unrest, 1911-1914' in his *Popular Politics and Society in Late Victorian Britain* (London 1968).

23. See Peter N. Stearns *Revolutionary Syndicalism and French Labor* (New Brunswick 1971) p. 70; for a colourful account of the 'labour unrest' which dwells on incidents like these see George Dangerfield *The Strange Death of Liberal England* (London 1966 imp.) 'The Workers' Rebellion'.

24. Paul Lloyd *The Influence of Syndicalism in the Dock Strikes of 1911 in Hull and Manchester (and Salford)*, University of Warwick M.A. thesis, esp. p. 64. Lloyd in an analysis of the prosecutions for rioting during the strike in Manchester has shown that strikers were involved in the riots, and that the riots were not, as was so often said at the time, solely the work of the 'hooligan' element, see esp. p. 67.

25. See Raymond Postgate *The Life of George Lansbury* (London 1951) p. 135. The *Daily Herald*, according to Postgate, regularly sold between 50,000 and 100,000 copies; and at times more.

26. Philip S. Bagwell *The Railwaymen* (London 1963) p. 339, and *Daily Herald* February 24th, 1913.

27. P. S. Bagwell, op. cit., p. 340.

28. Kenneth Hudson *Working to Rule* (Bath 1970) pp. 12-13; see also P. W. Kingsford *Victorian Railwaymen; the emergence of Railway Labour 1830-1870* (London 1970) esp. Chapter 2, 'Discipline'.

29. Kenneth Hudson *Working to Rule*, p. 13. Anyone who doubts the efficacy of 'working to rule' on the railways would be advised to recall the railwayman's pay disputes of Spring 1972 and the winter of 1973-74. In the 1972 dispute the newly formed National Industrial Relations Court ruled that working to rule was an 'unfair industrial practice'.

30. *Daily Herald* February 25th, 1913.

31. *Daily Herald* February 25th, 1913. Richardson was soon re-instated, after 90,000 railwaymen had voted in favour of strike action to secure his reinstatement. The Midland Railway Company took Richardson back into their employ after they accepted that he had had no intention to wilfully disobey the orders of his superiors. The Company also began to consider revising its rules, *Daily Herald* March 4, 6, 7, 8, 1913.

32. Lapworth was dismissed from the editorship in December 1913, on the grounds that he preached class hatred, see R. P. Dutt *The Rise and Fall of the Daily Herald* (Pamphlet, n.d., reprinted from *Labour Monthly*, March 1964) pp. 11-12.

33. *Daily Herald* November 22nd, 1913. The work to rule still has great potential in the Post Office. In the early 1960s, the Union of Post Office Workers realised this, and published a *Brief Guide to the Regulations Governing the Performance of Post Office Work*, see Mark Fore *Strategy for Industrial Struggle* (*Solidarity* pamphlet 37, 1971) pp. 14-15.

34. *Daily Herald* December 16th, 1913.

35. See J. F. C. Harrison *Learning and Living 1790-1960* (London 1961) pp. 275-277, and G. H. T. (George Thompson) 'Leeds University and the Tutorial Class Movement' in *The W.E.A. Education Year Book, 1918* p. 296, where he writes of 'the rupture between the Workers' Educational Association and the University during the Leeds municipal strike'.

36. Special Committee of Leeds Corporation, *Report of Special Committee on the Strike of Municipal Workmen*, 11th December 1913 to 13th January 1914, quoted in J. E. Williams, 'The Leeds Corporation Strike in 1913' in *Essays in Labour History 1886-1923* (London 1971) eds. A. Briggs and J. Saville, p. 94. My account of the Leeds Strike draws heavily on this source, esp. pp. 94-95.

III

The Industrial Workers of the World

Syndicalist ideas migrated round the world in pamphlets and books and in the heads of men and women. Just as sabotage was discussed by the syndicalists in Britain, so too it was discussed in the syndicalist and near syndicalist movements all over the world. Not surprisingly, because of the common language, the traffic in ideas and in personnel between the Industrial Workers of the World in America and their counterparts and associates in Britain was particularly flourishing. There is, in fact, no better way to illustrate this 'cross-fertilisation' than by noting the respective contributions of the American I.W.W. leader, William D. Haywood, and the leading British syndicalist, Tom Mann. A few words on Haywood also enable us to look briefly at the very lively discussion of sabotage in America itself. But before doing that it should be noted that Haywood, in the period before the First World War, made several visits to Europe where he took the opportunity to make contact with the French revolutionary syndicalists and with the handful of syndicalists in Britain gathered round Tom Mann. He was, indeed, to some extent involved in the events in South Wales which have just been discussed. During a visit to Britain in 1910, Haywood found his way to, among other places, the South Wales coalfield on the eve of the Cambrian Combine strike. Here he urged that the miners should increase the 'bite' of their proposed strike by withdrawing the pump men—thus causing the pits to flood. The effect of the miners using this tactic was that, in his own words, 'as the water came up in the mine, so the spirits of the owners went down in the office.'[1] When the strike took place the advice was followed. Haywood, indeed, explicitly claimed credit for the withdrawal of the pump men. He said of the South Wales strike, during a speech in New York City on March 16th, 1911, that : 'Some new methods had been injected into the strike. I had spoken there on a number of occasions previous to the strike being inaugurated, and I told them of the methods we adopted in the West.'[2]

Haywood was born in 1869 in Salt Lake City, Utah. By the time he reached manhood he was no stranger to the violence and hardship of frontier life. At this 'pre-political' stage of his life he set up as a homesteader in Nevada, only to be deprived of his land when the U.S. Government took it to form part of an Indian Reservation. Forced to return to working in the metal mines he quickly became radicalised, and helped to form the Western Federation of Miners in 1893. He soon rose to the leadership of the W.F.M., and led a remarkable series of violent strikes. In 1905 Haywood was one of the group of people who founded the Industrial Workers of the World. At the founding convention Haywood explained to the delegates what sort of an organisation it was to be. 'We are here today,' he told them, 'to confederate the workers . . . into a working class movement that shall have for its purpose the emancipation of the working class from the slave bondage of capitalism.'[3]

The I.W.W. set itself up as an avowedly revolutionary organisation based on industrial unionism, in contradistinction to the conservative craft unionism of the American Federation of Labor. Whereas the A.F. of L. unions were comprised of skilled men, the I.W.W. tried to organise the many working people who were ignored by the A.F. of L. The I.W.W. organised women workers, black workers, and unskilled and often migratory workers of all sorts. Joe Hill, the Wobbly songwriter and martyr, was in some respects an archetypal I.W.W. member—leading a life of a bum riding trains from one stint of seasonal work to another. Indeed, the doctrinaire followers of Daniel De Leon (who for a short while co-existed in the I.W.W. with the more anarchistic direct-actionist majority of Wobblies) soon began to call the members of the Chicago I.W.W. the 'bummery'.[4]

Haywood's visit to Britain followed his having attended the Stockholm Congress of the Second International. He was a delegate from the Socialist Party of America, of which he was at the time an Executive Councillor. Haywood was widely seen as being the chief instigator of the sabotage policy in America. As one contemporary observer put it : 'The most forceful and active spokesmen of these methods was Mr. William D. Haywood, and largely as a result of his agitation, *la grève générale* and *le sabotage* became the subjects of the hour in labour and socialist circles.'[5] The Lawrence Strike of 1912, it has been suggested, gave national currency to the words, 'Syndicalism', 'direct action', and 'Sabotage'. Haywood and Jos. Ettor attracted particular notoriety for themselves and the I.W.W. there by their open advocacy of sabotage at Lawrence.[6] Indeed, Haywood's advocacy of sabotage was the key factor in enabling the right wing of the Socialist Party of America to expel those S.P.A. members who supported the I.W.W. At the S.P.A.'s 1912 Convention a resolution was proposed by Victor Berger, campaigning under the slogan 'the syndicalists must go', which stated that anyone who advocated 'violence, sabotage, and crime' should be denied membership of the party. Berger got his way.[7]

'Sabotage' became the scare word in a period of a general scare about the I.W.W. It was not surprising, therefore, that Tom Mann, when he visited the U.S.A. in 1913, was tackled on this subject during the very first interview he gave to the American press. Mann was asked to give his views on sabotage. He replied :

'We can't get away from this fact—that when the enemy fights he fights to do damage to his opponent, and when I fight I shall not be such a fool as not to damage mine. Syndicalism does not countenance injury to human life, but it does not hold the property of the enemy sacred. As a general rule it is not necessary to resort to sabotage even in the destruction of property. I am not advocating it, but I do say that there are forms of sabotage which could be used more frequently and to excellent purpose.

'One of the most just and now most common forms of sabotage is the refusal of workers to turn out inferior products or to tolerate adulteration. That cuts into the profit of the capitalistic employer. If applied universally it would affect a large percentage of production, especially of foodstuffs.

'The employers resort to sabotage habitually—that is they take advantage of their power to make the workers' condition uncomfortable or unbearable.'[8]

There is one main conclusion to be drawn from that passage : that is that the explicit advocacy of sabotage had a relatively minor place in British syndicalist thinking. The British syndicalists, and Mann more than anyone, concentrated their energies on trying to build less sectional and, ultimately, industrial unions, through the amalgamation of existing unions. The well-planned strike with extensive sympathy action was the main tactic of industrial action that was being used, and this was highly successful.

Mann's main message to the I.W.W. in the U.S.A. was that it should drop its tactic of dual unionism, replacing it instead with the 'boring from within' approach—working inside the old unions to revolutionise and transform them—that was seemingly so successful in Britain.[9] In his interview with the New York paper, Mann seems to put forward a surprisingly mild version of sabotage. He does not, for instance, advocate the wholesale destruction of property. This mildness, however, is not just another example of an alleged British moderation. Mann was merely talking about sabotage in the sense that it had been used from Pouget onwards. The I.W.W. in America shared Pouget's views. Arturo Giovannitti, a 'Wobbly' of Italian origin, translated Pouget's pamphlet in 1913.[10] In his introduction to the translation, Giovannitti gave the following definition of sabotage :

'Any conscious or wilful act on the part of one or more workers intended to slacken and reduce the output of production in the industrial field, or to restrict trade and reduce the profits in the commercial field, in order to secure from their employers better conditions or to enforce those promised or maintain those already prevailing, *when no other way or redress is open.*

'Any skilful operation on the machinery of production intended not to destroy it or permanently render it defective, but only to disable it temporarily and to put it out of running condition in order to make impossible the work of scabs and thus to secure the complete and real stoppage of working during a strike.'[11]

The other main pamphlets on sabotage which were published by the I.W.W. owed just as much to Pouget's formulations.

Walker C. Smith's *Sabotage: Its History, Philosophy, and Function*, which was also published in 1913, drew heavily on Pouget's ideas, and reproduced many (though badly translated) passages from Pouget's classic.[12] Elizabeth Gurley Flynn's pamphlet, *Sabotage: the conscious withdrawal of the workers' industrial efficiency* tried to make things clear right from the sub-title itself. Gurley Flynn defined sabotage as 'the withdrawal of efficiency . . . either to slacken up and to interfere with the quantity, or to botch in your skill and interfere with the quality, of capitalist production. . . . Sabotage is not physical violence, sabotage is an internal, industrial process . . . it is simply another form of coercion.'[13] But in spite of all this clarification and the insistence that sabotage was not exclusively or even mainly concerned with the destruction of the means of production, it was frequently interpreted to mean precisely that by many adherents of the I.W.W. as well as by the I.W.W.'s political opponents and the national press.

Gurley Flynn's pamphlet was withdrawn from circulation by the General Executive Board of the I.W.W., because there was some concern that it encouraged the smashing of machinery and the burning of grain in the harvest fields.[14] An observer reported in 1913 that I.W.W. adherents in the saw mills of the North West carried out acts of industrial sabotage like changing the timber lengths so that only misfits were left for the planned structure; laying logs so that in sawing half the value was lost; and driving nails in such places as to damage the saw. In the hauling from the woods the teams, harnesses, and tools were 'skilfully injured'.[15] From the summer of 1913, for a year or more, the I.W.W. leadership called vigorously for sabotage. In part this was related to the fact that around this time it became illegal to use the tactic of the boycott in industrial disputes.[16] Sabotage, which anyway had long been practised though not called such, became more popular with some industrial workers.[17] Giovannitti put it like this :

'Now that the bosses have succeeded in dealing an almost mortal blow to the boycott, now that picket duty is practically outlawed, free speech throttled, free assemblage prohibited, and injunctions against labor are becoming epidemic—

45

Sabotage, this dark, invincible, terrible Damocles' sword that hangs over the head of the master class, will replace all the confiscated weapons and ammunition of the army of toilers. And it will win, for it is the most redoubtable of all, except the general strike. In vain may the bosses get an injunction against the strikers' funds—Sabotage will get more powerful against their machinery. In vain may they invoke old laws and make new ones against it—they will never discover it, never track it in its lair, never run it to ground, for no laws will ever make a crime of the "clumsiness and lack" of skill of a "scab" who bungles his work or "puts on the bum" a machine he "does not know how to run".[18]

In the summer of 1913 the I.W.W. ran a press campaign to popularise sabotage, which, if some of Giovannitti's statements are anything to go by, was regarded as a panacea in some quarters. The I.W.W. locals around Los Angeles, for instance, began to publish a semi-official weekly paper, *The Wooden Shoe*. On the front page of each issue there appeared slogans and mottoes in the following vein : 'A kick in time saves nine'. 'Kick your way out of wage-slavery.' 'Our coat-of-arms : The shoe rampant.' 'Immediate demands; Wooden shoes on all jobs.' 'The foot in the wooden shoe will rock the world.' 'A kick on the job is worth ten at the ballot-box.'[19] Frank Little, a member of the I.W.W. General Executive Board, was quoted in 1914 as having said : 'Wherever I go, I inaugurate sabotage among the workers. Eventually the bosses will learn why it is that their machinery is spoiled and their workers slowing down.'[20]

But, it was not only the bosses who disapproved of sabotage. The industrial unionist followers of Daniel De Leon, the Detroit I.W.W., certainly did not agree with their former comrades. One Detroit I.W.W. leaflet, 'Two Enemies of Labor,' stated unambiguously that : 'The working class cannot sabotage, cannot dynamite itself into possession of the plants of production.' One of the reasons behind the decision of the Detroit I.W.W. to change its name to the Workers' International Industrial Union was that it thought the name I.W.W. was too frequently associated with what were considered the irresponsible tactics of the Chicago I.W.W., who were characterised as 'shouters of "sabotage" and "direct action".'[21] In taking this attitude the

Detroit I.W.W., ironically, found itself in full agreement with its long-standing enemy, the American Federation of Labor. An article in the A.F. of L's magazine, *The American Federationist*, in July 1913, under the title, 'Destruction the Avowed Purpose of the I.W.W.' stated that although 'The propagandists say sabotage is a slang word used figuratively in the sense "to work clumsily" . . . Sabotage is just another term for destruction.'[22]

'Just another term for destruction' : that is certainly the way in which the I.W.W.'s advocacy of sabotage was most commonly interpreted in the public mind. Strikes led by the I.W.W. usually received anything but a 'good press', and it was common for the I.W.W.'s activities to be met with brutal repression. This was most marked from 1917—after the Russian Revolution and America's entry into the First World War. Most middle class, respectable Americans, according to Patrick Renshaw, shared the view of Senator William H. King, that the I.W.W. was 'a treasonable organisation . . . because it is giving aid and comfort to the enemies of the Republic.'[23] There is not much evidence that this accusation was true, but a mixture of war hysteria and anti-union feeling led to a Government sponsored investigation of the organisation. Things now developed quickly. Early in September 1917, the Department of Justice raided I.W.W. premises throughout the country, and by the end of the month 165 I.W.W. leaders were charged with, amongst other things, combining 'by force to prevent, hinder, and delay the execution' of eleven different Acts of Congress and Presidential proclamations dealing with the war effort.[24] During the subsequent Federal Trial of the I.W.W. in 1918, the question of sabotage was frequently raised. Wagon loads of papers were seized by the police from the I.W.W. offices. According to Philip S. Foner (who has made a careful analysis of the proceedings at the trial) : 'Some of the I.W.W. correspondence, especially letters relating to sabotage, written by C. R. Lambert who dismissed them during the trial as "just bluff", found its way into the Transcript of the Trial and the brief of the Appeals to the U.S. Circuit Court of Appeals.' Foner goes on to point out that in spite of the inadequacy of the evidence against Haywood and his comrades, it was 'elaborated' upon by the jury. 'Not a single act,' he writes, 'was cited to justify the charges in the indictment.' Correspondence was quoted indicating that Haywood directed an I.W.W. organiser to visit a particular factory, mill or mine. The purpose of the visit is not made clear in the correspondence, but this did not prevent the grand jury from concluding that the objective was either to sabotage plant operations or to interfere in some way with production. In general, the indictment was based on I.W.W. expressions of opinion on a wide variety of issues ranging from capitalism, the class struggle, strikes and sabotage, to patriotism, war and conscription.[25] A journalist, Robert Bruere of the New York *Evening Post*, had done several months research in the West to see if he could find evidence of I.W.W. sabotage in the lumber camps, but had to report in articles in February and March 1918 that he found none. Some years later E. F. Dowell of John Hopkins University in a 1300 page study of the criminal syndicalism laws in 1939 stated that, although the I.W.W. between 1912 and 1918 had undoubtedly advocated sabotage, no case of an I.W.W. saboteur caught practising sabotage or convicted of its practice was available.[26] But the prosecution, evidence or no, frequently talked during the trial of the I.W.W.'s involvement in sabotage—which it interpreted exclusively as the destruction of the means of production.

The I.W.W.'s defence lawyers countered this by insisting that when the I.W.W. talked about sabotage it did not mean the destruction of property. Haywood himself at one stage in the trial was emphatic that it merely meant slowing down on the job if the employers refused to make concessions.[27] J. T. (Red) Doran echoed Haywood's reply when he too was asked at the trial if he had ever discussed sabotage. He said that he had, but added, 'Well, I explained that sabotage did not mean destruction of property. Sabotage meant the withdrawal of efficiency, industrial efficiency . . .'[28] But by this time anti-I.W.W. hysteria was at its peak. Frank Little had been lynched at Butte, Montana in August 1917, and for the next three years Wobblies in various localities had been brought to 'justice' by bands of worthy citizens. The high point of this anti-I.W.W. feeling was probably reached with the lynching of Wesley Everest at Centralia on Armistice Day in 1919. The State authorities took a hand in this persecution. California had its own I.W.W. conspiracy trial in

1918 which was the prelude to the enactment of the State of California's criminal syndicalism law of 1919. Shortly afterwards twenty-three other states followed suit. All the criminal syndicalism laws contained sections making sabotage a criminal offence. The State of Montana was fairly typical when it defined sabotage to be 'malicious, felonious, intentional or unlawful damage, injury or destruction of real or personal property, of any form whatsoever. . . .'[29] Slowing down on the job, or the conscious withdrawal of the workers' industrial efficiency did not, as far as the respective States were concerned, enter into it. But the draconian Criminal Syndicalism Laws by no means erased all traces of sabotage (at least in the I.W.W.'s own understanding of it) from the consciousness of the American worker. To bear out this first point one need only look at the time that Louis Adamic, a Slovenian who had arrived in the U.S.A. in 1913, spent in I.W.W. in the 1920s. After his discharge from the army in 1920 Adamic went 'on the bum', in search of work, and came into contact with I.W.W. supporters. It was not long before, in an I.W.W. reading room, he was given a copy of Giovannitti's translation of Pouget's *Sabotage* to read. Adamic describes the pamphlet as 'a sort of Wobbly gospel'. He recalls that there was frequent and open discussion and advocacy of sabotage in the I.W.W. ranks, and that while working as a labourer on a construction job at Joliet, Chicago, one Wobbly 'sab cat' in particular frequently urged him to take it easy :

'For days the man kept close to me, continuing to urge me to slow down. "Put the brakes on, kid," he would say. Or, "Go take a sip of water." Or, "Say, don't you think it's about time you went to the can again?" Or, "Tomorrow's another day, boy".'

Adamic claims that on the Joliet job there was trouble with concrete mixers and other equipment every few days. The 'sab cat' and three others were eventually paid off, but not before they had already laid a section of concrete road in such a way that it would crack within three weeks—which it did. In the Kansas wheat fields, where Adamic also worked, there was much stalling and 'striking on the job.' Threshing machines and other harvesting machinery would often break down in the midst of work. Between 1923 and 1927 Adamic worked in a dozen jobs, from Philadelphia to Los Angeles—in steel, furniture, shoe and textile factories, on farms and ranches, in a restaurant, a stone quarry, print shop, auto plant, docks, and construction sites— and he states that 'practically everywhere I found some sort of sabotage. Nowhere did I find any real zest for work, any pride in labor.' In a furniture factory in Cleveland, groups of workers made things for themselves out of the employer's materials. In a lace mill near Scranton, 'The management was speeding up the machines, forcing the employees to work faster and faster for the same pay, with the result that there was much sabotage on the machinery. Looms were injured; on the large machines leather bands were cut with safety-razor blades.' In a Milwaukee shoe factory at least one worker so hated machines that he had 'all sorts of devices to damage them.' Activities of this sort were by no means restricted to I.W.W. supporters. Adamic contends that in spite of repeated urgings by orthodox labour leaders to steer clear of radical agitators, 'during the last decade, sabotage and "striking on the job" have become part of the psychology and behaviour of millions of American workers who would resent being called Wobblies or Communists.'[30] At about the same time an academic researcher was reaching similar conclusions after making a detailed examination of restriction of output amongst unorganised workers. He wrote that :

'Restriction [of output] is a widespread institution, deeply entrenched in the working habits of American laboring people . . . Underworking and restriction are greater problems than over-speeding and overwork. The efforts of managers to speed-up working people have been offset by the ingenuity of the workers in developing restrictive practices.'[31]

Paul F. Brissenden, the first serious historian of the I.W.W., noted that the Chicago Headquarters in its publications occasionally made reference to foreign 'jurisdictions'—in Britain, New Zealand, Australia, and South Africa. The British Administration, he pointed out, was weak, but in the British colonies the I.W.W. made more headway.[32] The Australian I.W.W. was probably the most successful of the non-American administrations of the I.W.W. Wherever I.W.W. ideas and modes of organisation went, so too did the ideas and practice of sabotage.

In Australia, the I.W.W. not only frequently advocated sabotage, but was also regularly accused by its opponents of fostering and carrying out acts of sabotage.[33] The imprisonment of Tom Barker, a leading figure in the I.W.W., under the War Precautions Act, was met by a number of threats to burn down Sydney. In June and July 1916, a number of business premises in Sydney were destroyed by fire—and the I.W.W. was implicated. The struggle soon widened into a general one against conscription, and a further round of fires was planned, and some of them attempted, by the I.W.W. Peter Larkin (brother of James), one of the twelve I.W.W. leaders imprisoned for conspiracy for these fires, had previously told an audience on the Sydney Domain, that it was 'Far better to see Sydney melted to the ground than to see the men of Sydney taken away to be butchered for any body of infidels.'[34] But according to Ian Turner, Australian I.W.W. propaganda seems to have emphasised 'the lazy strike and the many varieties of industrial sabotage'[35] after it became clear that propaganda for the general strike was not making very much headway. The secretary of the Amalgamated Railway and Tramway Servants Association complained of his members in February 1915, that 'a relatively large number . . . are inclined to view sabotage proposals seriously.' Such proposals included the regulations strike (the Australian term for working to rule), switching destination signs, slow running and cutting off the power. Early the following year posters which read as follows appeared in the railway workshops at Randwich :

'SLOW WORK MEANS MORE JOBS
MORE JOBS MEANS LESS UNEMPLOYED.'

There were also complaints that at the workshops men were going through the motions of work, but were not producing anything. In the I.W.W. paper, *Direct Action*, of January 22nd, 1917, Tom Barker commented on the official announcement that the workers had slowed down by 15% in the previous seven years. Barker commented :

'At the present rate . . . the boss will be in dungarees about 1955 . . . [Slowing down] is a more effective way of dealing with the working class nightmare [of] unemployment than soup kitchens or unemployment parades.'[86]

I.W.W. ideas had some influence in the British Trade Union movement. The British organisations which favoured I.W.W. ideas were small, and they tended to fragment, matching the splits that occurred in America. The American I.W.W., as is well known, split into two main groups : the strict De Leonists, having a 'two arm' policy of industrial unionism and the revolutionary political party, based at Detroit; and the Chicago based 'anti-political' grouping. The Socialist Labour Party in Britain—which first imported industrial unonist ideas into Britain—underwent the same division. The De Leonists remained inside both the Socialist Labour Party and its industrial wing, the British Advocates of Industrial Unionism; whereas a smaller 'anti-political' group mirrored the Chicago grouping by ruling out the revolutionary political party and concentrated on industrial unionism alone through the formation of the Industrialist League in 1908. The British Advocates of Industrial Unionism, and its Socialist Labour Party-influenced successor, the Industrial Workers of Great Britain, in keeping with De Leonist hostility to sabotage, ignored it.[87] The Industrialist League, however, gave some attention to it. The Industrialist League was a very small organisation dominated by E. J. B. Allen, who later became the assistant secretary of the Industrial Syndicalist Education League. In the outstanding pamphlet issued by the Industrialist League Allen stated that :

'The orthodox trade-unionist only knows one form of struggle, that is, to leave the works and see which will give way first, his empty pocket and stomach or the full ones of the employer. Needless to say it is generally the employer who gets home on this run.'[88]

Allen was scathing about trade unions which acted primarily as benefit societies, ridiculed the widespread practice of giving the employers long periods of notice of strikes, and argued for the 'determined, decisive, and short' strike. He contrasted the inefficiency of sectional strikes in Britain with the 'general strike of a whole industry, of a whole town, and of all industries' that was widely talked of in France. The 'irritation strike', in particular, he felt could be used to advantage in Britain. Discussing this he drew on the pamphlet, *Industrial Unionism*, written by W. E. Trautmann of the Chicago I.W.W. Another idea that Trautmann put forward commended itself to Allen who wrote of it :

'The other instance was of some navvies who had their pay reduced, and had promptly cut a strip about an inch to an inch and a half wide, off their shovels, saying, "Short pay, short shovels." Then again, where the open strike is not advisable, either in the shop or by leaving it, there are the tactics known to the French workers as "Sabotage". This is a course of systematic "ca'canny" or "miking" supplemented by waste of material, doing faulty work, and having "accidents" with the machinery, until, for economy's sake, the employers give way. The more skilled a workman is, the greater his knowledge of how to spoil work without it being immediately detected and thus blamed to him. Moulders can turn out casts full of bubbles, electricians make faulty insulating or put in weak fuses, carpenters putting in windows need only slacken the sash cord instead of stretching it, and in a week or two another carpenter will have to go and put it right. Shop assistants, by giving full weight and measure and an accurate and truthful description of the goods supplied, can damage trade during the excessive hours they have to work, and make the employer realise it would be more economical to shut up at a reasonable time than to keep open so long. Numberless devices can be adopted in the guerrilla warfare, according to the ingenuity and daring of the individuals concerned.'[39]

The Industrialist League produced another noteworthy pamphlet : A. Elsbury's *Industrial Unionism: Its Principles and Meaning*, which, it was claimed, was the first pamphlet on the subject to be published in Britain. It depended very heavily on Chicago I.W.W. material, and its remarks on sabotage as on much else probably came from this source. Elsbury wrote, after discussing the work to rule on the Italian railways, that :

'The Rules of many other bodies if enforced in detail has the result of stopping the system. . . . The principle of Sabotage, or "Ca'canny' as it is called in England, if worked in a systematic manner, has usually the effect desired.'[40]

The Industrialist League seems not to have been very successful. In February 1913, an I.W.W. member from Chicago called Gelder took the chair at a meeting at 108 City Road, London, when it was decided to set up a British Administration of the I.W.W.[41] This meeting was attended by a number of members and former members of the Industrialist League. They were rather annoyed, for the Industrialist League itself had been chartered by the Chicago I.W.W. in 1910 as being the British Administration of the I.W.W.[42]

The newly formed British Administration soon began to make something of an impact. It issued a paper, the *Industrial Worker* (the title itself was borrowed from that of the American I.W.W.'s Western official organ, published in Spokane), from November 1913. The British *Industrial Worker* is full of American I.W.W. terminology—it contains many references to 'scabs' and 'sab cats' (practitioners of sabotage). This probably shows the influence of the British I.W.W.'s resident American Wobbly, George Swasey. In the first issue of the *Industrial Worker* there is an article by Swasey on sabotage. In it he rehearsed the history of sabotage : from the Glasgow dockers' strike of 1889, through the Italian railway workers' work to rule, and the deliberate creation of chaos by the French railway workers after their unsuccessful strike in 1910. Swasey's concluding words were : 'We kind of guess it's about time some of the English speaking rail-slaves studied their regulations a little more attentively ! !'[43] Another article by Swasey on sabotage appeared in the December 15th, 1913 issue of the paper. By this time Swasey had been appointed general organiser of the British I.W.W., and the flamboyant orator, Bonar Thompson had become the organisation's National Propagandist.[44] Early in 1914 the *Industrial Worker* carried another article on sabotage, this time by an anonymous author. This one advocated 'open-mouthed' sabotage : the exposure of shoddy goods and the leaking of manufacturers' secrets :

> 'The workers carry with them the secrets of the masters. Let them divulge those secrets, whether they be secret methods of manufacture that competitors are striving to learn, or acts of repression directed against the workers.'[45]

Swasey frequently commended sabotage to those who listened

to his speeches. In Hyde Park, for instance, he would often get his audience to sing the songs of Joe Hill, and he made up for his lack of knowledge of socialist theory with an appealing and direct advocacy of class war. Employers were described as 'middle class cockroaches' as he preached strikes and sabotage. He would declaim :

'Every inch of fat on the boss's belly means another wrinkle in yours. Waiters, put oil in their soup : Dishwashers, break their dishes : Stop their machines, put sand in their bearings !'[46]

Another group which owed much to the Chicago I.W.W., but which did not, like the British or American I.W.W., advocate 'Dual unionism', was the Industrial Democracy League. This organisation was formed out of a split in the Industrial Syndicalist Education League in 1913. The League published the paper *Solidarity* (again the title was borrowed from the Chicago I.W.W.) from September 1913 until just before the outbreak of the First World War. *Solidarity* gave a good deal of attention to sabotage. The October 1913 issue, for instance, contained an item noting that a £50,000,000 combine intended 'to fight strikes'. *Solidarity* asked : 'How many millions will they require to fight Sabotage?' In the same issue it was advertised that Giovannitti's translation of Pouget's *Sabotage* was available from the Literature Secretary of the Industrial Democracy League. In a later issue, G. D. H. Cole's *The World of Labour* was reviewed. The reviewer thought that it was quite good, in spite of the fact that it had a 'middle class' attitude to sabotage. The reviewer did not elaborate on this, but it is highly likely that he did not approve of Cole's differentiation between the acts of sabotage which did not involve the destruction of property and those which did. Cole wrote that 'ca'canny', working to rule, and the 'stop-in' strike and so on were 'a very different matter from the actual destruction of machine or life.'[47]

NOTES

1. *Bill Haywood's Book* (London 1929) pp. 284-285, and W. Kendall *The Revolutionary Movement in Britain* (London 1969) p. 147.

2. William D. Haywood *The General Strike* (Chicago n.d.) quoted in Joyce L. Kornbluh (ed.) *Rebel Voices, An I.W.W. Anthology* (Ann Arbor 1964) p. 47. K. G. J. C. Knowles *Strikes* (Oxford 1952) p. 14. n. 2., points out that 'the policy of deliberately flooding the mines was discussed regularly in South Wales, but does not seem to have been carried out except in 1910.'

3. Quoted in Patrick Renshaw's essay on Haywood, 'The Lost Leader', in *History Today* September 1970, p. 612. I have drawn heavily on Renshaw's essay for this account of Haywood's life. Other accounts can be found in J. R. Conlin *Big Bill Haywood and the Radical Union Movement* and in Haywood's putative autobiography, *Bill Haywood's Book* (London 1929). Haywood died in 1928 in exile in the Soviet Union, to where he fled in 1920 while on bail following the Federal Trials of Haywood and other I.W.W. members.

4. A good description of the I.W.W. 'Bummery' can be found in Kenneth Allsop *Hard Travellin': the hobo and his history* (Harmondsworth 1972 edn.) Part Four. Chapter 27 of Allsop's book is largely about Joe Hill.

5. Robert Hunter *Violence and the Labor Movement* (London 1916 edn) p. vii.

6. P. Brissenden *The I.W.W.: a study in American Syndicalism* (New York 1919) p. 282 and p. 284.

7. Patrick Renshaw *The Wobblies* (Garden City, New York 1968 edn) pp. 122-123; see also David A. Shannon *The Socialist Party of America: A History* (New York 1955) pp. 69-73 and pp. 77-80 for the debate in the S.P.A.

8. 'Tom Mann in the U.S.A.' in *Daily Herald* August 16th, 1913, quoting an interview that Mann gave to the New York daily paper *The World*. For a discussion of the I.W.W.'s reputation for violence and sabotage see J. R. Conlin *Bread and Roses Too* (Westport, Conn. 1969) Chapter 4, 'Men of Beautiful Countenance.' Thorstein Veblen in his *On the Nature and Uses of Sabotage* (1919) devotes himself to the last point Mann made, and deals at length with employers' sabotage. For instance (p. 3): '. . . manoeuvres of restriction, delay and hindrance have a large share in the ordinary conduct of business; but it is only lately that this ordinary line of business strategy has come to be recognised as being substantially of the same nature as the ordinary tactics of the syndicalists.'

9. See, for instance, Mann's article in the *International Socialist Review* January 1914, and Haywood's rejoinder in the March 1914 issue.

10. It was published by Charles Kerr and Co.

11. A. Giovannitti, introduction to translation of E. Pouget *Sabotage*

(Chicago 1913), pp. 13-14, quoted in Harry W. Laidler *Boycotts and the Labour Struggle* (New York and London 1914) p. 341.

12. An edition of Smith's pamphlet was also published by the I.W.W. in Australia: see Ian Turner *Industrial Labour and Politics* (Canberra-Cambridge 1965) p. 262. Smith's pamphlet has recently been republished in Britain by the Anarchist Syndicalist Alliance, February, 1972.

13. Elizabeth Gurley Flynn *Sabotage: the conscious withdrawal of the workers' industrial efficiency* (Cleveland, I.W.W. Publicity Bureau, April 1915) p. 5, quoted in P. Renshaw *The Wobblies* p. 139.

14. P. Renshaw *The Wobblies* p. 139.

15. John Graham Brooks *American Syndicalism: The I.W.W.* (New York 1913) p. 143.

16. Harry W. Laidler *Boycotts and the Labour Struggle* p. 340.

17. Paul F. Brissenden *The I.W.W.: a study in American Syndicalism* p. 34 and p. 53. But P. S. Foner in his *History of the Labor Movement in the U.S.*, Vol. 4, 'The I.W.W., 1905-1917' (New York 1965) pp. 160-166, concludes, after a review of the evidence, that although sabotage was certainly much spoken of and written about, it was in fact little practised, and that the I.W.W.'s reputation for it was largely a product of hysteria from the public and the press.

18. A. Giovannitti, quoted in Harry W. Laidler *Boycotts and the Labour Struggle* p. 341.

19. P. Brissenden *The I.W.W.*, pp. 277-278.

20. *Chicago Daily News* September 22nd, 1914, quoted in P. Brissenden *The I.W.W.* p. 328.

21. P. Brissenden *The I.W.W.* p. 252 and pp. 253-254.

22. Quoted in D. Bloomfield (ed.) *Selected Articles on Modern Industrial Movements* (London 1920) p. 80.

23. P. Renshaw *The Wobblies* p. 173.

24. P. Renshaw *The Wobblies* p. 174.

25. P. S. Foner, introduction to 'United States of America Vs. Wm. D. Haywood, et al: The I.W.W. Indictment' in *Labor History* Vol. II, No. 4. Fall 1970, pp. 502 and 505. The indictment is reproduced in full on pp. 506ff, and contains (p. 513) a letter of August 13th, 1917, from Haywood to the Workers' Socialist Publishing Bureau at Duluth, Minnesota. Here Haywood advised that Pouget's *Sabotage* and Woodruff's *Advancing Proletariat* be translated into Finnish. Haywood then sent a copy of Pouget's pamphlet. I am indebted to the late John Williamson for the loan of an off-print of this article.

26. Joyce L. Kornbluh *Rebel Voices*, p. 38.

27. Philip Taft and Philip Ross, 'American Labor Violence: Its Causes, Character, and Outcome, in *Violence in America: Historical and Comparative Perspectives*, edited by H. D. Graham and T. R. Gurr (New York 1969) p. 285.

28. Quoted in Joyce L. Kornbluh *Rebel Voices*, p. 61.

29. P. Brissenden *The I.W.W.*, Appendix X, p. 383, see also Renshaw *The Wobblies*, pp. 189-191.

30. Louis Adamic *Dynamite. The Story of Class Violence in America* (New York 1931) pp. 377, 390, 382. For more details on Adamic see his autobiography *Laughing in the Jungle: the autobiography of an immigrant in America* (New York 1932).

31. S. B. Mathewson *Restriction of Output among Unorganised Workers* (New York 1931) pp. 4-5.

32. P. Brissenden *The I.W.W.* pp. 340-345.

33. See Ian Turner *Industrial Labour and Politics*, pp. 116, 124, 126, 189, 211. I have drawn heavily on Turner's excellent book in this section.

34. Ian Turner, op. cit. pp. 127ff, and for more graphically presented details of these events, see Ian Turner *Sydney's Burning*. (London 1967.)

35. Ian Turner *Industrial Labour and Politics* p. 140.

36. Ian Turner *Industrial Labour and Politics* pp. 142-143. Barker spent his lifetime in the labour movement. He died in England in 1970, not many years after having been Labour Mayor of St. Pancras and having from that office played a leading role in resisting a Conservative Government's policy of raising council house rents. For more details on Barker, see 'Self-Portrait of a Revolutionary' in *Bulletin of the Society for the Study of Labour History*, No. 15. Autumn 1967, pp. 18-27; E. C. Fry (ed.) *Tom Barker and the I.W.W.* (Australian Society for the Study of Labour History), (1965); and an obituary article on Barker by David Mitchell in *Tribune*, January 1st, 1971.

37. See W. Kendall *The Revolutionary Movement in Britain*, esp. Chap. 4.

38. E. J. B. Allen *Revolutionary Unionism* (London 1909) p. 16.

39. E. J. B. Allen *Revolutionary Unionism* p. 17.

40. A. Elsbury *Industrial Unionism! Its Principles and Meaning* (Bradford n.d.) p. 11.

41. *Daily Herald* February 20th, 1913.

42. See letter from T. O. Montgomery of the Industrialist League in *Daily Herald*, February 25th, 1913.

43. *Industrial Worker*, November 1st, 1913.

44. Bonar Thompson *Hyde Park Orator* (London 1934) pp. 152-153. Thompson recounts that Swasey was once arrested at Leeds for inciting the unemployed to steal.

45. *Industrial Worker*, January 15th, 1914.

46. R. M. Fox *Smoky Crusade* (London 1938) pp. 134-136.

47. G. D. H. Cole *The World of Labour* (first published London 1913, 1920 edn.) p. 96. The book was reviewed in *Solidarity*, December 1913. Cole also makes the interesting suggestion (p. 108) that Sabotage was so much talked of and practised in France because of the difficulty French unionists had in preventing 'scabs' from taking their places during a strike. He suggested that the British labour movement was fortunate in this respect because of the legalisation of picketing—the French law on this subject being, by contrast, 'highly unsatisfactory.'

Since writing this chapter, James Green has drawn my attention to an excellent article on this topic: 'The Stop Watch and the Wooden Shoe: Scientific Management and the Industrial Workers of the World', by Mike Davis in Radical America, *Vol. 9, No. 1, Jan.-Feb. 1975.*

Part Two

THE BACKGROUND TO SCIENTIFIC MANAGEMENT

IV

WORK-DISCIPLINE, MACHINES AND OUTPUT IN 19TH CENTURY BRITAIN

Pretensions to 'scientific management' began to emerge around the end of the 19th century and the beginning of the 20th century—with the United States and the work of Frederick Winslow Taylor setting the pace. In the period before the First World War the ideas and practice of scientific management spread into Britain, arriving into a situation in which, for over a century, British labour and British capital had been at odds with each other, as a result of their divergent objectives. Consequently, when, in 1912, the British Junior Institution of Mechanical Engineers listened to a paper on 'Scientific Shop Management on the Taylor System', one of the Institution's members forcibly reminded his colleagues that the greatest obstacle to the introduction of scientific management into British industry was that 'organised labour here is antagonistic.'[1] The background to that antagonism—in the dialectical relationship between the attitudes of labour and the responses of management and between the initiatives of management and the re-actions of labour—must, therefore, be explored.

Sidney Pollard has written that 'In many respects the rational and methodical management of labour was the central management problem in the industrial revolution, requiring the fiercest wrench from the past.'[2] But, as central as that problem was, the solutions to it were for the most part unsystematic and by no means 'scientific'. The early factory masters had a 'problem' with labour before they even started. Before they could manage labour they had first to recruit it, and then to retain it. The skills that the enterprises of the early factory masters required were in short supply in the labour market, and to make things worse there was a frequent and strong aversion on the part of many workers to entering the new enterprises, which involved

61

a work discipline and a work experience very different from that to which the vast majority of people were accustomed. Work in factories, to give the most well-known 'vanguard' feature of the rapid growth of industrial capitalism, was often associated with lack of freedom and was naturally unpopular with free born Englishmen. Early factory owners were often forced to go to great lengths, sometimes literally, to establish their enterprises with a stable labour force.[3] Once this no mean task was achieved the entrepreneur frequently had to confront the problem of, as some industrial sociologists call it, lack of labour commitment. One of the main concerns of the entrepreneur was 'to gain a high commitment from labour to the goals of management.'[4] The American industrial sociologist, W. E. Moore, in awkward but revealing language, puts it like this :

'Commitment involves both the performance of appropriate actions and the acceptance of the normative system that provides the rules and the rationale. Whether such commitment can be achieved in a single generation is debatable . . . the uncommitted worker is likely to quit or perform minimally, and to require much supervision.'[5]

This meant that workers, to be 'committed', had to learn the new work discipline desired by their employers. This new work discipline was based on the importance of time rather than task, as Edward Thompson has so eloquently demonstrated.[6] What was involved in this can best be shown negatively by looking at the old work discipline. We must, in short, look at what Edward Thompson has called 'the characteristic irregularity of labour patterns before the coming of large-scale machine-powered industry.' He goes on to point out that in the pre-industrial society work was often irregular and orientated to the task and not to time. 'Within the general demands of the week's or fortnight's tasks—the piece of cloth, so many nails or pairs of shoes—the working day might be lengthened or shortened.' An extremely graphic, though possibly to some extent exceptional, illustration of this point comes from the diary of a Pennine small farmer-cum-weaver in the 1780's. It shows the variety of his tasks, a large degree of freedom from externally imposed constraints, and an absence of that differentiation between work and leisure/play that has ever since characterised the life of most people under industrial capitalism. Thompson describes the life of Cornelius Ashworth as follows:

'In October 1782 he was still employed in harvesting, and threshing, alongside his weaving. On a rainy day he might weave 8½ or 9 yards; on October 14th he carried his finished piece, and so wove only 4¾ yards; on the 23rd he "worked out" till 3 o'clock, wove two yards before sun set, "clouted [mended] my coat in the evening". On December 24th "wove 2 yards before 11 o'clock. I was laying up the coal heap, sweeping the roof and walls of the kitchen and laying the muck miding [midden] till 10 o'clock at night." Apart from harvesting and threshing, churning, ditching and gardening, we have these entries:

January 18, 1783 : 'I was employed in preparing a Calf stall & Fetching the Tops of three Plain Trees home which grew in the Lane and was that day cut down & sold to john Blagbrough.'

January 21st : 'Wove 2¾ yards the Cow having calved she required much attendance.' (On the next day he walked to Halifax to buy a medicine for the cow.)

On January 25th he wove 2 yards, walked to a nearby village, and did 'sundry jobs about the lathe and in the yard & wrote a letter in the evening.' Other occupations included jobbing with a horse and cart, picking cherries, working on a mill dam, attending a Baptist association and a public hanging.'[7]

It was from human 'raw material' with life experience of this sort that the early factory masters had often to create their labour force. This sort of irregularity and variety of labour had to be replaced with regularity and lack of variety of labour in the overall context of a tight time discipline. But the old traditions died hard—and in many cases did not die completely. The tradition of St. Monday, to give one significant instance, was widespread in many occupations—and remained common in some trades well into the late 19th century and even into the early 20th century. One Scottish handloom weaver writing in 1845 and recalling the late 18th century wrote of that time as follows :

'Then was the daisy portion of weaving, the bright and midday period of all who pitched a shuttle, and of the happy one whose luck it was to win a weaver's smile. Four days did the weaver work, for then four days was a week, as far as working went and such a week to a skilled workman brought forty shillings. Sunday Monday and Tuesday were of course jubilee. Lawn frills gorged freely from under the wrists in his fine blue, gilt-buttoned coat. He dusted his head with white flour on Sunday, smirked, and wore a cane. Walked in clean slippers on Monday. Tuesday heard him talk war bravado, quote Volney and get drunk. Weaving commenced gradually on Wednesday . . .'[8]

In some industries in mid-Victorian Britain, St. Monday was so common that some employers, while disapproving of it, were forced to concede defeat formally. In some Sheffield steel mills Monday became the day 'that is taken for repairs to the machinery of the great steelworks.' In some mining districts the pits were kept open on Mondays for repairs with only 'dead work' taking place. Other employers, however, kept up their resistance to the custom. In the Staffordshire potteries—where there was 'a devout regard for Saint Monday' amongst the potters—in the 1850s employers brought many successful prosecutions under the Master and Servant Acts against workers who failed to turn up for work on Mondays and Tuesdays.[9] Similarly in the Derbyshire coalfield in the 1860s the practice of St. Monday was so widespread that some colliery owners began to use the same legislation in an attempt to reduce it. The West Staveley Colliery Company prosecuted no fewer than seven men in one week for leaving work without notice. Some of the colliers were sentenced to 14 days hard labour. In 1863 one colliery owner took a positive approach to the problem and offered, to those who did not neglect their work on Mondays and Tuesdays, 'an allowance of wages.'[10] In Stourbridge, St. Monday and even St. Tuesday, was commonly observed in the 1840s by the nail makers—and Wednesdays, Thursdays and

Fridays were 'days of incessant labour.'[11] St. Monday was also common in the local glass and coal industries as well as in nail making in the 1850s and after. Changes in the nature of the industries in the late 19th and 20th centuries did not completely eradicate the old pattern of the working week. Eric Hopkins has written that: 'By 1914 St. Monday had declined somewhat, but might still be observed in some mines and iron works, in most glass houses, and sheet metal works.'[12] In 1840 a writer in the *Birmingham Journal* complained that Monday was 'generally kept as a holiday by a great portion of the working classes.'[13] In the 1860s the Third Report of the Children's Employment Commission stated of Birmingham that:

'. . . an enormous amount of time is lost, not only by want of punctuality in coming to work in the morning and beginning again after meals, but still more by the general observance of "Saint Monday".'[14]

But in the twenty years between those two statements much happened in Birmingham. In the 1840s St. Monday was so common that little hostile criticism was made of it, but by the 1860s St. Monday was vigorously and frequently attacked. Part of the attack on St. Monday came from the upper working class elements who were active in the campaign to substitute the Saturday half-holiday for St. Monday. The needs of Birmingham's capitalists were, however, central to the decline of St. Monday: for it was in these decades that an important part of Birmingham's industries began to be organised on a factory basis using expensive installations of steam power. If capital equipment was to be utilised to the full then work attendance had to be regularised. In the industries organised on this basis St. Monday became less and less common—but in the many small workshops of the Birmingham trades it persisted. As Douglas Reid has written it seems likely that 'wherever small independent production survived then St. Monday might accompany it.'[15] In another industrial centre, Sheffield, where small trades persisted, St. Monday lingered too. In the Sheffield steel industry, in spite of constant attempts by the steel masters to regularise the working week, the tradition remained strong for generations. In 1874 it was said that it had become 'a settled habit and custom',[16] and as late as 1907 one Sheffield manufacturer was complaining that 'It is now Wednesday and five men in one department have not turned in yet.' Another manufacturer stated that he 'lay awake at night devising ways of circumventing them and setting them to work.'[17] For at least 100 years before that statement was made employers had engaged their minds on trying to think up ways of getting workers to work at the times, and with the intensity and regularity, laid down by managers. A number of approaches were made to the problem—with varying degrees of success.

One of the major ones was to attempt to impose a contract of service on employees : a contract which clearly stated the hours and conditions of labour. Breaches of the contract could result in legal action. T. S. Ashton states that in industries such as metal mining, iron smelting, glass making, and paper and chemical manufacture, skilled workers in the late 18th century had to enter into contracts for periods of from three months to seven years.[18] This sort of thing was often a partial solution to the problem at the 'macro' level, but it did nothing about smaller periods of irregular attendance during the period of the contract. To deal with this latter problem it was common for employers to institute a system of fines on workers who failed to keep to the times laid down. A typical list of rules dealt not only with lateness but with a whole host of other things relating to the performance of work and to the general behaviour of workers. Such a list existed in a Tyldesley cotton mill in the 1820s. It included the following rules, with the fines imposed for infringements of them :

'Any spinner found with his window open   1s. od.
Any spinner found dirty at work   1s. od.
Any spinner found washing himself   1s. od.
Any spinner heard whistling   1s. od.
Any spinner being sick and cannot find another
spinner to give satisfaction must pay for steam per
day   6s. od.
Any spinner being five minutes after last bell rings   1s. od.'

This list was published by Cobbett in the *Political Register in* 1823. It had come to light as the result of a strike at the mill and the publication of a pamphlet by the spinners outlining their grievances. The pamphlet added that 'At Tyldesley they work fourteen hours per day, including the nominal hour for dinner; the door is locked in working hours, except half an hour at tea time; the workpeople are not allowed to send for water to drink, in the hot factory; and even the rain water is locked up, by the master's order, otherwise they would be happy to drink even that.'[19]As late as 1851 employees at Water-foot Mill, near Haslingden, were expected to abide by a set of rules of much the same sort. Rule 2 stated that 'Any person coming too late shall be fined as follows :—for 5 minutes 2d., 10 minutes 4d., and 15 minutes 6d., &c.'; Rule 9 : 'Any Person leaving their work and found talking with any of the other workpeople shall be fined 2d. for each offence'; Rule 14 : 'Any person wilfully or negligently breaking the machinery, damaging the brushes, making too much waste, &c. they shall pay for the same to its full value.'; Rule 18 : 'Any persons found smoking on the premises will be instantly dismissed.'; Rule 21 : 'Any person wilfully damaging this notice will be dismissed.'[20] This essentially negative and punitive approach to factory discipline was especially marked in relation to the employment of children. Sidney Pollard has tabulated the answers given by firms employing children to a question asked by the 1833 Factory Commission : 'What are the means taken to enforce obedience on the part of the children employed in your works?' 575 firms took negative approaches to the problem. This 575 was divided as follows : Dismissal— 353; Threat of dismissal—48; Fines, deductions—101; Corporal punishment—55; Complaints to parents—13; Confined to mill— 2; Degrading dress, badge—3. Only 34 firms used positive means : Kindness—2; Promotion or higher wages—9; Reward or premium—23.[21]

One of the most important general factors in establishing the new work discipline was the growth of the market economy itself. Workers were not only important to industrial capitalism as producers, but also as consumers. The growth of domestic consumption, the transformation of luxuries into necessities, and the sheer variety and quantity of new commodities which were becoming available depended to a great extent on working class purchasing power and was vital to Britain's economic growth.

Workers needed cash to be able to satisfy their needs and their wants. This was of immense importance. As early as 1775 Bishop Berkeley had asked rhetorically 'whether the creation of wants be not the likeliest way to produce industry in people?' Many of the early factory masters had agreed. Richard Arkwright, for instance, gave prizes to those small traders in Cromford who 'best furnished the Market.'[22] In the early Industrial Revolution wage levels began to adjust themselves not only to the state of the labour market, but also to some extent to the new patterns of consumption. In the pre-industrial period wages had more often than not been customary and not market calculations. The pre-industrial economy's custom was that the more a worker was paid the less likely it was that an employer would get a full working week out of him, since it was felt that the pre-industrial worker's needs were soon satisfied and his wants were few. What Adam Smith wrote on this question in the 1770s, in his chapter 'Of the Wages of Labour', in *The Wealth of Nations* was very much in conflict with the prevailing conventional wisdom. Smith was striking the new note when he suggested that a workman's wage must at least be sufficient to maintain him, and that during the period in which a family was being brought up there needed to be 'somewhat more'. There were, Smith observed, certain circumstances in which labourers were enabled to raise their wages above such a basic subsistence rate. Labour shortage often meant that employers had to bid against one another to get workmen, thus breaking down 'the natural combination of masters not to raise wages.' In countries where the national wealth was continually increasing, the wages of labour tended to rise. This led to a situation in Adam Smith's Britain where 'the wages of labour seem . . . to be manifestly more than what is precisely necessary to enable the labourer to bring up a family.' Smith further contested the conventional wisdom when he wrote :

'A plentiful subsistence . . ., it has been concluded, relaxes, and a scanty one quickens their industry. That a little more plenty than ordinary may render some workmen idle, cannot be well doubted; but that it should have this effect upon the greater part, or that men in general should work better when they are

ill-fed, than when they are well fed, when they are dis-
heartened than when they are in good spirits, when they are
frequently sick than when they are generally in good health,
seems not very probable.'[23]

As the 19th century progressed there were, of course, many things
on which workers could spend what money they had. The range
and quantity of commodities was immense, and assiduous efforts
were made to create wants among the people. But by mid-
Victorian times the dominant ideology found it convenient to
try to channel working class expenditure in particular directions.
In this case the old 'problem' could reproduce itself in a different
form. Workers might in times of prosperity earn from a full
working week more in wages than they needed, and so they
might stay away from work after they had met their expenditure
requirements. The corollary of this was that they would not go
to work until they had spent the wages earned in the previous
week. The complaint of Samuel Smiles in 1875 was typical of
many :

> 'During prosperous times, Saint Monday is regularly observed.
> The Bank Holiday is repeated weekly. "Where are all the
> workmen?" said a master to his foreman on going the rounds
> among his builders,—"this work must be pushed on and covered
> in while the fine weather lasts." "Why sir," said the foreman,
> "this is Monday; and they have not spent all their money
> yet." '[24]

Workers came to want time in which to spend their wages,
and this could mean that after a certain level of income labour
supply was sharply curtailed. The chance of extra wages was
often traded off for leisure time. The *Derbyshire Times*, for
instance, in its issue of August 3rd 1872 complained that : 'The
colliery or foundry hand finds that in four days a week or less
he can earn as much as he can spend, and consequently he will
not work more, although the whole country is crying out for
coal. . . .' One entrepreneurial solution here might have been,
had the demand for coal in 1872 been small and the bargaining
power of labour therefore weak, to have reduced wages per day
and thereby necessitated colliers doing a full five day week in

order to keep up their desired level of expenditure. But in this case this was not a feasible strategy since it may well have produced an absolute labour shortage, as colliers looked elsewhere for employment which would satisfy their requirements more congenially. The solution adopted was to exhort the miners to increase their propensity to save, since saving (unlike spending) was an activity which did not necessitate the use of non-work time. As the *Derbyshire Times* continued 'The output is checked and diminished because the collier is not a saving man, and must therefore occupy his time by spending what he has earned, instead of working to earn more.'[25] To have tried to solve the problem by encouraging the Derbyshire miner to want to spend more was also unacceptable because the spending was highly likely to be on that thing which was anathema to all good Victorians, drink. The same paper on the 17th February 1872 had rejected that horrible and unacceptable course of action when it pronounced : 'We must see less worship of St. Monday, fewer scores at the beer-house and greater moderation in dress and expenditure.'[26]

This last statement sums up both the widespread rejection among the working class of the idea of working to accumulate small sums of capital by saving and also the strong disapproval by the middle class of the way in which many workers spent their leisure time. Working in order to save is, of course, a thoroughly Smilesian notion. The Victorian emphasis on hard work, on saving, on temperance, on self-improvement and the rest is epitomised in the works of Samuel Smiles. His books, *Self-Help*, *Character*, *Duty*, *Thrift* and others were, of course, not only highly typical of contemporary middle class attitudes, but also on account of their prodigious sales highly influential on working class values. The works of Samuel Smiles and his lesser imitators were part of a generalised onslaught of ideas of 'time-thrift', and of the vigorous attempt to 'internalise' work discipline among the working class, that characterised mid and late Victorian Britain. One recent writer, in a vigorous attack on 'restrictive' practices in the 1960s, calls Smiles the 'anti-thesis of restrictionism' and even suggests that paperback reprints of his works would have an important effect in eradicating the contemporary problem of 'restrictionism.'[27] Smiles' work *Thrift* is the most significant of his books for our present discussion. Smiles, indeed, when he produced *Thrift* in 1875 as a sequel to *Self-Help* (1859) and to *Character* (1871), himself said that it might have better appeared as a preface to those volumes 'for Thrift is the basis of Self-Help, and the foundation of much that is excellent in Character.'[28] The object of *Thrift* was to :

'induce men to employ their means for worthy purposes, and not to waste them on selfish indulgences. Many enemies have to be encountered in accomplishing this object. These are idleness, thoughtlessness, vanity, vice, intemperance. The last is the worst enemy of all.'

Thrift was one of the best methods of 'abating the Curse of Drink.'[29] Thrift was within the reach of everyone, it merely involved 'the power of resisting selfish enjoyments.' Self-denial was the cornerstone of Thrift; though it was a characteristic far from widely distributed in society : 'The majority prefer the enjoyment of pleasure to the practice of self-denial. With the mass of men, the animal is paramount. They often spend all that they earn.'[30] The expenditure of all a worker's income was *possibly* excusable in times of low wages, but definitely not in times of prosperity and higher wages. The reality showed that the workman had other ideas : 'the higher wages when obtained, are spent as soon as earned. Intemperate habits are formed, the habit of intemperance continues. Increased wages, instead of being saved, are for the most part spent in drink.'[31]

Savings were in Smiles' work given a place of supreme importance in the process of economic growth. Thrift was, therefore, the basis of civilisation and the foundation of economic progress :

'It is the savings of the world that have made the civilization of the world. Savings are the result of labour; and it is only when labourers begin to save, that the results of civilization accumulate. . . . Thrift produces capital; and capital is the conserved result of labour. The capitalist is merely a man who does not spend all that is earned by work.'[32]

Smiles in his typical fashion attempted to prove this assertion (and the related one that most great industrialists of the day had 'sprung directly from the ranks') by rehearsing the life stories of numerous individuals from humble origins who, by dint of 'saving' and other virtues, had elevated themselves from rags to riches. This strange view of how most industrial capital had been accumulated is, of course, at variance with the reality which had not so many years before been trenchantly described by Marx to name no others.[33] The sentence which reads 'The capitalist is merely a man who does not spend all that is earned by work', should be revised to read something like 'The capitalist is merely a man who does not give to the workers he employs all the value from that which is produced by their labour, but who expropriates a portion of it.' That sort of 'saving' is easy. Smiles confused this sort of 'saving' with the saving that might be done by the worker from his wages. In one place he suggested that 'There is no reason why the highly-paid workman of today may not save a store of capital. It is merely a matter of self-denial and private economy.'[34] It was in this way, Smiles maintained, that some workers could move up the social scale and become employers of labour themselves ('The men who economise by means of labour become the owners of capital which sets other labour in motion. Capital accumulates in their hands, and they employ other labourers to work for them. Thus trade and commerce begin.')[35] After that point had been reached no doubt they could really begin to 'save'. Even Smiles realised that not all workers could take this primrose path—if they did, we might ask, out of whose labours could the capitalists 'save'? The less fortunate individuals could however still save out of their meagre earnings—it was indeed the duty of every man to provide for the future, against bad times, and old age. They should 'lay by a store of savings as a breakwater against want'.[36] There were institutions in plenty, set up by the more provident section of the working class, into which these savings could be put : Penny Banks, Friendly Societies, Building Societies, Co-operative Societies, Savings Banks and the rest, all lovingly documented.[37]

At roughly the same time as Smiles was writing *Thrift*, Karl Marx was in the winter of 1857–58 filling notebooks (mainly for the purpose of self-clarification) with the notes and observations which are now known as the *Grundrisse*. In his second notebook, in 'The Chapter on Capital', he has a number of observations which were 'exoteric' to his main purpose there, but which are central to the notions we have just discussed. He pointed out, for instance, that the capitalists demanded that 'The workers should save enough at the times when business is good to be able more or less to live in the bad times, to endure short time or the lowering of wages. . . . That is, the demand that they should always hold to a minimum of life's pleasures and make crises easier to bear for the capitalists etc. Maintain themselves as pure labouring machines and as far as possible pay their own wear and tear.'[38] This motive, as we have seen above, is certainly present in Smiles. Some sentences later Marx points out that workers' savings, if they were substantial enough to 'surpass the piggy-bank amounts of the official savings banks', might well earn interest for capitalist bankers 'thereby merely increasing the power of his enemies and his own dependence' as a result of having 'foregone all life's pleasures in order to increase the power of capital'. The worker 'thus has saved in every way *for* capital, not for himself.' But he also points to the dilemma raised for the capitalist on the question of workers' savings. If all workers saved and did not spend, the capitalist's market would be greatly diminished. Marx stated that 'each capitalist does demand that his workers should save, but only *his own*, because they stand towards him as workers; but by no means the remaining *world of workers*, for these stand towards him as consumers. In spite of all "pious" speeches he therefore searches for means to inspire them with new needs by constant chatter etc.'[39]

Smiles, of course, would have been the last person to have suggested that money was everything, and that all the worker's time should be devoted to the earning of money. More time should, though, be devoted to work (and therefore potentially to saving) than to leisure. Leisure should certainly not be devoted to mere spending nor to idle pursuits—he explained 'But time may also be spent in doing many good and noble actions. It may be spent in learning, in study, in art, in science, in literature.'[40] These two sentences were, however, preceded by the following three :

'Thrift of Time is equal to thrift of money. Franklin said, "Time is gold." If one wishes to earn money, it may be done by the proper use of time.'[41]

73

Benjamin Franklin was a paradigm of the sort of person in whom resided positively all the virtues—he was hard working, thrifty, punctual, keen for self-education. His life and struggles against the baser human instincts were frequently alluded to in the works of Smiles and others. For instance, a volume called *Success in Life: A Book for Young Men* published in 1859 and containing such chapters as 'Perseverance', 'Integrity and Diligence', 'Industry', 'Economy', 'Employment of Leisure Hours' and so on, told its readers that 'The homely proverbs of Franklin, the fruits of his own experience, abound in maxims relating to this indispensable virtue. Punctuality, with regard to time and money, is one of those good old fashined virtues which Franklin delighted to honour.' *Success in Life* then proceeded to point out just how many of the common aphorisms of the day—like 'Time is Money'—in fact had their origins in Franklin's *Poor Richard's Almanac*.[42] The same book in its chapter on 'Employment of Leisure Hours' quoted at length, and with immense approval, from Franklin's autobiography the thirteen virtues to each of which Franklin accorded 'a short precept, which fully expressed the extent I gave to its meaning.' Precept 1, Temperance, read : 'Eat not to dullness, drink not to elevation.' Precept 6, Industry, read : 'Lose no time; be always employed in something useful; cut off all unnecessary actions.'[43] Franklin, let it be noted, had encountered St. Monday and a lot of other undesirable traits in London in the 1720s when he had been employed as a printer. Franklin thoroughly disappproved of the habits and customs of his fellow workers. He soon began to propose 'some reasonable alterations in their chappel [sic] laws, and carried them against all opposition.' For instance, it was at his example that

'a great part of them left their muddling breakfast of beer, and bread, and cheese, finding they could with me be suppl'd from a neighbouring house with a large porringer of hot-water gruel, sprinkled with pepper, crumb'd with bread, and a bit of butter in it, for the price of a pint of beer, viz., three half-pence. This was a more comfortable as well as cheaper breakfast, and kept their heads clearer.'

Franklin, embodiment of the Protestant Ethic and the Spirit of Capitalism as he was, even profited from those of his colleagues who would not forsake their beer for his gruel. When these poor unfortunates had run out of credit at the alehouse, according to Franklin, they 'us'd to make interest with me to get beer.' At the pay table on Saturday night Franklin collected the money that they owed him for beer. This, coupled with the fact that he was regarded as a 'pretty good' 'jocular verbal satirist', enabled him to become well liked amongst his fellows. He got on equally well with his employer, largely since the notions of time thrift and diligence which he was later to immortalise in his writings were already showing through. He wrote:

'My constant attendance (I never making a St. Monday) recommended me to the master; and my uncommon quickness at composing occasioned my being put upon all work of dispatch, which was generally better paid. So I went on now very agreeably.'[44]

Max Weber in his *The Protestant Ethic and the Spirit of Capitalism* quotes liberally and often from the writings of Benjamin Franklin. He quotes from Franklin's writings to show, as J. E. T. Eldridge has put it, 'how honesty, thrift, frugality, punctuality and hard work, because they promoted economic gain, were extolled as moral virtues.'[45] Franklin is taken to represent the fully developed spirit of capitalism, the latter being understood as 'accumulation for its own sake.' This spirit of capitalism is in sharp contrast to the 'traditional spirit', which involves, as far as the worker and the employer are concerned, the desire merely to earn enough money to be able to sustain an already established style of life. The traditional worker, therefore, was not interested in maximising his earnings beyond a level which allowed him to lead a life based on subsistence. As we have seen this notion was widespread in Britain at the onset of the rapid growth of industrial capitalism, and worker resistance to the regularisation of work was one manifestation of it. Another manifestation, with which we shall deal shortly, was the marked lack of interest both by workers and employers in forms of payment by results up to the late 18th century. Edward Thompson quotes Weber's statement on 'traditionalism' as follows: 'a man does not "by nature" wish to earn more and more money, but simply to live as he is accustomed to live and to earn as much as is necessary for that purpose,'[46] and he (Thompson) goes on to argue that if the new work discipline required of the workers by the capitalist employer is to be successful then workers must become possessed of an 'inner compulsion' which would supplement, and ultimately be more successful than, any managerially imposed work disciplines. Thompson reiterates the emphasis that Weber had put on this point, drawing attention to the influence of the 17th century Presbyterian, Richard Baxter, who specified the connection between his religious teaching and work discipline. Thompson moves the argument forward into the early 19th century by depicting Andrew Ure, the important ideologue of early industrial capitalism, as the Richard Baxter of Cottonopolis.[47] Ure in his book *The Philosophy of Manufactures* (1835) makes abundantly clear the importance of religion in creating this inner compulsion on the part of workers. He states that work should be carried out as a 'pure act of virtue . . . inspired by the love of a transcendent being, operating . . . on our will and affections', and he locates this 'transforming power' 'in the cross of Christ . . . it atones for disobedience; it excites for obedience; it makes obedience practicable; it makes it acceptable; it makes it in a matter unavoidable, for it constrains to it; it is, finally, not only the motive to obedience, but the pattern of it.' Ure urged employers to pay great attention to 'moral discipline'. He advised them :

'It is, therefore, excessively the interest of every mill-owner to organize his moral machinery on equally sound principles with his mechanical, for otherwise he will never command the steady hands, watchful eyes, and prompt co-operation, essential to excellence of product. . . . There is, in fact, no case to which the Gospel truth, "Godliness is great gain", is more applicable than to the administration of an extensive factory.'[48]

Thompson argues that Methodism was crucially important in creating this acceptance of the new work discipline in the emerging factory proletariat. Young children at Wesleyan Sunday Schools were taught these notions from infancy. Adults who were converted to Methodism typically underwent a 'psychic ordeal in which the character structure of the pre-industrial labourer or artisan was violently recast into that of the submissive industrial worker.'[49]

But, it must be stated that even Ure himself, being nothing if not a realist when it came to the interests of capital, for all his emphasis on the importance of getting the 'moral machinery' right, made it quite clear that this was not sufficient if the objectives of the employer were to be fulfilled. Consequently he has nothing but praise for the straightforward, external imposition of the new work discipline on workers. Possibly he could see in the real world of industry with which he was familiar signs that the moral machinery did not always work very well; and that the attempt to foster the 'inner compulsion' in the factory worker was either inadequate or else strongly resisted. The very dichotomy about the role of Methodism in early 19th century Britain makes this a possibility. As Eldridge has suggested, Thompson's attempt to explain away the fact that there were many class conscious and politically active Methodists by invoking the 'reactive dialectic' may well be just a neat side step of an awkward problem. Eldridge suggests it may well be better to analyse this side of Methodism in terms of 'an alternative formulation which, so to speak, existed in its own right.'[50] Or else, if the spread of the new work discipline by 'internal compulsion' was *so* successful, why did employers need the whole draconian panoply of rules that they exerted upon their workers, and why did Ure think it impossible to turn anyone past the age of puberty into a 'useful factory hand.'? Ure wrote that the main difficulty of the factory was 'in training human beings to renounce their desultory habits of work, and to identify themselves with the unvarying regularity of the complex automaton.' He went on to say :

'To devise and administer a successful code of factory discipline, suited to the necessities of factory diligence, was the Herculean enterprise, the noble achievement of Arkwright. Even at the present day, when the system is perfectly organized, and its labour lightened to the utmost, it is found nearly impossible to convert persons past the age of puberty, whether drawn from rural or from handicraft occupations, into useful factory hands. After struggling for a while to conquer their listless or restive habits, they either renounce the employment spontaneously, or are dismissed by the overlookers on account of inattention.'[51]

Thompson seems to suggest that this discipline, enforced by the overlooker, and coupled with the disciplining nature of machinery itself might be adequate for children, but that for adults it was not. Those past the age of puberty required rather 'inner compulsions.'[52]

It must be said, however, that inner compulsions, in workers of all ages, were no doubt, as far as the employer was concerned, nice stuff if you could get them. Weber's point on this seems to be more satisfactory. He merely notes that an entrepreneur was likely to be greatly helped if his workforce had had its character moulded by religion. It was a happy employer indeed who had such 'sober, conscientious and unusually industrious workmen, who clung to their work as a life purpose willed by God.'[53] If an employer was not fortunate in this respect—and many clearly were not—he would need to use actively the other stratagems of negative discipline and, increasingly as the 19th century proceeded, of positive inducements to secure compliance with managerial objectives. An employer, therefore, would be relying on a mixture of rules (with fines for infringing them) and incentive payment schemes like piecework. Piecework, offering as it did the opportunity for a worker to maximise his earnings, made great sense especially as the market expanded and there were many more things on which a worker could spend his money and, as Carlyle put it, cash payment became the 'universal sole nexus of man to man', the 'sole relation of human beings.'[54] Is it so surprising, indeed, that in the capitalist economy of 19th century Britain, material incentives were bound to be much more successful than moral ones? Workers were after all inexorably trapped in the labour market, utterly dependent on the receipts they earned from their labour power. To respond to the carrot of the financial incentive became in itself an entirely rational, secular response on the part of the worker. This 'secularisation' of the work ethic, via the transforming power of the cash nexus, was such that unless labour was well rewarded, time might be 'stolen' from the employer by reduction of effort and restriction of output. 'Time thrift' was much more likely to be called forth by material rather than moral incentives. Thompson's later characterisation of the process of change is memorable :

> 'The first generation of factory workers were taught by their masters the importance of time; the second generation formed their short-time committees in the ten-hour movement; the third generation struck for overtime or time-and-a-half.'[55]

The practice of rewarding labour commitment to managerial objectives with higher wages or bonuses began to become quite common by the 1830s but mainly amongst adult workers. In 1833, 47.1 per cent of the 67,819 cotton mill workers were on piecework, as against 43.7 per cent who were paid by the day.[56] The cotton industry in this respect was well in advance of other industries but as in so many other respects it was a harbinger of what was later to be common elsewhere. Pollard has reminded us that the use of payment by results systems marked a sharp break with the 18th century view that 'the hands worked the better the less they were paid', though he goes on to add that 'the slow breakdown of this dogma forms one of the most significant developments in the field of labour management in the industrial revolution.'[57] In the pre-industrial economy, and in the early stages of industrialisation, wages were, more often than not, customary and not market calculations, and 'the worker's labour effort, or standard of output per unit of time, was also determined by custom rather than market calculation. . . .'[58] As Eric Hobsbawm has pointed out, in the early stages of industrialisation, employers of time-workers knew roughly how much piece-output that would bring them, and the employer of piece-workers realised that they weren't likely to get more than the standard level of output from the normal working week.[59] In this sense, therefore, output was also customary. But, as industrialisation progressed, so too did the belief in the efficacy of incentive payments. Many employers developed piecemeal systems of bonus payment for extra output. This, of course, whilst solving the problem of quantity of production could easily raise the other one of quality of production. Charles Babbage, writing in the 1830s, indicates that this problem was sometimes solved by the imposition of fines for poor work :

'In some few factories, in which the men are paid by the piece, it is usual, when any portion of work, delivered in by a workman, is rejected by the master on account of its being badly executed, to fine the delinquent. Such a practice tends to remedy one of the evils attendant upon that mode of payment.'[60]

Babbage, indeed, in his celebrated work *On the Economy of Machinery and Manufactures* was one of the few individuals in the early 19th century to provide anything like a total, systematic view of management—and one which in many respects foreshadowed in main outline many of the developments embodied in the scientific management of the early 20th century. For one thing Babbage laid much stress on the importance of material incentives. In the first place this involved the recommendation that workers should be paid entirely in money; the Truck system was sharply criticised. The reasons for advocating money payment were remarkably perceptive, involving as they did the realisation that workers liked to know exactly what their work was going to produce in wages at the end of the week. (Wage stability and wage predictability are still important objectives of industrial workers.) Babbage advised :

'Workmen should be paid entirely in money;—their work should be measured by some unbiased, some unerring piece of mechanism;—the time during which they are employed should be defined, and punctually adhered to. The payments they make to their benefit societies should be fixed on such just principles, as not to require extraordinary contributions. In short, the object of all who wish to promote their happiness should be, to give them, in the simplest form, the means of knowing beforehand, the sum they are likely to acquire by their labour, and the money they will be obliged to expend for their support : thus putting before them, in the clearest light, the certain result of persevering industry.'[61]

Above all Babbage urged his readers, budding industrial capitalists no doubt, to be systematic in everything they did and thereby to minimise the risk of loss and maximise the chance of profit. In a remarkable chapter headed 'On the Method of Observing Manufactories' Babbage gave his readers detailed instructions on how to make the best out of visits to factories. Before the visit, questions should be carefully prepared, and sheets of paper drawn up on to which the answers should be put. This in itself shows all the signs of sophisticated social survey method. In his suggested 'skeleton' of questions Babbage, after some questions to establish the basic background of the industry and the particular enterprise, suggests that specific points should now be tackled. Questions here include :

'The weight of a given quantity, or number, and a comparison with that of raw material?
'The wholesale price at the manufactory?   £   s.   d.
'per
'The usual retail price?   £   s.   d.
'Who provides the tools? Master, or men? Who repair tools? Master, or men?
'What is the expense of the machinery?
'What is the annual wear and tear, and what its duration?
. . . . . .
'Is the capital invested in manufactories large or small?
. . . . . .
'Does the manufacturer export, or sell, to a middleman, who supplies the merchant?'

A separate 'skeleton' was then produced for each process in the factory. Questions included the following :

'The number of persons necessary to attend the machine.
'Are the operatives men, (   ) women, (   ) or children? (   )
'If mixed what are the proportions?
'What is the pay of each? (s.   d.) (s.   d.) (s.   d.) per
'What number (   ) of hours do they work per day?
'Is it usual, or necessary, to work night and day without stopping?
'Is the labour performed by piece or by day-work?
. . . . . .
'The number of times the operation is repeated per day or per hour?
'The number of failures (   ) in a thousand?
'Whether the workmen or the master loses by the broken or damaged articles?'[62]

This scrupulous attention to detail and to the importance for the aspiring entrepreneur to make accurate calculations of the costs of all the processes involved can also be found in Babbage's chapter headed 'Inquiries previous to commencing any manufactory.' Here he dealt with the expense of tools, machinery, raw materials and 'all the outgoings necessary' for the production of a new article. Market research was also advised.[63] In a later chapter Babbage went even one step further by suggesting that under an ideal system of factory management it might be possible to eradicate the 'most erroneous and unfortunate opinion' that prevailed among workmen—that 'their own interest and that of their employers are at variance.'[64] Babbage rejected this view, and held instead that 'the prosperity and success of the master manufacturer is essential to the welfare of the workman'.[65] He then proceeded to outline a system which, if acted upon, he felt, would both 'permanently raise the working classes, and greatly extend the manufacturing system.' There were two general principles on which this system was based : first, that a considerable part of the wages of any employee should depend on the profits of the firm; and second, that every person connected with the firm should profit directly from any improvement he made to the production process. In such a factory 'it would be essential that the time occupied in each process, and also its expense, should be well ascertained; information which would soon be obtained very precisely.'[66] Three of the results of the installation in a factory of such a system would be :

'1. That every person engaged in it would have a *direct* interest in its prosperity; since the effect of any success, or falling off, would almost immediately produce a corresponding change in his own weekly receipts.
2. Every person concerned in the factory would have an immediate interest in preventing any waste or mismanagement in all the departments.
3. The talents of all connected with it would be strongly directed to its improvement in every department.'[67]

But, as Sidney Pollard has pointed out, this total, systematic view of management that Babbage put forward 'remained on paper only, and another half-century was to elapse before incentive schemes began to be made integral with general efficiency schemes.'[68] Babbage's ideas remained relatively untried, although many employers took up some of his ideas about the importance of financial incentives for workers. Piecework was already becoming common in some industries by the time Babbage was writing, and it was to become a good deal more widespread in a whole host of industries as the century progressed. We have observed that as early as 1833 nearly half of all cotton mill workers were paid by the piece but there were special historical reasons for this phenomenon.[69] Payment by the piece had in fact been the payment system in the textile industry under the domestic system. Many of the first power-loom weavers were paid by the piece— though some of them may have been paid by time until the development of weaving lists in the mid-19th century. The first generation of jenny spinners were almost certainly on a piece-rate system. Spinning lists seem to have appeared at least from the 1820s. By 1904 a historian of the Lancashire Cotton Industry could write that 'From the drawing-frame to the loom piece-rates are almost universal.'[70] The cotton industry, however, was exceptional in its widespread adoption of piece-work in the early phases of industrialisation. But, as the century progressed, so too did the spread of piece-work. The factory inspector, Leonard Horner, observed in 1851 that the proportion of piece-work to fixed weekly wages was 'daily on the increase.'[71] Some contemporary writers indeed attributed the superiority of British industry to the widespread use of piece-work. J. R. McCulloch, was one of these enthusiasts, and in one of his books he put the case for piece-work as follows : 'Large amounts of manufacturing, agricultural, and other labour are performed by the piece, and whenever it can be adopted, this is the preferable mode of hiring work people. Their strength, skill and assiduity are widely different. And when they are hired by time, it is often impracticable and is always a difficult, troublesome, and insidious task to arrange them in classes and adjust the wages of each according to their deserts.'[72]

The spread of piece-work around mid-century took place mostly in places of production that were brought under the Factory Acts—i.e. in the factories, where the hours of labour were strictly limited. As is well known Marx was extremely enthusiastic about the 'Ten Hours Act', which he regarded as a great victory for the working class—a triumph of the Political Economy of Labour over the Political Economy of Capital. But he was by no means oblivious to the attempts of the Political Economy of Capital to re-assert its dominance. Even if the law was not side-stepped or evaded, as it often was, then the intensity of labour in a shortened working day could be increased. As Marx put it : 'capital can only get more out of the working day by increasing the intensity of labour.'[73] Piece-work was often the tool by which this was done—and, as the remarks of McCulloch make clear, it meant that external supervision could be minimised since workers would often discipline themselves. The factory inspectorate reported in 1858 that 'Those who are paid by piece-work . . . constitute probably four-fifths of the workers in the factories.'[74] As Marx points out in his detailed analysis of piece wages, the pieceworker might well drive himself :

'Given the existence of piece-wages, it is, of course, to the personal interest of the worker that he should strain his labour power to the utmost, and this fact enables the capitalist all the more easily to raise the normal degree of intensity of labour.'[75]

A contemporary illustration of how piece-workers might tend to 'strain their labour power to the utmost' is provided by a letter to *The Times* in 1852 from the head of an engineering firm. The letter also provides an open admission of how employers' attempts to manipulate the disparity between output under day wages and under piecework could produce an intensification of labour for workers. The letter read :

'When work which has been done daywork is put on the piece, the employer usually regulates the piecework price a little under the price of it at daywork, knowing how production is increased by it. But he finds that men do work in quantity far beyond what they have been doing daywork, earning often 10s. per day, when at daywork they had done much less than half the work at 5s. 6d. per day. So much, indeed, is this the case, that manufacturers have made it a private rule that men for their extra work should earn "time and quarter" or "time and third", and have reduced the price accordingly; that is, where 5s. was the man's day pay, the price should be so arranged that ultimately he should earn 6s. 3d. or 6s. 8d. per day. This method we do not quite agree with, and we believe it has made men complain.'[76]

There is, in fact, very little doubt that this sort of accompaniment to piecework produced some very vociferous complaints. A writer in *The Trades Union Magazine* in the mid-1840s complained bitterly, not only about the greed generated by piecework (which he called task work) and the increased rate of labour, but also about piecework as a creator of unemployment. He wrote :

'The worst passions of our nature are enlisted in support of task-work. Avarice, meanness, cunning, hypocrisy, all excite and feed upon the miserable victim of task-work, while debility and destitution look out for the last morsel of their prey. A man who earns, by task-work, 40s. per week, the usual wages by day being 20s., robs his fellow of a week's employment.'[77]

These remarks were regarded as being so descriptive of contemporary reality that they went in turn from the pages of Disraeli's *Sybil* (1845)—where they were quoted almost verbatim—to James Ward's *Workmen and Wages at home and abroad* of 1868, and finally into the pages of one of the first really serious examinations of payment systems in British industry. David F. Schloss, in his *Methods of Industrial Remuneration* (first published 1892), quoted these remarks as an early example of the 'lump of labour' doctrine, which, he felt, so infected the minds of British workers around the turn of the century. The 'lump of labour' theory rested in his opinion on 'the utterly untenable supposition that a fixed amount of work exists.'[78] Schloss attributed the bulk of output restriction by workers to this view, citing only two cases in which output restriction was not due to it : those being output restriction by tinplate workers to prevent overstocking of the market and resultant wage cuts, and the explicit ca'canny policy of the National Union of Dock Labourers.[79] In his chapter headed 'Objections Entertained to Piece-Work by Working Men' Schloss commented that the workers' main objection was over-exertion; that piece-work might lead to scamping; that it encouraged employers to indulge in 'nibbling', cutting the rates 'by an insidious process of continual petty reductions'; and that it led employers to indulge in 'chasing', that was, using one exceptional worker to set the rates for the whole group. These, indeed, were precisely the criticisms levelled at piecework by W. G. Bunn of the Hearts of Oak Benefit Society during his attack on piecework at the Industrial Remuneration Conference in 1885. Bunn talked of 'the introduction of "piecework" with its attendant evils of slaving and scamping. . . .' He elaborated on this by asserting that :

> 'When a price was fixed, the fair average workman was not taken as a criterion. In every shop there were slow workmen and quick workmen, and very often the slow workmen turned out the best work, but frequently the time of the quick workman was adopted as the criterion by which the price was fixed. The natural consequence was that the slow man went to the wall.'[80]

On top of this there was the 'lump of labour' notion which Schloss illustrated graphically with an example of a workman employed in a dockyard in making washers with a boring machine. The workman told the investigator that : 'Now I am on piece-work, I am making about double what I used to make, when on day-work. *I know I am doing wrong. I am taking away the work of another man.* But I have permission from the Society.' Schloss's comments on this bear repeating :

> 'The words in italics are referable to the belief so firmly entertained by a large section of our working-classes, that for a man to exert his energies up to the point which just stops short of undue exertion—to do his level best—is inconsistent with his own interests and with loyalty to the cause of labour. The basis of this belief, which is in a large measure responsible for the unpopularity of piecework, is that noteworthy fallacy to which it is desired to direct attention under the name of "the theory of the Lump of Labour." '[81]

But, as E. H. Phelps Brown has pointed out : 'The "lump of Labour fallacy" was no fallacy in the experience of the workman. He found himself often enough in a position where there was only so much work going, and the more any one man did of it, the sooner the others would be sacked.'[82] The 'lump of labour' theory was widely held by working people in the second half of the 19th century. From about 1850 workers partially learnt the 'rules of the game', as Eric Hobsbawm puts it. After 1880, however, this learning process was largely complete and 'Workers began to demand what the traffic would bear and, where they had any choice, to measure effort by payment.'[83] This learning of the 'rules of the game' was also increasingly accompanied by workers being strong enough to be able to regulate to their advantage the degree of effort they put into their work. Phelps Brown points out that even unorganised labour had conventions by which the amount of work any man might do in a day was limited. Wages were paid for so much effort—though effort was something which could not be measured, though 'the results of it sometimes can be, and it might seem that at least when the wage-earner was paid by the piece the contract was explicit; but a piece-rate is judged by the amount it will enable a man to earn, and that depends on how hard he is to work.'[84] Even under piecework, then, there were important ways in which workers might regulate the 'effort bargain' in their favour. Further it seems to be the case—in spite of the fact that some unions remained hostile to piecework in this period and subsequently[85]—that the majority of trade unionists by the late 1890s had come to terms with piecework and were using it substantially to their advantage. As we saw earlier the dockyard worker quoted by Schloss had the permission of his union to work piecework, and this was increasingly typical of the trade union position in the 1890s. When the Webbs did their painstaking sums on the numbers of workers who were members of trade unions, which, respectively, 'insisted on piece-work', 'willingly recognise, in various departments, both piece-work and time work', and 'insisted on time work', they found that only 29 per cent of all trade unionists insisted on time work, as against 57 per cent who insisted on piecework, and 16 per cent who recognised either payment system. When these percentages for trade unionists are put alongside the percentages of *all* male wage earners (excluding those employed in agriculture or domestic service) who were estimated by the Board of Trade to be on the respective systems (33 per cent on piecework, and 67 per cent on time work) it is hard to avoid the Webbs' conclusion that organised workers were employed on piecework to a greater extent than unorganised workers.[86] Among the unions which favoured piecework were the miners, the cotton weavers, cotton spinners and the boot and shoe makers; and those main unions which opposed it were the Amalgamated Society of Engineers, the Ironfounders, the Carpenters and most of the main unions in the building trades. The point here is clear—by the turn of century it was by no means the case that piecework was inherently a 'bad thing' for workers, nor indeed that it was inherently a 'good thing'. Whether a trade union preferred one payment system to the other depended entirely on the extent to which it could achieve its object of securing a Standard Rate under a certain payment system. The piece-working cotton workers, employed in a work situation where the technology largely determined the output, used elaborate piecework price lists to ensure that 'every element by which the labour is increased effects an exactly corresponding variation in the remuneration. Only under such a system could any uniformity of rate be secured.'[87] Time work for the cotton workers would have been the high road to managerially determined work loads and speed up. Miners preferred piecework, not because it worked in their favour on this front, but rather because it offered freedom from close supervision and from the likelihood of being employed on time rates determined by butty masters and thereby suffering from constant speed up.[88]

The union which most bitterly opposed piecework, the A.S.E., similarly sought to achieve their objective of the Standard Rate through collective bargaining on time rates. The Webbs explain the engineers' objection to piecework as follows:

'The work of a skilled mechanic in an engineering shop differs from job to job in such a way as to make, under a piecework system, a new contract for each job. Each man, too, will be employed at an operation differing, if only in slight degree, from those of his fellows. If they are all working by the hour, a collective bargain can easily be made and adhered to. But where each successive job differs from the last, if only in small details, it is impossible to work out in advance any list of prices to which all the men can agree to adhere. The settlement for each job must necessarily be left to be made between the foreman and the workman concerned. Collective Bargaining becomes, therefore, impossible. But this is not all. The uncertainty as to the time and labour which a particular job will involve makes it impossible, for the foreman, with the best intentions in the world, to fix the prices of successive jobs so that the workman will obtain the same earnings for the same effort.'[89]

This 'effort bargaining' was a central part of the process of the learning of the 'rules of the game'. But new technology and new organisation of work could threaten the existing effort bargain. The constant introduction of new machinery and the transformation of the work situation upset previously held notions of what constituted a 'fair day's work.' We must now turn to a consideration of workers' attitudes to machinery.

The introduction of machinery on a large scale in some industries in the late 18th and early 19th centuries was itself responsible for large increases in production and in production per worker. This fact, of course, upset the customary relationship between output produced and the time taken. Machinery itself was also a force which disciplined the worker, since it might make regularity of work for the worker on a machine a thing about which he had little choice. This is precisely what the famous words of James Philips Kay signify:

'While the engine runs the people must work—men, women and children are yoked together with iron and steam. The animal machine—breakable in the best case, subject to a thousand sources of suffering—is chained to the iron machine, which knows no suffering and no weariness.'[90]

The need for the new work discipline itself derived very much from the use of machinery. Andrew Ure, for instance, had said that the main problem for the pioneer industrial capitalists was to get workers 'to renounce their desultory habits of work, and to identify themselves with the unvarying regularity of the complex automaton.' The reason why the manufacturers needed the 'complex automaton' to work with 'unvarying regularity' is quite simple. New machines are expensive pieces of capital equipment and a capitalist, true to his lights, will want to maximise the return from his capital outlay as quickly as possible. (We shall have more to say about the 'economics of capital utilisation' in a later section on the great expansion of shift working in the period since the end of the second world war.) The excellent work of Douglas Reid on mid-19th century Birmingham has amply shown this process at work. The growth of large factories in some sectors of Birmingham industry from the 1850s had brought about, as one large manufacturer told the *Morning Chronicle* in 1851, the need for 'stricter discipline and order'—a discipline and an order that were, as Reid puts it, 'required by manufacturers because of their heavy investments in steam power.' Whereas steam power in the city in 1800 amounted to only 127 h.p., by 1825 there was 1,400 h.p., and in 1835 2,700 h.p., in 1851 5,400 h.p., and in 1870 11,272 h.p. The demands of the industrial capitalists' use of steam power conflicted with the labour and leisure patterns of Birmingham's St. Monday-worshipping working class. A manufacturer of hooks and eyes said in 1862 that 'When we started a steam engine, I told the people that it would be necessary to begin at a fixed hour, instead of the irregularity which had been usual.'[91]

Reid has suggested, plausibly, that the successful introduction of this new factory discipline was greatly helped by the fact that an important social movement (involving many working class leaders) to drive out St. Monday and to replace it by the Saturday half-holiday coincided with the large scale introduction of steam power.[92] Reid points out that to trade-off St. Monday for the Saturday half holiday was an unfair exchange for the working class—$10\frac{1}{2}$ hours of free time was replaced by 3 hours. Many firms so re-arranged working hours that the length of the working week was unaltered, and in some cases increased. Areas of resistance to this new time discipline were mainly found in the small workshops, whereas in the factories the triumph of the political economy of capital, and of the profit maximising appetites of the 'complex automaton' seems to have been considerable. But this analysis ignores the important fact that to lengthen the working day or the working week is not of itself a triumph of the political economy of capital—and nor is the opposite, a reduction of working hours, necessarily a triumph of the political economy of labour. These things are only true if work loads, and therefore the rate of exploitation of workers, remain the same under the new arrangements as under the old. If hours are increased and the same work rate per hour is maintained then that represents a defeat for the workers. But if hours are increased and work rates fall, if effort slackens off, if output per hour is diminished, and if more leisure is taken *at work*, then the workers have in an important way scored a victory. If the complaints of employers and their allies at the turn of the century are anything to go by then this latter definitely happened in many industries and trades. Whether, and how soon, it happened in Birmingham after the virtual eradication of St. Monday in the factories, we do not know. But if Birmingham industry was at all like much of the rest of British industry then it probably did happen and happen fairly soon. The massive turn by employers to the use of piecework (with its effects on the intensity of labour that Marx and others talked of) is highly significant here. Piecework was made necessary from the industrial capitalists' point of view precisely because workers were allowing their effort at work to drop off unless it was propped up by material incentives. Reid himself cites piecework as being one cause of worker resistance to the attempted abolition of St. Monday in Birmingham—but piecework was only used in the small workshops[93] at the time that Reid is writing about. Since piecework soon began to be introduced in the large factories too, one imagines that, since here St. Monday had already been largely rooted out, it was a symptom of the fact that leisure was now being taken at work rather than away from work, that deliberate 'slacking' at work was taking place, and that these strategies were being used by workers to offset the effects of the formally longer working week.

The introduction of machinery into some industries in the early 19th century immediately brings machine breaking and Luddism to mind. But we should, as E. J. Hobsbawm in his article on the subject has shown, be extremely careful not to attribute these phenomena exclusively or even mainly to straightforward hostility on the part of workers to machinery. Machine breaking and Luddism are complex subjects. Hobsbawm has in the first place given considerable rationality to the actions of machine breakers and Luddites. He also points out that there are at least two main sorts of machine breaking. The first sort implying 'no special hostility to machines as such', but rather involving merely a means by which workers put pressure on employers for such things as wage increases or against wage reductions. To describe this he has coined the memorable phrase 'collective bargaining by riot'. Although this sort of machine breaking did not involve hostility to machines as such, the second sort did represent an 'expression of working class hostility to the new machines of the industrial revolution.'[94] In this case we should immediately remember that this sort of hostility to machinery is exemplified by the attitudes of framework knitters to the new knitting machines, of handloom weavers to the new power looms, and of agricultural labourers to the new threshing machines. We should remember that, as Alisdair Clayre has put it : 'Those who broke the machines were not in general the men who used them, but the men they displaced.'[95] Nor was machine breaking of this sort indiscriminate or ill thought out. The Nottingham correspondent of the *Leeds Mercury* at the end of December 1811 pointed out of the Nottinghamshire Luddites that :

'They broke only the frames of such as have reduced the price of the men's wages; those who have not lowered the price, have their frames untouched; in one house, last night, they broke four frames out of six; the other two which belonged to masters who had not lowered their wages, they did not meddle with.'

In Derbyshire villages such as Ashover and Pentridge, Luddite bands left untouched those frames which made 'full fashioned work, at the full price', destroying only those which contravened these requirements.[96] The machine breaking activities of these workers was often, as Hobsbawm has shown, successful in slowing down the introduction of those machines which displaced labour and reduced the living standards of the workers using the older technology. Power loom weavers, for example, we must conclude were by and large happy about the machinery they worked upon. Only occasionally do we find references to machine breaking on the part of the operators of the new machinery. Thus Charles Babbage in the early 1830s could write that as a result of 'a most erroneous and unfortunate opinion' amongst workmen 'that their own interest and that of the employers are at variance' 'valuable machinery is sometimes neglected, and even privately injured. . . .'[97] But even this he felt was dying out rapidly in Britain—'partly from the fact that good workmen had been promoted to foremen.' Hostility to machinery was not found in all parts of the emergent working class. It was only to be found where the changes brought about by the introduction of the new machinery disadvantaged certain groups of workers.

The detailed work of Hobsbawm and Rudé on the Swing riots of 1830 makes this point quite clearly. Other points of interest emerge also. The breaking of threshing machines (and to some extent of other agricultural machinery) while 'the most significant' was only 'one of the many forms that the labourers' movement assumed.'[98] Arson, wages meetings, attacks on overseers, parsons, and landlords, threatening letters and riotous assemblies were other forms of the movement.[99] The chief motive for the attacks on the threshing machines (if the demands of Swing bands themselves are anything to go on) was the fact that the machines displaced labour and lowered wage rates. Many incidents of machine breaking were carried out, therefore, in a context of tumultuous demands for the withdrawal of the machines *and*, often at least as important and sometimes more important, a general demand for wage increases. An example from West Sussex makes it quite clear that wage issues were very much in the forefront even where machine-breaking was widespread. Hobsbawm and Rudé write :

'From Chichester it was reported that, on 15 November, the labourers of Arundel, Bersted, Bognor, Felpham and Yapton had combined to destroy all threshing machines and to have their wages raised from the present 10s to 14s a week. As they marched from farm to farm they recruited new forces by intimidation or persuasion, demanded money, food and beer and compelled farmers to agree to increase their wages. Meanwhile, ran the report, "almost every machine is broke up".'[100]

An example from Basingstoke is particularly illuminating of the way that widespread machine breaking was used to force the pace on the wage issue, and how new agricultural machinery other than threshing machines was sometimes also a target of Swing bands. Fifty men armed with sticks having arrived at a farm, when asked what they wanted 'the answer was some money to support them, and then they were to rise in a body to have their wages risen.' The owner of the farm gave them money, but nevertheless her winnowing machine was smashed. Her subsequent testimony is revealing : 'They said it must go, as it was a machine; and it was broke to pieces.'[101] There are also on record between 20 and 25 cases of industrial machine breaking. Some of the main centres of industrial machine breaking were the Andover area, parts of Buckinghamshire and Berkshire, and also Norfolk. Some of this machine breaking damaged large amounts of property—for instance, an iron foundry near Andover and five paper mills at High Wycombe. At Fordinbridge in Hampshire two factories were destroyed.[102] At Hungerford, Berkshire, the Swing rioters destroyed all the machinery and wrought iron at an iron foundry.[103]

At first much of ruling class opinion was extremely worried that the machine breaking going on in the countryside would spill over and be reproduced in the urban areas and in industrial situations generally. Magistrates demanded that troops should be sent into the towns, arguing that if Swing reached the manufacturing districts 'no man can foresee the consequences.' But only a few days later *The Times* could point out that this threat was not materialising—'our manufacturing districts are unaffected by the surrounding commotions and the work people are in full employ and remunerative wages.'[104] In a county like Leicestershire, one of the strongholds of Luddism in the 1810s, such fears of the spread of the contagion amongst industrial workers were naturally strong. This feeling was nearly confirmed as reality when the Loughborough weavers went on strike for higher wages and to increase their bargaining power they threatened to fire the houses of two master hosiers. But the local magistrates found no direct connection between this threat and Swing, though they added the qualification that the language of the strikers 'certainly showed that they were emboldened by the present public excitement.'[105] But the general failure of urban workers to follow Captain Swing in 1830 is highly significant, and may well prove the point that was advanced earlier : that there was no widespread hostility to machinery as such among industrial workers. If there had been, 1830 would have been the obvious opportunity for the expression of such hostility on a large scale in the manufacturing districts. Not all machinery displaced or disadvantaged workers—and if it did then others benefited from the misfortunes of the displaced and disadvantaged. Frequently, and increasingly with the growth of trade unions and the processes of collective bargaining, workers threatened by new machinery began to bargain for their continued employment on the new machines. If workers did not begin to welcome new machinery, they certainly began to be able to cope with it. The introduction of new machinery gradually came to be accepted, as long as the existing workers were the ones allowed to operate it. Many groups of trade unionists successfully began to protect their living standards and their control of the labour market by adopting a policy similar to that of the engineers in the last quarter of the 19th century of 'following the work to the new machines.'[106]

A process of learning was going on here. Marx, as ever, had some perceptive things to say about this. In a section in Volume One of *Capital* called 'Struggle Between the Workers and the Machine', he points out that 'only since the introduction of the machine has the worker been at war with the instruments of labour itself, with the material embodiment of capital.' He goes on to give chapter and verse on this development, and commenting on Luddism he states that :

'Time and experience were needed before the workers could learn to distinguish between machinery itself and the use of machinery by capital; and until they could come to direct their attacks, not against the material instruments of production, but against the particular social form in which these instruments are used.'

In a footnote to this he adds that 'In old-fashioned manufactures we find that, even today, the revolts of the workers against machinery sometimes assume a savage form. This happened, for instance, among the Sheffield file-cutters in 1865.'[107] This late example of machine breaking (and it was by no means the last) should remind us that it is clearly wrong to suggest an evenness in the development in all trades of ways other than machine breaking to exert some job control. No doubt as a general cultural factor, machinery in general was much more acceptable, because it was much more normal as far as workers were concerned in say, 1880 than say, in 1810. But new, and potentially threatening machinery, hit workers and continues to hit workers at different times. The industrial revolution in cotton for example came a good deal sooner than the industrial revolution in shoe making or in hosiery. In those industries where the introduction of machinery came late there were often ways of handling it other than machine-breaking available to the workers. As Hobsbawm has pointed out, the policy of 'capturing' machinery for the benefit of the workers concerned through conventional trade union activity was patchily adopted from the 1840s and more generally adopted from the mid-1890s.[108] From the 1840s open advocacy of machine breaking was very rare. On one occasion in the 1830s when it was openly recommended as a tactic for securing the redress of a grievance it came from an unexpected quarter. Richard Oastler, 'Church and King Tory' that he was, during his vigorous campaign for the full implementation of the 1833 Factory Act, having heard from local reformers at Blackburn that a magistrate had dismissed a case against a local employer for contravening the Act, made a fierce speech at Blackburn on September 15th, 1836 during which he threatened to unleash a wave of machine-breaking. Oastler told his audience, which was made up of large numbers of enthusiastic working class people and also of a small number of less than enthusiastic mill-owners and magistrates, that unless the latter complied with the law he would be forced to ask them whether the lives of the factory children or the owners' spindles were 'the most entitled to the law's protection.' He told the magistrates present that if they again rejected factory cases he would instruct the children to apply old knitting needles to their spindles 'in a way which would teach these law-defying mill-owner magistrates to have respect even to "Oastler's Law", as they had wrongly designated the factory law.'[109] But in the mid-19th century this attitude was becoming increasingly rare. The message for instance, from, of all places, Sherwood Forest itself, was very different from what it had been a generation earlier. Christopher Thomson, a working man with great enthusiasm for the education and the emancipation of his class, writing from Edwinstowe in 1847, seems to epitomise the new attitude of conditional support for machinery. He wrote :

'Is the fact of hundreds being thrown out of employment by the introduction of machinery, a sufficient argument against its use? I would answer no! I believe that great, important as are its results already, that it is yet in its infancy, and that the most comprehensive mind can but dimly shadow forth its benevolent mission. I regard it as one of the great blessings of the Creator, who had destined the inanimate to conquer labour, by its iron bone and muscle—that man, the inventor and director . . . shall some day work by his mental might.'

For Thomson, the present disadvantages of machinery had to be set against that future. But between the unsatisfactory present and the satisfactory future a transformation in the relations between capital and labour was needed. The present system of labour would go on 'Just so long as the artisans will allow it, but no longer!'[110]

But, in 1868, James Ward could still write that 'there are a considerable number of the working-classes who have a lingering, lurking dislike to machinery, which they cannot rationally explain, and who look with the liveliest apprehension at any improvement which may be effected in that grand aid to human industry.' He singled out recent riots at Coventry against the application of steam power to ribbon manufacture, and the disturbances at Northampton, Kettering, and Wellingborough against the introduction of the sewing machine into the boot and shoe industry.[111] Similarly, the Manchester based Brickmakers' Society, according to a recent writer, achieved 'considerable notoriety in the 1860s with its policy of sabotage, boycott and machine smashing against machine-made bricks'.[112] But responses like these were, in fact, becoming less and less common. Increasingly, from the latter end of the 19th century, workers learnt to live with machinery, or rather found ways other than machine breaking to resist the full brunt of machinery's appetites. It was this change which Carter Goodrich was writing about in 1920 when he pointed out that : 'I suppose few accounts of restrictions on technique have been written without an emphasis on the objection to machinery. Historically of great interest, it is a nearly dead issue now.' By the time he was writing 'Bargaining over the conditions of change' had become far more important 'than a mere opposition to change.'[113] This transition from outright hostility to machinery to a qualified acceptance of it had already been noted by the Webbs in a chapter of their *Industrial Democracy* (1897) called 'New Processes and Machinery'. They wrote that :

'A generation ago it was assumed, as a matter of course, by almost every educated person, that it was a cardinal tenet of Trade Unionism to oppose machinery and the introduction of improved processes of manufacture.'

They go on to quote a critic of trade unionism as saying, as late as the 1860s, that 'Trade Unions have ever naturally opposed the introduction of machinery. . . .' To show that trade unionists themselves shared this view they quote the editor of *The Potter's Examiner* in 1844 as saying that :

'Machinery has done the work. Machinery has left them in rags and without any wages at all. . . . I look upon all improvements which tend to lessen the demand for human labor [sic] as the deadliest curse that could possibly fall on the heads of our working classes, and I hold it to be the duty of every working potter—the highest duty—to obstruct by all legal means the introduction of the scourge into any branch of his trade.'

But by the late 1890s the Webbs could say with great confidence (though without complete accuracy) that 'Nowadays we hear no such complaints. . . . The fact is that Trade Unionism on this subject has changed its attitude.'[114] In the main this statement is perfectly true. The Webbs themselves found only a couple of cases of outright opposition to machinery—amongst Birmingham pearl button and stud makers and Sheffield file and table-blade forgers. As A. L. Levine has pointed out, there were a few other cases in the period from the mid-1890s up to 1914. The Woolwich

Branch of the United Pattern Makers' Association in 1898 complained bitterly about the introduction of surfacing machines, though, significantly, the union's executive ignored the complaint. From the evidence given to the Royal Commission on Labour in the 1890s can be extracted at least two instances of old-fashioned hostility to machinery. As late as 1913 the Amalgamated Society of Farriers was urging the War Office to encourage hand-made rather than machine-made horseshoes. An analysis of the Board of Trade's Annual Reports on Strikes and Lockouts between 1900 and 1914 reveals only two (relatively unimportant and, as with most of the other examples, in peripheral sectors of the economy) strikes caused by rejection of mechanised processes. These were an unsuccessful strike of Limerick tailoresses in 1902 against button-holing machines, and again in Ireland a strike of Dublin bottle makers in 1913 who unsuccessfully tried to stop the spread of bottle making machines.[115] Similarly Carter Goodrich states that in 1911, 1912, and 1913 there were only two strikes against the introduction of machinery—that of glass bottle makers already mentioned and another of dockers. And there was a third strike against the use of a portable instead of a stationary drill amongst Boilermakers. Less than a thousand workers were involved in these three strikes.[116]

Arthur Shadwell, in his book *Industrial Efficiency* (1909), commented about the boot and shoe industry (which we shall use as a 'case study') that 'The boot and shoe trade has been revolutionised in late years by the introduction of machinery, and that has been accomplished with the help of the unions.'[117] The boot and shoe industry is particularly interesting for us here since its 'industrial revolution' (involving the substitution of machinery for hand labour and the organisation of the industry into factories) was a phenomenon not of the late 18th and early 19th century, but rather a product of the second half of the 19th century—the period in which, as the various testimonies given above indicate, the worker learnt to live with the machine. It is therefore, immensely rewarding to examine the process of change in workers' attitudes to the introduction of machinery into their industry over this period, culminating in Shadwell's statement. But, as we shall see, although by the period before the first world war boot and shoe workers no longer openly resisted machinery they still had ways to mitigate its worst effects. The historian of the National Union of Boot and Shoe Operatives (on whose work I rely heavily here), writes that by 1855–56, the Singer Sewing Machine Company was attempting to sell on the British market a sewing machine which would speed up the process of closing the uppers. From the workers' point of view, of course, this machine threatened to bring with it the unemployment of men and women hand-closers. In the mid-1850s the shoe workers in most of the British centres of footwear production were in no position to fight against the introduction of the machine—but, even so, in Stafford, Northampton, Kettering and Wellingborough, the bootmakers, in latter-day Luddite fashion struck in 1857 and 1858 in attempts to prevent manufacturers from introducing the machines.[118] But strike action only slightly impeded, and by no means prevented, the progress of the sewing machines into the industry. In fact, the intransigent attitude of the Northampton workers to the machine drove much of their former work to Leicester, where workers, in the main, welcomed the machines. The Leicester bootmakers and their counterparts in other areas failed to show solidarity with their Northamptonshire colleagues. John Ball, F.R.S., in a paper to the Social Science Association in 1860 discussing the strikes against the sewing machine, said that support was not forthcoming for the Northampton workers because it was felt by the rest of the workers in the industry that it was:

> 'neither desirable nor practical to resist the extension of mechanical improvements, although [the other bootmakers were] very sensible of the inconvenience and suffering that are sometimes caused by a rapid change in the nature and extent of the employment afforded in any particular trade.'[119]

And nor, indeed, was there any support for the Northampton bootmakers' stand against machinery forthcoming from workers in other industries. The Chainmakers' Union, for instance, had no hesitation in declaring that the strike was 'foolish'. But some employers in the industry, knowing full well the extremely serious consequences of the wholesale introduction of machinery, applied the hand-team system as a transitional phase in the process of full mechanisation.[120] Alan Fox comments of this system that:

'If, say, five men who previously worked separately were brought together in a team, and increased their total output as a result, then their increased output must be paid for at [piecework] statement prices.'

The result of this sort of system, allied with the old basis for payment, meant that labour costs for each pair of boots remained the same—the whole advantage of the more efficient organisation of production going to the workers.

By the 1890s the majority of the union's leaders were committed to the acceptance of full mechanisation in the boot and shoe trade. The attitudes of the union leaders on this issue fully bear out the Webbs' point that by 1897, trade unionists had abandoned the attempt to exclude machines, and instead 'claim, for the operatives already working at the trade, a preferential right to acquire the new dexterity and perform the new service.'[121] In 1892 the secretary of the union commented that 'we have had almost startling changes in the methods of working, machinery being the order of the day . . . with regard to the wholesale introduction of machinery, now being accomplished, this must be closely watched, so that our members may be induced to work in conjunction therewith, otherwise we shall find our membership rapidly decrease, and a compact body of men or youths working against our interests.'[122] In the short run, the introduction of machinery inevitably displaced some labour, and the union leadership responded to this by demanding the sharing of the available work amongst the members of the union. But, within the ranks of the union, particularly amongst the socialists in the industry at Leicester and Northampton, there was considerable straightforward opposition to the use of machinery. It was out of this hostility that a fairly explicit rank and file policy of output restriction evolved. The trade journal, *The Shoe and Leather Record*, in 1892 was quick to observe this trend and commented that:

'The men may . . . in too many cases, so contrive to idle away their time as to leave the manufacturer but a small return for his capital outlay. . . . They maliciously dawdle over their work so as to make it appear that hand labour is as good and as cheap as labour aided by machinery.'

The editor of the journal argued that :

'There exists among workmen a tacit understanding that only so much work shall be done within a certain time, and no matter what machines are introduced, the men conspire to prevent any saving being effected by their aid. . . . The Union are engaged in a gigantic conspiracy to hinder and retard the development of labour-saving appliances in this country.'

In Leicester, where socialists controlled the local branch of the union, restriction of output became an organised policy. The branch committee would calculate what output the earnings derived from the day wage payment system (which had been introduced with the machines) represented in terms of the piece-rates which had been applied under the hand work system. The calculation having been done, branch members were instructed to produce that much on their machines and no more. Those union members who failed to comply with the restriction on output were fined amounts ranging from 2s. 6d. to 20s. by the branch officials.[123] One union leader, T. F. Richards, openly admitted at a meeting of the Leicester Arbitration Board in 1893 that this policy existed—a point which even the more moderately inclined William Inskip could not deny. The employers' response was one of fury, a fury that was intensified by fears about foreign competition. This reaction took purposeful shape before very long, with the employers attempting to assert their 'right to manage'. The 1895 Lockout was the culmination of this.[124] The upshot of it all was that the union was comprehensively defeated, and a settlement was reached based on seven points (the 'Seven Commandments') which were largely in the employers' favour. The second commandment, in particular, epitomises the assertion of managerial prerogatives and the key importance of the machine question. It said, in effect, that every employer in the industry had full control over his factory, that he could choose day wages or piece wages, and that he could introduce machinery into the factory at will and without notice.[125]

As Alan Fox points out, 'the output-restriction issue was bound up with the question of the method of payment. The Union had to wage a long defensive struggle on this question against employers who tried to gain a competitive advantage by manipulating the system of payment.'[126] It was not until the end of the First World War that piecework was widely adopted throughout the industry. Resistance to piecework had been particularly strong in the town of Northampton. Whenever it was introduced there it was usually countered by organised restriction of output. During the 1913–1914 national negotiations, the activities of James Gribble and his comrades in the Northampton branch of the Social Democratic Federation in the local leadership of the union were singled out as being particularly irksome to the employers.[127] At the 1916 conference of the union, Gribble explained the long-standing resistance of the Northampton workers to piecework and compared it to the position in Leicester, where by then the workers accepted it. He said:

'in Northampton we take a different view. We don't want to go the pace, and are not desirous of killing ourselves. We have been opposed to piece-work rates, and we know full well what it will mean to our men when it is universally adopted. . . . We should have had numbers unemployed, whilst others would have received more than under the old system. That is why we are so far behind Leicester in getting out [piecework] Statements.'[128]

Even those branches which did not adopt piecework statements commonly exhorted their members not to maximise their earnings, and in the decade before the First World War there were still cases of branches disciplining workers who earned more than the old day-wage.[129] But machinery had arrived for good. Employers sought to introduce the payment systems which would minimise their costs and at the same time would offer some workers a chance of enhanced earnings. But work groups and union branches frequently adopted a contrary policy of work sharing and used collective pressure to limit the earnings of individual workers to what were regarded as customarily acceptable levels. Restriction of output was, by the First World War, a widely adopted and explicitly advocated union policy at branch level.

High demand for footwear during the First World War had allowed piecework to spread even more widely than before, and output restriction was pursued less vigorously by the boot and shoe workers. But, with return of bad trade in the early 1920s, rank and file pressure for the ending of piecework was building up. In 1921, according to Fox, 'the Union membership had voted decisively . . . in favour of day-work governed by Quantity Statements, with the individual worker limiting his output to that level required to earn his minimum wage (in other words, piecework with restriction of output).'[130] Although restriction of output was explicitly forbidden under the National Agreement, it was openly supported at local level. Len Smith, who for a long time was the Northampton leader of the union and who rose to become national General President between 1938 and 1944, openly supported the policy of restriction of output throughout his period of considerable influence in the union. What he told the union's 1918 national conference remained as one of his perspectives for the next twenty-five years or so : 'I have always believed in the restriction of output as one of the weapons of our class.'[131] Smith was by no means alone in holding to, and acting on, that belief.

NOTES

1. Quoted in L. Urwick and E. F. L. Brech *The Making of Scientific Management* Vol. 2. (London 1964 imp.) p. 99.
2. Sidney Pollard *The Genesis of Modern Management* (Penguin 1968 edn.) p. 189.
3. Much detail on all this can be found in S. Pollard op. cit., esp. Ch. 5 'The Adaptation of the Labour Force', and Stanley D. Chapman *The Early Factory Masters* (Newton Abbot 1967). Robert Owen wrote of the aversion to factory work as follows : 'Such was the general dislike of the occupation at that time, that with few exceptions only persons destitute of friends, employment and character were found willing to try the experiment.'
4. A. Tillett 'Industry and Management' in *Management Thinkers* eds.

A. Tillett, T. Kempner and G. Wills (Penguin 1970) p. 34.

5. Quoted in S. Pollard op. cit. p. 204.

6. E. P. Thompson 'Time, Work-discipline, and Industrial Capitalism' in *Past and Present* No. 38 December 1967.

7. E. P. Thompson 'Time, Work-discipline, and Industrial Capitalism', pp. 71-72.

8. Quoted in T. C. Smout *A History of the Scottish People, 1560-1830* (London 1972 edn.) pp. 394-395.

9. E. P. Thompson, 'Time, Work-discipline and Industrial Capitalism.' pp. 74-75.

10. J. E. Williams *The Derbyshire Miners* (London 1962) p. 60. A very similar stratagem to reduce the absence problem is still adopted by the National Coal Board.

11. Eric Hopkins 'Working Conditions in Victorian Stourbridge' in *International Review of Social History*, Vol. XIX, 1974, p. 410.

12. Ibid., p. 415.

13. Quoted in D. A. Reid 'The Decline of St Monday. Working-class leisure in Birmingham, 1760-1875', paper for Society of the Study of Labour History Conference on 'The Working Class and Leisure', Brighton, November 1975. Typescript p. 4.

14. Quoted by D. A. Reid, p. 4.

15. D. A. Reid, p. 9. We shall return in a later section to the question of the decline of St Monday on account of the economics of capital utilisation.

16. E. P. Thompson, 'Time, Work-Discipline and Industrial Capitalism', p. 74.

17. Sidney Pollard *A History of Labour in Sheffield* (Liverpool 1959) p. 211.

18. T. S. Ashton *An Economic History of England: the 18th Century* (London 1966 imp.) p. 211.

19. Quoted in J. L. and Barbara Hammond *The Town Labourer (1760-1832)* (London 1949 edn.) Vol. 1, pp. 32-33. See also C. Aspin *Lancashire: the First Industrial Society* (Helmshore 1969) pp. 71-73 for other sets of rules in Lancashire cotton mills.

20. From Plate 34 in C. Aspin *Lancashire: the first industrial society* (Helmshore 1969).

21. Sidney Pollard *The Genesis of Modern Management* p. 222.

22. Quoted from the diary of John Byng, 1790, in T. S. Ashton, op. cit., p. 214. The quotation from Bishop Berkeley comes from Ashton, p. 213.

23. Adam Smith *An Inquiry into the Nature and Causes of the Wealth of Nations*, Vol. 1, Chapter 8, p. 92 (London 1908 edn.). See also Ashton, op. cit., p. 213.

24. Samuel Smiles *Thrift* (London 1897 edn.) p. 27. Smiles goes on to cite Dean Boyd as having said that over £7 million per year was lost to workers in the woollen and cotton industries and the brick-laying and building trades on account of 'Idle Monday.'

25. Quoted in J. E. Williams *The Derbyshire Miners* (London 1962) p. 60.

26. Quoted in Williams, op. cit., p. 60.

27. J. A. Lincoln *The Restrictive Society* (London 1967) pp. 48-49.

28. Samuel Smiles *Thrift* (London 1897 edn.) p. v.

29. Ibid., p. vi.
30. Ibid., p. 13 and p. 15.
31. Ibid., p. 27.
32. Ibid., p. 8. Extremely similar sentiments appear on p. 184.
33. The importance of Smiles' analysis of thrift for his theory of society is dealt with by Asa Briggs in his fine essay 'Samuel Smiles and the Gospel of Work' in his *Victorian People* (Harmondsworth 1965 edn.) pp. 136-141. Briggs' whole essay is well worth reading. Another good analysis can be found in Reinhard Bendix *Work and Authority in Industry* (New York 1963 edn.) pp. 109-114.
34. Smiles, *Thrift*, p. 12.
35. Ibid., p. 10.
36. Ibid., p. 29.
37. Ibid., see Ch. VI 'Methods of Economy', Ch. VII 'Economy in Life Assurance', Ch. VIII 'Savings Banks'.
38. Marx *Grundrisse* (Pelican/New Left Review edn., Harmondsworth 1973), trans. Martin Nicolaus, p. 286. I owe these references to George Johnston.
39. Ibid., p. 287.
40. Smiles, *Thrift*, pp. 12-13.
41. Smiles, *Thrift*, p. 12.
42. *Success in Life: A Book for Young Men* (London 1859) p. 194.
43. Ibid., pp. 314-317. Franklin's writings were quoted in many works of this genre: see for instance Henry Southgate *Things A Lady Would Like to Know* (London and Edinburgh 3rd. edn. 1875) pp. 510-511.
44. *The Autobiography of Benjamin Franklin* (Collier Books edn. New York 1970 imp.) p. 52.
45. J. E. T. Eldridge (ed.) *Max Weber: the interpretation of social reality* (London 1972 edn.) p. 40.
46. E. P. Thompson *The Making of the English Working Class* (Penguin 1968 edn.) p. 392.
47. E. P. Thompson *The Making of the English Working Class*, p. 398.
48. Quoted in ibid., p. 397. The previous quotation from Ure comes from p. 398.
49. Ibid., p. 404, see also J. E. T. Eldridge, op. cit., pp. 48-49.
50. J. E. T. Eldridge, op. cit., p. 50. Robert Moore in his *Pitmen, Preachers and Politics: The Effects of Methodism in a Durham mining community* (Cambridge University Press, 1974) has taken this discussion a great deal further than previous writers. See, especially, Moore's Introduction for a critique of Thompson's views.
51. Quoted in E. P. Thompson *The Making of the English Working Class*, pp. 395-396.
52. Thompson, op. cit., p. 396.
53. Weber *Protestant Ethic*, quoted by J. E. T. Eldridge, op. cit., p. 48.
54. Thomas Carlyle *Chartism* p. 36 and *Past and Present* p. 185 (Chapman and Hall edn. London 1895). Sidney Pollard, *Genesis of Modern Management* p. 222 indicates that although financial incentives were seldom used with children they were widely used with adults. Perhaps Thompson's formulation should be revised to say

that for children discipline enforced by supervision might be adequate, but for those past the age of puberty material incentives were required.

55. E. P. Thompson, 'Time, Work-Discipline and Industrial Capitalism', p. 86.
56. S. Pollard *Genesis of Modern Management*, p. 222.
57. Ibid., pp. 223-224.
58. E. J. Hobsbawm 'Custom, Wages, and Work-load' in *Essays in Labour History*, eds. A. Briggs and J. Saville (London 1967 edn.) pp. 117-118.
59. Ibid., p. 119.
60. Charles Babbage *On the Economy of Machinery and Manufactures* (first published London 1832, third edn. 1833) p. 295.
61. Ibid., p. 310.
62. Babbage, pp. 115-117.
63. Babbage, Chapter XXV.
64. Babbage, p. 250.
65. Babbage, pp. 250-251.
66. Babbage, pp. 253, 256, and 257.
67. Babbage, p. 257. An important by-product, Babbage felt, of such a system would have been the removal of 'all real or imaginary causes for combinations.' (p. 258)
68. S. Pollard *Genesis of Modern Management*, p. 225.
69. Ibid., p. 222.
70. Sydney J. Chapman *The Lancashire Cotton Industry* (Manchester 1904) p. 272, and in general Chapter XI 'Methods of Paying Wages.
71. Leonard Horner, quoted in E. J. Hobsbawm 'Custom, Wages and Work-load', p. 132, n. 4.
72. J. R. McCulloch *A Treatise on the Circumstances which determine the rate of Wages and the Conditions of the Labouring Classes* (London, 2nd. edn. 1854) p. 70. See also Hobsbawm, 'Custom, Wages and Work-load' p. 131.
73. Marx, *Capital* (E. and C. Paul trans. London 1930) p. 608.
74. Reports of Inspectors of Factories, April 30, 1858, quoted in Marx, *Capital*, p. 608, n. 4.
75. *Capital*, p. 605.
76. Quoted in S. and B. Webb *Industrial Democracy* (first published 1897, London 1920 edn.) pp. 292-293 footnote. I have relied heavily in this section on the Webbs' superb analysis of piecework in their chapter 'The Standard Rate.' The Webbs commented on the illustration given that 'Thus the employer not only gets the advantage of an increased output upon the same fixed capital, but actually contrives also insidiously to alter, to his own profit, the proportion between the muscular energy expended by the workman and the amount of food which the latter obtains.'
77. This quotation originally came from *The Trades Union Magazine* in the 1840s. It was quoted shortly afterwards (with only minor alterations) by Disraeli in *Sybil* (1845), and in the 1860s was used by James Ward in his *Workmen and Wages at home and abroad* (London 1868) p. 244; and it appeared still later in D. F. Schloss's *Methods of Industrial Remuneration*.

78. D. F. Schloss *Methods of Industrial Remuneration* (3rd edn., London 1907) p. 84.
79. Ibid., p. 86, footnote.
80. *Industrial Remuneration Conference: the report of the proceedings and papers read*, etc. (London 1885) p. 169.
81. D. F. Schloss, op. cit., p. 80; see also D. Landes *The Unbound Prometheus* (Cambridge 1969) p. 321.
82. E. H. Phelps Brown *The Growth of British Industrial Relations* (London 1965 edn.) p. 98.
83. E. J. Hobsbawm 'Custom, Wages and Work-load' in *Essays in Labour History*, p. 114.
84. Phelps Brown, op. cit., pp. 288-289.
85. See, for example, Ernest Aves 'Methods of Remuneration: Time and Piece-Work' in Charles Booth (ed.) *Life and Labour of the People in London*, Vol IX, (London 1897) p. 314.
86. See the detailed tables and notes on them in S. and B. Webb *Industrial Democracy* (1897, London 1920 edn.) pp. 286-287.
87. Webb, *Industrial Democracy* p. 289.
88. Ibid., p. 290.
89. Ibid., pp. 291-292.
90. J. P. Kay *Moral and Physical Conditions of the Operatives employed in the Cotton Manufacture in Manchester* (1832) p. 24.
91. D. A. Reid 'The Decline of St. Monday. Working-class leisure in Birmingham, 1760-1875', p. 4.
92. Ibid., pp. 5-9.
93. Ibid., p. 9.
94. E. J. Hobsbawm 'The Machine Breakers' in *Labouring Men* (London 1968 edn.) p. 7.
95. A. Clayre *Work and Play: Ideas and Experience of Work and Leisure* (London 1974). For detailed studies of Luddism see E. P. Thompson *The Making of the English Working Class*, George Rudé 'Luddism' in *The Crowd in History, 1730-1848* (New York 1964), Malcolm Thomis *The Luddites* (Newton Abbot 1970).
96. E. P. Thompson *The Making of the English Working Class*, pp. 606-607.
97. Charles Babbage *Economy of Manufactures* p. 250.
98. E. J. Hobsbawm and George Rudé *Captain Swing* (Harmondsworth 1973) p. 71.
99. Ibid., p. 71 and p. 163.
100. Ibid., p. 85.
101. Ibid., p. 90.
102. Ibid., p. 189.
103. Ibid., p. 107.
104. Ibid., p. 98.
105. Ibid., p. 136.
106. See J. B. Jefferys *The Story of the Engineers* (London 1945 edn.) p. 142 for this practice amongst A.S.E. members.
107. Marx *Capital* (Eden and Cedar Paul trans., London 1932 imp.) p. 458.
108. E. J. Hobsbawm 'The Machine Breakers' p. 12.
109. Quoted in J. T. Ward *The Factory Movement 1830-1855* (London 1962) p. 161, see also J. L. and Barbara Hammond *Lord Shaftesbury*

(Pelican 1939 edn.) p. 50. Perhaps, in view of Hobsbawm's 'collective bargaining by riot' category of machine breaking, this sort should be categorised, in the style of the Webbs, as 'legal enactment by sabotage'.

110. Christopher Thomson *The Autobiography of An Artisan* (London and Nottingham 1847) pp. 167-168.
111. James Ward *Workmen and Wages at Home and Abroad* (London 1868) p. 240 in a chapter on 'Dread of Improved Machinery'.
112. W. Hamish Fraser *Trade Unions and Society* (London 1974) p. 19.
113. Carter Goodrich *The Frontier of Control* (London 1920).
114. Sidney and Beatrice Webb *Industrial Democracy* pp. 392-393.
115. A. L. Levine *Industrial Retardation in Britain 1880-1914* (London 1967) pp. 80-81.
116. Carter Goodrich *The Frontier of Control* p. 184.
117. Quoted in A. L. Levine, op. cit., p. 81.
118. Alan Fox *A History of the National Union of Boot and Shoe Operatives 1874-1957* (Oxford 1958) p. 13.
119. John Ball, F.R.S., 'Account of the Strike of the Northamptonshire Boot and Shoe-makers in 1857, 1858 and 1859' in *Report of the Social Science Association on Trade Societies and Strikes*, 1860, quoted in S. and B. Webb, op. cit., pp. 393-394.
120. Fox, op. cit., pp. 204-205.
121. Webbs, quoted in Levine, op. cit., p. 94.
122. Quoted in Fox, op. cit., p. 206.
123. Ibid., p. 208.
124. See Fox, op. cit., Chap. 22.
125. Ibid., pp. 221-222.
126. Ibid., p. 434.
127. Ibid., p. 346.
128. Quoted in Fox, op. cit., p. 269.
130. Ibid., p. 435.
131. Quoted in ibid., p. 411.

V

British Labour Productivity, 1890–1914

The end of the 19th century saw the British economy in serious straits. Britain had manifestly lost its hegemony over the world economy. The United States and some of the European countries were beginning to outpace Britain. In the twenty or so years before the first world war there was a marked reduction in the rate of growth of the British economy. The annual growth rate in the period just before the first world war was probably well under 2 per cent per annum—a rate which compared very unfavourably with the growth rate of the mid-Victorian economy.[1] Since this decline in the rate of increase of production was accompanied also by an increase in the number of people employed, it is quite clear that there was also a marked decline in the rate of increase of productivity, or output per worker. One index shows an actual decline in industrial output per employed person between 1900 and 1911.[2] From the vantage point of the present, as Sidney Pollard has pointed out, it is not very surprising that 'a mature industrial economy with its advanced industries would grow at a slower percentage rate than an economy in an earlier stage of growth, even though perhaps still at a high absolute rate.'[3] But however plausible this view may seem now, to employers and ruling class politicians at the time there was no such inevitability about Britain's slip from world economic dominance. They felt firmly that something could be done about the situation, and that the solution to the problem was mainly in their hands only in a negative sense: that is, they felt that organised labour had to be forced to cease and desist from its socialistic challenge to the right of employers to manage their enterprises as they thought fit. This challenge to managerial prerogatives was often, contemporaries felt, exerted through deliberate trade union restrictive practices and the wide-spread policy of restriction of output.

The 'new' unionism of the late 1880s and the early 1890s had seen the important expansion of trade unionism amongst many previously unorganised and (it was felt) unorganisable groups of workers. Much of this success in organising less skilled workers was short lived. The huge accessions of membership to the 'new' unions in the period of their origins were soon severely reduced with the down turn in the trade cycle which took place before the mid-way point of the 1890s. But, by and large, permanent organisations of less skilled workers had resulted, and many of them, during the next 30 or so years, established themselves suffi-ciently well to become the bases of the great general unions which were formed in the 1920s. The 'new' unions amongst the seamen, dockers and other waterside workers which in particular had had such explosive initial successes were the first to run into serious trouble. Not long after their foundation they ran foul of a serious counter-attack from employers in the industry—the latter quickly learning the lesson they had been taught by their employees about the value of organisation. By the autumn of 1890 the employers of seamen and related workers had organ-ised themselves into the Shipping Federation. The Shipping Federation quickly made serious inroads into trade union strength, taking on the ports one by one. Hull, which had emerged as the best organised of all the ports from the trade union point of view, was, for instance, the scene of a major confrontation between the employers and the unions in 1893. The result was a clear victory for the employers.[4] From the mid-1890s the employers' counter-attack became generalised as employers in a variety of industries took on the trade unionists in their employment. The craft unions, which had also grown and prospered in the boom years and which were thus often in a position to be better able to flex their muscles by means of craft control, were the subject of attacks by the employers as much as were the new unions. For example, trade unionists in the tailoring industry were locked out in 1892 by the Master Tailors' Association. The Association, in a circular to its member firms, put its case in terms which were to become common in many other trades :

'Keep before you the plain issue which the men's conduct has raised, viz., whether employers shall have reasonable liberty to conduct their businesses free from dictation and tyranny of their union, or from henceforth, be subjected to their orders and exactions, however unreasonable such may be.'[5]

We have already seen, in the previous chapter, how the same managerial desire to manage their enterprises unimpeded by the activities of trade unions led to a major clash in the Boot and Shoe industry, and how the issue had been, in the main, settled on terms distinctly favourable to the employers. Major set-piece battles of this sort occurred in a variety of industries throughout the 1890s, in minor sectors of the economy as well as in more major ones. In 1898 there was, for instance, a lockout in the Scottish furniture industry with employers demanding amongst other things the end to trade union limitation of output, the right to introduce time work or piecework, and an end to the practice of trade unionists refusing to work with non-unionists. In similar vein the following year saw a lockout in the plastering industry, with employers demanding that the union should abandon its policies of coercion of foremen, limitation of apprentices, and enforcement of union membership by boycott.[6]

The most important of all the episodes of what Clegg, Fox and Thompson call the employers' 'general counter-attack' is undoubtedly the Engineering Lockout of 1897. In this case the managerial prerogatives were contested on the two connected issues of which class of worker was to work the the new machinery which was greatly de-skilling the industry, and the question of payment by results. The new machinery was of a sort that could be operated by workers who were less skilled than the time-served skilled engineer. Piecework caused further resentment in the ranks of the skilled engineers since it was felt to involve speed-up and a reduction in the degree of craft control a skilled man could exercise over his job. At first the A.S.E. tried to impose a complete ban on piecework except in those districts where it had long been common. But this policy had to be revised, with some district committees attempting instead to regulate piecework prices with the aspiration of producing a situation such that the worker could earn at least his previous time rate plus 25 per cent, no matter what his output.[7] On top of this, in the face of heavy unemployment in the trade by 1892, the A.S.E. stepped up its traditional defences of the skilled men by more strict enforcement of the existing policies of the exclusion of non-unionists and the restriction of the number of apprentices entering the trade. In some places, Clegg and his colleagues tell us, more direct attempts were made on the shop floor to offset the disadvantages to the workers of new managerial methods. In Glasgow and in Manchester upper limits were set on piecework earnings and those A.S.E. members who exceeded the limits were fined. One Clydeside firm reported cases where shop stewards, to use the words of an engineering employers' exposé in 1897, 'repeatedly checked one of the turners for turning out too much work.'[8] On the machine question the A.S.E. again attempted, in the face of an increasing threat to existing work practices, to intensify the use of protective mechanisms they had already developed. In this case, the attempt was to continue to pursue the policy of 'following work to the new machine.' The A.S.E. Annual Report of 1897 justified this as follows :

'The proportion of machine to hand work is an increasing one. If skilled engineers are to retain a position in the trade, they must follow the work to the machine.'

In the previous year, 1896, the employers in the engineering industry had organised themselves into a body called the Employers' Federation of Engineering Associations. The objects of the Federation illustrate quite clearly the growing demand by employers to re-assert their managerial prerogatives against the encroachments on these by trade unions. The objects of the employers' federation talked 'in particular' of the need 'to protect and defend [their] interests against combinations of workmen seeking by strikes or other action to impose unduly restrictive conditions upon any branch of the engineering trades,' and to 'secure mutual support . . . on such questions as interference with foremen, unreasonable demands for wages, minimum rates of wages, employment of apprentices, hours of labour, overtime, limitation of work, piecework, demarcation of work, machine work, and the employment of men and boys on machines.'[9] Right from the very first meeting of the Federation there were complaints about trade union interference—with such a comprehensive list of things over which employers were claiming unilateral control this is not surprising. Nor is it surprising that, in the space of the year or so following the formation of the Federation, it threatened a lockout on two occasions before finally it imposed the Great Engineering Lockout in July 1897. The sense of the inevitability of a clash between the employers and the unions in the engineering industry comes out quite clearly in the statement made by the employers' leader, Colonel Dyer, at a conference held between the two parties in April 1897, ostensibly to discuss the machine question. Dyer (of Armstrong Whitworth) clearly demonstrated that whatever the immediate issues, deeper-seated ones were at the source of the conflict, when he asserted that 'of late years there has been a great number of aggressions made by your Society on the liberty of the employers.'[10]

Although the Engineering Lockout of 1897–1898 was eventually precipitated by the A.S.E.'s demand for the 8 hour day, it is quite clear that managerial prerogatives and the union's challenge to them were, in reality, the issues in contention. This, indeed, is what the Board of Trade itself was later to say when it pointed out that 'Though the immediate cause of the general dispute was the demand for the eight-hour day in London, the real questions at issue between the parties had become of a much more far-reaching kind and now involved questions of workshop control and the limits of trade union interference.'[11] The dispute was eventually settled with the employers scoring a clear victory. Apart from shoring up the right to collective bargaining, the A.S.E. was forced to concede much to the employers. Firms were to be given a free hand in the employment of non-unionists; over the question of manning new machines; overtime was to be virtually unrestricted, and the employers would be free to introduce piecework (though the prices were to be fixed by mutual agreement). On top of this a very precise grievance procedure for processing disputes was established, and this in itself seriously reduced the much prized autonomy of A.S.E. Districts, which now found themselves subject to the disciplining power of national control. Those districts where attempts were made to persist with the old policies which were now forbidden under the terms of the 1898 settlement now found themselves being ordered by their national officials to get into line with agreed procedure.[12] But in spite of these major setbacks for the engineers in terms of local autonomy and workshop control, there was some promise, as we shall see later, in at least two main directions. The union's defeat could have been much more comprehensive than it was. In the first place, as the historian of the engineers has put it, 'instead of the individual bargaining which some employers hoped would be the outcome of the struggle, the engineering industry henceforth was bound, in the workshop, locally and nationally, to organised collective bargaining.'[13] And secondly, alongside the employers' right to introduce piecework, the extremely important principle that 'The prices to be paid for piece-work shall be fixed by mutual arrangement between the employer and the workman or workmen who perform the work' had been established. This 'mutuality' principle was several generations and much struggle later to become the source of much shopfloor power in the engineering industry. The nature of the piecework bargain was such that, as the engineers' President was to say 70 years after the Great Lockout, 'with piece-work you have the man on the shop floor determining how much effort they will give for a given amount of money . . . once the piecework bargain is struck, the worker can work at the speed he chooses.'[14]

During the Lockout of 1897–98 the engineering employers made considerable use of a tactic of anti-unionism which had become a common feature of the employers' counter-attack of the 1890s—the use of 'Free Labour'. The National Free Labour Association which had been formed in 1893 was the most important of the bodies of non-union workers given encouragement by the employers in their struggle against the 'tyranny' of trade unionism. The N.F.L.A. had been established primarily for one purpose : to supply employers with workmen in place of locked-out or striking trade unionists. Free Labour exchanges were set up all over the country and registers of workers who had signed the Free Labour pledge were compiled. In the event of strikes or lockouts free labour workmen would be drafted in to keep work going for the employers.[15] William Collinson, the leading working class figure behind the N.F.L.A., claimed that during the Engineering Lockout his organisation had enabled twenty of London's leading firms to keep going.[16] As well as providing these practical services, the N.F.L.A. also gave an at least partly authentic expression to working class hostility to trade unionism. For instance, again during the Lockout, the N.F.L.A.'s president, John Chandler claimed, with some effect on 'public opinion,' that A.S.E. members were entering factories to destroy machines.[17] Collinson was particularly good at this general propaganda work. He was articulate, he had a coherent and usually well-documented case, and he knew how to spread his message through powerful means of communication and opinion. Collinson's case against the new, aggressive unionism hinged round his view that the trade union movement was being turned into 'a despotism for the enforcement of admittedly false and subversive doctrines' which, apart from intimidation and boycotting of non-unionists and unlawful picketing, also included 'undue restriction of the hours of labour and an arbitrary limitation of the output—a curtailment . . . of human industry . . . and a restriction of productive power in the working of mechanical appliances.'[18] Collinson was to give views of this sort a considerably wider currency when in late 1901 and early 1902 a series of articles appeared in *The Times* which gave chapter and verse to the opinion that there had grown up in Britain at that time a 'newer' trade unionism which had as its desire the promotion of restrictive practices and the deliberate restriction of production by workers. The series of twelve articles, which were published anonymously, appeared in *The Times* between November 18, 1901 and January 16, 1902 under the general title of 'The Crisis in British Industry'. In spite of the fact that they were not attributed to an author it is possible to ascertain quite clearly that Collinson had had an important part in their production.

The French institution, *le Musée Social*, which concerned itself with labour affairs had, as we saw earlier, in 1896 published a careful account of developments in British trade unionism. In 1903 the same institution published a follow-up to that work under the title of *La Crise du Trade-Unionisme*. The authors, Paul Mantoux and Maurice Alfassa, devoted the first half of their book to the legislative culmination of the general counter-attack on the trade unions, the Taff Vale Case. The second half consisted of a detailed examination of the claims made by *The Times* articles. Mantoux and Alfassa discovered that the articles had been written by Edwin A. Pratt (a gentleman who, incidentally, was later to become the honorary secretary of the Anti-Nationalisation League). Mantoux and Alfassa elicited this information, and much more, from an interview they had with William Collinson. Collinson told them :

'It was me who wrote those articles, or more exactly, I provided the information for them to a regular writer in *The Times*, Edwin A. Pratt. It was necessary to act in such a way in order to give the campaign an impartial character. All the facts published by *The Times* are scrupulously correct, but there could have been charges of exaggeration if I had signed those articles.'[19]

Having established the pedigree of *The Times* articles, we must now turn to what they said. The first article in the series asserted that the high costs of production in British industry and its loss of competitiveness with industry abroad, were largely the fault of trade union action in the past.

The 'new' unionism, 'with its resort to violence and intimidation' had been succeeded by a 'newer' unionism which :

'Although working along much quieter lines, is doing even more serious injury—by reason of the greater difficulty of coping with it—alike to trade, to industry, and to the individual worker.
'This "newer" unionism would pass among economists under the courtesy title of "restricting the output". Among trade unionists of the Socialist type, who have no regard for courtesy titles, it is better known as "Ca'canny".'

The article then gave chapter and verse from the original 'ca'canny' article in the *Seamen's Chronicle* of October 1896, and concluded with a number of examples of restriction of output and restrictive practices which were allegedly common in the building trades.[20] Other industries were dealt with in subsequent articles. From the first the articles caused a great deal of controversy, and there was a very full correspondence on the subject. Collinson covered his tracks by innocently contributing to the

debate with a letter to *The Times* on November 26, 1901. Here
he claimed that restriction of output was notorious in all sections
of the building trades. A 'great show of industry' was made, he
claimed, when an employer visited a site, but when he left the
men resumed 'their normal slow style of working.' In the
engineering industry, he stated, shop delegates frequently induced
workers to reduce the speed of their tools. He concluded dis-
ingenuously : 'We could furnish innumerable instances of the
petty tyrannies adopted by the trade union officials, but we fear
we should be trespassing on your valuable space.' But Collinson
did continue (though few knew it), through the information he
provided to Pratt, to trespass on *The Times*' 'valuable space'.
Numerous instances of slacking, ca'canny, restrictive practices,
and union control over entry into trades were given. Examples
from three trades will suffice here—they have been chosen
because they illuminate the importance of payment systems in
the employers' attempts to solve the problem of restriction of
output, and give some indication of workers' hostility to new
methods of work. When considering the Boot and Shoe Industry,
Pratt quoted from the Annual Report of the Incorporated Federated Associations of Boot and Shoe Manufacturers for Great
Britain and Ireland of 1900. 'Complaints of the limitation and
reduction of output,' the report stated,' are very general in the
trade, and come from manufacturers in all centres. . . .' The
manufacturers, realising this problem, had hoped to solve it by
replacing time payment by piecework. But the boot and shoe
workers had been able to manipulate the operation of the piecework system to their own advantage. The Report complained
that :

> 'The [piecework] statement has been used by the union for
> the purpose of regulating and limiting the amount of work to
> be done by workmen in weekly wages, and to supply a pretext
> for interference by union officials in the management gener-
> ally of lasting departments. . . . Under such a system of
> limitation and interference the workmen are not encouraged
> to work to the best of their ability, and the employers derive
> none of the advantages of piecework, but are subjected to all
> its disadvantages, with the result that the cost of production
> is materially increased.'[21]

In the Plate-glass and Sheet-glass industries, however, piecework had the effect desired by the employers. The workers in the glass industries who could really influence the levels of output were paid by the piece, and had no reason for restricting output.[22] The unions were weak in the industry, and they seemed to have owed what existence they had to piecework, the maintenance of a piecework scale being the main reason for the existence of the unions.[23] Tin-plate workers, on the other hand, commonly restricted output—to prevent an over-stocking of the market and the resultant falling of wages.[24] Restriction of output was also widespread in printing. One authority told Pratt that the tendency of men in printing 'to go easy in regard to the use of improved machinery, by never working it to the top of its capacity, is so widespread as to be almost universal. He finds that the tendency shows itself more especially in regard to the fast two-revolution flat-bed presses recently introduced from the United States, and to the use of composing machines.'[25]

How much substance was there in Pratt and Collinson's accusations? It seems highly likely that there was a good deal of truth in terms of their detailed, specific points. That much can be conceded. But to say that, however, is in no way to agree with their views about a socialistic conspiracy which they alleged was deliberately fomenting all the trouble; and nor is it to concede for one moment that the workers' attitudes and actions about which they complained were either 'irrational' or 'illegitimate.' Many of Pratt and Collinson's points are borne out by the observations of other, and often less inherently hostile, observers. This can be shown quite clearly in the case of one of the industries about which we have good documentation—that of printing. In the middle of the 19th century, time rates, or the 'stab' system as it was known in the trade, was almost universal in the provincial letterpress printing industry. By the end of the century, however, piecework was widely prevalent, though not completely widespread. Members of the print unions, as well as their employers, were by no means agreed about the relative merits of either payment system for the achievement of their different objectives.[26] Employers, for instance, by adopting a policy of close supervision of workers on 'stab' rates, and by ascertaining individual output, could weed out the less able workers and impose task work at workloads which would reduce the unit costs of production. Print workers were, quite naturally, determined that this sort of process should not take place, and as we shall soon see they frequently prevented it from happening. Piecework, the alternative payment system, on the other hand, was criticised by workers for creating unemployment, and for promoting selfishness. Vigorous bargaining over piecework prices, however, coupled with union demands for high piece rates often made it unwelcome to the employer. The introduction of composing machines into the industry especially from the 1890s led to a general reversion to 'stab'. To make it work in their favour and to ensure against unemployment of hand composers many branches of the Typographical Association adopted, as A. E. Musson has put it, 'a deliberate "limit system" on "stab" work, a policy of "ca'canny" or "go slow", restricting the amount of composition done by each man.'[27] This was done precisely to prevent employers from using the 'stab' system in the way outlined above. But Musson tells us there is no evidence at all to suggest that this policy received *official* backing from the union. Official union policy was 'a fair day's work for a fair day's wage'. What constituted a 'fair day's work' was never defined, and nor did the union give any encouragement to the introduction of the only thing that can monitor such a notion, the measurement of individual output. The union's view was that 'no guarantee must be given as to output, nor must there be any restriction.' Employers, not unnaturally, were reluctant to accept this, and tried many stratagems to circumvent it.[28]

Employers complained bitterly about these attempts to limit production. The Linotype Users' Association, for instance, claimed that employers had a right to exercise control over both the quality and the quantity of output, and they considered that the union's policy was 'undoubtedly intended as a means of restricting the output of the machine.' Some employers began to install indicators on the machines as a way of ascertaining a worker's output. The union executive in 1899 decided that it could not object to the simple registering of lines composed but they warned that 'the introduction of the appliance must be guarded in such a manner as to prevent its misuse for the purposes of establishing any system of task-work.'[29] Indicators, in short, were all right as long as the workers were the only ones to know from them what an individual worker's output per unit of time had been. The spread of indicators caused much resentment amongst the print workers. This attempt by employers to ascertain individual output was regarded by workers as the prelude to 'a system of slave-driving.' Attempts to increase production per head through the use of bonus systems were similarly villified by the print workers. The strong feeling in the union against these managerial methods came to a head at the Typographical Association's delegate meeting in 1908 where a resolution was passed saying that 'bonus-paid task-work, indicators etc., or any system by which type-setting machine operators' output may be gauged shall not be permitted under the auspices of the Association; nor shall members accept work on composing machines on terms under which they are called upon to produce a fixed amount of composition, or on a system of payment (except piecework pure and simple) which offers inducements to racing or undue competition between operators.'[30] During the debate on the question the deep resentment amongst print-workers of managerial attempts to regulate their speed of work was made quite clear. One delegate (with Chaplinesque forebodings?) said :

'in the old days they used to use a lash upon slaves; in these modern times I suppose they would use an indicator. . . . Why should we be asked to work under a system that indicates every movement of our elbow?'[31]

These strong words were clearly backed up by strong actions in the print shops for by 1911 virtually all mechanical indicators had been withdrawn, and in the same year the union secured the employers' agreement to their complete withdrawal.[32]

American management methods and the alleged hard working nature of American workpeople, as well as the superiority of much American machinery, aroused the interest and envy of British employers. Colonel Dyer, of the Engineering Employers' Federation for instance, had written to *The Times* in September 1897 stating that the engineering employers in Britain were 'determined to obtain the freedom to manage their own affairs which has proved to be so beneficial to the American manufacturer.'[33] Dyer had visited the U.S.A. and commented of the Carnegie works in Pittsburgh that 'for perfection of machinery, organisation, and completeness of installation, there is nothing in Europe to compare with them.' The strenuous opposition of the unions there to the new methods had, he stated, driven the managers to desperation, and the Carnegie managers became determined 'to manage their business as their experience and intelligence directed, and to free themselves entirely from the dictation of the Trade Union leaders.'[34] This had been carried out through an extremely violent attack on trade unionism by the Carnegie company; the 34 deaths during the notorious Homestead Strike of 1892 and the deployment of the Pinkerton Company made it one of the mobilising causes of the American labour movement.[35] One of Pratt's articles in *The Times* cited the observations of a manager of a large engineering firm in the North of England who had visited the U.S.A. specifically to discover why American industry was more productive than British industry. He found himself asking the following question :

'How is it that in Pittsburgh you find Lancashire and Sheffield men doing two and three times the work per day that they do in their native country?'

American employers he felt, had to face basically the same problem as British employers—unions were clamorous, strikes were often serious, and there had been a period in which American workmen had commonly restricted output. American employers, Pratt's informant stated, had managed to overcome the problem by organising themselves more efficiently and also by using payments systems more conducive to increased output. In short, in America straight piecework was being replaced by new forms of premium payment.[36] This development coincided with, and perhaps contributed to, a steady increase in production per head in the U.S.A. Lord Leverhulme stated that, according to Samuel Gompers, American workmen had abandoned restriction of output in the late 1880s,

'which was,' Leverhulme added, 'by a strange coincidence, about the very period the British workman first began to adopt extensively "ca'canny" and restriction of output . . .'

He had a certain amount of statistical evidence to back up this claim. During the First World War a census of production showed that of seven million workers in Great Britain, four million of these were employed in trades yielding a net increased annual value of only £75 to £100 per head over the value of the material used. In the United States, on the other hand, as far as most of the principal industries were concerned, the output per worker averaged from three to five times that amount.[37] The British and American censuses of production for 1907 had earlier demonstrated that in 26 leading trades there were roughly 4 British to 5 American wage-earners—yet the total production of the two countries was as 1:2.64. Comparisons of this sort are, of course, meaningless unless other things are measured too—such as the amount of capital behind each worker. The 1907 figures give some guide to this in terms of horsepower employed; the relationship between Britain and the U.S.A. being as 1:2.1. Although these last figures to a great extent might explain a good deal of the striking difference in output per workers they will not explain all of it. One contemporary commentator, by no means unsympathetic to labour, attributed these differences mainly to a combination of the 'failings' of both labour and capital. He attributed Britain's poor performance as being 'mainly due to bad organisation, restriction of output, and to deficient supply or abuse of machinery.'[38]

'The American comparison' was one that was often made in these years. The main burden of the argument was that of *The Times* articles—i.e. that labour, and especially trade unionism, was responsible for Britain's economic decline. One capitalist who shared this belief took the unusual but highly significant initiative of sending a group of British trade union leaders on a study tour of the U.S.A. in 1902. Alfred Mosely, a wealthy South African mine-owner, assembled a Commission of 23 trade unionists from a representative cross section of industries. Each member of the Mosely Commission was asked to pay particular attention to his own trade, and also to answer a questionnaire on the general industrial situation. According to Henry Pelling, Mosely 'had hoped that the delegation's visit would lead its members to take a strong stand against "ca'canny" and other restrictive devices on their return to Britain',[39] but this hope was to be largely unrealised. The general conclusion by W. C. Steadman makes this point quite clearly :

'The English worker has nothing to learn from America, but the employers have a lot. Let our employers realize that labour is as much a partner in the business as his capital, and that the success or failure of that business depends upon both. . . . High wages pay both the employer and the employed. In America they know this, and act up to it; hence the secret of their success. The trade unions in this country have been accused of driving the trade out of the country, yet the same forces are at work there, only more so, for trade unionism in that country is increasing by leaps and bounds as a purely industrial and fighting force, and yet America is going ahead.'[40]

The General Federation of Trade Unions had made a similar point—but had taken it further—in a reply they produced to *The Times* articles. The G.F.T.U. argued that high wages were indeed the secret of American economic superiority, since high labour costs meant that employers were forced to keep up to date through the introduction of new machinery in order to keep unit costs of production down.[41] The 'ca'canny' point was more difficult to dispose of, but Clem Edwards, former trade union official and lawyer and soon to become a Liberal M.P., in an article in 1902 called 'Do Trade Unions Limit Output?' confidently dismissed the question.[42] The most recent historians of British trade unionism, with the benefit of hindsight, agree with him : though this view has not gone unchallenged by other present-day writers.

Clegg, Fox and Thompson, whilst acknowledging the reality of the decline in British productivity per employed worker, discount entirely (but not very convincingly) the 'explanation popular at the time . . . that productivity declined because of the restrictive practices of the trade unions', and here refer explicitly to Pratt's 'alarmist account'. They go on to claim that 'Most economic historians have hesitated to attribute much importance to this factor.'[43] One economic historian who, without by any means seeking to isolate worker restriction as a sole or even a main cause, has sought to examine this aspect of the problem is E. J. Hobsbawm. Hobsbawm, with some care, has claimed that from the 1890s :

'It is at least possible that certain groups of workers now began systematically to allow their output to sink unless held up by incentives, or else that the weakening of older forms of labour discipline or tradition produced the same result.'[44]

Clegg and his co-authors counter this statement with an extremely brief rehearsal of suggested reasons for decline in productivity in the coal mining, building, and cotton industries, and then *assert* that :

'There is accordingly no need to turn to trade union restrictions as a causal factor, and no evidence that they will serve as an explanation. The workers were not the authors of their own difficulties but the victims of economic circumstances outside their control.'[45]

This view, of course, is precisely the view that contemporary trade unionists often took when faced with the accusation. It is no surprise that trade union leaders, faced with accusations of ca'canny, should reject the charge—that quite clearly is the prerogative of trade unionists at any time when they are faced with charges an even partial admission to which will weaken their case. Similarly it is clear that Pratt and his like, no friends to labour, would seek to maximise the amount of blame that could be placed on labour and minimise the culpability of capital. That, surely, is the way of the world. But, with the benefit of hindsight, the claims and counter claims of contemporaries can in my opinion be seen each to have elements of truth in them. The interpretation of Clegg and his colleagues it seems to me is vitiated by their view that workers and trade unions are rather passive objects—for ever on the receiving end of changes; a permanent opposition which not only can never become the government of industry, but which also cannot even, it seems, propose a motion.

E. H. Phelps Brown and Margaret Browne have, unlike Clegg and his colleagues, gone into considerable detail on this question of the extent and causes of the decline of productivity per worker in this period. Their view is worthy of consideration. They establish, first of all, that Britain did, after 1900, experience a 'sudden and sustained check to the rise of productivity' both in manufacturing industry and in the whole economy.[46] Britain alone of the five countries they studied (the others were France, Germany, Sweden and the U.S.A.) experienced this check to productivity, though all the five countries had experienced very similar rises in productivity up to 1890. They state with considerable caution that :

'The check to the rise of productivity in Great Britain after 1900, however, stands out, and if our price index did import a bias, it would be to just that effect; but that the check is a fact and no statistical illusion is strongly supported by its undoubted presence in the physical output of some British industries of this time . . .'[47]

In a long and careful section (Section 12. 'The Springs of Productivity : a comparative study of the U.K. 1890-1913', pp. 174 ff.) they address themselves to the causes of the phenomenon, by asking why it happened at this time in the U.K. alone of the countries they looked at. Having dealt in detail with the industries for which adequate figures are available, and having examined the influence of investment, they conclude that fluctuations in investment do not provide the explanation, since 'when the check to productivity came the level of equipment was rising.' What, then, is left can only be the implication of 'a fall in the output per unit of capital.' A change of this sort can only come about as a result of one or both of two sorts of change : first, a decline in the effective input of labour, and second, with the efficiency of the human factor unchanged, the introduction of greater quantities of capital equipment of the existing type, yield diminishing returns. Phelps Brown and Browne believe that both of these things happened in the British economy from the 1890s.[48] They are prepared, having said that, to attribute a good deal of the decline in productivity to 'the changed attitude of the worker, which to many contemporary observers was unmistakable.'[49]

One thing that had emerged quite frequently from the observations of the Mosely Commission was the American superiority in management techniques. When members of the Commission were asked whether they thought that American factories were better managed than those in Britain two of them replied as follows : 'The American manager is more enterprising and more ready to introduce the latest and best of everything.' (G. N. Barnes of the Engineers); 'American employers interest themselves in the management of their business to a great and more intimate extent than is the custom in England.' (T. A. Glynn of the Tailors.)[50] There is, in fact, little doubt that these impressions were in general correct. British interest in management and management technique was far less well-developed than it was in America, where the work of Frederick Winslow Taylor and his disciples was making a considerable impact. One of Taylor's best known axioms, in his first major work *Shop Management* (1903), was published in the year after the Mosely Commission had visited America : 'High wages and low labour costs are not only compatible, but are, in the majority of cases, mutually conditional.' Of this statement the members of the Mosely Commission would have, in principle, approved. The practice of Scientific Management, however, was to prove less comforting.

NOTES

1. See Table 54 in W. G. Hoffman *British Industry 1700-1950* (Oxford 1955). A good review of the subject is S. B. Saul *The Myth of the Great Depression 1873-1896* (London 1969) esp. the section on 'Industrial Production' pp. 36ff. Saul rejects the argument that the depression can be dated as having taken place between 1873 and 1896, but is certain that 'at some time during the last quarter of the nineteenth century Britain . . . went through unusual and worrying economic experiences. . . .' p. 54.
2. W. G. Hoffman, op. cit., p. 38, table 6, see also H. A. Clegg, Alan Fox and A. F. Thompson *A History of British Trade Unions Since 1889*, Vol. 1. 1889-1910 (Oxford 1964) p. 474.
3. S. Pollard *The Development of the British Economy 1914-1967* (Second Edn. London 1973 imp.) p. 4. The fullest account of this economic decline and an analysis of the reasons for it is A. L. Levine *Industrial Retardation in Britain 1880-1914* (London 1967).
4. See John Saville 'Trade Unions and Free Labour : the background

to the Taff Vale Decision' in *Essays in Labour History*, eds. A. Briggs and J. Saville (London 1967 edn.) pp. 328-330. Saville's fine article is indispensable reading for the understanding of this period.

5. Quoted in Clegg, Fox and Thompson, op. cit., p. 136. I have relied heavily on this work for some of the detail that follows.

6. Clegg, Fox and Thompson, op. cit., pp. 160 and 158.

7. Ibid., p. 139.

8. Ibid., p. 141 and footnote. The quotation comes from *First Series of Examples of Restriction and Interference*, produced by the Federation of Engineering and Shipbuilding Employers, November 4th, 1897.

9. Quoted Clegg, Fox and Thompson, p. 161.

10. Eric Wigham *The Power to Manage: a history of the Engineering Employers' Federation* (London 1973) p. 35. See also p. 44 where another employer, Sir Benjamin Browne blames the impact of the new unionism on the A.S.E. for the development of policies that sought 'to interfere in the management of engineering works, and to encroach upon the employers in a manner not done previously.'

11. Quoted in Wigham, op. cit., p. 55.

12. Wigham, op. cit., p. 63, for details of the settlement see Wigham, op. cit., p. 61 and Clegg, Fox and Thompson, p. 167.

13. J. B. Jefferys *The Story of the Engineers* p. 149.

14. Hugh Scanlon, interview in *New Left Review* No. 46, November-December 1967.

15. On the N.F.L.A. see John Saville 'Trade Unions and Free Labour' pp. 336-339.

16. E. Wigham *The Power to Manage*, p. 51.

17. J. B. Jefferys, op. cit., p. 146.

18. Collinson quoted in Clegg, Fox and Thompson, op. cit., p. 171.

19. P. Mantoux and M. Alfassa *La Crise du Trade-Unionisme* (Bibliotheque du Musée Social, Paris 1903) p. 184. The same point is repeated on p. 316. *The Times* articles were shortly afterwards produced as a booklet, the authorship of which was attributed to Pratt.

20. *The Times*, November 18, 1901.

21. *The Times*, December 3, 1901.

22. *The Times*, December 14, 1901.

23. Ernest Aves, 'Methods of Remuneration: Time and Piecework' in C. Booth, (ed.) *Life and Labour of the People in London*, Vol. IX (London 1897) p. 324. Tank and basket makers also favoured piecework, because it brought them independence.

24. D. F. Schloss *Methods of Industrial Remuneration* (3rd. edn. London 1907) p. 86, based on information in the Board of Trade *Labour Gazette*, January, February, and March, 1895.

25. *The Times*, December 27, 1901.

26. A good and detailed discussion of this can be found in A. E. Musson *The Typographical Association* (London 1954) pp. 169-170.

27. A. E. Musson, op. cit., p. 172.

28. Ibid., p. 172. The same ground is covered by Musson in more detail on pp. 192-195.

29. Ibid., p. 211.

30. Quoted in Musson, op. cit., p. 212.

31. Quoted in P. N. Stearns *Lives of Labour* (London 1975) p. 219.

32. Musson, op. cit., p. 337.

33. Quoted in Clegg, Fox and Thompson, op. cit., p. 164.
34. Ibid., p. 172.
35. The Anarchist Alexander Berkman attempted to kill Carnegie's right hand man, Henry Clay Frick, as a reprisal for the company's violence: see biographical sketch of Berkman in A. Berkman *ABC of Anarchism* (first published 1929, London 1964 edn.).
36. *The Times*, December 30, 1901.
37. Lord Leverhulme *The Six-Hour Day and Other Industrial Questions* (London 1918) p. 11.
38. C. S. Myers *Mind and Work* (London 1920) p. 127.
39. H. Pelling 'The American Economy and the Foundation of the Labour Party' in *America and the British Left* (London 1956) p. 83.
40. Quoted in Ibid., p. 83.
41. Ibid., p. 77.
42. Ibid., p. 78.
43. H. A. Clegg, Alan Fox and A. F. Thompson *A History of British Trade Unions Since 1889*, Vol. 1., 1889-1910 (Oxford 1964) p. 475.
44. E. J. Hobsbawm, 'Custom, Wages and Work Load', p. 122. This masterly article should be consulted for much detail and argument on the general problem.
45. Clegg, Fox and Thompson op. cit., p. 476.
46. E. H. Phelps Brown and Margaret Browne *A Century of Pay: the course of pay and production in France, Germany, Sweden, the United Kingdom, and the United States of America, 1860-1960* (London 1968), Fig. 17. p. 123, and p. 124.
47. Phelps Brown and Browne, op. cit., p. 124.
48. Phelps Brown and Browne, op. cit., p. 183.
49. Phelps Brown and Browne, op. cit., p. 185 and also p. 189. They cite the findings of G. T. Jones in his book *Increasing Returns* (1933) about the British Building industry where efficiency rose by only 17 per cent between 1850 and 1910 as an epitome of the situation in British industry generally. The rise in efficiency came almost entirely from the introduction of machinery into joiners' shops.
50. Quoted in A. L. Levine *Industrial Retardation in Britain 1880-1914* (London 1967) pp. 57-58.

Part Three

TAYLORISM

VI

Frederick Winslow Taylor and Scientific Management

In 1878, at the age of 22, a young man called Frederick Winslow Taylor started work as a labourer in the machine shop of the Midvale Steel Company works in Philadelphia. Taylor started at the bottom, in spite of the fact that he had just completed an apprenticeship as a patternmaker and machinist—and, even more strangely, in spite of the fact that he came from a well established and well connected middle class family in Philadelphia. Taylor had, indeed, at one time been expected to follow his father's footsteps and become a lawyer. To this end he had gone as far as to take and pass the entrance examination for Harvard. Then, for medical and other reasons which have never been adequately explained, he abandoned the idea of university study and began to serve his time as an apprentice.[1] Taylor's training and obvious ability soon enabled him to rise to positions of progressively greater responsibility in the machine shop. Before long he had become clerk of the shop, taking over from the previous incumbent after the latter had been caught stealing. Later he was given work as a machinist running one of the lathes. Since he turned out rather more work than the other machinists he was within a few months made gang boss over the lathes. Almost all the work done in Taylor's shop was done on piecework. He recalled : 'As was usual then, and in fact as is still usual in most of the shops in this country, the shop was really run by the workmen, and not by the bosses. The workmen together had carefully planned just how fast each job should be done, and they had set a pace for each machine throughout the shop, which was limited to about one-third of a good day's work.' Each newcomer to the shop, Taylor asserts, was told by his workmates how much work they should do, and if this was exceeded it would not be long before the offending worker was driven out of the shop. Taylor also recalls that as soon as he became gang-boss he was in fact approached by the men who told him unambiguously that if he attempted to increase the pace of work 'you can be mighty sure that we'll throw you over the fence.' Taylor, however, now felt himself to be part of the management, and therefore he told the men in his shop that he proposed to do whatever he could to get a fair day's work out of the lathes. A 'war', which became progressively more bitter, ensued. He tried every expedient to get his workers to do a 'fair day's work'. He sacked some of the stubborn men; he lowered the wages of others; he reduced the piece-work price; he hired green men whom he personally instructed in the work and from whom he extracted the promise that once taught they would do a 'fair day's work'. Worker-resistance, however, continued unabated, both inside and outside the works, and those who toed Taylor's line were soon compelled by their fellows who resisted it to conform to the shop norms or to leave the shop. Taylor noted that in a war of this kind there was one weapon which the resisting workers employed with considerable effect; they contrived ways in which the machines in their charge were either broken or damaged, apparently accidentally or in the regular course of work. These breakages, the workers alleged, were the result of the foreman's insistence that the machines be driven hard, so hard in fact that they quickly deteriorated. Taylor suggests that most works' superintendents would have little alternative but to take the workers' word for this, but in Taylor's case 'the Superintendent accepted the word of the writer when he said that these men were deliberately breaking their machines as a part of the piece-work war which was going on.' The Superintendent allowed Taylor to counter this machine-breaking (which he did successfully) by putting up notices threatening to fine workers if their machines were broken. Taylor held that the reason why the superintendent believed him was because he (Taylor) 'was not the son of a working-man', and, therefore, had the employers' interests at heart. His class position also helped Taylor to successfully wage his war against worker-resistance in another way. He recorded:

'If the writer had been one of the workmen, and had lived where they lived, they would have brought such social pressure to bear upon him that it would have been impossible to stand out against them. He would have been called "scab" and other foul names every time he appeared on the street; his wife would have been abused, and his children would have been stoned.'[2]

Taylor, then, unlike most other gang bosses, had sufficient things in his favour due to his unorthodox origins to be able to continue to fight the good fight. He struggled away for about three years—with some success. Output increased, and in some cases it doubled. Taylor was rewarded with further promotion and eventually became chief engineer. The continuing struggle led Taylor to begin to think out and develop his system of 'scientific management'. Soon after his elevation to chief engineer he decided that he would try to change the management system in the works, attempting to produce a working environment in which 'the interests of the workmen and the management should become the same, instead of antagonistic.'[3] At Midvale Taylor was sufficiently successful to be encouraged to develop his ideas further, both in practice and in theory. His work began to attract outside attention, and before long he left Midvale to go to the Bethlehem Steel Company where he was brought in to reorganise the plant. At Bethlehem, however, he met nothing but opposition—not only from the workers but also from other managers. In April 1901 he was sacked. For Taylor, however, there were as many lessons from defeat as there were from success; and immediately after the Bethlehem fiasco he began to set his ideas down on paper. The result was his first book, *Shop Management*.

In this book and its elaboration and successor, *The Principles of Scientific Management*, one of the chief themes is the output question. The starting point for Taylor's view of management was clearly his virtual obsession with restriction of output or what he called 'Soldiering'. In *Shop Management* he had taken pains to differentiate between 'natural soldiering' and 'systematic soldiering'—the former deriving from the natural instinct of men to take it easy and the latter (for him far more serious, if not evil and criminal) proceeding from the workmen's 'more intricate second thought and reasoning caused by their relations with other men.'[4] This point came out quite clearly in his bigger and more famous book, *The Principles of Scientific Management*, which was first published in 1911 'for confidential circulation among the members of the American Society of Mechanical Engineers'. Taylor there asserted that the majority of workers believed that the 'fundamental interests of employees and employers are necessarily antagonistic. Scientific management, on the contrary, has for its very foundation the firm conviction that the true interests of the two are one and the same . . .' 'Maximum prosperity,' he continued later, 'can only exist as a result of maximum productivity,' and this involved getting the worker to work 'at his fastest pace and with the maximum of efficiency.'[5] He went on to contrast the great effort an English worker might put into a game of cricket and an American worker might put into a game of baseball with the poor effort they both habitually put in at work. He complained :

'When the same workman returns to work on the following day, instead of using every effort to turn out the largest possible amount of work, in the majority of cases this man deliberately plans to do as little as he safely can—in many instances to do not more than one-third to one-half of a proper day's work. And in fact if he were to do his best to turn out his largest possible day's work, he would be abused by his fellow-workers for so doing, even more than if he had proved himself a "quitter" in sport. Underworking, that is, deliberately working slowly as to avoid doing a full day's work, "soldiering" as it is called in this country, "hanging it out" as it is called in England, "ca cannae" [sic] as it is called in Scotland, is almost universal in industrial establishments, and prevails also to a large extent in the building trades; and the writer asserts without fear of contradiction that this constitutes the greatest evil with which the working-people of both England and America are now afflicted.'[6]

That, for Taylor, was the problem. The solution was his system of scientific management. In extremely brief detail it involved careful observation, analysis and timing of workers' movements; measurement of the labour cost of each operation; and the establishment of norms based on these calculations. Applying the information derived from these measurements it was possible (and economically desirable) to bring about an increased speed of work, a relaxation of restrictive practices and elimination of 'wasteful' movement. The workers to whom the system applied were to be at one and the same time recompensed with financial incentives, favourable piece-rates if output norms were reached (but very unfavourable ones if they were not), premium payments and so on. To use the words of David Landes 'the effort to maximise the product of labour led to a careful study of the worker as an animate machine'[7]—and on top of this a payment system was specifically designed to make that animate machine operate as an individual economic man. Taylor had no doubt that it was possible to determine scientifically all these elements. He stated that :

'The writer has found, through an experience of thirty years, covering a large variety in manufactures, as well as in the building trades, structural and engineering work, that it is not only practicable but comparatively easy to obtain, through a systematic and scientific time study, exact information as to how much of any given kind of work either a first-class or an average man can do in a day, and with this information as a foundation, he has over and over again seen the fact demonstrated that workmen of all classes are not only willing, but glad to give up all idea of soldiering, and devote all his energies to turning out the maximum work possible, providing they are sure of a suitable permanent reward.'[8]

Taylor's book was published for open circulation in 1914, and it became immensely influential in American management circles. Taylor's death at the height of his powers in 1915 only increased the virtual deification of him that took place in American industry. Taylor's words were invested with scriptural authority; and a fervent band of his disciples devoted themselves to spreading the theory and practice of Taylorism throughout industry both at home and abroad.[9] To a remarkable extent they were successful, though at first, as will be seen, there was considerable resistance from organised labour.[10]

Although Taylor thought that the application of his system would generate 'harmony, not discord' there is a great deal of evidence to suggest that it produced considerable resentment amongst workers. In the decade beginning in 1910 especially profound waves of opposition to the application of Taylorism in American industry were forthcoming. The application, for instance, of Taylorism to the U.S. Navy's Arsenals caused a good deal of trouble. The best illustration of this is given by the events at Watertown Arsenal. After a couple of years of preliminaries the first bonus was offered in the Arsenal in May 1911. Within two years nearly half the machine shop was under the premium system. It was estimated that the productivity of individual workers was about two and a half times what it had been under day work. The success at Watertown Arsenal was such that the Navy recommended that scientific management be introduced into other navy arsenals. At this stage the American Federation of Labor and the International Association of Machinists protested vigorously—and there were some hearings on the subject in Congress. When an attempt was made to introduce the premium bonus system into the foundry at Watertown arsenal in the summer of 1911, the entire labour force walked out and even though the strike lasted only a few days, it was enough to lead the House of Representatives to appoint a special committee to carry out an investigation. In June 1913 the majority of the Watertown workers, backed by their union representatives, filed petitions calling for the abandonment of what they called the 'Taylor' or 'stop watch' system. Congressmen at various times during 1915 and 1916 introduced bills trying to ban the use of the stop watch, time study, and the paying of bonuses on government work; and from July 1916 time studies and premium bonus systems were banned from Watertown and all other branches of Government service.[11]

The extension of scientific management to private industry brought a similar response. In April 1914 some hearings on Scientific Management before the U.S. Commission on Industrial Relations—where it was found that 'the representatives of organised labor stand in almost unqualified opposition to what they regard as scientific management'—led the Commission to order a full investigation.

This was carried out under the direction of Robert F. Hoxie, Associate Professor of Political Economy at the University of Chicago. Hoxie looked in considerable detail at the operation of scientific management in about 35 plants named by Taylor, Gantt and Emerson, (the leading proponents of the system), themselves. Amongst the plants studied were the Watertown

Arsenal; the Remington Typewriter Plant at Ilion, New York; and the Westinghouse Electric and Manufacturing Company at East Pittsburgh.[12]

Criticism of Taylorism was not the preserve of the I.W.W. and other radicals in the trade union movement. Even the usually cautious and conservative American Federation of Labor ('the one body' according to Hoxie which could seriously claim the right 'to voice the prevailing sentiment of organised labor in America') was deeply opposed to Scientific Management. Hoxie's summary of the A.F. of L.'s attitude runs in part as follows: that Scientific Management was 'a device for the purpose of increasing production and profits; and tends to eliminate consideration for the character, rights and welfare of the employees. It looks upon the worker as a mere instrument of production and reduces him to a semi-automatic attachment to the machine or tool. In spirit and essence, it is a cunningly devised speeding-up and sweating system, which puts a premium upon muscle and speed rather than brains, forces individuals to become "rushers" and "speeders"; stimulates and drives the workers up to the limit of nervous and physical exhaustion and over-speeds and over-strains them; shows a constant tendency to increase the intensity and extent of the task; tends to displace all but the fastest workers; indicates a purpose to extract the last ounce of energy from the workers; . . . It intensifies the modern tendency towards specialisation of the work and the task; . . . splits up the work into a series of minute tasks tending to confine the workers to a continuous performance of one of these tasks; . . . degrades the skilled worker to the condition of the less skilled; . . . weakens the bargaining strength of the workers. . . . It displaces day work and day wage by task work and the piece-rate, premium and bonus systems of payment.

'It tends to set the task on the basis of "stunt" records of the strongest and swiftest workers without due allowance for the human element or legitimate delays, so that only a few of the strongest and most active workers are capable of accomplishing it, and has devised and established modes of payment, usually arranged so that it is greatly to the advantage of the employer to prevent the workers from equalling or exceeding the task, and which usually result in giving the worker less than the regular rate of pay for his extra exertion, and only a portion and usually the smaller portion of the product which his extra exertion has created. . . . Puts a limit upon the amount of wages which any man can earn; offers no guarantee against rate-cutting; is itself a systematic rate-cutting device; . . . leads to over-production and the increase of unemployment. . . . It greatly intensifies unnecessary managerial dictation and discipline. . . . It increases the spirit of mutual suspicion and contest among the men, and thus destroys the solidarity and co-operative spirit of the group. It has refused to deal with the workers except as individuals. It is incompatible with and destructive of unionism; destroys all the protective rules established by unions and discriminates against union men. It is incompatible with and destructive of collective bargaining. . . . It is unscientific and unfair in its determination of the task and furnishes no just or scientific basis for calculating the wage rate. . . . "Scientific management" intensifies the conditions of industrial unrest. . . . It increases the points of friction and offers no guarantee against industrial warfare and is conducive to strikes.'[13]

There was, indeed a great wave of strikes and much industrial warfare in America around this time. David Montgomery has recently argued that the period between 1909 and 1922 saw 'the transformation of workers' consciousness'. The U.S. Commission on Industrial Relations which had commissioned Hoxie's special investigation was one response to that transformation of workers' consciousness. Although Hoxie and his colleagues were in general condemnatory of Scientific Management they did not attribute to it all the blame; prefering to conclude that 'Scientific Management is but one factor in the broad industrial problem.'[14] Some labour leaders, however, like J. P. Conlon, the Vice-President of the Machinists' Union, were more sure of their ground. In his evidence to the Commission on Industrial Relations in 1916, Conlon squarely put the blame for the massive labour unrest on the spread of new managerial practices through much of American industry. The workers' response to this had been 'sabotage, syndicalism, passive resistance.' And he added that : 'We did not hear of any of these things until we heard of scientific management and new methods of production.'[15]

All this, of course, was said before 1917, the year in which

America entered the war. The putting of the American economy on a war footing led to demands for extra production similar to those made in Britain. Taylorism began to come into its own, to gain much respectability and also support even from the American Federation of Labor unions which had bitterly denounced it only a short time before. The same Samuel Gompers, President of the A.F. of L. who had, for instance, 'vigorously attacked' the plan to introduce scientific management into the Rock Island Arsenal in the spring of 1911,[16] was in September 1920 stating that 'The trade union movement welcomes every thought and plan, every device and readjustment that will make expended effort more valuable to humanity . . .'[17] In the ten years between those two statements a revolution in the attitudes of the A.F. of L. towards Taylorism had taken place. H. B. Drury, the author of an academic apologia for Taylorism felt obliged, indeed, to contribute a long introduction to the third edition of his book (which had been first published in 1915, at the height of labour attacks on the system) in 1922 pointing out that since 1915 Taylorism had become acceptable in Government circles and amongst trade union leaders. He wrote :

'The American Federation of Labor, as a body, has, however, gone quite far towards committing itself to the general principle that production is a concern of the worker. No doubt the war-time labor policies of the government, under which there was a considerable amount of cooperation between the unions, the government, and the leaders of industry, had something to do with bringing the different groups to a point where they could consider a closer tying together of interests.'

In 1919 the A.F. of L. had a conference with 'a number of the leading scientific management engineers with reference to the co-operation which labour could give in making industry more efficient.'[18] And in 1925 Taylorism was fully embraced when the A.F. of L. president at a reception given by the Taylor Society stated that: 'The A.F.L. recognises that the worker's welfare depends on the efficiency of management.'[19]

It was not, however, just a question of organised labour moving closer to Taylorism. The Taylorites themselves, after the death of the messiah in 1915, had become a good deal more sympathetic to the aspirations of labour. The *Bulletin of the Taylor Society*, for instance, came out in support of the workers in the bituminous coal strike in 1919, and also supported the workers' demand for the eight hour shift in the steel industry. The *Bulletin* also, around the same time, attracted perhaps by the importance placed on a 'Practicable Soviet of Technicians', reprinted part of Thorstein Veblen's series of articles from *The Dial* in 1919 which were later collected together under the title of *The Engineers and the Price System.*[20] Veblen's book contained chapters called 'On the Nature and Uses of Sabotage', and 'On the Danger of a Revolutionary Overturn.' In the latter chapter he sought to disabuse those with vested interests in the maintenance of the existing social order of the notion that a revolutionary overturn was a serious possibility, by arguing that the social forces did not exist to bring it about. The nearest thing 'to a practicable organisation of industrial forces, just yet,' Veblen wrote, 'is the A.F. of L.; which need only be named in order to dispel the illusion that there is anything to hope or fear in the way of a radical move at its hands.' Veblen made the point that the A.F. of L. itself had vested interests in the maintenance of the existing order, and that it was designed for bargaining and not for organising production. This stricture applied even more to the labour movement organisation of which Veblen was more fond, the I.W.W.—about which he said that 'this flotsam of industry is not organised to take over the highly technical duties involved in the administration of the industrial system.'[21] Some members of the I.W.W., especially after Lenin's newfound enthusiasm for Taylorism as one of the cures for the poor economic performance of the Soviet economy immediately after the Revolution, began around 1919 to move closer to a qualified support of some of Taylor's ideas. There was talk among them of training workers to take over and run the industrial machine, thinking that the industrial chaos which followed the revolution in Russia might be avoided in the U.S.A. if workers had more knowledge of scientific technique.[22] At least one American paper had noticed the irony of this partial acceptance of Taylorism from what seemed like the most unlikely quarter. The non-socialist paper, *The Independent* on March 8, 1919 noted of Lenin's pamphlet

The Soviets At Work (which was a socialist best-seller in the U.S.A., quickly going through five editions, and in which Lenin wrote enthusiastically about scientific management) that :

'Lenin's advice to the Bolsheviki in the pamphlet "Soviets At Work", might be published in any of our efficiency magazines with some changes of phraseology, for it is devoted to urging increase of production, speeding up of process, iron discipline during work, careful accounting, business devices, the Taylor system of scientific management, and the like . . .'[23]

The impact of Taylorism was not just restricted to the United States. It spread to most of the other industrialised countries, usually taking hold first in the most advanced sectors of the economy. In France, for instance, it was introduced before the First World War into the Renault works. On this occasion it led to an important debate in the French syndicalist movement which is worth reiterating in view of the important general points its raises. The debate, which was conducted largely in the columns of Pierre Monatte's paper *La Vie Ouvrière*, emerged against the background of the introduction of Taylorism into the Renault car works at Billancourt and Douai. This itself led to several strikes, some of them violent, in late 1912 and early 1913, with the strike leaders touring the Paris region and according to one of them 'holding meetings almost every evening, at the gates of the factories, in the great industrial centres, to prepare our comrades to resist the application of a system, the purpose of which is clearly set forth in F. W. Taylor's works.'[24] Alphonse Merrheim, the secretary of the Metal Workers' Federation and then very much a revolutionary syndicalist, opened the debate in *La Vie Ouvrière* of February 20, 1913, in which he spelt out the instinctive objections of workers to Taylorism. Friedmann states of this article, correctly in my view, that 'in spite of the lack of accurate knowledge of the details of the system, the workers' instinct was not deceived as to the effective use of the method by capitalist rationalisation and its long-term implications.' In a later article Merrheim asks the question : 'How can it have been thought that unionism would even tolerate the Taylor method? What does this method do? What is it intended to do? Is it not clearly the sharpest expression of capitalist disdain for the working class?'[25] In similar vein our old friend Emile Pouget, in a pamphlet of 1914 called *L'organisation du surmenage, le système Taylor*, talked about Taylorism being a system of 'organised over-work' involving the turning of the worker 'into a brute and a moron' and reducing him to being 'only the extension of the machine which he must run blindly and ignorantly!'[26]

Friedmann suggests that these opinions overlooked what we might call the Lenin point—that is, they overlooked 'the positive aspects of Taylorism in the technical field as an effort for more accurate and rapid production. They did not distinguish clearly between certain progressive suggestions of Taylor and the char-acteristics of the capitalist system which was exploiting them.' But if Merrheim and Pouget did not realise this point then at least one other contributor to the debate in the French syndicalist movement did. A militant called Ravaté in an article in *La Vie Ouvrière* of April 5, 1913 argued that Taylorism was in many respects 'progressive' and he argued :

'Trade unionists cannot be opposed to a better employment of human energy in production. On the contrary. Then why take up arms against certain principles? We might as well give up machinery. The whole argument against the Taylor system could be used, and was used against machinery at the time of its first appearance, but my trade union ideal is not a return to nature.'

For Ravaté it was not the Taylor system that had to be fought against, but rather the use of the system under capitalism. This, of course, raises large problems, but the general point is well-taken, and Ravaté's argument seems to have led to something of a revision in Merrheim's views.[27] The sort of view expressed by Ravaté, of course, rests on the traditional Marxist assumption that only in the most advanced capitalist economies, using the most advanced methods of production, was there the economic basis for socialism. It was also thought to be the case that it was in countries with these features that the social contradictions were bound to be most acute, thus generating the social forces to transform society. In capitalist societies Taylorism was part of the problem, but in a sense a necessary one. In infant socialist societies, however, such as the Soviet Union, a new use of Taylorism was seen as part of the solution. Taylorism, as we shall see later, was introduced in the Soviet Union on a large scale in the wake of Lenin's statements on the subject, as a major part of the attempt to industrialise the economy. But the implied hope that under a new form of ownership the Taylorist mode of production would take a substantially new form was not realised.

NOTES

1. Thomas Kempner 'Frederick Taylor and Scientific Management' in *Management Thinkers* eds. A. Tillett, T. Kempner and G. Wills (Pelican 1970) p. 75. An interesting analysis of Taylorism can be found in Harry Braverman *Labor and Monopoly Capital: the degradation of work in the twentieth century* (New York 1974) esp. Ch. 4.
2. F. W. Taylor *The Principles of Scientific Management* (New York 1911) pp. 28-30. Taylor was begged by his friends not to walk the two and a half miles from work to his home since they felt he would be at risk for his life. But Taylor rejected their advice, arguing that it would be tactically best not to appear to be timid, and he continued to walk from work to home unarmed.
3. Taylor *Principles of Scientific Management* p. 31.
4. *Shop Management* quoted in F. B. Copley *Frederick W. Taylor: Father of Scientific Management* (New York 1923) p. 208 in a chapter (Book III, Chapter 1) called 'The "Systematic Soldiering" He Had to Overcome'.
5. F. W. Taylor *The Principles of Scientific Management* (New York 1911) p. 9 and p. 11.
6. Ibid., p. 11.
7. David Landes *The Unbound Prometheus* (Cambridge 1969) p. 321.
8. F. W. Taylor *Principles of Scientific Management* quoted in T. Lupton ed. *Payment Systems* (Penguin 1972) p. 20.
9. On Taylor and his disciples see especially Samuel Haber *Efficiency and Uplift: Scientific management in the Progressive Era* (Chicago 1964).
10. To some extent, as H. G. Aitken has commented, another of Taylor's projects—the development of high-speed steel—'spread much more quickly through American industry than did the innovation of scientific management': quoted in *Management Thinkers*, p. 40. High-speed steel also had adverse effects on labour, for instance in de-skilling some jobs and making greater work-speeds possible.
11. This account is based on the section on Watertown Arsenal in H. B. Drury *Scientific Management* (first pub. 1915, New York 1922 edn.) pp. 172-176. There is also Hugh G. J. Aitken *Taylorism at the*

Watertown Arsenal: Scientific Management in Action 1908-1915 (Cambridge 1960) which I have not been able to consult.

12. R. F. Hoxie *Scientific Management and Labor* (first published 1915, New York 1966 edn.) p. 3.

13. Hoxie, op. cit., pp. 15-19. An even fuller list of Trade union objections to Scientific Management is given in Appendix V of Hoxie's book. On union attitudes generally to scientific management see M. J. Nadworny *Scientific Management and the Unions 1900-1932* (1955).

14. Hoxie, op. cit., p. 139.

15. Conlon to U.S. Commission on Industrial Relations *Final Report and Testimony*, 64th Congress, 1st session, Senate Doc. 415, I, 874. Washington 1916. Quoted in David Montgomery 'The "New Unionism" and the Transformation of Workers' Consciousness in America, 1909-1922' in *Journal of Social History* Summer 1974, Vol. 7, No. 4, p. 518.

16. H. B. Drury Scientific Management (3rd. edn. New York 1922) p. 174.

17. Quoted in Drury, op. cit., 'Introduction to the Third Edition', 1922, p. 27.

18. Drury, op. cit., Introduction to the Third Edition, p. 26. Drury also maintained that scientific management itself had changed since 1915: 'the center of gravity in scientific management has now definitely shifted away from the idea of making men work harder to the idea of making their work more effective.'—an interesting enough admission in itself. But in the same introduction Drury added that 'the changes of recent years have been additions to, rather than subtractions from, the scientific management whose origin and development are described in the body of this book. (p. 28)

19. Georges Friedmann *Industrial Society* pp. 269-270.

20. Samuel Haber *Efficiency and Uplift. Scientific Management in the Progressive Era* (Chicago 1964) p. 133.

21. Thorstein Veblen *The Engineers and the Price System* (New York 1921) p. 88.

22. S. Haber, op. cit., p. 155.

23. Quoted in S. Haber, op. cit., p. 152. Lenin's *Pravda* article of April 1918 in which he said the same things was reprinted with great glee by Taylor's official biographer: see F. B. Copley *Frederick Winslow Taylor: Father of Scientific Management* (New York 1923) p. xxii.

24. Quoted in Georges Friedmann *Industrial Society* (Glencoe, 1955) p. 266—on which this account draws heavily.

25. *La Vie Ouvrière* March 5, 1913, quoted in Friedmann, op. cit., p. 267.

26. Quoted ibid., p. 268.

27. Quoted ibid., p. 268. A point of view similar to Ravaté's was put forward by Gramsci: see *Selections from the Prison Notebooks*, eds. Q. Hoare and G. Nowell-Smith (London 1971), for instance p. 292 where he states that skilled workers in Italy had never, individually or collectively, 'actively or passively opposed innovations leading towards lowering of costs, rationalisation of work or the introduction of more perfect forms of automation and more perfect technical organisation of the complex of the enterprise. On the contrary.' As

G. Nowell-Smith points out (p. 278) Gramsci thought that resistance to 'Americanism and Fordism' came largely from backward economic groups and reactionary intellectuals: 'The working class, by contrast, he saw not as opposed to Americanism as such, nor even to its attendant effects in social life, but rather to the specific form it would take in conditions of intensified economic exploitation and authoritarian cultural repression.'

Since I wrote this chapter James Green has drawn my attention to an exceptionally useful article on some of the themes of this chapter in Katherine Stone's 'The Origin of Job Structures in the Steel Industry' in Radical America, *Vol. 7, No. 6, Nov.-Dec. 1973.*

VII

SCIENTIFIC MANAGEMENT IN BRITAIN BEFORE 1914

Scientific management made only a relatively small impact on British industry before the First World War. But that is not to say that no attention was given to new management methods by British employers and managers in the period. This attention mainly took the form of considerable interest in new wage incentive systems—a direct response to the widespread ca'canny problem. In 1932 W. F. Watson, a skilled engineer and former syndicalist militant, could write with considerable justification that for over 50 years British employers had been 'groping for an incentive that will successfully induce the maximum number of workers to maintain the maximum output of which they are capable.'[1] Watson himself had lived and worked through these attempts to impose payment systems which would bring about increases in worker productivity. For him the rapid extension of payment by results systems before the First World War was scientific management, even though F. W. Taylor would not have dignified it with that label. Watson tells us that 'Scientific Management' came to Britain around 1900, and that 'for some years the employers were scientific system mad.'[2] Some, but by no means all of this 'madness', was imported from America. According to Georges Friedmann, Taylorism proper itself was first introduced into Britain in the Huddersfield Works of J. Hopkinson Ltd. 'where it was badly received.'[3] Arthur Paterson, the author of a book hostile to trade unionism called *The Weapon of the Strike*, gives another illustration of how the system was imported into British industry. In 1921 he recalled an incident which took place in about 1910 or 1911 when he was called in by a large firm which already paid good wages to a largely non-unionised workforce. Paterson was asked to give advice on what would be a fair minimum wage for the lowest grade workers, and also about the desirability of introducing the premium bonus system which the works manager 'fresh from experience' in the U.S.A. wanted to introduce. In this case a meeting to explain the premium bonus system was held with the workforce, and a number of workers volunteered for time study. Rates were thus established, the system applied and production doubled.[4]

Things did not always go so smoothly for Britain's embryonic scientific managers. There is clear evidence that many workers greatly resented the attempts to introduce new payment systems and new methods of workshop organisation. Alice Foley has recalled of the invasion that took place in the cotton spinning industry that:

'Young scientific experts came into the mills armed with slide-rule and stop-watch to statistically measure individual "work-loads" with the object of stimulating productivity and reducing costs. But with the rapid application of time and motion techniques much resentment and suspicion arose on the shop-floor.'[5]

In the engineering industry at least, planning was replacing improvisation in many aspects of work. High speed steels, new machines and production techniques were becoming rather more common. Works engineers, rate-fixers, progress men, 'work hustlers', and 'speed and feed men' began to arrive in the works office and on the shop floor. Time clocks appeared at the gates, and as one writer has put it:

'Once the worker was safely inside he was faced by clocks in each of the shops and in the rate-fixer's hand, and was many times reminded that "a good job done in my own time" was no longer the criterion of the workshop.'[6]

Alongside these changes, new payment systems were being developed particularly in the engineering and boilermaking trades. Roughly speaking, until the end of the 19th century 'straight piecework' was the alternative system of payment to a time-based system. In the engineering and boilermaking trades for instance, in 1886, only five per cent of workers were on piece-work. By 1906 the figure was 27.5 per cent. At the same date

4.8 per cent of all adult males in these trades were on premium bonus. In 1914, 46 per cent of the fitters, 37 per cent of the turners and nearly 50 per cent of the machine men were employed under some system of payment by results.[7] Although A. L. Levine is doubtless right to contend that 'the spread of premium bonus and similar schemes forms a slender basis from which to argue that a revolution in management techniques had swept over British industry during these pre-war years, or that the purer forms of Taylorism began to enjoy a secure foothold in Britain',[8] it must be said that the one element of Scientific Management which interested British managers more than any other was precisely the premium bonus system.[9] It was this fact which allowed Edward Cadbury with perfect justification to say in a paper which urged great caution in the application of Scientific Management to British industry that 'some attempt has been made by English firms to adopt the American system of payment on the differential bonus basis.'[10] And in 1917 when the American trade journal *Iron Age* noted the growth of interest in scientific management in Britain by then, it had to add that most of the English discussion was about premium methods of wage payment.[11]

The major problem with any sort of piece work system as far as the workers themselves were concerned, was the continual cutting of piece rates.[12] In engineering, the employers admitted that this was their practice, and the Amalgamated Society of Engineers opposed piecework because of this. The A.S.E., therefore, when presented with the carrot of a method of payment by results which, they thought, would not lead to reductions, jumped at the chance. In 1902, the A.S.E. leadership agreed to the removal of all restrictions on the operation of the premium bonus system, in return for guarantees from the employers about overtime rates for piece-workers, a minimum wage, and an assurance that once prices were fixed they 'should only be changed if the methods or means of manufacture' were changed. There was much opposition to the new system from the A.S.E. branches, but the Executive urged that it be given a fair trial, and solicited a contribution from Sidney Webb to the October 1902 issue of the *Monthly Journal*, in which he stated that the premium bonus system was 'an admirable expedient'.[13]

All payments systems of this sort following Taylor, were based on the theory that low wages did not necessarily connote low costs. Taylor was the pioneer of payment systems which rewarded high output with high wages, but which severely hit those who failed to reach the set standard. To quote W. F. Watson once again :

'This system marked a new departure in methods of remunerating labour. Under piecework the workman received the full value of extra effort, the price of the job remained constant regardless of the time taken. But with Taylor's system the quicker a man does a job, after reaching standard performance, the less he actually gets for it. This principle has been sedulously followed by all other designers of bonus systems.'[14]

The actual working of this type of system soon disillusioned many in the trade union movement. As early as 1902 A.S.E. members in a Patricroft machine shop, clearly accustomed under straight piecework to having each increment of output rewarded by a uniform increment of earnings, were complaining that 'the employers are not justified in taking one-half of the men's earnings due to their extra effort.'[15] On top of this 'built-in' rate cutting, conventional rate cutting also continued. John Hodge, the first Minister of Labour, recorded that the Premium Bonus System had never worked smoothly in the engineering industry. 'Whenever a man begins to earn too much money,' he wrote, 'some pettifogging alteration is made to the machine and an alteration of the rate is called for on the grounds of altered methods of working.'[16]

In 1909 the T.U.C. appointed a sub-committee to investigate the system. The sub-committee came out strongly against it. Amongst the criticisms made of it were the following : 'that it destroys the principle of collective bargaining'; 'that it is destructive of trade-unionism and discourages organisation'; 'that it is one of the causes of unemployment'; 'that it leads to scamping of work' and that it promoted selfishness among the workmen in a shop.[17] There seems to have been strong rank and file agreement with the opinion expressed by W. Salisbury, a boilermaker and delegate of Derby Trades Council to the Manchester Conference on Industrial Syndicalism held on November 26, 1910—

that the evil of the Premium Bonus System should be eradicated by strong 'combined action.'[18]

In 1911 the A.S.E. voted overwhelmingly in favour of the withdrawal of the premium bonus system from the engineering industry, with the union's *Monthly Journal* declaring in an editorial in August 1911 that:

> 'Those who believed that it was introduced to benefit the workers must by this time realise that they were either deceived or misinformed . . . premium bonus has only one use . . . it enables the employer to keep back from the worker . . . that which would be his due under a piece-work system.'

The historian of the A.S.E. has described the impact of these aspects of Taylorism into the engineering industry using the words of union officials and members themselves in the years 1910 to 1913:

> 'Inside the shops startling changes had taken place. At the gate, clocks and time-cribbing had been widely introduced. One member remarked that "the employers would like to put a micrometer on the clocks if they could." In the yards, "policemen in various shapes and forms and under different names" had made their appearance. In the shops the workers were "watched and dogged by a whole army of non-producers." Piece-work and premium bonus systems, speed-and-feed men, operations inspectors, work-hustlers—elements of the Taylor system "one of the last stages of lunacy"—and the general speed-up with the new machines and improved cutting steels, altered the character of the engineer and the type of problem facing the Society.'[19]

It is interesting to note, however, that by 1912, one half (at least) of the Webb partnership had become critical of scientific management. Beatrice Webb had by then read Taylor's *Principles of Scientific Management*, and reached the conclusion that American syndicalism was a reaction to rash experiments in scientific management. She advised her friend, Lady Betty Belfour:

> 'Do not go and send this book to English Labour and Socialist friends. It is the only justification I have yet read for the policy of Sabotage.'[20]

For those actually subjected to aspects of Taylorism at work the practice of it was often sufficient. They did not need to read the book in order to justify their responses. W. F. Watson's experience as a working engineer makes this quite clear. At one time before the First World War he was working under the Rowan System at Thorneycroft's Torpedo boat yard in London. Time-recording clocks had been installed in the shops; work had to start at the sound of a hooter; and 'feed and speed bosses' were employed to see that this was done. Fixed to every machine was a chart indicating the speeds to be employed, and the feed and speed men, armed with feedometers perambulated the shop to ensure [that] both men and machine [were] working to their utmost capacity.'[21]

Engineering workers had lost their customary job control. They were, for instance, no longer allowed to grind their own tools—all emery wheels were removed from the shop. On starting a man was given six standardised tools, 'ground to theoretic angles on special machines, which were changed for new ones when worn.' But there was a degree of worker resistance to this. Watson tells us that:

'Passive resistance and sabotage were practised at Thorney-croft's. We persuaded the man in the tool room to allow us in "just to touch this tool up, Jim," and ended by walking in and out at will. Time limits, fixed by theoretic charts, were invariably all wrong. When excessive—as they sometimes were—we ca'cannied so as not to earn too much; if insufficient, we "went slow" just the same, and lodged a complaint to the foreman, who sent for the rate fixer. When he arrived there ensued a wordy war between the three, then the rate-fixer timed the job with a stop-watch; but it was easy to "swing the lead" on an inexperienced clerk by providing that the tool would not cut properly. We seldom got the increase we demanded—we didn't expect to—but we usually got enough to suit our purpose.

'The charts disappeared from the machines—no one knew where they went.'[22]

A feed and speed man might instruct a worker to increase his rate of working. Adopting a sabotage tactic the worker would comply with the request in such a way that an overloading was caused, or too much was taken off, so that the job had to be scrapped. It was through the use of such tactics that, Watson claims, the employers began to realise 'the futility of such methods.' But it was only a partial victory. Scientific management as such could not be halted. The systematisation of production proceeded, and only 'the harsh repressive features' were withdrawn.[23]

It is absolutely clear that, as far as engineering workers were concerned, the whole tendency of scientific management was precisely in the direction which Taylor had been talking about when he urged that 'all possible brainwork should be removed from the shop and centred in the planning or layout department.' Watson and his colleagues were able to fight back to some extent, but even Watson himself was forced to admit that changes in management practice allied with changes in the structure of industry were fundamentally altering the status of the skilled engineer. He tried in fact to use these changes to persuade the skilled engineers to come down off their pinnacle and to show solidarity with—rather than hostility to—the semi-skilled workers, who were increasingly employed in engineering. In an 'Open Letter to Engineering Workers' published in 1912, Watson called on his fellow members of the A.S.E. to work for amalgamation of the various unions in the engineering industry. The open letter began as follows: 'Time was when you were known as "the aristocrats of Labour", when you swelled your chest with pride and told everyone you were an Engineer.' Watson went on to claim that it it was now extremely foolish for A.S.E. members to maintain this attitude: the growth of the cycle and motor industries, the decreasing importance of skilled labour, the premium bonus and other payment by results schemes, and the speed up generally, had in reality knocked the skilled engineer off his pedestal. He gave a telling example of just how seriously the skilled engineer had been humbled, probably recalling his Thornycroft days:

'When I worked some years ago in a big yard in West London, I saw a notice in the w.c. to the effect that no one was to stay more than seven minutes and only twice a day.'

He had also heard of a Lancashire firm where the time limit was four minutes. This led him to comment 'I put it to you, my comrades, is it not absolutely degrading that we should have to tolerate such conditions.'[24]

The railway workshops were another place where scientific management made considerable headway in the years before the First World War. Here there is less evidence of the sort of resistance that Watson talked of. Great changes took place in the organisation of work in the railway workshops between 1900 and 1914. Alfred Williams in his classic *Life In A Railway Factory*, first published in 1915, wrote about these changes from first hand :

'A decade and a half ago one could come to the shed fearlessly, and with perfect complacence; work was a pleasure in comparison with what it is now. . . . The workman was not watched and timed at every little operation. . . . The supervisory staff has been doubled or trebled, and they must do something to justify their existence. Before the workman can recover from one shock he is visited by another; he is kept in a state of continual agitation and suspense which, in time, operate on his own mind and temper and transform his whole character.'[25]

Williams gives a striking example of how new tools from the U.S.A. were introduced into the stamping shed. A man called Pinnell, 'by far the hardest working man' in the shed, was chosen by management to pioneer the operation of the machinery. According to Williams :

'He had to demonstrate what the machines were capable of doing, and upon his output would be based the standard of prices for those to follow after or work beside him. . . . Every operation was correctly timed. The manager and overseer stood together, watches in hand."

Pinnell was measured by the minute, and from that the rates for the hour and for the day were worked out. If Pinnell paused or checked something the overseer would quickly get him back to work. Even the time he spent in the lavatory was recorded. Another important thing was that the overseer and manager only timed Pinnell in the morning after breakfast, when his speed of work was greatest. Poor old Pinnell soon found it impossible to keep going at the same rate all day—and ended up wishing himself dead.[26] But not all workers in railway workshops were as gullible as Pinnell. At least one other example is at hand to illustrate that the introduction of new techniques and new machinery into railway workshops were resisted by workers. In July 1914, the *Railway Review* tells us that 'the employees at Wolverton . . . struck work towards the end of last week against the attempt of the L. & N.W. to introduce speediators in to the works there. The strike appears to have been short and effective, and we understand the speediators were withdrawn pending a discussion of the whole question with the men.'[27] Edward Cadbury of the cocoa firm, who was conditionally sympathetic to some aspects of Scientific Management, pointed out in April 1914 that the 'Labour Unrest' of the time was one of the 'expressions of the workman's demand to control his own life.' He added that this demand would have to be reckoned with, 'for as we have seen there have already been strikes arising out of the attempt to introduce the mechanism of scientific management into various establishments.'[28] And six months later Cadbury in another contribution on the subject pointed out (again perceptively) that any introduction of scientific management into British industry had to take into account the attitude of the trade unions. 'Already,' he pointed out, 'the unions are beginning to discuss the problems raised by various aspects of Scientific Management. It is not merely the question of wages that interests them, but the status of the worker and the trade-union under the system, and such questions as the control of the workshop. In the *Workers' Union Journal* (Midland Edition), for example, there has been running in recent issues a series of articles on Scientific Management and the workers' attitude towards it. . . .'[29] The British working class was by no means entirely populated by Pinnells.

Edward Cadbury contributed those remarks to a debate on Scientific Management in *The Sociological Review*. The debate had started in July 1913 when J. A. Hobson contributed a paper on the subject in which (and this was symptomatic of the lack of knowledge of Taylor's ideas before the First World War) he attempted to set out a simple summary of Taylor's main points, backed by ample quotations from Taylor's writings. Hobson was not completely uncritical of Taylorism, arguing in particular that the extreme division of labour that came about under scientific management was bound to 'squeeze out of the labour-day some human interest, some call upon initiative, reason, judgment, responsibility, surviving under previous conditions even in the most routine and subdivided toil.'[30] Cadbury's paper 'Some Principles of Industrial Organisation : The Case for and against Scientific Management' appeared next, in the issue of April 1914. Cadbury was one of the few British employers who had read any Taylor. He was, however, by no means over-awed by it—seeking instead to point out the problems and disadvantages of scientific management in the British context. He went on to expound at considerable length on the more 'scientific', more paternalistic, less anti-trade union, and more English approach to management which had been developed at his firm's Bournville works over several years. 'We have always believed,' he stated, 'that business efficiency and the welfare of the employees are but different sides of the same problem.' Slow workers in the Bournville works were not, Taylor style, driven from the works but sent to the company doctor and checked for things like keeping late hours, inadequate sleep and malnutrition; if such things were discovered benevolent remedial action was taken. In contradistinction to Scientific Management's attempts to make trade unionism irrelevant, the Cadburys chose to work 'through and with the trade unions'. Extra output came not so much from wage incentives as from 'the moral incentive of increased respect generated between worker and employer.'[31]

The same issue of the *Sociological Review* also carried a number of short comments on Cadbury's paper : from J. A. Hobson, G. D. H. Cole, Walter Hazell (of Hazell, Watson and Viney Ltd.) and C. G. Renold of the Manchester firm of Hans Renold. Renold's contribution is perhaps the most interesting since he was probably Taylor's strongest supporter in Britain as well as one of the few practitioners of something like a fully fledged American-style Scientific Management system in Britain. Renold consequently believed that the Taylor system could be applied to the British engineering industry and that it would bring about substantial increases in productivity. But even

Renold, interestingly, chose to disabuse people of the view that there was something completely new in this alien, American management system. He stated :

'For many years works jobs have been closely studied, workmen have been carefully selected, detailed instructions for doing work have been given, tools and appliances have been standardised, even "functional" foremen—notably inspectors have been used. . . . The novelty of Scientific Management (he concluded) lies, not in the fact that these principles have been set to work, but that they have now achieved consciousness.'[32]

Renold was, no doubt, an advanced management thinker as far as British industry was concerned; nevertheless there is some substance in his view. Taylorism as such may not have received much attention in the British trade press but it was argued there that Taylorism was merely common sense, good management practice which only fools did not already apply in some measure. *The Engineer*, one of the two leading trade journals, commented in November 1913 that :

'No works manager would be worth his salt who did not endeavour ceaselessly to make his labour bill per unit of output lower. To call this scientific management is simply to give a high-sounding title to an old and well-understood thing. . . . It is the ordinary doctrine of works that better methods must be adopted as soon as they present themselves. It is scientific, of course, but to call it scientific is like speaking of the common pump as a philosophical instrument.'[33]

This was perhaps one of the more charitable of the very few acknowledgements and discussions of Taylorism that appeared in *The Engineer* and other discussion points in the British engineering world. Other comments were mostly hostile.[34] The one or two home-produced manuals on factory administration and management methods published before 1914 were given a good deal more attention and praise than any work of Taylor's or his disciples. A review of one of the British works was sometimes an excuse for a side-swipe at Taylor. A review of E. T. Welbourne's *Factory Administration and Accounts* (a book which sold more copies than any previous work on British management) in *The Engineer* in May 1914 praised its English sentiments and attacked the irrelevant ideas emanating from the other side of the Atlantic.[35] One of the few favourable receptions of Taylor's ideas was that by G. C. Allingham in a paper called 'Scientific Shop Management on the Taylor System' given before the Junior Institution of Mechanical Engineers in 1912. But even then one of the members reminded the meeting that the greatest obstacle to the introduction of Scientific Management into British industry was that 'organised labour here is antagonistic.'[36]

The marked coolness of British management towards scientific management was, however, transformed into a veritable heatwave of enthusiasm for it after the outbreak of the First World War. As H. B. Drury put it 'This early interest, however, seems almost casual compared with the outburst of enthusiasm which succeeded the opening of the war.'[37] The war, of course, produced many social changes on the home front but none were more far-reaching than those in industry through the application of new management techniques. The First World War was, in an important way, a laboratory of and testing ground for the development of British scientific management practice : regressive payment systems, time and motion study, welfare work, fatigue study, all developed apace.

NOTES

1. W. F. Watson *Bedaux and Other Bonus Systems Explained* (London 1932) p. 3.
2. W. F. Watson *Machines and Men: the autobiography of an itinerant mechanic* (London 1935) p. 90.
3. Georges Friedmann *Industrial Society* p. 262, see also p. 42.
4. Arthur Paterson *The Weapon of the Strike* (London n.d. ? 1921) pp. 232-233. Paterson may have been the 'A. H. Patterson', an ardent enthusiast for Taylorism, who as a member of Social Welfare Association of London corresponded enthusiastically with the secretary of the Taylor Co-operators: see letter from Patterson quoted in H. B. Drury *Scientific Management* (New York 1922 edn.) p. 189.
5. Alice Foley, *A Bolton Childhood* (Manchester 1973) p. 90.
6. J. B. Jeffreys, *The Story of the Engineers* (London 1945) pp. 124-125.

7. J. B. Jeffreys, op. cit., p. 129 and A. L. Levine, op. cit., pp. 67-68. Levine contends that 'the spread of premium bonus and similar schemes forms a slender basis from which to argue that a revolution in management techniques had swept over British industry during these pre-war years, or that the purer forms of Taylorism began to enjoy a secure foothold in Britain.' (p. 68)

8. A. L. Levine, op. cit., p. 68.

9. See, for instance, William Graham *The Wages of Labour* (London 1921), in chapter 4 on 'Scientific Management', who said that in Britain 'there has been, in the main, more interest in the premium bonus system' than in other aspects of Scientific Management. (p 116).

10. Edward Cadbury in *The Sociological Review*, April 1914, p. 104.

11. Cited in H. B. Drury, *Scientific Management*, (New York 1922 edn.) p. 189 and p. 191.

12. See J. B. Jeffreys, op. cit., p. 154; and E. J. Hobsbawm 'Custom, Wages, and Work-load' p. 137; Alfred Williams in his *Life in A Railway Factory* (first pub. London 1915, Newton Abbot 1969 edn.) complained that 'Piecework prices are cut to the lowest possible point' (p. 42) and 'The prices have been cut again and again.' (p. 78)

13. J. B. Jeffreys, op. cit., pp. 154-155.

14. W. F. Watson *Bedaux and Other Bonus Systems Explained* (London 1932) p. 15. Other systems include those devised by Merrick, Gantt, Emerson, Halsey, Rowan, Priestman—and later Bedaux: see Watson, p. 17ff, and I.L.O. *Payment By Results* (Geneva 1951) Ch. 1.

15. A.S.E. Monthly Report May 1902, quoted in Peter Stearns *Lives of Labour* (London 1975) p. 212.

16. John Hodge *Workman's Cottage to Windsor Castle* (London n.d. ? 1931) pp. 194-195, and see also W. F. Watson *The Worker and Wage Incentives* (London 1934) pp. 40-41.

17. Quoted by Edward Cadbury in *The Sociological Review* April 1914, p. 104: see also L. Urwick and E. F. L. Brech *The Making of Scientific Management* Vol. 2 (London 1949) pp. 105-106.

18. See *The Industrial Syndicalist* Vol. 1, No. 6, December 1910, p. 31.

19. J. B. Jefferys, op. cit., p. 132.

20. Beatrice Webb to Lady Betty Balfour, 16 October 1912, Webb Papers, quoted in H. Pelling 'America and the British Labour Unrest' in *America and the British Left*, p. 96.

21. W. F. Watson, *Machines and Men*, p. 90.

22. W. F. Watson, *Machines and Men*, p. 92.

23. W. F. Watson *Machines and Men*, p. 93. An interesting present day account of the shop floor battle with the rate fixer can be found in Phil Higgs' essay 'The Convenor' in *Work*, Volume 2, edited by R. Fraser (Penguin 1969) pp. 114-115. See also W. F. Watson *The Worker and Wage Incentives* (London 1934) pp. 39-41 on 'going slow', 'swinging the lead', and 'soldiering' in the face of scientific management systems.

24. *Daily Herald* December 28, 1912. More recently Brian Jackson has indicated the importance of lavatories at work. Writing of a Huddersfield mill he says: 'Because they were the only places where a man could reasonably expect to be free from the surveillance of authority, the lavatories occupied a unique place in the mill's social life.' *Working-Class Community* (Penguin 1972 edn.) p. 75.

25. Alfred Williams *Life in A Railway Factory* (first pub. London 1915, Newton Abbot 1969 edn.) p. 304.
26. Alfred Williams *Life in A Railway Factory* pp. 183-184.
27. *Railway Review* July 14, 1911. A 'speeder' (according to the definition given in the Concise Oxford Dictionary) is a device for quickening or regulating the speed of machinery.
28. Edward Cadbury 'Some Principles of Industrial Organisation. The Case for and against Scientific Management' in *The Sociological Review* Vol. VII, No. 2, April 1914, p. 105.
29. Edward Cadbury in *The Sociological Review* Vol. VII, No. 4, October 1914, p. 329.
30. J. A. Hobson 'Scientific Management' in *The Sociological Review* Vol. VI, No. 3, July 1913, p. 210.
31. Cadbury in *The Sociological Review* April 1914, quotations from pp. 106, and 116. Cadbury's book *Experiments in Industrial Organisation* (London 1912) gives a fuller account of Cadbury's system.
32. Renold in *The Sociological Review* April 1914 p. 122.
33. Quoted in A. L. Levine *Industrial Retardation in Britain* p. 64.
34. A. L. Levine, op. cit., gives a full account: see pp. 60-68; for a fuller account see L. Urwick and E. F. L. Brech *The Making of Scientific Management*, Vol. 2., Ch. VII, 'The Acceptance of F. W. Taylor by British Industry'.
35. A. L. Levine, op. cit., p. 65, and A. Briggs 'Social Background' in *The System of Industrial Relations in Great Britain* eds. A. Flanders and H. A. Clegg (London 1964 imp.) p. 36.
36. Urwick and Brech, op. cit., p. 99.
37. H. B. Drury, *Scientific Management*, (New York 1922 edn.) p. 189.

Part Four

THE FIRST WORLD WAR AND THE WAR
AFTER THE WAR

VIII

The First World War

The Labour Unrest of the pre-war years soon abated with the arrival of war in August 1914. The revolutionary threat to the stability of the British state evaporated. The British trade union movement, and its leaders in particular, 'rallied round the flag' in exemplary fashion. The leaders were rewarded with a new status, and the rank and file members were cajoled and exhorted with varying degrees of success to make great sacrifices in the national interest. In the early part of the war many male industrial workers volunteered for the forces, thus leaving serious gaps in the labour force, which was already under great pressure to produce vast quantities of armaments and associated war-waging commodities. Women and less skilled male workers stepped into the breach. The Government, taking on a new and growing role of overseeing industrial production, soon came to see one of its major problems as being that of extracting from the then existing labour force an output uninterrupted by strikes and stoppages and unhampered by the persistent use of the wide range of written and unwritten protective rules and restrictions employed by workers and their organisations. Or, as Arthur Marwick puts it, 'There were other obstacles to the maximising of labour power. The most important of these was the elaborate structure of trade union rules and restrictions built up over the years of struggle with the employing classes.'[1]

Under the Treasury Agreement of March 1915 the leaders of the main men's unions engaged in war production (with the exception of the miners) agreed on behalf of their members to forgo many of their customary trade union practices. The right to strike was surrendered; an arbitration procedure was established for disputes; and it was agreed that there should be a relaxation of 'present trade practices' for the duration of the war.[2] One of the positive concessions in favour of workers and their organisations (and there is some significance in this, as we shall see later) was the undertaking from the employers' and the Government's side that piecework prices should not be cut.[3] There was pressure from all sides on the rank and file to forgo the considerable degree of hard won craft and job control that had been established over the years. The Government, the employers, outside agencies, as well as trade union leaders all engaged themselves in the task of putting this pressure on the rank and file of the industrial labour force. A typical plea for the workers to drop their customary resistance to full production (the most significant of all labour's 'restrictive practices') was that made by the Section of Economic Science and Statistics of the British Association. A report issued by a working party (which included Charles Booth, C. W. Bowerman, Harry Gosling, Archdeacon Cunningham and Professor E. C. K. Gonner) on industrial unrest acknowledged quite clearly the widespread pre-war tendency of workers to restrict output, and how this was being carried through into wartime.

'There is a need for greater productivity in all our leading industries. This greater productivity is a possibility, for we have not yet in normal times, worked our hardest or produced our maximum.'[4]

George Barnes, the former secretary of the Amalgamated Society of Engineers and shortly to be incorporated in the war cabinet, was one of the many trade union leaders who joined this chorus of people and institutions which was urging workers to increase production and productivity during the war. In an interview in the *Daily Express* in 1916 he indicated what he regarded as being one of the trade union movement's responsibilities on this score :

'Trade union rules have undoubtedly had the effect of restricting the output. Speeding-up does nobody any harm in itself; it is speeding-up under a sense of injustice that causes of mischief. Let us get rid of this miserable makeshift of ca'canny which does nobody any good.'[5]

The problem of output restriction and its prohibition was, indeed, explicitly enshrined in the Munitions of War Act, Section

IV(3) in July 1915. 'Any rule, practice, or custom,' it said there,
'not having the force of law which tends to restrict production
or employment shall be suspended, and if any person induces
or attempts to induce any other person (whether a particular
person or generally) to comply with such a rule, practice or
custom, that person shall be guilty of an offence under this
Act.'[6] All the exhortation and legislation seems to have had
some effect. There was a sharp reduction in the number of
strikes beginning in 1915 and 1916 compared with the immediate
pre-war years, and there was similarly a sharp reduction in the
number of working days lost through strikes—nearly 10 million
working days had been lost in both 1913 and 1914, whereas in
1915 and 1916 the figures were nearly 3 million and nearly 2½
million respectively.[7] If, in the early stages of the war, the Munitions Act coupled with the general de-radicalising effect of the
spirit embodied in the Treasury Agreement was relatively successful in leading to a reduction in strikes, the same cannot be said
for the related attempt to persuade workers at shop floor level
to drop their restrictive practices and to cease restricting output,
or in plain words to work harder. It soon came to be realised by
employers and by certain sections of the Government that workers
responded better to financial inducements than to rhetoric. But
rhetoric there was—constantly—and no better exponent of it
than Lloyd George. When he was Minister of Munitions he
treated the 1915 Trades Union Congress to a long display of
it in the shape largely of a homily on the sins of restricting the
output.

He told the delegates (who gave him a warm reception) that :

'This country at the present moment is not doing its best. It
is not doing its utmost, and it is almost entirely a labour problem, and you alone can assist.'

According to Lloyd George, three things had to be done. First of
all dilution had to be accepted; secondly there had to be no
strikes or stoppages in essential industries for the duration of
the war, and thirdly, restriction of output had to stop. Or, as
Lloyd George put it :

'The next direction in which Trade Unionists can help us is
by suspending during the war, again, all practices and customs

which have the effect of preventing men from turning out as much work as their strength and skill permit. I am going to speak very plainly about that later on. What I tell you now is that the reports we get from our own offices, the Admiralty, the War Office, and the Munitions Department, show that if we had a suspension during the war of these customs which keep down the output we could increase it in some places by 30 per cent, in other places by 200 per cent.'

He reminded the Congress of what had been decided at the Treasury Conference, and of the bargain that had been made there by the representatives of the Admiralty, the War Office, the Treasury, and the trade unions. The bargain was that 'if Trade Union restrictions and customs were suspended during the war, we also on our part should take steps to restrict the profits of employers'. He reminded Congress of the definite undertaking to restore trade union restrictions and customs after the war. A further point was that :

'no increase in the output should be used as an excuse for putting down the piece rate, that the unskilled man or woman whom we employ should be put on exactly the same wage for piecework as skilled workers for the same class of work.'

Lloyd George insisted that the Government had kept its side of the bargain—715 munitions establishments, the great majority, had been brought under Government control by Act of Parliament. The trade unions' side of the bargain, he claimed, was frequently not being kept. He gave examples of men at Woolwich Arsenal refusing to accept semi-skilled men, and of workers in South Wales refusing to allow unskilled labour to work lathes. But the most important respect in which he stated that the trade unions were not keeping their part of the bargain was over restriction of output :

'I come now to the promised part of the agreement that there must be no effort to restrict the output. I am sorry to say that part of the bargain has not been carried out. I have had a number of cases represented where men who have turned out more than the customary output were warned to desist. . . . In some places the usual Trade Union restrictions of output are rigidly maintained. . . ."

He illustrated his point by citing cases from Enfield, where one man had been fined £1 by the Friendly Society of Ironfounders for working too quickly; the case of C. Hewitt in Coventry who had been intimidated by fellow workers for taking only 8½ hours on a job which usually took 31½ hours; and the general finding of the Labour Party Advisory Committee's investigation at Woolwich Arsenal in which it was stated that :

'The Trade Union witness regretted having to acknowledge that the workmen in several departments restricted output in order to maintain the prices obtained before the war, and this was continued up to the present time.'[8]

The executive committee of the engineering unions undertook an investigation into these charges. The cases mentioned by Lloyd George were dealt with as follows. According to Lloyd George, a workman at the Enfield Ordnance Factory had been obliged by workshop pressure to regulate his output so that he did not earn more than one shilling per hour, although he could easily have earned two shillings and sixpence an hour. The engineering unions' National Advisory Committee on War Output stated in its report that this incident did take place, but before the Treasury Agreement was signed, and that since that time A.S.E. officials had withdrawn restrictions on output when the authorities definitely adhered to their promise not to cut piece rates. Lloyd George had similarly said that there was 'a deliberate attempt to keep down the output' at Woolwich Arsenal. He had backed this up by the testimony of an A.S.E. member that the workers in his department at the Arsenal were attempting 'to deliberately restrict output . . . notwithstanding the exhortations of Lord Kitchener.'

The investigators found that the A.S.E. member who had said this, was in fact, unable to sustain the charge. Another witness, however, had replied, when asked if workers at the Arsenal were doing their utmost to accelerate the output of work, that the men were only working normally and that they could increase output, but were still afraid that piece rates might be cut. The case of C. Hewitt at the Coventry Ordnance works, which Lloyd George had outlined so tellingly at the T.U.C., was defused in similar fashion. It had been alleged that a note which had cir-

169

culated among the men in the works had read : 'Will you kindly note that C. Hewitt has started on a howitzer for finishing jacket and screwing for B hoop at 7 p.m. and in all probability will have it finished at 5 a.m., which means eight and a half hours on a thirty-one and a half hour's job?' The note concluded by inviting the men to go and 'practically to mock at this man, to watch him, to keep their eye on him. The Committee.' The A.S.E. claimed that no such committee existed, and that the note was circulated by a non-unionist. Hewitt, a member of the A.S.E., had taken 14 hours not 8½ hours on the job. His usual time for the job was between 17 and 18 hours, and 'the basic time allowed for the job on the premium bonus system being 31½ hours. Therefore,' the report concluded, 'there is no evidence in support of the statement that members of the A.S.E. were attempting to restrict output.'[9] But, given the climate of the times, the Advisory Committee on War Output felt obliged to condemn restriction of ouput. The report, therefore, concluded with an appeal for increased production though it added some general hints as to why there seemed to be a degree of resistance to the dropping of restrictive practices. Part of this appeal read :

'The justification of restrictive practices is usually the fear that prices will be cut if too much money is earned, and that the increased output will be made the standard of production after the War. It is also feared that there will be reductions in piece work prices, and an increase in the amount of work demanded from time workers.

'Even were these likely to be justified, that would be no excuse for deliberate slacking, when the need for munitions is so imperative, and when upon their unrestricted and abundant supply, the fate of this country depends.

'That the existence of this country should be imperilled and the lives of its soldiers squandered, because a minority of workmen are apprehensive that their workshop conditions may be threatened if they turn out too much work at this time is unthinkable and would be a serious reflection on the intelligence and patriotism of the great majority of workmen connected with the Engineering and Shipbuilding Industries.'[10]

Not long after his speech to the 1915 meeting of the T.U.C., Lloyd George was in Glasgow trying to get a hearing for his

views amongst the Clydeside munitions workers. On Christmas
Day 1915 about 3,000 workers packed into St. Andrew's Hall.
According to John Maclean's paper, *The Vanguard* : 'Seldom
has a prominent politican, a leading representative of the Governing Class, been treated with so little respect by a meeting of
the workers. It is evident that the feeling of servility towards
their masters no longer holds first place in the minds of the
Clyde workers. . . .'[11] The meeting was a marked success for the
Clyde Workers' Committee, and a clear defeat for Lloyd George.
He was able to get his revenge—the Clyde Workers' Committee
was comprehensively defeated within the next four months as
the result of 'a well-planned offensive directed by the Labour
Department of the Ministry of Munitions.'[12] Lloyd George was
on Clydeside because the Clyde Workers' Committee appeared
to be the major obstacle to the Government's carrying through
its campaign for increased output. As we have seen from Lloyd
George's T.U.C. speech the main hope in this direction was
through dilution—the process of introducing less skilled men
and women into jobs which had been traditionally thought of as
the exclusive preserve of skilled male engineering workers. But,
as we have also noticed, that was not the Minister of Munitions'
only concern. He sought also to make a general appeal to workers
to drop the whole range of restrictive practices, including restriction of output. This aspect of the drive for increased output
emerged quite clearly in the couple of days before the Christmas
Day speech. During these couple of days Lloyd George planned
to visit some of the local munitions factories to talk directly to
the workers. The Clyde Workers' Committee leaders, William
Gallacher and John Muir, by visiting the factories ahead of
Lloyd George and urging the shop stewards in them to refuse
to meet him, for the most part spoilt the Minister's plans. At the
Parkhead Forge, however, Gallacher and Muir were unsuccessful. They were not able to prevent David Kirkwood, the shop
stewards' leaders there, from taking the opportunity of Lloyd
George's visit to make his views known to him. John Maclean
in his famous 'Speech from the Dock' in May 1918 commented
on the Lloyd George/Kirkwood encounter in the following way :

'Now David Kirkwood, representing the Parkhead Forge
workers, at the end of 1915, when the dilution of labour began,

put forward a printed statement for the benefit of Mr. Lloyd George and his colleagues, the first sentence of which in big type was "What you wish is greater output". He said that the Parkhead Forge workers were then prepared to give a greater output and accept dilution if they, the workers, had some control over the conditions under which the greater output would accrue.'[13]

Maclean went on to observe that in the ensuing years Kirkwood was indeed able to boast that the Parkhead Forge Workers had generated a considerable increase in output. At one of his public meetings (for making seditious statements at which he was now on trial) Maclean had been asked whether Kirkwood's 'achievement' was 'consistent with the position and with the attitude of the working class.' Maclean told the court that he had replied to his questioner that it was not consistent with the attitude and position of the working class, and that Kirkwood's business was not to increase output but rather that :

'his business was to get right back down to normal to "ca'canny" so far as the general output was concerned.'

The analysis that followed is worth quoting from at length :

'The country has been exploited by the Capitalists in every sphere, to get the toilers to work harder to bring victory. I said at the commencement of the war that while this was being done, and while assurances were being given that at the end of the war the people would get back to normal, I said that circumstances would make such a return impossible. Now I have ample evidence to support that belief; I have used it at my meetings at Weir's of Cathcart—that they were asking the workers to toil harder not only during the war, but after the war they wish them to work harder and harder, because there is going to be "the war after the war", the economic war which brought on this war. You see therefore the workers are brought into a position where they are speeded up, and they are never allowed to go back again. They are speeded up again and again.'[14]

The capitalist, Maclean pointed out, applied the principle of 'ca'canny' in his own way. Wages were kept low during the war, in spite of big price rises, thus robbing the workers of some of their purchasing power. But at the same time the workers were asked in the name of the country to work harder, without being compensated by higher wages. 'If it was right,' Maclean argued, 'for the employer to get the maximum of energy from workers while paying them the minimum in wages was it not equally right for the worker to give the minimum of his energy and demand the maximum of wage?' Because of this diametrical opposition of interests between workers and employers,

'The worker has therefore in the past adopted this policy of "ca'canny" and I have, in the interests of the working class, advocated the policy of "ca'canny", not because I am against the war, but knowing that after the war the worker will have the new conditions imposed upon him, I hold still to the principle of "ca'canny".'[15]

Sir George Askwith, the Government's conciliator, writing shortly after the end of the war, lamented that the section of the Munitions of War Act outlawing the restriction of output had been thoroughly flouted, in spite of the efforts of the arbitrators to enforce it. He concluded that it was impossible to legislate ca'canny away, and added that 'unless a common purpose and a better feeling can be and is obtained, with direct interest of a man in the result of his work, the blows which ca'canny has received will have no more effect upon its strength than the flip of a boxer's glove.'[16] Askwith did suggest however, that the war had reduced the influence of ca'canny, and that the war had shown what level of production was possible without it. If he is right then one must assume that in wartime—when there is so much emphasis on increasing production—that even a decreased amount of it showed up more than in peacetime. It should be noted here that Askwith thought the problem serious enough to devote a separate chapter of his book to 'Propaganda and Ca'canny'. In this chapter Askwith quotes at length from a report on ca'canny in wartime made by Sir Lynden Macassey of the Department of Shipyard Labour, in January 1918. It is worth reproducing in full:

'A discharged soldier who returned to work for a motor-car firm at Birmingham found that in turning cylinders he could do a job in forty-three minutes, and he maintained this speed for three weeks. The man was warned that the official time was seventy minutes. The warning being ignored, on November 4 last the union stopped the shop until the man was moved to other work. The same kind of intervention seems to take place on most engineering work on which piece-rates are paid.

'In the collieries the restriction is exercised indirectly. If a miner exceeds a certain output per day, varying from four to seven tons, he finds himself delayed by the "shunt" men, who cut his supply of tubs and props. In South Wales and Lancashire the output laid down is a fixed number of tubs per day, called a "stint", and if this were regularly exceeded the pit would be stopped to enforce it. The same applies to the docks. Recently a ship discharging grain in bulk in Birkenhead was stopped because the union considered that 150 tons a day was an excessive rate, though the rate was laid down both in the ship's charter-party and the sale contract: the result is that the elevators are now running at 25 per cent below full speed. In Cardiff and elsewhere carters are not now allowed to load more than one tier of team wagons. On November 10 last a team lorry was stopped in Bute Street, Cardiff, by the union delegate, and the carter made to unload eight bags which were in a second tier. At Immingham a motor-lorry was stopped because it had a full six ton load. The driver asked the delegate what the limit was, and he said: "I don't know, but you have got too much on there anyhow."

'Sometimes the restriction appear to be applied by the men more than by the unions. At the Cardiff coaltips the men are turning over one truck every seven minutes, compared with two minutes before the War; they will not keep their machines running at full speed. The ships' painters in Liverpool and Birkenhead are working 16 per cent. per hour below the pre-war rate. In leather-stamping at Leicester, the men refuse to cut more than a certain number of pieces at a time, and this amounts to a loss of effort by the machine of 4 per cent. In bushelling wheat at Barrow, the men will not allow any more than two bushels to be made up every three minutes, and the unions have adopted this agreement among the men as a definite rule. In shipbuilding on the Clyde an attempt was made to limit the output of riveters by keeping the boy rivet-heaters to a set number.

'The restriction is of special moment when we find it applied to house-building. At Huddersfield, during the building of an extension, four men were stopped by their union for three days because they laid 480 bricks in a day of eight hours. A slater was warned at the same place because he fixed a gutter—a plumber's job—in order that he might get on with his work. Instances might be multiplied indefinitely.'[17]

In a book of his of 1922, Macassey gave more examples of what he then referred to as 'the appalling extent to which the false doctrine of limiting output' was 'rampant' in war-time industry. Once again Macassey's observations are worth repeating :

'In one instance some boys straight from a board school were put on to do a simple operation from which men had been withdrawn for more arduous duty. Working at the men's piece-prices, they averaged £4. 15s. per normal working week against the men's £2. 10s. That meant the boys turned out—nor were they any the worse for it physically—almost twice the men's output. Women I put on to replace men at some simple machining operations made, after a short period of training, £6-£10 per week, against the men's £4-£5. The women were paid the men's piece-prices for the operation. In another case men who were working on piece-work, after learning of the announcement of the Minister of Munitions that under no circumstances would piece-prices be "cut", speeded up their output by 120 per cent.'[18]

The output performance of 'dilutees' clearly threatened to undermine the traditional output norms of skilled workers—and this may well be an insignificantly appreciated reason for the opposition amongst skilled engineering workers to the introduction of less skilled male and female labour into jobs which had formerly been the exclusive preserve of time-served male skilled engineers. Something more than a narrowly conceived struggle for the protection of a male craft preserve was at stake here. 'Dilutees' were bound not to know the 'rules of the game' in relation to customary restriction of output, and, since they could only be minimally brought into line by the skilled workers on this question, they were in effect acting as 'rate-busters', thus giving support to the employers' long-standing accusations of ca'canny, and allowing the intensity of labour on a wide range of jobs to be considerably increased, possibly permanently. A couple of other 1915 cases, one involving skilled engineering workers and another involving 'dilutees', make this point quite clearly. In an engineering firm doing munitions work a job in the production of shells was being done, as it would have been done traditionally, by male turners. 'Almost at once they reached an output of forty shells per day, and there they stuck.' The firm at this point realised that the men wanted higher piece-rates. On account of the great shell shortage these were granted, with the result that output went up to 44 shells per day and stayed at that new level. The next developments have been recorded as follows :

'Shortly afterwards this firm started its own shell shop, and, as a result of this experience, determined to exclude all trade unionists from it. Girls were engaged, and were trained by draughtsmen from the drawing-office. They were taught the operation of grooving and waving R.T.H.E. shells—the work which had previously been done by the turners. Beginning with an output of ten per girl per day, they worked up to eighty per day. At this point the men approached one of the best girls and said that this rate of production must not continue. She was very indignant, and said she was aiming at a hundred shells per day. Actually she eventually reached a daily output of one hundred and forty.'[19]

Exhortation and legislation, then, seem not to have produced the desired result. Payment systems involving financial incentives for extra output seem to have had a good deal more success, though they did bring with them further problems. Piece-work and other payment by results systems became increasingly widespread during the war. G. D. H. Cole in his book about the workshop movement in the first world war, *Workshop Organization*, commented that 'the tendency from 1914 to 1916 was indeed all in the direction of an increasing substitution of payment by results for time work. . . .',[20] but he went on to emphasise that this was only a trend, and that payment systems were subject to much variation between areas, industries, and unions. The spread of payment by results systems in the early years of the war was most common amongst less skilled workers, most notably dilutees. Resistance to payment by results persisted amongst skilled workers, who preferred the independence and job control deriving from time payment. This fact led to the phenomenon of dilutee labour often being able to make better money than skilled workers—which in itself was a source of considerable workshop friction and of militancy amongst skilled workers.[21] Mrs. Humphrey Ward, the novelist, who had been given 'some special opportunities of seeing what Great Britain is doing in the war, and in matters connected with the war'[22] by the British Government, visited a number of munitions works in early 1916 and commented of one of them ('a small workshop for shell production—employing between three and four hundred girls') that the female workers there were 'working so well that a not uncommon wage among them—on piece-work of course—runs to somewhere between two and three pounds a week.'[23] The 'of course' about piece work as well as the high levels of earnings, makes the point quite succinctly.

Another of Mrs. Ward's observations illustrates a further problem (and a more important one for us) attendant upon piecework even amongst those who worked it willingly. It is clear that output could not be maximised under straight piece-work systems if workers felt insecure, particularly about the possibility that increases in the production per worker would lead to the cutting of piece rates by management. Mrs. Ward visited a large shell factory in Yorkshire which had a labour force of 1300 women and a small staff of skilled men. The employers had had no problems in recruiting a labour force which apparently had what might be called the 'war-effortist' mentality that she found so commendable. 'But when the factory began', she recounts, 'the employers very soon detected that it was running below its possible output. There was a curious lack of briskness in the work—a curious constraint among the new workers. Yet the employers were certain that the women were keen, and the labour force potentially efficient. They put their heads together, and posted up a notice in the factory to the effect that whatever might be the increase in output of piece-work, the piece-work rate would not be altered. Instantly the atmosphere began to clear, the pace of the machines began to mount.'[24] The reason given by Mrs. Ward for the output restriction is interesting but it is scarcely adequate. According to her, 'A small leaven of distrust on the part of the men workers was enough, and the women were soon influenced.' The real point, it seems to me, is just how quickly and easily even 'green' and 'war effortist' workers learnt the defensive tactic of output restriction, and how their output went up when they were sure they would benefit personally and collectively from increasing it—i.e. when the piece-rates were made secure. This insecurity engendered by rate-cutting was extremely widespread—we have already seen that Lloyd George mentioned it at the 1915 T.U.C. ('no increase in the output should be used as an excuse for putting down the piece-rate'), and we have already noticed that this was conceded, though clearly to little practical effect, in the Treasury Agreement. Indeed, it was felt to be necessary to amend the Munitions Act in January 1916 to the effect that no reduction in piece-rates could be made as a result of increased output.[25]

The result of the amendment was, according to James Hinton, 'a very considerable rise in output.' But it wasn't long before employers were up to their old tricks again. At Barrow-in-Furness in March 1917, the firm of Vickers was accused by the workers of systematically cutting the time allowances under the Premium Bonus system since October 1916. On March 21st a strike began which quickly involved about 8,000 workers. In spite of the attempts of the Ministry of Labour and the executives of the men's unions to persuade the men to return to work pending arbitration, the men were initially adamant and voted by an overwhelming majority to stay out on strike until a settlement was reached on rate-cutting. But not long afterwards, following considerable pressure from the A.S.E. Executive, and Government threats to detain the strike leaders under the Defence of the Realm Act, the men voted for a return to work.[26] In theory, of course, under the Premium Bonus system the base time on a job should not be altered 'unless', in J. T. Murphy's words, 'it was challenged by the worker as inadequate. But (he continues) the employers were not satisfied. They began to force the pace and to cut the base rates.' The great advantage for the employer of the Premium Bonus system was meant to be that unlike straight piecework, the rate cutting was, so to speak, built into the system itself. Employers, of course, tended to cut piece rates partly because in absolute terms labour costs could become prohibitive under straight piecework even though the relative cost per unit of output remained the same. It was not long, as we shall see later, before some employers began to introduce new systems of wage payment which from their point of view had the merit of stimulating increased labour productivity and yet at the same time did not become too expensive for employers : that is, a payment system in which systematic rate cutting was, in effect, built-in from the start.

But in the absence of such systems, and before the amendment to the Munitions Act, the position was frequently as it had been described by Cole :

'When a piece-work price was being fixed, the object of the management was that of finding the shortest possible time in which it could be done, while that of the men was to take long enough in the doing of it to ensure that, on future occasions, it would always allow the worker to earn a good piece-work balance. Moreover, when a job was highly priced, the workers felt that, if they did it in the least possible time, and so made high earnings, the only result would be that the management would find some way of "cutting" the price, or of balancing the account by fixing the prices for other operations at correspondingly low level. The employer, therefore, usually "speeded up" and the workers usually "speeded down". The result was a widespread prevalence, in shops working on systems of payment by results, of mutual antagonism, "speeding up" and "ca'canny", *which often more than neutralized the incentive to increased output which the piece-work system was designed to provide.*'[27]

After the amendment to the Munitions Act, to borrow Cole's words again, 'the immediate reason for "ca'canny" ' was removed and 'the need for increased production for war purposes adding a fresh incentive, output on certain operations went up to an amazing extent.'[28] But since the wording of the amendment was somewhat ambiguous it was still possible for employers to find ways of cutting rates. Around the same time there were strong governmental initiatives taken to encourage the extension of payment by results throughout industry as a whole. The impulse for this came from John Hodge shortly after he took up office as the first ever Minister of Labour early in 1917. From the outset it was widely reported that he intended to try to tackle two long-standing problems : how to increase production, and how to synchronise agreements and contracts. The extension of payment by results over the whole of industry, irrespective of production processes or of trade union attitudes, was his main if not sole suggestion for buying out restrictive practices and ending ca'canny.[29] Hodge, who had previously been secretary of the Steel Smelters' Union (which encouraged payment by results) called a conference in February 1917 between representatives of the trade unions and of the government in a situation in which (in Sir George Askwith's words) 'the fate of the whole country might depend upon the largest possible production.' But Hodge made no headway at the conference. 'He was too blunt. Instead of proposing an inquiry, he spoke from his own experience of steel, and practically intimated that no other system but that which succeeded in the steel trade was worth anything. He told the whole of the delegates that they must have payment by results. The usual objection against appearance of dictation at once came to the front from trades such as carpenters and joiners, and the ironfounders.'[30]

The effect of this wrong-headed single-mindedness on Hodge's part was to rule out even the possibility of trade union co-opera-tion in an enquiry into the matter. But the Government by no means abandoned its efforts, rather it sought other ways to bring about the same object. Ministry of Munitions and Admiralty local officials were instructed to try as hard as they could to bring about the spread of payment by results in the munitions factories and the shipbuilding yards.[31] There was, however, nothing new in this. It amounted merely to an intensification of an existing tendency, as can be seen by recommendations made earlier by arbitrators considering disputes brought to compul-sory arbitration. For instance, the *Board of Trade Gazette* in the summer of 1916 detailed a case concerning an engineering firm in the Clyde District :

'With a view to increasing their output, Messrs. Scotts Ship-building and Engineering Company Ltd., Greenock, introduced a system of piece-work into their sheet iron department, where the work had hitherto been done on time. This innovation was resisted by the Sheet Iron Workers' and Light Platers' Society, on behalf of their members and the parties being unable to agree on the matter, the difference was reported to the Department. . . .'

The case was referred to Sir Lynden Macassey to produce a decision in accordance with the relevant sections of the Munitions of War Act. On May 27, 1916 Macassey issued his award, 'deciding that the custom of payment on time in the case of workpeople concerned does tend to restrict production, and that the system of piece-work should be at once introduced.'[32] A more traditional method of trying to buy out restrictive practices was with straight wage increases. The Liverpool Dock employers tried to do this, but, it seems, met with little success. A Liverpool paper was complaining late in 1916 that 'ca'canny seems to be rife at the docks'. Since the war began Liverpool dockers had had increases in wages of 40 per cent., but the employers were complaining that the dockers were in fact doing 30 per cent less work than they did before the war.[33]

But from early 1917, according to Cole, 'the process of introducing payment by results advanced rapidly, often attended by considerable workshop friction.'[34] In engineering payment by results made most progress in those districts where it already had some hold previously. Where payment by results did have a considerable impact it frequently led to a growing preoccupation of shop stewards with the problems arising from it. Cole concluded that this state of affairs arose not simply because of the mere extension of payment by results but also because 'attempts were constantly being made to apply new, and often "fancy", systems of wage-payment.'[35] This further range of new, almost 'new-fangled', payment systems, breaking with tradition much more than straight piecework did, was another product of the war economy's insatiable appetite for more production. As has been mentioned already, there was a major problem with straight piecework—namely that labour costs tended to become prohibitive where output was high, which in turn tempted the employer to cut piece rates and thus induce restriction of output by workers once again.[36] The object of the exercise for many employers especially those in engineering and shipbuilding became the finding of a payment system which increased output, and at the same time reduced labour costs, and yet still gave financial incentives to workers. One of the leading devisers of this sort of payment system—the premium bonus system—was William Rowan Thomson, of David Rowan and Co., Marine Engineers, Glasgow and President of the North West Engineering Trades Employers' Federation. He put the problem this way :

'I am convinced that any system of Payment by Results which does not provide, along with an inducement to the workmen to save time, a similar equally powerful inducement to the employer to help towards that saving, is bound in the long run to be inoperative or at most only partially successful. If, therefore, an increase in output, along with a reduction in labour cost, can be obtained, and, at the same time, handsomely increase the total earnings of the workman himself, surely he should have nothing to object to or complain of, from his point of view.'[37]

The various versions of the Premium Bonus system solved these problems in the following way. Instead of the employer fixing a piece-work price for a job, he fixed a 'basis time' in which it was felt the job ought to be done. If the job was then performed in less than the basis time the worker got a bonus proportionate to the time saved on top of a standard time work rate. The effect of this method was that, in all Premium Bonus systems except one, the labour cost of the job to the employer falls with every increase of output, while at the same time the earnings of the worker increase, but not in proportion to the increased output.[38] This last is clearly an important point. Some managers clearly wondered how they would ever manage to get away with that one. This is certainly the impression one gets from a leader in the 16th March 1917 issue of *The Engineer*, a trade journal with a long-standing commitment to the extension of premium bonus systems. The leader began :

'A correspondent has raised the question that has always to be faced sooner or later by the manager who proposes to introduce the Premium system of paying wages. Why should not the workmen be paid for all the time saved? . . . in view of the importance of the matter, and of the need that managers should be in a position to meet arguments of the kind, it may be as well to consider the problem in more detail. Let us admit that it is an extremely difficult one to handle, because a variety of economic questions is involved, and, if we once get outside certain narrow limits, we are led into an interminable train of arguments. On the other hand, the faulty view of the workman is due to the fact that the limits he puts to his investigations are too narrow, and unless we give ourselves a somewhat wider field, we cannot hope ever adequately to understand the position, yet we must use some care not to be lured too far from the main point.'

The main point rested on the need to be able to compete in the world markets : 'In order to compete in the markets of the world we must manufacture cheaply, and we must constantly endeavour to keep the total cost per piece—on cost, material, and labour—as low as possible. . . . The object to be obtained is the cheapening of our products. That we know can be achieved by increasing the output per man and reducing the labour cost per piece.' According to *The Engineer*, the workman had the wrong end of the stick if he took the view that 'the saving effected by his increased output goes directly to swell profits. As a matter of fact, it does nothing of the kind, save in cases where the profits have been originally too low.' Another criticism that workers tended to make about premium bonus systems and all payment systems other than time work was that they all involved speeding-up on the part of the worker. G. D. H. Cole put it this way in 1913 : 'the dullness of mechanical processes is such that an artificial stimulus to greater exertion seems to be required. This is found in some sort of bonus system, appealing to the individual cupidity of the worker, and making him do more work than he would do on time rates. . . . The premium bonus system is a method of applying piece-work to labour engaged in time rates : it is a particularly bad form of speeding-up. . . .'39

Employers using premium bonus and piece work systems were, however, not unaware of the dangers of speed-up induced by payment systems. There was after all the problem of killing, or at least, tiring out the worker-goose who laid the golden egg. Even William Rowan Thomson realised this when he asked in his book : 'To what extent, then, can a workman speed up his ordinary time rate of working, increase his output, and maintain same, without injury to his physical or mental conditions?'[40] David Lloyd George himself realised that there was a problem here too. In his foreword to Miss E. D. Proud's book on Welfare Work of 1916 he outlined some of the problems attendant upon the 'advent of the women' into munitions works. 'The conditions of their work,' he wrote, 'soon engaged my attention. If a maximum output was to be reached—still more, if it was to be maintained for a protracted period—it was all-important that the health and well-being of the workers should be carefully safeguarded.'[41] Attention to 'welfare' and 'fatigue study' became increasingly important managerial concerns towards the end of the war. As the authors of one of the best primers on Scientific Management, published in London in 1917, put it 'In England the promulgation and furthering of welfare work has, of course, received an extraordinary impetus since the war.'[42] Thus the Chief Inspector of Factories and Workshops could write in his Annual Report for 1918 that:

'The prominence given to safety, health and welfare, including the reduction of hours of labour has perhaps been—apart from the special war work—the principal feature of the work of our Department not only during the past year but also during the whole period of war.'[43]

A few paragraphs later, he added that:

'Few questions affecting the industrial worker have been brought more prominently forward during the war than that of Welfare. Long before 1914 there had been an increasing desire on the part of enlightened individual employers to improve the conditions of employment in their works beyond the statutory requirements.'[44]

There had indeed been some development of welfare work before the war—the Cadburys and the Rowntrees in particular had interested themselves in it—but on the whole it was a concern of a small minority of employers. Something like only a couple of dozen firms were known to have set up Welfare Departments before the war, and when the Welfare Workers' Association was founded in 1913 it had a membership of 35.[45] By 1917 when the Welfare Workers' Association became the Central Association of Welfare Workers its membership was 600—a level which was not reached again until 1935. (The really great growth of the association—then known as the Institute of Personnel Management—took place after the Second World War.) The First World War transformed welfare from being an expression of the conscience of a few paternalistic and high-minded employers to a widespread managerial device. At the end of 1915 Seebohm Rowntree—one of the old school—was invited by Lloyd George to head a Welfare Section of the Ministry of Munitions.[46] In April 1916 the appointment of welfare workers in all state controlled factories where women and young people were employed was made compulsory. Over 1,000 welfare workers (a motley crew: clergymen, overlookers, teachers, cooks, ex-constables, organists, doctors, gymnasts) were working in munitions factories by the time of the armistice.[47]

Welfare workers in the factories were meant to concern themselves with the physical, mental and moral well-being of the workers under their charge. Dorothea Proud, a member of Rowntree's welfare section at the Ministry of Munitions, stated in her big book on the subject that the British tradition and practice of welfare work was centred on the workers' best interests, and, unlike the welfare aspects of American scientific management, was not directed towards the efficiency of enterprises and employers' profits. She wrote that 'two distinct motives' had led to specialisation in welfare work, and these were 'the motive of pity and the motive of profit. Undoubtedly,' she commented, 'the former has been the more powerful in England; the latter, it would seem is the only one tolerated in America.'[48] John Maclean, for one, did not agree with that judgement, and in his pamphlet of 1918, *The War After the War*, commented that:

'The whole object of the "Welfare Work" organisation is to help in keeping the workers up to highest pitch of "efficiency"; and "efficiency" is now coming to be understood as meaning "the output per hour".'

He was scathing about the extension of welfare work, adding that some capitalists had found that 'a certain standard of comfort above the animal level increases efficiency, and is therefore advantageous to them. These are urging their class,' he contended, 'to adopt the policy of "enlightened capitalism" to save capitalism from the establishment of a Socialist Republic.'[49] Most munitions workers, though probably not agreeing with all of Maclean's analysis, seem to have found themselves more in agreement with him than with Dorothea Proud. They did not like welfare work at all—whether it was motivated by profit or by pity.

In May 1917 women's sections of the Labour movement gathered together at a conference of the Standing Joint Committee of Women's Industrial Organisations to discuss welfare work. Mary MacArthur told the conference 'that there is no word in the English language more hated amongst the women workers of today than that of "welfare".'[50] Most welfare workers, the conference report stated, 'discourage organisation, and only try to increase output.' Many welfare workers were accused of interference, not only in the factory where it was their function, but also outside working hours. A good supervisor might try to do everything for the girls, but this merely undermined their own self-reliance and sapped their will to take collective action. The report added :

'It was stated that girls object to even a good welfare supervisor, because they think her goodness will not last, and they wonder what the game is. . . . The bad supervisor disciplines and is always interfering. She interferes if the girls are out at night (especially if they are with a man in khaki), she interferes if boots are dirty, or blouses low at the neck, or stockings thin. But she hardly interferes as thoroughly as it is done in America, where the welfare supervisors fill up charts with particulars about the parents, religion, taste in books, etc., etc. In America this scheme is part of scientific management, where the essence of scientific management is centralization of authority and the subordination of the workers.'

The welfare supervisor, it was felt, could not serve two masters. A welfare worker either had the interests of the girls at heart (in which case she would, for instance, protest against the cutting of piece rates—which had been known to lead to the sacking of the supervisor); or else she was part of the management. The report continued :

'There was plenty of evidence that the girls think it is really a dodge to get more out of them, and there is no doubt that welfare pays. For instance, an employer thought of increasing wages to retain the services of his employees, but instead gave them cocoa and a bun in the middle of the morning, and the output was greatly increased at a trifling expense. It is all right to try and get a big output on the employers' side, but there is no need for hypocrisy and interference.'

The instinct of the British working class to distrust employers' attempts to do things 'in the best interests' of the workers was working strongly, as it has done on countless occasions before and since. A resolution (which read in part as follows) was carried by the conference protesting 'against any extension of control over the private lives of the workers, and asserts that in every factory the welfare, social and physical, of the workers is best looked after by the workers themselves.'[51]

Throughout the war the Health of Munitions Workers Committee (which continued in being over the following thirty years, first as the Industrial Fatigue Research Board and later as the Industrial Health Research Board) issued memoranda and carried out research, the recommendations of which Rowntree and his team tried to persuade employers to carry out. One of the Committee's first memoranda (in January 1916) made it clear that, for all the altruism of Rowntree and his like, the need for increased production was the key force behind the spread of welfare. The early years of the war had seen the adoption of a simple solution to the problem of increasing production—the extension of the working day. But it did not take long before it was realised that fatigue from working more hours was sometimes detrimental to overall production but always detrimental to output per hour. The Committee's memorandum read :

'If the present long hours, the lack of healthful and sympathetic oversight, the inability to obtain good wholesome food, and the great difficulties of travelling are allowed to continue, it will be impracticable to secure or maintain for an extended period the high maximum output of which women are undoubtedly capable.'[52]

Before long a policy was adopted of encouraging the reduction of working hours. In one munitions factory, for instance, men engaged on the sizing of fuses had their hours reduced from 58.2 to 50.6 per week. This 13 per cent reduction of working hours was accompanied by an increase in the hourly output of 39 per cent. The increase in the total output was 21 per cent.[53] The Health of Munitions Workers Committee issued several reports on Industrial Efficiency and Fatigue in which similar points were made. One of their Interim Reports in 1916 gave an example of how five munitions workers in an eight hour day exceeded the average output of eight men working a fourteen hour day. 'It is impossible to resist the conclusion,' the Interim Report commented, 'that the paid week day workers at this factory, who have been working their long hours for many months, might have greatly improved their output and their comfort under a better chosen system of special efforts alternating with suitable rests.'[54]

Fatigue study did not merely involve the reduction of working hours, but also the careful study of work and the elimination of as many of the fatigue causing elements of it as possible. The international expert on Fatigue Study was an American, Frank B. Gilbreth. Gilbreth as a young man had made detailed studies of work processes in the building industry, vastly rationalising the work involved in bricklaying for example. Taylor at one stage wanted Gilbreth to collaborate with him on a book on bricklaying, but Gilbreth declined largely because he disliked what he regarded as Taylor's misuse of time study and his general inattention to improving the design of jobs.[55] In 1916 Gilbreth and his wife Lillian M. Gilbreth published their book *Fatigue Study*. The object of fatigue study was firstly to find out what fatigue resulted from what work, and secondly to eliminate all unnecessary fatigue to the lowest possible amount. Fatigue study was not, of course, carried out primarily to make the workers' job easier—though it could do that—but to increase output and productivity. Thus the Gilbreths could state that after the elimination of fatigue 'Usually, in practice, the output increases as a result of the fatigue recovery periods.'[56] If the worker was less tired at the end of the day that only enabled him to work just as hard the following day. The Gilbreths put it like this :

'Many employers have resolved that, so far as their plants are concerned, needless fatigue must be eliminated. They have resolved that the day is coming when every worker shall go home from work happy in what he has done, with the least amount of unnecessary fatigue, and prepared to go back in perfect condition on the morrow.'[57]

That even the elimination of fatigue could wrest some control at the point of production away from workers towards management is clear from the following passage taken from the McKillops' 1917 book, *Efficiency Methods*:

'The old-fashioned type of management has been accustomed to dispose of the question of fatigue to a very large extent, by giving some "change of work", which was believed to be "as good as play". It allowed, indeed expected, the workman to stop his work to hunt up some implement, to grind a tool, or to carry something somewhere. These forms of relaxation are certainly not part of scientific management. The workman tackled the matter of fatigue quite simply and naturally by slacking when he felt inclined; but the votaries of efficiency disapprove of slack work at all times, and particularly when expensive machinery is running.'[58]

The Gilbreth's work on fatigue study was a continuation of Frank Gilbreth's earlier work on motion study, about which he published a book in 1911. At the beginning of *Fatigue Study* the Gilbreths pointed out that *Motion Study* had already shown the way by pointing out that the biggest waste in industry was in 'needless, ill-directed, and ineffective motions.'[59] The Gilbreths were widely followed in their assumption that fatigue could only be eliminated after a job had been thoroughly investigated and broken into component parts. This process of investigation (which in the hands of others usually involved the use of the stop watch) would usually expose the fact that the way in which a job was being done was inefficient and could be improved. From this point changes in jobs could be most usefully made, and a new payment system introduced to carry through and reinforce the changes. Again it was in the munitions factories in Britain that motion study and its allied approaches were pioneered. A good example, which includes practically every other aspect of fully fledged scientific management, comes from the Derwent Foundry Company in Derby which during the war was making Mills' hand grenades and fuse-hole plugs for shells. The foundry's managing director had concluded that it was possible to bring about enormous increases in output without inducing greater fatigue in his workers. Taking two or three trusted men the managing director set out to :

'analyse each small job . . . into its essential component movements, and to time these movements with a stop-watch in order to see how he could improve the movements. Having done this to his satisfaction, and having drawn up a list of the "standard times" of each separate unit movement and the "standard time" in which the whole job should be performed, he devised instruction cards on which these estimates were entered. He deducted 10 per cent. from what he had evolved as standard times, so as to allow the worker 45 minutes during the day to attend to his personal needs, and also to allow for accidental waste of time; and then, after making various improvements in the arrangement of materials, in the efficiency of the machining, and in the co-ordination of the moulders' and labourers' work, he turned to the workers and asked them to allow themselves to be trained. He said : "We are out for shorter hours, higher wages, and more output; will you help us?" They said they would.'

After the workers were trained their hours were reduced from 54 to 48 per week. At this point the workers were given wages 25 per cent higher than the ordinary day wage in the district to induce them to continue to be trained. Motion study and fatigue elimination were not enough :

'When the men began to produce at the standard rate, they were put on to a special system of payment which he had devised, in which piece-rate and bonus systems were combined. In the early days they did not fully appreciate the working and the advantages of this system, and some of the older men were disinclined to give up the older methods; they were in a groove from which it was difficult to escape.'

The managing director dealt with such 'grumblers' by saying that if they did not like the new system they could go back to the old—at the old working hours and at the old wages. But it was, apparently, more due to tact than to threats that some of them agreed to carry on with the new system. The new system thus installed brought spectacular increase in output: whereas the Ministry of Munitions had estimated that the foundry could turn out 3,000 articles a week, it eventually produced 20,000.[60]

NOTES

1. Arthur Marwick *The Deluge: British Society and the First World War* (Harmondsworth 1967 edn.) p. 59.
2. Sidney Webb *The Restoration of Trade Union Conditions*, (London 1917) Chapter 2, gives a full account of the pledges to restore pre-war practices and conditions.
3. See G. D. H. Cole *Workshop Organization* (Oxford 1923) p. 60.
4. *Labour, Finance, and the War* (London 1916) ed. A. W. Kirkaldy, p. 21.
5. Quoted in *Industrial Worker* November 1916.
6. Quoted in Lord Askwith *Industrial Problems and Disputes* (London 1920), p. 303. See also James Hinton *The First Shop Stewards' Movement* (London 1973) chapter one, on the passing of the Munitions Act and its background.
7. For a brief discussion of the effectiveness of the anti-strike legislation of the Munitions Act see James Hinton *The First Shop Stewards' Movement*, p. 37 note 2. Hinton argues that it probably had a limited effect in reducing strikes in 1915 and 1916, but that it clearly failed seriously in 1917 and 1918 when the numbers of working days lost due to strikes were about $5\frac{1}{2}$ million and nearly 6 million respectively.
8. David Lloyd George, speech to 1915 TUC, in Trades Union Congress, *Annual Report*, 1915, pp. 354-359.
9. Engineering Unions' National Advisory Committee on War Output, *Report*, 1915, quoted in *The Marine Caterer*, December 1915.
10. Quoted by W. F. Watson, 'Engineers and the War' in *The Trade Unionist*, November 1915.
11. Suppressed issue of *Vanguard*, quoted in James Hinton *The First Shop Stewards' Movement* (London 1973) p. 135.
12. James Hinton 'The Clyde Workers' Committee and the Dilution Struggle' in *Essays in Labour History 1886-1923*, (London 1971) eds. A. Briggs and J. Saville, p. 153.

13. *Condemned from the Dock. John Maclean's Speech from the Dock 1918* (originally published by the Clyde Workers' Propaganda Defence Committee, Glasgow, 1918; reprinted with introduction by Bob Purdie, n.d. ? 1970) p. 16. On Maclean's life see the biography by his daughter Nan Milton *John Maclean* (London 1973), see especially pp. 167-175 for an account of the trial at which Maclean made the remarks quoted above.

14. *Condemned from the Dock*, pp. 16-17.

15. *Condemned from the Dock*, p. 17.

16. G. R. Askwith *Industrial Problems and Disputes* p. 304.

17. Sir Lynden Macassey, January 1918, quoted by G. R. Askwith *Industrial Problems and Disputes*, pp. 302-303.

18. Lynden Macassey *Labour Policy—False and True* (London 1922) p. 295.

19. *Are Trade Unions Obstructive? An Impartial Inquiry* eds. John Hilton, J. J. Mallon, Sam Mavor, B. Seebohm Rowntree, Sir Arthur Salter, and Frank D. Stuart (London 1935) pp. 152-153. The evidence as to whether, in general, the output of women was greater than that of men on the same work is conflicting—for a contemporary view of this question see A. W. Kirkaldy (ed.), *Labour, Finance and the War* (1916) pp. 82-83.

20. G. D. H. Cole *Workshop Organization* (Oxford 1923) p. 62.

21. See Cole *Workshop Organization*, pp. 62-63, and Hinton *The First Shop Stewards' Movement* pp. 86-87.

22. Mrs. Humphrey Ward *England's Effort* (London 1916) p. 7.

23. *England's Effort*, pp. 49-50.

24. *England's Effort*, p. 67.

25. See Hinton *The First Shop Stewards' Movement*, p. 87.

26. Hinton, op. cit., p. 189. See also J. T. Murphy *Preparing for Power* (London 1972 edn.) p. 135.

27. Cole *Workshop Organization* p. 59. My italics. Cole, in his useful small book, *The Payment of Wages* (Fabian Research Department 1918) p. 22, also there stated that restriction of output commonly accompanied piecework and premium bonus systems, but added: 'I do not mean to suggest that payment by results necessarily leads to restriction of output, but I do suggest that it very often does so, especially where it is applied to non-standardised trades, or without being accompanied by a complete system of collective bargaining.'

28. Cole *Workshop Organization*, p. 60.

29. See, e.g., 'The Abolition of Ca'canny' in *Liverpool Weekly Post* January 20, 1917.

30. Lord Askwith *Industrial Problems and Disputes*, p. 422.

31. Cole, *Workshop Organization* p. 63.

32. At the same time Macassey ruled that the Premium Bonus system should be brought in at Messrs. Beardmore at Dalmuir, and at Messrs. Bow, Maclachlan at Paisley, *Board of Trade Gazette*, quoted in *The Marine Caterer* August 1916.

33. 'Ca'canny at the Docks', in *Liverpool Post and Mercury*, November 23, 1916.

34. Cole, *Workshop Organization*, p. 63.

35. Cole, op. cit., p. 64.

36. G. D. H. Cole *The Payment of Wages* p. 48.

37. Wm. Rowan Thomson *The Rowan Premium Bonus System of Payment by Results* (Glasgow July 1917) p. 9, wrote that systems like his 'offer little temptation to the employer to "cut" prices.'

38. I have here drawn heavily on the concise account in Cole's *The Payment of Wages*, p. 49. See also James Hinton *The First Shop Stewards' Movement*, p. 89.

39. G. D. H. Cole *The World of Labour* (London 1920 edn. first published 1913) pp. 321-4.

40. Wm. Rowan Thomson *The Rowan Premium Bonus System* p. 11.

41. D. Lloyd George, preface to E. Dorothea Proud *Welfare Work: Employers' Experiments for Improving Working Conditions in Factories* (London 1916) p. x.

42. M. McKillop and A. D. McKillop *Efficiency Methods: and introduction to scientific management* (London 1917) p. 150.

43. *Annual Report* of the Chief Inspector of Factories and Workshops for Year 1918, Cmd. 340, 1919, p. iii.

44. Op. cit., p. v.

45. Ian McGivering 'The Development of Personnel Management' in *Management Thinkers*, eds. A. Tillett, T. Kempner, and G. Wills (Harmondsworth 1970) pp. 176 and 197.

46. *War Memoirs of David Lloyd George* (London 1938 edn.) Vol. 1. p. 206; McGivering in *Management Thinkers* p. 177; see also Asa Briggs *Social Thought and Social Action: A Study of the Work of Seebohm Rowntree* (London 1961) p. 113, and chap. v. passim.

47. *War Memoirs of David Lloyd George* p. 208. The details of the previous occupations of welfare workers come from E. D. Proud *Welfare Work* p. 67.

48. E. D. Proud, *Welfare Work* pp. 59-60.

49. John Maclean *The War After the War* (first pub. Glasgow 1918, London 1973 edn.) p. 12 and p. 23.

50. Quoted in Appendix on 'The Attitude of women trade unionists to welfare work, 1917' in *Management Thinkers* p. 193.

51. Quotations from Appendix in *Management Thinkers* pp. 193-197. The report orginally appeared in *Journal of the Confederation of Iron and Steel Workers*, June 1917. See also Barbara Drake *Women in Trade Unions* (London, n.d., ? 1920) pp. 102-103. Drake, p. 103, argues that 'Under cover of "welfare supervision", women saw themselves threatened with a new form of "scientific management" carried by means of the "welfare supervisor" into their most private and personal affairs.'

52. Quoted in *War Memoirs of David Lloyd George* p. 207.

53. C. S. Myers *Mind and Work* (London 1920) p. 75. Other examples are given on pp. 75-76.

54. *Interim Report* of the Health of Munitions Works Committee on Industrial Efficiency and Fatigue, Cd. 8511, 1916, p. 13.

55. For details on Gilbreth see Anne G. Shaw *The Purpose and Practice of Motion Study* (Manchester 1960 edn.) pp. 1-5, and Michael Thickett 'Gilbreth and the Measurement of Work' in *Management Thinkers*, pp. 97-107.

56. F. B. and L. B. Gilbreth *Fatigue Study* (New York and London 1916) p. 7 and p. 51.

57. Quoted in McKillop and McKillop *Efficiency Methods* p. 154.

58. McKillop and McKillop *Efficiency Methods* p. 100.
59. *Fatigue Study* p. 3.
60. This account comes from C. S. Myers *Mind and Work* (London 1920) pp. 6-9. Other studies of motion study carried out by the Industrial Fatigue Research Board are C. S. Myers *A Study of Improved Methods in an Iron Foundry* (1919), and Eric Farmer *Motion Study in Metal Polishing* (1921).

IX

THE WAR AFTER THE WAR

The most powerful critique of the application of scientific management in British industry during the First World War was produced by John Maclean in his remarkable pamphlet *The War After The War* of 1918. For Maclean scientific management was a proof of the Labour-Time theory of value :

> 'Scientific management is the resort to any and every expedient to increase output, or, to put it another way to reduce the time taken to do a piece of work or turn out the completed commodity. Scientific management was undoubtedly more thoroughly applied in the United States than in the British Empire prior to the war, the hindrance in the Empire being largely due to the conservatism of the capitalists and the "ca'canny" policy of the powerful trade unions.'[1]

He noted how, at first during the war extra output was sought by increasing working hours, but how this soon proved to be counter-productive and consequently set fatigue study in train. The redesigning of jobs subsequently allowed the reduction of hours and spectacular increases in production per head. Welfare work was designed to help to keep up 'efficiency'—or as Maclean preferred to put it 'the output per hour'. Piece-work, premium bonus and the like had similar effects.[2] But these developments on the labour front were not the only developments of importance. As Maclean pointed out : 'Increased efficiency does not depend solely on the "live machines", the "human cows", but on increased sub-division of labour, the use of better machinery, applied science, use of waste material, trustification, improved office and business methods, etc.'[3] In all this the United States was still in advance of Britain—he cites, for instance, the facts that in Chicago a bullock passed through the hands of about a thousand workers before it was canned, and describes the Ford Company's car assembly line[4]—but Maclean was quite sure that British industry would continue to proceed in the same way as it had begun to develop in the war years. There would, in short, be a 'War after the War.'

This perspective was, of course, in marked contrast to that of the leaders of the trade union movement who were, in one way, committed towards trying after the war to get the Government to honour its bargain and to restore pre-war conditions, but who were, in another way, even before the war had ended, committing themselves to a continuation of the policies of output exhortation after the war. Employers, trade union leaders and the Government all showed signs at least by 1917 of being virtually obsessed with the need for the very same things which had originally been regarded as temporary expedients for the duration of the war (state control being, of course, the major exception). Consequently in 1917 the authors of a British primer on scientific management could quite sensibly open their book with the following observation :

'Every article or essay dealing with the situation which will follow immediately after the war begins by raising this cry : Improve efficiency, increase output, make the very most of men, materials and equipment in industrial organization.'[5]

The industrial side of the Reconstruction debate was dominated by this theme. Dr. Christopher Addison, having lost his post as Minister of Munitions to Churchill, was appointed Minister of Reconstruction in 1917 and took the major concern of his previous post with him to his new one. He proclaimed (for neither the first nor the last time) that in post-war, 'reconstructed' Britain :

'there must be a new outlook on the part of both employers and employed : the old jealousies between firms must be abandoned once and for all, and what is equally important, the "Ca'canny" methods must be dis-continued.'[6]

The same message emanated from many less eminent sources. 'Scrutator', for instance, writing in the *Liverpool Weekly Post* early in 1917, asserted that :

'Restriction of output, one of the main effects of trade union regulations has long been the bugbear of manufacturers. It stood directly across the path of victory in the war, and when the war is over it will, without the shadow of a doubt, if persisted in, be a fatal obstacle to national recovery. It must go now. Ca'canny, slacking, and time-losing must all go.'[7]

In November 1918, the month of the armistice, *Solidarity*, one of the papers of the shop stewards' movement, appeared on the streets and in the workshops containing amongst other things, a polemical review article of a book by an American, Walter Dill Scott. The book, *Increasing Human Efficiency in Industry*, was reviewed in an article headed 'Reconstruction. The Human Element in Industry.' Fully aware that the exhortation for 'the abolition of ca'canny' and for extra effort from the workers was not going to end with the cessation of hostilities between Britain and Germany, the article addressed itself squarely to Maclean's theme of 'the War after the War.' One of the battles in the continuing class struggle would be precisely about the demand for 'increased efficiency' in industry. Sentiments in Scott's book were singled out as warning signs for British labour. One such passage was that in which Scott suggested that production could be increased if workers who were content with 'a mere living wage earned by piecework' were weeded out and replaced by hard working men who set an example to others. *Solidarity* commented that: 'America is the home of Scientific Management, and has given us its F. W. Taylors, F. B. Gilbreths, Gantts, Emersons, Halseys, and Rowans . . . nothing succeeds like success, we are likely to be Americanised as well as Prussianised.'[8] In a way *Solidarity* was right—the American influence on British management methods continued throughout the 1920s and 1930s to be very strong. But in a way it was wrong, since scientific management, as it came to be applied in Britain, developed a peculiarly British flavour with strong emphasis on welfare and on industrial psychology. In the immediate post-war years such was the insistence of the demand for more output that the spread of the new management techniques owed less to the importation of American ideas than to the exhortations of trade union officialdom. *Solidarity* sensed this too and in December 1918 commented on the fact that trade union leaders as well as government officials

and employers were all saying 'we must have greater output.' It
added :

> 'Years ago George Barnes and Sidney Webb were the medium
> through which the employers foisted the "Premium Bonus
> System" upon the engineers, and it seems as if they are now
> going to use the Trade Union officials as "feed-and-speed"
> men.'[9]

As it happened, since most of the readers of *Solidarity* were
engineering workers, they had soon to look no further than to
some of the officials of their union, the Amalgamated Society of
Engineers. On August 25, 1919, their union President, J. T.
Brownlie sent a letter to C. W. Bowerman, the secretary of the
Parliamentary Committee of the T.U.C., appealing to the Parliamentary Committee to disseminate material about the need
to increase production. At the same time Brownlie wanted the
T.U.C. to allay fears amongst trade unonists that increased production would necessarily add more people to the growing ranks
of the unemployed. Not surprisingly this letter attracted a good
deal of publicity in the press and caused quite a stir among trade
unionists.[10] By accident or design Brownlie's activities coincided
with a period of considerable debate on payment by results inside
the union. By this time Tom Mann had become the union's
General Secretary, his election to that office being a considerable
victory for the shop stewards' movement; and Brownlie consequently was under pressure from the Left.[11] The background
to the debate on payment systems was that in 1919 there had
been agitation amongst the engineers for a shorter working week,
and this had resulted in an agreement between the Engineering
Employers' Federation and the A.S.E. which established a 47
hour week. But the agreement that was signed was regarded by
the employers as being ambiguous, and they used this fact as an
opportunity to try and get payment by results introduced once
again—the Premium Bonus agreement that had been signed in
1902 having been repudiated by the union before the outbreak
of war. The employers now stated that they would refuse to
consider or adjust any grievances arising out of the 47 hour
week unless the A.S.E. Executive recommended to the union
membership that 'the employer should have freedom to intro-

duce into his works, in agreement with his workpeople, any or
all of the following systems of payment by results :—

   (a)   straight individual piecework.
   (b)   company or collective piecework.
   (c)   individual premium bonus or any other bonus system.
   (d)   company or collective output bonus.'[12]

Brownlie, given his views on the need for extra output, tended
to favour the adoption of some sort of bonus scheme. But Mann
did not, and although under the constitution of the union he was
without a vote on the Executive Committee, he campaigned
vigorously against payment by results in the union's journal
(which he edited), at numerous union branch meetings and the
like, and through a specially written pamphlet. The pamphlet
included the following sentences :

'There is no room for misunderstanding as to what the employers are after—IT IS INCREASED OUTPUT. . . . There
should be no room left for any misunderstanding as to what
the workmen want and mean to have—IT IS INCREASED
COMFORT.'

There were two sides to that comfort. The first was the need to
prevent the further discomforting of the engineers' work situation. Premium bonus, he argued, would lead to speed-up and a
further diminution of the skilled man's control over his own
job. The second was material comfort derived from the possibility
of higher earnings. These were possible under premium bonus
and similar systems, but only for some workers. Mann, unlike
Brownlie, was certain that increasing the output would lead to
even more unemployment; and this was a severe problem for
engineering workers as the war economy wound down. Consequently Mann recommended A.S.E. members to vote for the
employers' payment system package only on condition that the
employers guaranteed responsibility for all unemployment in
the industry, by adjusting working hours accordingly (a favourite
theme of his since 1910). As if that demand wasn't utopian
enough he also demanded that all war wages, bonuses and percentages be merged into a consolidated flat rate.[13] As *Solidarity*

pointed out, Tom Mann must have realised that there was extremely little chance of the employers' conceding these counter-demands. As it happened the vast majority of A.S.E. members agreed both with Mann and *Solidarity* on the unemployment and speed-up issues. Payment by results systems, *Solidarity* asserted, were 'only introduced with the definite object of speed-ing up the worker, and in many cases setting one man to compete against his fellow.'[14] It was no surprise that the membership voted by three to one against even negotiating on the payment by results question.[15]

But, while all this was going on, Brownlie was using his position in the A.S.E. and in the wider trade union movement to urge on his campaign for extra output. He was responsible in January 1920 for convening a conference at the Memorial Hall, Farring-don Street, London, at which he read a paper on 'The World Need for Increased Production.' At the very time when the majority of his union members were arguing strongly for sharing out what work there was through the further reduction of work-ing hours and so on, Brownlie was, amongst other things, con-demning ca'canny. This policy could, he felt, only be justifiable as long as employers used a similar tactic. 'If practised by the workers,' he said, 'it is certainly not unknown to employers. Who has not heard of short time to make possible the disposal of surplus stocks?'[16] But, this apart, Brownlie was of the opinion that the vast majority of objections to the increase of production by workers were untenable. The only occasion on which ca'canny might be justifiable was if it was a response to 'speeding-up.'[17] W. F. Watson, the syndicalist militant who was coming to specialise in the 'ins' and 'outs' of payment systems, had been at the conference. Feeling that he had not been able to get his point across, Watson tackled Brownlie's views head on in a pamphlet published by the East London Workers' Committee. Here he stated that Brownlie's attempt to distinguish between justifiable and unjustifiable ca'canny was rather lame; and he singled out a statement of Brownlie's (wherein the latter said that 'There are *some* men in *perhaps* most industries who practise "ca'canny" with the deliberate object of checking production, and that form of "ca'canny" is not justifiable') as being both an understatement and a folly. Watson replied :

'Ca'canny is always the outcome of the attempts of the employers to cut rates and screw the last drop of sweat out of the workers, and, in consequence, is always justifiable.'[18]

There are examples from other industries in the early 1920s of trade union leaders condemning ca'canny. Ben Tillett, Robert Williams, Harry Gosling and Arthur Pugh were amongst those members of the Shaw Enquiry of 1920 into dock labour who signed the Majority Report, Paragraph 40 of which, under the heading of 'Slowing Down of Output', made it quite clear that ca'canny was a problem and also that the trade union officials did not sanction it :

'The Court cannot be blind to the fact that there is, not arising from exceptional causes but as a part of a deliberate policy, the adoption in not a few cases of a system of slowing down of output. . . . The system known as "ca'canny" is loss on every side. The workman gains nothing in time. . . . The system may be difficult to eradicate; it may need courage and great manliness to resist the temptations to it. Yet the Court is impressed with the fact that the responsible leaders of the men do not sanction it, and treat it not only as wrong but as a mistake.'[19]

Sir Lynden Macassey K.C. (who, as we saw earlier, had been during the war in the Department of Shipyard Labour and one of the Government's chief opponents of ca'canny) was the employers' counsel and he had a field day in presenting the many cases of ca'canny that existed in the country's ports. He showed that there had been, for example, a decline of output of 22 per cent in Bristol since 1917; that a Hull shipping firm reported a drop of 33 per cent since 1914; and he cited a case from Glasgow of men refusing to use electric grain-weighing machines. According to a recent writer, 'Numerous instances were given of restrictive practices, bad time-keeping, piecework and overtime disputes.'[20] Ernest Bevin, the 'Dockers' K.C.' having made his famous 'fodder basis' speech, eventually triumphed over Macassey in the sense that the dockers' claim for 16 shillings a day across the board was conceded by the Enquiry. But Macassey's instances of ca'canny were not, as the quotation from the report given above makes clear, gainsaid. The report of the Enquiry, indeed, located the root cause of ca'canny among the dockers in casualism itself, and at one point went on to quantify part of the problem by estimating that bad time-keeping cost over 9 million man-hours a year, and it recommended that more machinery and more piecework should be introduced to increase output.

Macassey's debacle at the Shaw Enquiry did not prevent him in 1922 from pronouncing on *Labour Policy—False and True*, and in a section of his book called 'The Right Relationship between Employers and Employed' he deals with 'The Workers' Belief in Restricted Output.' This belief he regarded as a 'dangerous and widespread fallacy.' He complained that 'When the day's work is completed the workman, if paid on time, will frequently remain at work, but doing nothing until the "hooter goes." ' In other cases if paid on a piece-work basis, the workman will sometimes leave the shop after the day's work or 'stint' is finished. He claimed to have investigated cases where workmen starting work at 7.00 a.m. had finished their work and left for home by 10.30 or 11.00 a.m. Where this was not possible workers would 'with nice calculation slow down all day long so as to spin out the allotted day's work more or less uniformly over the working day. Industrial experience during the war has proved the existence, to an almost inconceivable extent, of this latter method of limiting production.'[21] Macassey's wartime experience, as well as showing him the size of the 'problem', also seems to have led him to be sceptical about the effectiveness of straightforward exhortation in driving it out. The only way, he concluded in 1922, of attacking the 'heresy' was from 'the concrete illustration drawn from the United States of America'—where, he claimed, restriction of output was not merely 'unknown', but also 'definitely repudiated' by the trade unions. But there was a problem : many British workers, Macassey alleged, had been given the impression by labour intellectuals that Scientific Management was 'cunningly devised slavery.' But Macassey claimed that he had been able to get round this and that he had managed to persuade groups of workers of the benefits of scientific management on the grounds that increased output per worker per hour, by reducing unit costs of production, resulted in 'a larger percentage increase in the amount available for division between workmen and employer.' Even Macassey, however, admitted that there would be some difficulties in persuading British employers to cease their rate-cutting practices.[22]

Most miners' leaders, unlike their counterparts in the docks industry, were, for the most part, unwilling to concede any truth in the many charges of ca'canny that were brought against the members of their unions. Accusations and denials about ca'canny and restriction of output were quite close to the centre of the conflict between capital and labour in the coal industry in the early 1920s. This is certainly the case in the debate over the ownership and control of the industry after the end of the First World War. The owners wanted a speedy abolition of the wartime state control, and a return to full private ownership and control. The Miners' Federation of Great Britain on the other hand, wanted to keep and extend state control and to bring about the full nationalisation of the industry. This latter course had been recommended in principle to the Government by the Sankey Commission—but only by the casting vote of its chairman—on account of the inefficiency of the industry and the 'present atmosphere of distrust and recrimination' between owners and men.[23] In this situation both sides sought to use the ills of the industry to make their precisely opposite points—the owners to argue for decontrol and the continuation of private ownership, and the miners to argue for state ownership and control. The industry's poor output performance was a rather prominent political football in this argument. As Frank Hodges, the General Secretary of the M.F.G.B., put it in a book which was one of the miners' contributions to the debate :

'Is the decline in output due to decreased effort on the part of the workmen? Is it due to ca'canny? To this the employers would answer with a unanimous "Yes". The workmen with equal unanimity would answer, "No".'[24]

That, at least, was how the argument boiled down when the miners' representatives were on their best behaviour and mindful of 'public opinion'. In those circumstances they firmly denied the existence of ca'canny and like Hodges here attributed low output and poor productivity to poor geological conditions, the natural working out of old seams and the reduction in the number of coal-getters as a proportion of the total mining labour force (necessarily augmented as seams got deeper and more men were needed to handle the coal after it had been won from the seam).[25]

But Hodges, without accepting the sort of blame for poor performance of which they were accused by the owners, to a certain extent contradicted himself and admitted that some miners 'could do more and are content to do less'. He went on to attribute in considerable measure the decrease in output per miner to the bad industrial relations and bad management engendered by the owners' attitudes and actions—or as Hodges put it to 'the spirit pervading his [the miner's] whole relationship with the employers rather than to any consciously directed attempt to keep output down.'[26] Robert Smillie, the M.F.G.B. President and star of the Sankey Commission, on the occasion of a deputation to the Prime Minister in 1919 drew the obvious conclusions from this state of affairs and stated that the output situation could and would be improved only if the owners were forced to relinquish their ownership and control. This now became an argument for nationalisation. Smillie said:

'I want the mines nationalised, in order that, by the fullest possible development on intelligent lines, with the assistance of the engineering power which we know we possess and the inventions which we know we possess, we might largely develop the mines and increase the output. That is one of our first claims.'[27]

Smillie said exactly the same sort of thing in November 1919 when he rejected an invitation to attend a convention of employers at Central Hall, Westminster, which was discussing scientific management. In his letter of rejection (which was read out at the meeting) he had said: 'I am not against scientific management. I know it is a good thing, but I do not want it or any other good thing in the mines until the miners are in possession.'[28] These remarks were considered by the owners to be so damning of the miners' case and so supportive of the owners' case that they were quoted in evidence against the miners' union up to thirty-five years later, when they appeared in an apologia for the performance of the coal industry under private enterprise written by William Alexander Lee, the Mining Association of Great Britain's chief executive between 1917 and 1947. The left wing writer, Gerald Gould, in 1920 put forward a similar point to that made by Smillie. He argued that 'with the socialisation of industry, enormous new forces of production will be immediately let loose. There is a difference of productive energy according to the *motive* to work. Wherever there is "ca'canny" or deliberate slackness in any industry, it can almost always be traced to suppressed resentment. And if the workers are more and more convinced (as they are) that the product of their energy is unjustly confiscated by the few, they will be more and more unwilling to increase that product.' Gould went on to point out that those people who were most clamorous for increased production were usually hostile to nationalisation. There was, Gould argued, 'a certain sense in which everybody wants more production' and also 'a certain sense in which everybody wants scientific management, in order that the production may be accompanied by as little waste of energy as possible.' More, however, had to be said :

'But just as the very words "scientific management" stink in the nostrils of the ordinary working man, because the phrase has come to be associated for him with the inhuman suggestion that the worker is to be treated like a well-kept and well-oiled machine, to produce ever greater and greater profits for his owner—so the continued clamour for more production, coming from people who are determined that the result of that production shall be reaped by the profit-making capitalist, only infuriates the worker, and certainly will not lead to the increased production to which it incites.'[29]

Views of this sort, though common in the debate on the nationalisation of the coal industry, were by no means universal in the labour movement. Indeed, some waverers in the ranks of the Executive of the M.F.G.B. itself were sorely troubled by those remarks of their colleagues which in their opinion amounted to open advocacy of output restriction with a view to forcing nationalisation. Vernon Hartshorn, for instance, one of the South Wales miners' leaders, and to become Postmaster General in the

First Labour Government, in an article in *Reynold's Newspaper*
on November 14th 1920 complained that :

> 'Throughout the coal negotiations the one thing that has
> dominated my policy is the knowledge that decreased output,
> the result largely of the policy of trying to ruin the present
> system by direct action and deliberate restriction, has brought
> the industry to the verge of complete economic collapse.'[30]

With the sudden coming of economic slump at the end of 1920,
the Government came down firmly in favour of the owners by
advancing the date already agreed for decontrol of the mines to
March 31st, 1921. The Coal Strike of 1921, culminating disas-
trously on 'Black Friday', began immediately Government control of the industry ended—on April 1st, 1921.[31] On April 12th,
a Scottish member of the M.F.G.B. Executive, Duncan Graham,
in a meeting at the Kingsway Hall, London let forth another
'incitement to restriction of output' (to use W. A. Lee's words),
no doubt greatly upsetting his colleague Hartshorn. Anticipating
the serious defeat for the miners which was only a couple of
days away, Graham, as the *Morning Post* of the following morning reported, said :

> 'that when the miner went back, even if he were forced back,
> they would only get the coal he chose to give. While he (Mr.
> Graham) was prepared to recommend an honest day's labour
> for an honest day's wage, yet if they did not get that honest
> wage he was going to advise a policy of "ca'canny". The result
> of this civil war, or attempt at civil war, would be to bring
> about nationalisation. When the leaders said "Reduce Out-
> put" output would be reduced. He was a believer in
> "ca'canny". This war might last one month, two months or
> six months, but if the miners had to go back on conditions,
> they would fix the price of coal, and the public would have to
> pay the price.'[32]

William Alexander Lee, the chief officer of the owners' organisation at the time, commented some years later that it was not
easy to assess how successful the miners' leaders were in instilling
the ca'canny policy into their members' minds. We, of course,
must share his difficulty. But Lee was certain that some effect

was had—even after the de-control issue settled by the miners' defeat in the 1921 strike. He noted that cases of restriction of output continued to occur, for instance in the Nottinghamshire coalfield. He cited a case involving J. G. Hancock, M.P., the senior agent of the Notts miners, who, in a report to a mass meeting of miners at Brierley Hill (Sutton Colliery) in July 1922 about the result of a deputation to the owners, the Blackwell Colliery Company, regarding a threatened pit closure, said that losses for a fortnight were £1,129 and that output per man had gone down by half since before the war. Hancock then proceeded to go overboard in his recommendation of wage cuts and his criticism of 'ca'canny'. He told the Sutton miners:

'He had been reluctant to admit to the charge of "ca'canny", but evidence was so clear that he could not deny it. He was convinced that a reduction in wages was inevitable, but if the pre-war output had been maintained, it would have gone far towards meeting the present difficulty.'[33]

It should be said, however, that the Frank Hodges point also applies. Sutton Colliery had been a difficult and usually unprofitable pit ever since it was sunk in 1873. It was working an area of coal where there had been many workings before, and to find fresh coal the company had to sink deeper which necessitated heavy capital expenditure which it could ill afford. On top of this, according to A. R. Griffin, the wage costs at the colliery were high, largely because of geological difficulties.[34] The Blackwell Company found it an unprofitable enterprise and to some extent seem to have attempted to reduce unit costs of production by 'squeezing' the workers. As Griffin puts it: 'Because profits were low, ruthless economies were practised and Sutton acquired the nick-name "The Bread and Herring pit"'[35]—a breeding ground for ca'canny if ever there was one. The claims and counter-claims over output would not lie down in the mining industry in the early 1920s. Consequently one can detect an almost school-masterly tone in the following recommendations of the Royal Commission on the Coal Industry, 1925:

Recommendation 2. 'The owners should discontinue charging the miners as a body with deliberate attempts to destroy the prosperity of the industry, in order to compel its nationalisation. . . .

Recommendation 3. 'The owners should also cease to countenance accusations against the miners of restriction of output. Here again there may be sporadic cases, and when rates of pay for new classes of work are under discussion, production may sometimes be purposefully kept at a low level. But viewing the effect upon the industry as a whole, this point is quite unimportant.

Recommendation 4. 'The miners on their part should cease to attach exaggerated weight to the loss of output due to failures of the management to provide the colliers with proper supplies of tubs, rails, timber or other requisites. . . .'[36]

Carter Goodrich, an acutely sensitive observer of the British industrial scene around the end of the First World War, made some exceptionally wise and perceptive remarks on this subject in 1920 in his superb book, *The Frontier of Control*. There is little doubt in my mind, when all is said and done, that Goodrich gets it right about ca'canny and restriction of output. His remarks are therefore worth quoting :

'There is no doubt at all that a ca'canny (go slow) policy is a serious problem in many industries—and a ca'canny that cannot be explained as a mere natural difference between the employer's and the worker's idea of a "fair day's work". Very likely the extent of this policy is exaggerated in certain current exhortations to hard work, but its existence is admitted by too many trade union leaders to be a matter of doubt. . . . The use of ca'canny or the "stay in strike" as a conscious form of militant labour policy—either as a weapon in a particular dispute or with the fixed idea of making capitalism impossible by making it unprofitable—is another matter and surely of much rarer occurrence.'[37]

NOTES

1. J. Maclean *The War After the War* (First published Glasgow 1918, reprinted by Socialist Reproduction, London 1973) pp. 10-11.
2. Ibid., pp. 12-13.
3. Ibid., p. 14.
4. Ibid., p. 15.
5. M. McKillop and A. D. McKillop *Efficiency Methods: an introduction to scientific management* (London 1917) p. 1.
6. Quoted in Paul Barton Johnson *Land Fit For Heroes: The Planning of British Reconstruction, 1916-1919.* (Chicago 1968) p. 7. See also pp. 480-481 for the remarks on ca'canny by Sir Robert Horne in 1919.
7. *Liverpool Weekly Post*, January 20, 1917.
8. One of the shop stewards' movements' chief themes during the war had been resentment against the growing power of the bourgeois state: see on this James Hinton *The First Shop Stewards' Movement*, Chapter One 'The Servile State'. *Solidarity* was incorrect to call Rowan an American.
9. 'For Whose Benefit?' in *Solidarity* December 1918.
10. *The Trade Unions and Output* (published by the Council of Ruskin College, Oxford 1920) p. 6.
11. On the significance of Mann's election to the General Secretaryship of the A.S.E. (to become the Amalgamated Engineering Union in the summer of 1920) see B. Pribicevic *The Shop Stewards' Movement and Workers' Control* (Oxford 1959) pp. 49-53.
12. Quoted in the A.S.E. *Monthly Journal* March 1920.
13. Tom Mann *Payment by Results: Piece Work and Time Work* (London 1920) p. 12.
14. 'Payment by Results' in *Solidarity* April 1920.
15. See J. B. Jefferys *The Story of the Engineers* pp. 188-189.
16. *The Trade Unions and Output* p. 16.
17. *The Trade Unions and Output* p. 12.
18. W. F. Watson *Should the Workers Increase Output?* (London 1920) p. 12.
19. Shaw Enquiry, Report, Cmd 936, 1920, pp. xvi-xvii.
20. David F. Wilson *Dockers: the impact of industrial change* (London 1972) p. 76.
21. Lynden Macassey *Labour Policy—False and True* (London 1922) pp. 294-295.
22. Macassey, pp. 296-297.
23. C. L. Mowat *Britain Between the Wars* (London 1966 imp.) p. 33.
24. Frank Hodges *Nationalisation of the Mines* (London 1920) p. 77. The case for workers' control rather than mere 'nationalisation' of the

industry was put by the South Wales Socialist Society in their pamphlet *Industrial Democracy for Miners* (Rhondda 1919) and they pointed out that 'Every effort he [the coalowner] makes to decrease the financial cost of production tends to increase the intensity of labour performed by the miner. . . . Since his desire is for unlimited production, it is bound to clash with that of the miner, who desires a limitation of effort.' The full document is reprinted in the compilation by Ken Coates *Democracy in the Mines* (Spokesman Books 1974) see p. 108.

25. Hodges, op. cit., pp. 50-51.
26. Ibid., p. 78.
27. Quoted in Carter Goodrich *The Frontier of Control* (London 1975 edition, first published 1920) p. 215.
28. Quoted in W. A. Lee *Thirty Years in Coal, 1917-1947* (London 1954) p. 61.
29. Gerald Gould *The Coming Revolution in Great Britain* (London 1920) pp. 190-191.
30. Quoted in W. A. Lee, op. cit., p. 61. Lee also quotes another letter of Hartshorn's in the same vein.
31. C. L. Mowat, op. cit., pp. 119-120. The owners also announced wage cuts and district wage scales.
32. Quoted in W. A. Lee, op. cit., p. 62.
33. Quoted in W. A. Lee, op. cit., p. 63.
34. A. R. Griffin *Mining in the East Midlands* (London 1971) p. 162.
35. Ibid., p. 178 note 13.
36. Quoted in Appendix I in W. A. Lee, op. cit., pp. 216-217.
37. Carter Goodrich *The Frontier of Control* pp. 178-179. For a similar contemporary view see Elie Halevy, introduction to *Imperialism and the Rise of Labour* (London 1961 edn.. first published 1926) p. x; and R. C. K. Ensor *England 1870-1914* (Oxford 1936) pp. 501-502.

Part Five

BETWEEN THE WARS

X

'THE HUMAN FACTOR'

'There can be no doubt that Labour is rightly opposed in this country to the introduction of the early American methods of scientific management. . . . The impartial observer cannot regard with satisfaction the huge profits reported from the early use of scientific management in America and, at the same time, the relatively insignificant advance in wages paid therefrom to the workers. The impartial observer cannot countenance motion study if its ideal is to encourage types of workers who "more nearly resemble in their mental make-up the ox than any other type", or if the worker is to be told—"You know just as well as I do that a high-priced man has to do exactly as he's told from morning till night". Nor can he deny the justice of the worker's demand for greater industrial control in these days of government by consent, of increasing democratic spirit in education, and of growth of personality and responsibility. Especially after the experience of the war, for good or evil, class distinctions are everywhere breaking down, and the former hard-and-fast cleavage and opposition between management and labour must disappear in the course of social evolution.'[1]

This criticism of scientific management was made in 1920 by Charles S. Myers, director of the Psychological Laboratory at Cambridge University, and member of the Industrial Fatigue Research Board. In 1921 Myers was to found the National Institute of Industrial Psychology, thus setting in train an important British tradition of the application of psychological investigation and knowledge to the problems of industry and industrial relations. Myers had been strongly influenced by the lectures on Industrial Psychology given in 1916 by an investigator for the Industrial Fatigue Research Board, Bernard Muscio. In these lectures Muscio 'defined the subject area which, he felt, could incorporate the scientific management movement.'[2] This sub-ordination of industrial psychology to the emphasis on increased output which vitiated scientific management was profoundly unpopular with trade unionists. Myers, however, was sufficiently sensitive to the aspirations of labour and astute enough to realise that 'scientific management', especially in its undiluted American form, was likely to intensify industrial unrest. He, therefore, rejected much of it and chose instead a psychologically based management style informed by traditional British empiricism and a reasonable degree of openness and honesty. In short, he pioneered a British approach to industrial psychology which set out to occupy the middle ground 'between efficiency promoting and welfare.'[3] Myers, for example, was critical of both the F. W. Taylor and the F. B. Gilbreth schools, seeking to distance himself even from Gilbreth by talking of 'movement study' and avoiding time study wherever possible. Throughout *Mind and Work* Myers kept up a thinly veiled attack on Taylorism—the quotation on the ox-like worker came from Taylor. Myers was bitterly opposed to rate-cutting and bonus systems where rate cutting was built into the payment system after the norm had been reached. In one passage he made a strong criticism both of the arrogance of Gilbreth and of Taylor and of the follies of welfare work stating that :

'To argue that there is but *one* best method, suitable for all purposes and adapted to all types of worker, is a psychological fallacy of the first exponents of so-called scientific manage-ment, and only justifies the workers' fears that motion study will convert them all into blind, soulless machines. . . . The workers fear that motion study will rob them of all craftsman-ship and will result in all craft knowledge passing into the hand of management. They fear that they will be deprived of "craft skill" and reduced at most to the possession of the "job skill". Such fears are reasonable only if the study is applied solely in the interests of management. The deplorable history of the welfare movement shows what may happen when a scheme which will benefit the workers is imposed on them without their co-operation or by persons improperly trained for the work. Ample causes must arise for complaint, and a (generally baseless) suspicion is engendered that the employer is introducing the "welfare" movement in his own interests, so as to throw dust in the eyes of the workers which shall blind them to a view of their helplessness and dependence, or so as to administer a narcotic which shall lull them with a sense of false security.'[4]

Only the fullest consultation with workers, and even a degree of workers' control over the introduction of new techniques, would ensure success. Such was the strength of Myers' fears about the likelihood of new techniques back-firing and causing more of the problems that they were intended to eliminate, that he and his National Institute of Industrial Psychology tended throughout the inter-wars to stay well clear of motion study, new payment systems and associated things, concentrating instead on the less contentious areas of ability measurement, personnel selection, training techniques and vocational guidance.[5]

But the use of psychologists, even in the best regulated factories, initially aroused the suspicion of workers. Seebohm Rowntree, who had encouraged Myers to establish the National Institute of Industrial Psychology when the latter stayed with him in York in 1920, and who served on the executive of the Institute from its inception, wanted in the early 1920s to set up a Psychological Department and to appoint a Works Psychologist at the Cocoa Works in York.[6] In March 1920 Rowntree set up a committee (which included three representatives of the workers) to consider the appointment of a psychologist, but such was the strength of suspicion about this proposal that it took two years of coaxing and reassurance before the Psychological Department was established, an event which Asa Briggs has called a 'landmark in British industrial history.'[7] Recalling the problem in the late 1930s, Rowntree wrote that 'In 1921 a few of us came to the conclusion that a trained psychologist could help in selecting employees for different kinds of work, but to adopt such a course would have caused endless suspicion among the workers unless the whole thing was explained to them in the greatest detail.' The project was, therefore, discussed at length in the works council, and psychologists frequently went to York to explain the mysteries of their profession. 'At first,' Rowntree went on, 'there was strong opposition to our proposal, but gradually, as the workers came to understand just what was involved, the opposition died down' and the first psychologist was appointed.[8] His job consisted largely of instituting vocational selection tests. Even then suspicion had not completely died down. In Rowntree's words :

> 'When vocational tests were first introduced they were regarded with a good deal of suspicion, and in some quarters were resisted for a short time, but by handling the situation carefully, and maintaining the closest co-operation between the psychologist and the official representatives of the workers, the suspicion soon died down, and the workers came to realise that they had nothing to fear from the innovation.'[9]

Another management innovation in the Rowntree works in the 1920s was the introduction of time study. Time study was first used in the Cocoa works in 1923. It also met opposition from the workers. Two of Rowntree's labour staff later recalled of its introduction that :

> 'Unfortunately, the workers' attitude to time study was at that time prejudiced by the general hostility shown to it by trade unions. This hostility was undoubtedly due to the manner in which many employers had attempted to apply a few of the principles of scientific management to their own particular business.'[10]

The objections that the workers raised to time study were as follows : that it was inequitable because it made the output of the fastest worker the standard for all; that it was undemocratic because the studies were made by management alone; and that it was not scientific as was claimed. Representatives of the workers were allowed to discuss these criticisms with the management, and out of these discussions an agreed procedure for time study was established. The procedure was that 1) only workers of average ability were to be chosen for time study; 2) that normal working conditions should prevail; 3) that standards of quality should be clearly defined; 4) that tests should be long enough to cover normal fluctuations in conditions affecting output; 5) that shop stewards and management should ratify the standard output determined by the time study observer before it was put in operation; 6) once the rate was established there should be no cuts unless there were changes of machinery, materials, or processes used.[11]

These exemplary conditions for the introduction of time study by no means existed in much of the rest of British industry. This being the case indeed, there was good cause for the initial reaction of the Rowntree workers. It had been common, ever since the development of time study and the use of the resultant times to set work norms, for the 'scientific managers' to choose 'the best and most promising men'. Taylor certainly did this— and also paid time study subjects twice their usual wages. A colleague of Taylor's, Sandford Thompson, who specialised in time study, stated in a paper on the subject published in the *Journal of Political Economy* in May 1913, that this was standard practice. Other places paid workers 25 per cent extra. It was concluded in one discussion of the subject in 1917 that : 'The custom of making it worth the worker's while to have "the stop-watch put on him" (as the workers who have been irritated have phrased it), seems fairly well established, and worthy of imitation—though with some forethought and caution.'[12] At the Cocoa Works at York a different conclusion was quickly arrived at.

One writer has suggested that from the 1920s onwards, building on both his experience in welfare work during the war and the traditions of his family firm, Rowntree engaged in 'a continuous process of innovation and experiment.'[13] In his book *The Human Factor in Business*, which was published in 1921, Rowntree set out his philosophy and his practice of industry. In the cocoa works at York Rowntree had applied, and continued to apply, most of the elements of management thought (though tempered with his own humanitarian concerns) which the First World War had thrust to prominence. In *The Human Factor* Rowntree dealt with wages, hours, security of life, good working conditions, and the joint control of industry. Adequate wages, the role of financial incentives in industrial efficiency, the reduction of working hours, fatigue study and motion study, welfare work, and the role of the trade unions in management were themes that he had investigated and applied. In the opening passages of the book he set out the philosophy underlying and informing his work at York :

'Broadly, it may be said that in framing that policy our objective has been to raise the status of the workers of all ranks from that of servants to that of co-operators; in other words, to introduce into the management of the business, in all matters directly affecting the workers, as great a measure of democracy as possible without lowering efficiency.'[14]

Rowntree, for all his advanced thinking and practice, and all his concessions to the consultation of workers, believed quite clearly that ultimately management had the right to manage. The object of increasing the amount of democracy in the management business was not just to avoid 'lowering efficiency', but rather in the long run to increase the efficiency of the firm. One admirer of Rowntree was later somewhat perturbed by the fact that Rowntree told him that the better he treated his workpeople the more profits he made.[15] But this, of course, was perfectly consistent with Rowntree's views, believing as he did that it was possible, if capitalist enterprises were conducted on his lines, to give the worker a standard of life and a status which many in that labour movement felt was only possible under socialism.[16] No wonder that the reviewer of the book in *The Labour Leader* of September 29, 1921 wrote that 'There can be little doubt that if all employers acted on the Rowntree ideal one half of the efficacy of socialist propaganda would disappear.'

Shortly after the publication of *The Human Factor in Business* Rowntree made his first visit to the home of scientific management, the United States. In the course of his two month visit Rowntree addressed many audiences of academics and industrialists, and at one meeting met American hostility to trade unionism head on.[17] Much of Rowntree's visit was spent in going round American factories. In general he was impressed by the advanced management methods applied in American factories and the modern equipment in them. But he was by no means uncritical of scientific management. He wrote in his journal of one factory where Taylorism held sway that: 'Every single job in the factory has been time studied, and the work upon it must be performed according to carefully written instructions. Even spittoons are cleared by instruction. So far as we could judge, the mechanics did not resent the system, and the labour turnover in the factory is much below normal. It struck us, however, that the system had been carried to excess, though the authorities would not admit this.'[18] Rowntree did, however, find some kindred spirits in American industry—men like Henry Dennison and Robert B. Wolf—with whom he kept up correspondence for many years. Between 1921 and 1937 he visited the United States on sixteen occasions, and his enthusiasm for much of what he saw prompted him to contribute an article to *The Cocoa Works Magazine* in 1923 in which he sought to allay some of his employees' fears about the consequences of this enthusiasm. After commending the virtues of exchange visits between American and British industrialists, he commented:

'I sometimes hear the fear expressed that we are trying to "Americanise" our methods at the Cocoa Works, and to introduce the bustle and heartless drive which many people, often quite wrongly, associate with the idea of an American factory. But let any who fear this, be comforted. None of the directors would be a party to relentless "speeding up". Our object is something very different, namely to eliminate all useless or ineffective expenditure of energy and all other kinds of waste.'[19]

That Rowntree's fellow directors and his other managerial staff were not prone to follow blindly methods which had been applied in America is clear from a book which four of Rowntree's management staff produced in 1928. This book, *Factory Organization*, by Clarence H. Northcott, Oliver Sheldon, J. W. Wardropper and L. Urwick, represented a pioneering and thoroughly British treatment of the subject, and was (as its title implies) not primarily concerned with increasing the efficiency of an enterprise by speeding up or driving workers in an unchanged industrial environment, but rather by attending first and foremost to the organisation of production. This, of course, was partly a question of 'so directing and motivating men and women as to secure their co-operation in the plans and purposes of those responsible for the direction of the factory.'[20] Northcott's chapter in the book on 'Principles and Practice of Industrial Relations', dealt most directly with problems of 'man-management'. Materials, as Northcott pointed out, were 'more tractable' than were men and women. 'Men and women protest against being made the sport of chance or circumstance. They claim for other elements of their natures than the physical or material. Their humanity and vital energies lift them above the level of commodities and enable them to make a dynamic contribution, either positive or negative, to the problem of organization.'[21] Industrial relations problems were human problems, and the first question in the organisation of industrial relations was that of wages. Northcott put it this way : 'what rates of wages must the employer pay, not merely to satisfy the law, but also to obtain a sufficient supply of labour and prompt his employees to the fullest output?'[22] The perennial problem of payment systems and increasing output raised its head again. The discussion on this point is informative. There were basically three different forms of wage payment : time wages, piece wages, and bonus systems. Time rates gave the worker a known and calculable wage, and gave the employer a stable and calculable total labour cost, but there were some important disadvantages. Time rates 'fail to supply any intrinsic incentive to greater effort or harder work. There is no additional reward for effort greater than the customary "stint", and no inducement to work faster than the pace which the overlooker will tolerate. Consequently, the employer is compelled to rely upon the driving power of his foremen or the fear of unemployment to obtain an output necessary for him to balance his cost of production with the prices he can obtain upon the market.'[23] Piece-rate systems got round these problems, and bought out ca'canny practices. But there were other problems.

First of all, it was difficult to 'find a fair output basis for the fixing of piece rates.' And since in most trades there were agreements that the earnings of efficient piece workers should be about a quarter or a third greater than time rates, it was necessary to 'discover what output can normally or reasonably be given.' 'In most cases,' Northcott continued, 'any such effort begins a struggle between the workers and the management, the former having an obvious interest in having this quantum set as low as is feasible.'[24] Ca'canny was a problem here too, under a payment system designed deliberately to prevent it. Further ca'canny was highly probable if the employer was tempted (as he frequently was) to cut the rates to offset the fact that the workers had limited their effort while the rates were being set.

As Northcott put it : 'The lowering of any rates initially fixed too high is generally regarded as dishonest by workers, who retaliate by restriction of output to avoid such contingencies. One evil thus leads to another, costs of production remaining high under either alternative.'[25] One of the reasons for ratecutting, which Northcott called 'the arbitrary raising of the amount of output required for a standard sum of money,' was that workers had shown that 'they can give an output greater than the figure originally fixed.' In practice, this could mean that labour costs per unit of production were higher than they need have been, and, since the abiding concern of managers was and is to reduce unit costs of production, this was obviously an important temptation. But it has often been noted in British industry that there is a strong but erroneous tendency amongst managers to equate high wages with high labour costs per unit of production.

A major enquiry into 'restrictive practices' came out of this stable of enlightened British management thinkers in the 1930s. In 1935 Seebohm Rowntree and others (including J. J. Mallon and John Hilton) produced a book called *Are Trade Unions Obstructive? An Impartial Inquiry.* It was not completely lost on the authors that it was rather odd (since higher labour productivity was bound in the short run to lead to even higher unemployment) to enquire into the extent of union-condoned restriction of output in the face of three million unemployed. But the authors chose to study restrictive practices, not because they were the only or even the most important problem of British industry in the 1930s, but because they wanted to focus their attention on one manageable theme. They acknowledged that it was widely said that trade union inspired 'restrictive practices' were important, and more specifically they pointed out that 'it is alleged that these restrictive practices have been an important fact in encouraging the drift of industry to the South. Employers have felt that it would be advantageous to move to fresh ground, where traditions and practices are not so firmly rooted.'[26] The enquiry was carried out in October 1934 into the Coal, Building, Cotton, Docks, Electrical Engineering, Iron and Steel, Glass, and Furniture industries—an interesting mixture of old, declining industries and new, growing ones. The enquiry involved four things : 1) an introduction on the state of each industry; 2) the employers' views on restrictive practices; 3) the trade unions' reply to these charges; and 4) a summary by the authors. In their general conclusion, the authors point out that they did not invent the term 'Trade Union restriction', but took it as 'found' and they also observe that there were wide differences of opinion between employers as to what trade union restrictions were—some employers indeed thought that 'the most grievous of all restrictions' was the refusal of trade unions to agree to wage cuts. The authors did not accept this :

> 'Our position is that the trade-union policy of standing out for the highest general level of wages and working conditions that can be got without general hurt is not, for our purposes, a "trade-union restriction".'[27]

But that statement should not mislead anyone into thinking that Rowntree and his colleagues were entirely sympathetic to the aspirations of labour—as their attitude to the highly important switch to new machinery makes clear. This changeover was the root of much tension in industry at the time : the tension being produced by attempts by craft unions 'to stipulate what shall happen to their members' earnings, when a job formerly done by a skilled man with hand tools begins to be done on a machine or with the aid of mechanical appliances.'[28] The bargaining power of craft unions was so low that they could not prevent the process taking place, rather the best they might do was to influence the conditions on which the new machines were to be introduced : 'their members can hold things up for a while : but they cannot hope to win a lasting victory. It is not on the cards.' Our authors regretted the fact that craft unions did not limit their case to 'sound' arguments—for instance, that skilled men still had a very important place under the new technology. They were, however, extremely unhappy where craft unions had been strong enough to bring about a situation in which the introduction of new, higher output technology had not led to the displacement of labour. It was to be regretted that trade unions only agree to accept new machines if the craftsmen are still employed 'and receive the same payment per unit of output as they did before' . . . . 'To say that this kind of claim is "unreasonable" is hardly adequate.'[29]

In general Rowntree and his colleagues felt that 'restrictive practices' were less numerous and less important than they had been. They wrote :

'It is, moreover, clear to us that restrictive practices imposed by trade unions are actually fewer than they were, and of less importance. Employers in a number of industries have referred to conditions in their father's or grandfather's time, and have admitted that, comparatively, their own grounds for complaint are small. Restrictions which were imposed in the days when the social conscience was less active have been rendered obsolete and have disappeared. Both trade unions and employers have learnt through experience, and there is a deal more reasonableness than there used to be.'[80]

This analysis is obviously naive—unless what they call 'reasonableness' and 'the social conscience' grows and flourishes in situations in which the bargaining power of labour is greatly reduced. The known positions of our authors would not allow them to admit this openly. But it is quite clear that the reduced bargaining power of labour made it extremely difficult for workers to maintain, let alone extend, those practices designed to increase their control over the work situation. There is, in fact, much evidence in the book itself which bears this analysis out. In the section on the cotton industry, for instance, in a discussion on the cotton finishing trades it is noted that restriction was greatly reduced, and the comment is made : 'It is suggested, however, that this is due to the present economic conditions,' and that, 'if trade was good, and they [the workers] were allowed to do so they would revert to a lot of their old methods of restriction.'[31] True 'reasonableness', surely, should outlast the exigencies of the trade cycle. Similarly in a discussion of the Dock Industry it is pointed out that in London there was a wharfingers' rule that 'Men are to transfer their labour—ship to shore, shore to ship, ship to ship, and hold to hold, as may be customary.' But the employers complained that : 'in some places the men absolutely refuse to transfer from ship to shore, and in others they say that none of these transfers may take place during overtime hours. That was never contemplated when the rule was drawn up. . . . We have asked them to honour their agreement, *but they have consistently refused to do this where they are strong enough.*'[32] Or take this example from the building industry, of which it was observed that 'The small employer, in a district where unions are strong, complains that he is considerably handicapped.'[33] The whole section on the coal industry is dominated by the effects of the loss of bargaining power of the miners after 1926—and it was precisely this that led Rowntree and his colleagues to report that 'Employers in most districts are agreed that there is very little that can be regarded as restrictive action by the trade unions in the industry today.[34] The great 'problem' of absenteeism had, in the face of unemployment and short time working, virtually disappeared.[35] One of the few restrictions about which employers continued to complain was that of men going slow when a new piece price list was being fixed.[36] The miners were, in general, however, so greatly on the retreat that they had even lost their full rights to concessionary coal—with employers in Yorkshire, especially, wanting some payment for it. In a revealing phrase a Yorkshire miners' leader said that the miners had been forced to meet the employers half way on this question *'owing to our reduced power of resistance'.*[37]

The Miners' Federation of Great Britain had also been persuaded to give their official support to mechanisation, though in some districts this was unpopular with the membership—'the men are said to show a marked antipathy to machine mining.'[38] Mechanisation was, indeed, one of the most dramatic changes in the organisation of work in mining, bringing with it many other important changes, in the inter-war years.

In *The Human Factor*, the significantly titled journal of the National Institute of Industrial Psychology (with which a number of the authors of *Are Trade Unions Obstructive?* were intimately connected) in April 1933, a mineworker, J. H. Mitchell, published an article called 'The Mechanization of the Mines' in which he contrasted the old and the new work situations in the industry. In the past 'The work was unhurried . . . [the miner] could organise work to suit himself—work as hard as he liked, and, to a great extent as long as he liked.' Mitchell continued : 'Now compare the lot of this worker with that of a miner in a modern colliery. All is hurry and bustle.' Machine coal cutting, conveyors, and extra supervision (which was highly disliked) had led to a situation in which 'the leisurely isolated worker of some years ago has been displaced by the hurrying squads of today.' Mitchell's impressions received striking confirmation in a critical comment on his article by Herbert Greenwell, an employers' representative :

'As Mr. Mitchell observes, one thing which workmen may boggle at is supervision. The miner of pre-machinery days was to a large extent his own master, and he takes very ill to the supervision to which he now finds himself subjected. . . . Machinery has created an excess of leisure, which the workman has been unable so far to plan to his best advantage, but it does not permit of leisure on the job itself, for almost the whole merit of a conveyor system, in either a factory or a mine, is that it connotes a constantly moving cycle with which the human element must comply.'[39]

Similar changes were taking place in engineering—this also being documented in *The Human Factor* by W. F. Watson in an article called 'The Machine and the Individual'. Watson similarly could contrast the old with the new work situation.

'I have been associated with machinery all my life—I am master of the lathe. When I entered the industry in 1896, mass production and machinery were in their infancy. The following year I saw the first capstan machine installed in Chater Lea's cycle works, then in Golden Lane, London. Indeed, I was its first operator, and after a few day's tuition, I was turning out more crank bolts in a day than ten turners could do in a week. Then came the automatic machines, and I vividly recall a protest meeting being held by the turners when nearly all of them were discharged because of the machine.'[40]

In a further contribution to *The Human Factor* (February 1935) Watson gives just a small hint of the extent to which these changes undermined the craftsmanship and craft control of the skilled engineer. In this instance he is describing one of the archetypal centres of the 'New Industries' of the 1930s :

'A fellow turner, working in a thoroughly up-to-date American factory along the Great West Road, asked me the other day if I had a boring bar I could lend him! Imagine it! An Americanised factory without a boring bar in its maintenance shop. In the course of a conversation he told me that although his lathe was not too bad, there were no spanners, few small tools, and it was the greatest difficulty in the world to get a bit of tool steel.'

Engineering was certainly one of the industries where accusations of restriction of output under piecework were still common in the 1930s[41]—as, indeed, were cases of it, though the A.E.U. could justifiably argue that there was nothing in their rules which might condone the practice. Other engineering unions were, however, prepared to admit that their members had not in the past always given of their best—largely because of the fear of rate-cutting. But with the 1922 agreement in the industry, where rates could only be altered if the method of manufacture or materials used were changed 'the unions believe that there is now no ground for charging their members with restriction of output.'[42] Rate cutting was endemic in British industry, British managers having failed to learn from Taylor that high wages did not necesssarily connote high unit costs of production. As early as 1904 the Special Report of the Commissioner of Labor on Regulation and Restriction of Output in America in 1904, made some comment on British managerial attitudes on this point, and expressed some astonishment at the strength of the British doctrine that a certain wage is 'enough for a workman.'[43] William Denny, a Dumbarton shipbuilder, suffered from the consequences of this attitude being held by the managers he employed in the late 19th century. Denny had frequently denounced the folly of his workmen in resenting payment by results, but later came to appreciate the rationality of his workers' attitudes when he discovered that his managers regularly cut rates when they thought that workmen were 'getting too much.'[44] There is little doubt that rate-cutting persisted strongly into the present century (and it is by no means unknown today) in spite of the fact that virtually every book on management worth anything—from Webb's *The Works Manager Today*, to Myers' *Mind and Work*, the book by Northcott and his colleagues, *Factory Organization*, and not least Rowntree's three editions of *The Human Factor in Business*—spent many words condemning the practice.[45] Not only did rate-cutting persist, but so did the attitude that often prompted it, a moralistic view about what was an adequate wage for workers. As a result of a visit to the United States in 1925 Bertram Austin and W. Francis Lloyd published *The Secret of High Wages* in which, in the course of chapters with titles like 'No Limit to a Man's Output', and 'No Limit to Payment by Results', they made unfavourable comparisons between British and American managerial attitudes on this and other points. Examples of their comments are : 'In Great Britain it is felt, in some quarters, that high wages are not desirable.'; 'It is unfortunate that British management is too often deceived by the high proportion that wages bear to the total costs of production and generally jumps to the conclusion that the only way of reducing costs is to reduce the rate of wages and to lengthen the working hours'; 'Employers must give up the theory that the only proper rate of wages that the men can claim is one which borders on a subsistence level or fodder basis, or that a "reasonable" wage is the equivalent of the *real* wages obtaining before the war.'[46]

Rowntree and colleagues in 1935, in a general discussion of restriction of output induced by fear of rate-cutting, concluded that employers 'here and there' grumbled about the existence of output limits in some piecework industries—in spite of the fact that these restrictions did not appear in collective agreements or union rules. 'But,' they pointed out, 'among the members of many unions such limits are said to be an understood thing,' and unions argued anyway that such restriction of output was 'necessary and right' since it prevented rate-cutting.[47] Rowntree and colleagues were, in fact, reasonably sympathetic to this, and, in a thinly disguised plea for work study, argued that employers were often at fault :

'Employers who do not know how to arrive at sound basic rates, or who will not take the trouble to do it, must expect and put up with limitations of output, for such employers cannot help cutting rates on which earnings are unduly high, and the men know it. . . . The way to avoid the imposition of these restrictions is to make a sound job of estimating basic times, to price each job in time instead of in money, and to put it down in writing that basic times will be subject to alteration, and then only in consultation between employers and men.'[48]

They returned to this theme a few pages later :

'Slack masters make slack men, and it needs no trade-union villainy to account for men putting very little into their part of the joint busines of production when the employer sets the example. An employer should know just what is a fair day's work for each and every man; if he does not, he can neither praise, blame, nor judge aright. His intelligence section is broken down and he better get it mended. He should see that work is not held up by staff bungling and sloppiness. It might almost be said that the employer who suffers "ca'canny" has asked for it and deserves what he gets. But that does not exonerate the trade union that gives the wink and the nod to slacking. The right sort of trade union has standards of working conduct independent of the virtues or failings of employers. The dry-rot of "ca'canny" can moulder a union more surely than it can ruin an industry.'[49]

This sort of statement—with its judicious blows handed out both to 'bad' employers and 'bad' trade unionists and with its emphasis on efficient but responsible management—was entirely character-istic of the school of enlightened, and very British, management centred round Rowntree and the National Institute of Industrial Psychology. This school always spurned the brash and ruthless appeals of Taylor and his American disciples. But many British managers in the 1930s were not the exemplars of good manage-ment that the 'Human Factor' school would have liked—rather the reverse. Many British managers seem to have made consider-able use of the opportunity and the reduced power of resistance of the trade union movement to drive home their advantage and to make a concerted attempt to speed up labour. A striking example of this was in Cotton weaving—already extremely hard hit by unemployment—which was the scene of an exceptionally bitter strike in 1932 against wage reductions and against the introduction of six and more looms per weaver instead of the traditional four.[50]

NOTES

1. C. S. Myers *Mind and Work* (London 1920) pp. 175-177.
2. Michael Travis 'Psychology in Industry' in *Management Thinkers* p. 275, and on Myers and the N.I.I.P. see pp. 277-279.
3. C. A. Oakley *Men at Work.* (London 1945) pp. 6-7.
4. Myers *Mind and Work* pp. 192-194.
5. Travis in *Management Thinkers* pp. 279-280, and Anne G. Shaw *The Purpose and Practice of Motion Study* p. 7.
6. See A. Briggs *Social Thought and Social Action* p. 231.
7. Briggs, op. cit., p. 235.
8. B. Seebohm Rowntree *The Human Factor in Business* (3rd. edn. London 1938) p. 113.
9. Rowntree, op. cit., pp. 117-118.
10. Patricia Hall and H. W. Locke *Incentives and Contentment: a Study made in a British Factory* (London 1938) p. 112.
11. Ibid., pp. 113-115.
12. M. McKillop and A. D. McKillop *Efficiency Methods* (London 1917) pp. 85-86.
13. Dennis Chapman 'Seebohm Rowntree and Factory Welfare' in *Management Thinkers,* p. 204.
14. *The Human Factor in Business* 1921 edn. quoted in *Management Thinkers* p. 124.
15. A. G. Woodward 'Personnel Management' in *Efficiency Magazine* 1938, cited in *Management Thinkers* p. 182 footnote.
16. See extracts from *The Human Factor in Business* 1921 edn. in *Management Thinkers* p. 215.
17. See A. Briggs, op. cit., pp. 165-166.
18. A. Briggs op. cit., p. 169.
19. Quoted in Briggs op. cit., p. 184.
20. C. H. Northcott, O. Sheldon, J. W. Wardropper and L. Urwick *Factory Organization* (London 1928) p. 6. These men, along with some others like William Wallace, were among the group of Rowntree's employees and ex-employees who became extremely influential in the world of management: see Briggs op. cit., pp. 226-227.
21. *Factory Organization,* p. 106.
22. Ibid., p. 116.
23. Ibid., p. 119.
24. Ibid., p. 121.
25. Ibid., p. 122.
26. *Are Trade Unions Obstructive? An Impartial Inquiry* under joint editorship of John Hilton, J. J. Mallon, Sam Mavor, B. Seebohm Rowntree, Sir Arthur Salter, Frank D. Stuart, assisted by Vida M. S. Heigham (London 1935), pp. 7-8.
27. Ibid., p. 312.

28. Ibid., p. 320.
29. Ibid., pp. 321-322.
30. Ibid., p. 335.
31. Ibid., p. 73.
32. Ibid., p. 97, my italics.
33. Ibid., p. 24.
34. Ibid., p. 45.
35. Ibid., p. 49.
36. Ibid., p. 50.
37. Ibid., p. 52, my italics.
38. Ibid., p. 51.
39. H. Greenwell 'The Man and the Machine' in *The Human Factor*, May 1933.
40. W. F. Watson in *The Human Factor*, July-August 1933.
41. *Are Trade Unions Obstructive?* p. 152.
42. Ibid., pp. 158-159.
43. See R. H. Tawney *Equality* (first published 1931, London 1971 imp.) p. 36.
44. A. B. Bruce *The Life of William Denny* (1889) cited in S. Webb *The Works Manager To-day* (London 1917) p. 69.
45. Webb: *The Works Manager To-day* (1917) pp. 45-49, 76-79 and elsewhere; Myers *Mind and Work* (1920) pp. 112-115; C. H. Northcott and others *Factory Organization* (1928) pp. 121-126; B. S. Rowntree *The Human Factor in Business* (1938 edn.) pp. 51, 181, 204.
46. B. Austin and W. F. Lloyd *The Secret of High Wages* (London 1926) pp. 43, 75, 107.
47. *Are Trade Unions Obstructive?* p. 319.
48. Ibid., p. 320.
49. Ibid., p. 332.
50. N. Branson and M. Heinemann *Britain in the 1930s* (London 1973 edn.) pp. 108-114, and *Are Trade Unions Obstructive?* pp. 70-71.

XI

THE BEDAUX SYSTEM

The 1920s and the 1930s were a period of wage cuts in many industries, accompanied by mass unemployment and mass short-time working. The trade unions lost membership at an alarming rate : the six and a half million affiliated membership of the T.U.C. in 1919 and 1920 turned into three and a quarter million by 1933. The bargaining power of labour was, in general, extremely low and the post-General Strike labour movement was neither in the mood nor in the shape to resist the full-scale capitalist rationalisation of industry which characterised the inter-war years. It was in this climate that the ideas of a new management messiah, again from America, arrived on the British industrial scene—and his methods were frequently ones which were anathema to men like Rowntree and his colleagues. The man in question was a naturalised American, Charles E. Bedaux (1887–1944), who began his career as an industrial consultant in the U.S.A. in 1911. The first substantial arrival of the Bedaux system into Britain came in the 1920s when some of his ideas were adopted by I.C.I. and some other firms. By 1926 the demand for technical consultants trained in the Bedaux method was large enough for a company under the name of Charles E. Bedaux Ltd. to be registered in London to meet that demand.[1] If a speaker at the meeting of the British Association in 1931 was right when he said that there were two methods open to the employer in dealing with withholding of effort—justice or cunning—then there were plenty of British employers who opted for cunning. By 1931 some two hundred men, according to R. M. Currie, had been trained in the Bedaux methods and had applied them in some five hundred plants. By 1932 it was estimated that about 50,000 employees in thirty-two firms were covered by the Bedaux system.[2] The firms involved were frequently, though not

231

always, in the new and expanding industries of the 1930s—
chemicals, food processing, motor vehicles, light engineering and
so on. But the system spread also to some firms in, for instance,
the iron and steel, textile, and hosiery industries. In 1936 a
publicity brochure issued by Charles E. Bedaux Ltd. from their
Bush House Offices in Aldwych, London, showed that 240 firms
were operating the system. Amongst them were I.C.I., Joseph
Lyons, Carreras, Hoffman Ball Bearings, Mullard Radio and
Kodak.[3]

R. M. Currie, a patent admirer of Bedaux and the *eminence
grise* of British work study, wrote less than candidly of the
application of Bedaux to British industry that :

'A certain amount of resentment towards the Bedaux consultants arose owing to the fact that the introduction of the
system coincided with the general depression of 1929 and the
early thirties, when employers appeared to be largely concerned with economies in labour. There is no question that
certain employers brought the Bedaux system into disrepute
by adopting the extremely bad practice of cutting properly
established values after the Bedaux consultants had completed
the application.[4]

Bedaux was an extremely unpopular system with workers, and
its unpopularity stemmed not only from the cutting of 'properly
established values' but also from the very fact that the basis on
which those values were established was secret. On top of this,
to most workers who experienced the system it felt like 'speed
up' and it often involved an unwanted intrusion by management
in the workers' conduct of his own job. In theory the Bedaux
System involved a good deal more than time study plus a
related incentive payment system. Indeed, like most management systems, it claimed to embrace a total approach to the
questions of raising productivity and decreasing unit costs of
production. It claimed to deal with the more efficient use of
capital—factory lay-out, supplies of materials, adequate machinery and so on, as well as with the increased productivity of
labour as such. But there is no doubt that in practice its most
important emphasis was on the speeding up of work, of increasing
the exploitation of labour. When the Bedaux Company pre-

pared a survey in July 1932 for the Manchester wiredrawing factory of Messrs. Richard Johnson and Nephew Ltd., it was stated that 'The principal objective of Bedaux is the elimination of all ineffective effort and losses at present hidden.'[5] The document went on to say that 'the underlying principle' of Bedaux work measurement was that 'all human effort can be measured in terms of a common unit made up of effort and relaxation, in proportions governed by laws controlling strain.'[6] There, cloaked in the language, but not in the reality of science, stood what was, as far as the workers on whom the system was used were concerned, the basis for increasing the intensity of their labour.

Under the Bedaux system, work was regarded as being made up of a series of movements and manipulations which required on the part of workers the expenditure of a certain amount of effort. These things it was argued could be measured and known accurately. The unit of measurement employed was called the 'B'. This represented the amount of work which could be performed by a worker in normal circumstances in one minute. This work minute was then regarded as being made up of work and of rest. The average worker, then, should have been able to get an output of 60 'B's an hour—though Bedaux consultants regarded a standard of 80 'B's as being attainable where workpeople and management were 100 per cent efficient. 'B's produced beyond 60 an hour were called Premium 'B's, for which a bonus was paid as an incentive. The bonus for each premium 'B' was 1/60th of the base rate of wage, and the Bedaux organisation recommended that three quarters of the bonus be paid to the workpeople directly concerned and the remaining quarter to supervisors and to indirect labour whose work has facilitated production in excess of the 60 'B' standard.[7] If all this sounds rather complex and technical that should cause no great surprise. In the initial stages of Bedaux's introduction into plants bewilderment was one of the most common responses which it produced in workers. The utter strangeness and complexity of the system, involving as it did an appeal to scientific accuracy, led, for instance, to one of the first companies which used the system in Britain preparing a booklet on it for its employees. In July 1928 the Hoffman Manufacturing Company of Chelmsford issued a pamphlet, full of reassuring phrases and bewildering calculations, called *The Bedaux Method of Wage Payment*. The booklet began as follows :

> 'After very careful consideration the Bedaux Wage Payment Plan is being introduced into these works. It is designed to obtain the best practical results by offering to the employees concerned a fair incentive to increase their effort.'

At the end of the booklet 'Ten Distinctive Features of Bedaux' were listed. Amongst them were the following : that the normal effect of Bedaux was to increase workers' earnings; that work standards include allowances for relaxation; that the 'B' values are absolutely guaranteed by the management, and that they would only be changed when materials, methods of production or types of product are changed; that speed and quantity is not the object of Bedaux.[8] A present day work study specialist has suggested that the Bedaux system succeeded for three main reasons. Firstly, that it produced management-control information; secondly, that it gave managements an excuse for sacking roughly half their direct labour force; and thirdly, that it persuaded workmen to restrict output at a new and higher level in return for more money, at a time when basic pay was often not enough to support a family properly. He goes on to demystify Bedaux as follows :

> 'The mathematics of a Bedaux scheme were straightforward. In concrete terms, if a man earned £3 a week for producing 40 articles, Bedaux offered him £4 a week if he produced 80. Put in these terms, the confidence trick is too obvious, but the logic was confused by jargon and a certain amount of downright untruth. For instance, Bedaux always started from the premise that the man should have been producing 60 articles for his £3, and thus if he produced a third more— 80—he got a third more pay—£4. What could be fairer? The man with the £1 didn't complain, and the man with the sack couldn't make himself heard in the crowd.'[9]

Many workers in the 1930s did see through Bedaux, and realised that it brought 'speed-up', caused unemployment, and involved time study and increased supervision. At the 1932 T.U.C. in Newcastle a resolution was passed calling on the

General Council to carry out an enquiry into the system. By the time the T.U.C. met the next year, a pamphlet *Bedaux: the T.U.C. examines the Bedaux System of Payment by Results* had been published. Of the 104 unions approached by the T.U.C. for information only 13 had experience of it. But on the basis of their replies it could be asserted that 'in almost every case' the unions concerned had opposed the introduction of the system. The report claimed that :

'In the first place, such methods have the effect, and in some cases, the intention of speeding-up the individual worker to the greatest possible extent, regardless of his health, comfort and individuality. The object of such systems is to produce the maximum output per worker and carried to extremes, this has very undesirable results both physiologically and psychologically. Overstrain and fatigue may follow and may, over a long period, cause serious injury to the health of the worker. Moreover, the worker under such systems is made to feel that he is a cog in an inhuman machine for increasing output. The tendency is to obliterate individuality and craftsmanship and to make the worker merely a machine.'

To conclude it noted that : 'A final criticism is that the Bedaux System by increasing output per head, results in the displacement of labour.'[10]

The T.U.C. called for greater consultation between unions and employers when the latter proposed to introduce Bedaux. As the 1930s progressed a greater degree of trade union consultation was established and this, allied with other factors led *Labour Research* in June 1936 to comment that Bedaux was no longer 'meeting the militant opposition so characteristic of the institution of the system three or four years ago.'[11] In the early years of the decade however, there had been a good deal of militant opposition to the system. In 1932 there had, for instance, been a strike against it by hosiery workers in the Wolsey Works at Leicester. The strikers were, for the most part, non-unionists before the strike began. The General Council of the T.U.C. in its report for 1932 felt moved to comment that 'The effort made by the union was notable for the remarkable solidarity displayed by the employees, the majority of whom were girls.'[12] Unorganised women workers displayed the same determined and militant characteristics in many of the other anti-Bedaux strikes, for example in the fierce strike (involving substantial solidarity action by London bus workers) at the Venesta Plywood Factory in the East End of London in the spring of 1933. Disguised Bedaux, bringing with it considerable speed-up, had led in 1932 to a one day protest strike in the Birmingham motor accessories factory of Joseph Lucas.[13] Speed-up following the introduction of the system in the Morris Motor works at Cowley led to considerable resentment from the workers, and it was a contributory factor in the important strike at the nearby Pressed Steel works in July 1933.[14] Resentment caused by Bedaux also led to strikes at the Caledonian Linoleum works, at the metal window firm of Henry Hope, and at Elliots Engineering. Opposition from workers at Rover Motors and at Hornes, the clothing firm, led in those cases to the abandonment of the system.[15] The intensification of labour which accompanied Bedaux was, in most of these cases, the most common cause of militant action by workers.

Perhaps the most important centre of criticism of Bedaux was the rump of the National Minority Movement which, by 1933, was grouped round a particularly good monthly newspaper, *The Militant Trade Unionist*, edited by Tom Mann. The second issue of *The Militant Trade Unionist*, that of June 1st 1933, was devoted to 'Hours and Speed Up', and its centre pages contained a big feature called 'Speed-up Systems Can Be Smashed.' *The Militant Trade Unionist* claimed that it had already made a practical contribution to the struggle against speed-up, by, for instance, issuing strike bulletins during the Venestas strike, and by giving financial aid (from collections) to the strikers at Hope Brothers in Smethwick. The centre page feature was illustrated by photographs of blacklegs being protected by police at Venestas at West Ham and of women strikers at Lucas Accessories. There was also a cartoon of 'the man with the stop-watch', the caption to which read 'He stands behind you at the bench; he sits in a glass cage near the roof; he stands at the street corner timing your bus. His job is to save time—for time is money to the employer. It cuts his wage-bill. It raises his profits. To the worker, speed-up is the

very devil. It exhausts his strength. It undermines his health.'
Figures were put forward detailing how speed-up had been
introduced : the London bus conductors used to collect £6 or
£8, each per day in fares—now they were collecting £16 and
£18, but their wages stayed the same; thirteen years previously
the miner cut 14½ cwts of coal a day, in 1932 he cut 22 cwts.
It was calculated that this increase in productivity was sufficient to allow hours to be cut to 5 per day—but instead they
had increased from 7 to 7½, and wages had dropped from
£4 5s. 9d. to £2 1s. 11d. The general conclusion was : 'It is
the same in every industry. The effects of speed-up are felt
in every nook and corner of working-class life.' The solution
to this state of affairs was set out as follows :

'Sanity demands that unless we are to be reduced entirely to
the level of short-lived machines, we must win back those
stolen hours; must stand solid against speed-up; must send the
Bedaux, Taylor, Luvex and other "efficiency" systems to hell,
where they belong.'

The Bedaux system was given special attention, in view of the
fact that it was relatively new and because many workers were
struggling against its effects at the time. The following explanation of it was given for those who were unfamiliar with it :

'A representative of the Bedaux firm stands behind a worker
with a stop-watch. At every turn of the hand or movement
of the foot which he considers unnecessary, he stops his watch
for the duration of the "unnecessary" period—even for split
seconds. The time taken for the operation, less the time occupied in "unnecessary" movements, is regarded as the "normal"
time required. This time, however, is further reduced on the
calculation that if you repeat an operation several times you
get a faster rhythm. Piecework rates are adjusted accordingly.
This time is then divided up into "B units", the idea being
that a worker should be able to produce 60 B units per hour.
A bonus is given for extra output. But 25 per cent. of the
bonus earned is handed over to the foreman of the shop—to
encourage him as well.'

Higher wages were offered, but 'hardly ever materialise',
although output might double or treble. A worker at Hope

Brothers provided detailed documentation of this point—he stated that after trying to get his 'Bs' in, he found that after doing 3,500 he earned just over 11 shillings. He calculated that under the previous payment rate of 3d. per dozen he would have earned £3 12s. 11d. A worker at Silvers Chemicals, Silvertown, who previously had to mould 63 tyres a day, now had to mould 76 tyres a day, for the same money. A worker at Venestas commented of Bedaux that 'What affects us chiefly is that we don't get any rest. . . . We are working twice as hard for the same money.' She claimed that one week she got 2/6d. less than she did before she was timed, although she did a lot more work under Bedaux.

In many firms where Bedaux was introduced the workers engaged in something like guerrilla warfare against it. The full scale strike at Hopes in Smethwick, had, for instance, been prefaced by six months of struggle by the workers there who had been only 5 per cent organised in January 1933. Protests and short strikes came first—but brought no redress. The chairman of the strike committee said that on March 29th, 'We drove the Bedaux expert out by physical force. From that time until now we have been outside the factory, and still determined to stay until the system is withdrawn.'

The sheer crudity of the measurements involved in Bedaux, coupled with the mysterious nature of the system, frequently led to trouble. Georges Friedmann, in his superb book, *Industrial Society: the Emergence of the Human Problems of Automation*, points out that by and large workers' reactions to the new system were usually very unfavourable. Friedmann writes :

'I was able to verify this at Birmingham in 1933, in an important machine shop in which a strike occurred. The workers were made particularly suspicious by the mystery enveloping the procedures which were imposed upon them, without any satisfactory explanation (the management itself claimed not to understand them).'

Since also, under Bedaux, perhaps 25 per cent of any bonus generated by workers was distributed to foremen and supervisors, the latter had a direct interest in driving the workers.

Resentment at the extra supervision involved, coupled as it was with the fact that Bedaux was for most workers the first experience of the stop watch and of time and motion study, meant that hostility could be immediate and could involve workers with strong traditions of craftsmanship and high levels of 'company loyalty' as well as non-unionised workers in the new industries. Just such a case, involving such workers, took place at the Manchester wiredrawing works of Richard Johnson and Nephew. It is worth recounting in some detail.

Richard Johnson and Nephew introduced Bedaux into the stranding shop of their Manchester plant in November 1932 after a pilot study had been undertaken by the Bedaux company earlier in the year. A Bedaux field engineer was installed in the shop, and it was his very presence that was the original source of trouble. As Tom Seed, full-time official of the Amalgamated Society of Wire Drawers and Kindred Workers put it in February 1933 : 'there is general discontent and unrest among the work-people . . . as a result of being beset and watched for the purpose of procuring their trade secrets and methods of working, which normally, we think, legally belong to themselves.'[16] This initial reaction led to the postponement of the introduction of Bedaux for six months whilst talks were held between the union and the firm. Simultaneously however the firm was receiving plentiful advice from the Bedaux Company about how to deal with the men's arguments in readiness for the time when the system was tried again. The firm produced a number of documents, suitably laden with calculations and blandishment about higher wages and the maintenance of existing employment, in order to reassure its employees about the system. On March 2nd, 1933, however, unknown to the workers the Board of Directors decided unanimously that 'a new system of wage payment and shop control, based on a specialised time system, should be put into operation, even if this course of action involves a stoppage of work.' The Works Manager was empowered to negotiate with the employees about the introduction of the system, but was told that if the workers refused to accept it then 'the necessary steps should be taken to enforce the adoption of the system, even if this course involves a stoppage of work.' From this point onwards a confrontation was inevitable, for the men and their union were firm in their opposition to Bedaux. Their opposition, however, was conducted in a remarkably gentlemanly fashion, based not so much on an explicitly held notion about the class struggle, but rather on a belief in 'the rights and liberties of British subjects resident in this country.'[17] Alf Bywater, the strike leader, told a meeting with the employers and the Lord Mayor of Manchester that 'the principle of timing interfered with the liberty of free Englishmen. He, himself, had been timed and he was quite overcome after even five minutes of it.'[18] It was this belief in the rights of free born Englishmen which led to the union to take their case to the law; their case being heard in the Court of Chancery in November 1934. It was dismissed, the judge remarking that he was satisfied that 'what was done by way of observation was well within the legal rights of Richard Johnson.'

By this time the inevitable strike was six months old. Sixteen men in the Cleaning Shop had stopped work immediately after the Bedaux engineer had entered the shop, restarting work only after he left the shop. The management, true to its intentions, sacked the sixteen men on the grounds that they had consistently refused to give the output required. Against the advice of the union about 500 of the other employees struck in sympathy with the sixteen. The five hundred stayed out throughout the summer and early autumn of 1934 in spite of attempts by the firm to destroy their solidarity by offering them their jobs back 'without any change in the pre-existing conditions, which latter includes a continuance of the reorganisation of the works.'[18] The workers remained united in their opposition to Bedaux, and they successfully enlisted the aid of Manchester and Salford Trades Councils, other trade unions, the National Unemployed Workers' Movement, and the General Council of the T.U.C. as well as other labour movement organisations in Lancashire and Yorkshire. But defeat was on its way, for by the end of March 1935, the firm could issue a statement saying that the works were fully staffed and that no more men could be taken on. Most of the strikers had by then found other jobs or had been recognised as being unemployed, although some few stayed out hoping for reinstatement. Not until June 1937 did the union close its book on the strike. It was then recorded that 'it would appear that all our members who came out in dispute and who were available for employment had been placed at other firms'; that the rest were past working age; that the management at Richard Johnson and Nephew Ltd., had 'likewise changed almost completely since the dispute began; that the Bedaux Company's experts had been withdrawn from the works; [and] that attempts were being made to run the works under the old system but with imported labour and improved labour saving devices.'[20] As Mick Jenkins rightly puts it, in his account of the strike, it ended 'in defeat for the men, but not a victory for the firm.'[21]

Although the Bedaux system had to be withdrawn at Richard Johnson and Nephew, its spread throughout much of the rest of industry in the 1930s was frequently unchecked. Other workers subjected to Bedaux elsewhere came to learn to live with it. That their labour was intensified is clear from Bedaux's own figures. The introduction of Bedaux usually had the following results—a dramatic rise in productivity; a marked fall in labour costs; and some rise in workers' earnings. For instance, it was claimed that, in a large cycle and motor cycle firm, productivity went up 122 per cent, labour costs went down 38 per cent, and operator earnings went up 18 per cent. A teleprinter and radio firm showed results, respectively, of 171 per cent, 57 per cent, and 15 per cent.[22] Some disinterested investigators employed by the Industrial Health Research Board in 1938, while failing to find such dramatic results from Bedaux, claimed on the basis of their enquiry into six firms using the system that: 'there is not the least doubt that the Bedaux system increases output.' They found an average increase in output of 52 per cent, ranging from 27 per cent to 95 per cent.[23] For Labour the spread of Bedaux was a clear setback: work was speeded up, supervision was usually intensified, and, in short, workers took another step back from receiving the full fruits of their output. After a while workers came to limit their criticisims of Bedaux to its application in their own workplaces, rather than, as in the early 1930s, exhibiting full-blooded opposition to the system as such. The criticisms of Bedaux that were made often related to the fact that its pretensions to scientific accuracy were frequently unfounded. This, indeed, was the conclusion of the Industrial Health Research Board's investigation of 1938 of over 500 male and female workers in five different factories using the Bedaux system. Over eighty per cent of the 500 workers stated that it was 'more difficult to earn their money on some kinds of work than on others.' If scientific work measurement had existed then variations of this sort should not have occurred. The investigators stated that in most cases these variations could be put down, as one departmental manager told them, to a time-study man having 'slipped up on his studies.' The great majority of workers were 'emphatic that variations in earnings were due to unequal standards and not to differences in practice or experience.' There was no doubt, the investigators added, that this sort of inaccuracy represented 'a genuine grievance and was a serious cause of discontent.'[24]

In 1945 an industrial psychologist pointed out that workers' opposition to the Bedaux system came, not so much from their fear of being speeded up, as from their dislike of being timed and from the worker's disinclination thereby to let the 'office know too much about what he does and could do.'[25] This desire by workers to do *their* jobs in their own way was widespread; as was its corollary, the dislike of management strategies which increased the amount of interference in the worker's conduct of his job. This is exactly what was implied in the statement of Tom Seed during the Bedaux dispute at Richard Johnson and Nephew when he stated that unrest was being caused among the workers 'as a result of being beset and watched for the purpose of procuring their trade secrets, which normally, we think, legally belong to themselves.'

Workers commonly adopted what Reinhard Bendix has termed 'strategies of independence'—in the shape of 'output restriction, co-operative teamwork, or indifferent neutralism.'[26] These strategies were applied even (if not especially) against those managerial directives and actions precisely designed to eradicate them. As we saw in the discussion of payment systems made by the Rowntree Company's Labour Manager, Clarence Northcott, this often seemed like sheer perversity on the part of workers. Piece work could be introduced to eliminate the restriction of output common under time wages, only to see the re-emergence of ca'canny when the rates were being set; and later, when employers were tempted to cut piece rates to compensate for what was regarded as underworking and over-earning, the workers would merely intensify their ca'canny whenever the rates for a job were being established on a future occasion. The Rowntree team were not unaware of this problematic side to incentive payments.

This point emerged again in a study carried out at the Cocoa Works and published under the title of *Incentives and Contentment* in 1938. In an analysis of what motivated employees to work hard a whole host of factors was looked at—but it was concluded that the financial motive remained the most important. Hence, for one thing, the fact that, whereas 60 per cent of the cocoa workers had been on payment by results in 1919, the figure in 1936 was 85 per cent. But for all the importance of payment by results schemes it was added that they had also been 'responsible for much unrest and strife in industry.'[27] To some extent the study broke new ground by dealing in some detail with all the other factors which influenced the degree of job satisfaction experienced by workers. The enquiry had been undertaken to discover how to bring about a greater sense of co-operation between the company and its employees. This, of course, was a sort of Holy Grail for Seebohm Rowntree and one which he felt to be an indispensable accompaniment of company profitability and not just an optional extra. In his foreword to the book Rowntree had pronounced that:

'Probably the greatest single source of waste is that which arises from lack of cordial co-operation between employer and employed. Strikes and lockouts, serious though they are, only account for a small part of it. Infinitely more important is the day-to-day waste to which it gives rise in every factory. If *this* could be avoided, then it would be possible substantially to raise the workers' standard of living.'[28]

One of the findings of *Incentives and Contentment*, though by no means one that was made much of, was that group feeling among workers could negate the objectives of individual incentive schemes.

As Asa Briggs has pointed out this enquiry bears a certain amount of comparison with the experiments carried out by Elton Mayo and his colleagues at the Hawthorne works of the Western Electrical Company in Chicago throughout the inter-wars.[29] The Mayo work is well-known and has been the subject of many accounts. The following points are, however, worth making about the Bank Wiring Room and Relay Assembly Test Room observations.

The Relay Assembly Test Room was a small section employing six women who sat on a long bench cut off from the main department. Mayo and his associates recorded their output over a period of five years. Throughout this period an observer sat in with the workers and generally kept them informed of what was happening. During the five years a series of changes were introduced to their work situation—for example, piecework, shorter working hours, rest pauses and the like. For the most part, the changes coincided with (or caused?) a rise in output. And to everyone's surprise, when, towards the end of the experiments two of the original conditions of long hours and absence of rest pauses were reverted to for a twelve week period, the output rose to a record level. Mayo in his early comments on this in his book *The Human Problems of an Industrial Civilization* (1933) felt that this result, combined with the general improvement that had come about in the women's attitude to their jobs, could be more logically attributed to 'a betterment of morale than to any of the alterations made in the course of the experiments.'[30] By the time that long hours were restored and rest pauses eliminated the workers'

'apprehension of authority was almost entirely dissipated. In this period the girls expressed full confidence toward those in charge of the experiment. They were no longer afraid that they would be the losers from the experimental changes.'[31]

On top of this the six girls had become a thoroughly cohesive group—one which had become 'bound together by common sentiments and feelings of loyalty.'

Mayo and his associates now turned to the Bank Wiring Room for their next major piece of observation. They were seeking to investigate the behaviour of social groups at work, and especially the strong controls that groups exercised over the work behaviour of their individual members. In a series of studies in 1931 and 1932 it was found that the 14 men (9 wiremen, 3 soldermen, and 2 inspectors, who were paid as a group) who made up the Bank Wiring Observation Group brought about no increase in production as the result of any changes that were made. Output remained pretty well constant from week to week—and it was clear that the workers were by no means working to their full capacity. Mayo's colleagues in a detailed account of the experiment made the following observations :

That each member of the group was restricting his output. That restriction of output manifested itself in two ways : first, the group had a standard of a day's work which was considerably lower than the 'bogey' and which fixed an upper limit to each person's output. That this standard had been formulated by the men themselves, and as such flew straight in the face of the ideas underlying the financial incentive system they were paid under 'which countenanced no upper limit to performance other than physical capacity.' That individual output was fairly constant from week to week. That it was admitted by most of the wiremen that 'they could easily turn out more work than they did.' That the observer said that 'all the men stopped work before quitting time.' That many methods were used by members of the group to ensure that other members did not attempt to reach production targets set down by the firm or in any other way vary their production level from the informal norm. That these methods included punching the recalcitrants on the upper arm, 'binging'. About this it was commented :

'In addition to its use as a penalty and as a means of settling disputes, binging was used to regulate the output of some of the faster workers. This was one of its most significant applications and is well illustrated in the following entry :

W(orker)8 (to W6) : Why don't you quit work? Let's see, this is your thirty-fifth row today. What are you going to do with them all?
W6 : What do you care? It's to your advantage if I work, isn't it?

W8 : Yeah, but the way you're working you'll get stuck with them.
W6 : Don't worry about that. I'll take care of it. You're getting paid by the sets I turn out. That's all you should worry about.
W8 : If you don't quit work I'll bing you. (W8 struck W6 and finally chased him around the room.)
OBS(erver) (a few minutes later) : What's the matter, W6, won't he let you work?
W6 : No. I'm all through though. I've got enough done. (He then went over and helped another wireman.)'[32]

The great hope of the extremely influential 'Human Relations' school that Mayo's work spawned was that industry's numerous Bank Wiring Room work groups could be, by dint of the development of management's 'social skills' and 'good communications', transformed into work groups of the type which inhabited the Relay Assembly Test Room. Such was the enthusiasm for this idea that those findings in the reports on the work itself which contradicted it were conveniently overlooked for many years. Roethlisberger and Dickson themselves (who wrote the account of 'binging' quoted above) had warned in 1939 in that report of 'the inability of supervisory human relations training to have any significant influence on the fundamental conflict situation found in the Bank Wiring Room.'[33] Many of the findings and extrapolations from the findings of the Hawthorne work are now seriously discredited,[34] though they remained influential for many years.

But one 'discovery' of Mayo and his colleagues that continues to hold water is the very basic one about the existence of the work group itself. The Hawthorne experiments showed conclusively that workers could not be regarded as wage maximising individuals in isolation from their fellows, even when payment systems were based on an assumption that a worker would act out his role as 'economic man' and seek to maximise his own earnings. What Mayo did in his attempt to explore the causes of low productivity and output restriction was to discover the importance of the work group. As Reinhard Bendix has put it, Mayo's research confirmed his belief that 'workers acted in natural solidarity with their fellows, not as isolated individuals.'[35] The job of the manager in this situation was not, as F. W. Taylor might have held, to undermine the group, but on the contrary to attempt to build positively on its existence, and to turn it from work-group-hostility-to-management (and restriction of output) towards work-group co-operation-with-management (and increased output). It was a matter for management to try to provide an environment in the organisation in which, in Mayo's words, the workers could fulfil their 'eager human desire for co-operative activity.' The existence of work groups and their internal loyalties had to be recognised and the positive aspects of them (from the firm's point of view) encouraged and enhanced. This 'human relations' approach involved the realisation that

> 'Change, to be acceptable to a group, must come from within, and must appear as the visible need of its present activities. . . . So management in industry can lead its groups to just that extent to which it is itself accepted by those groups, and it can lead no further; anything beyond that will be resisted as compulsive interruption to social living.'[36]

These words were written by Mayo's colleague, T. N. Whitehead, and appeared in his *Leadership in a Free Society* (1936), a book which, according to one authority, was in Britain 'the most influential book of the Mayo school.'[37] The book received a very cordial reception in advanced British management circles. *Industry Illustrated*, for instance, in an editorial called it 'a tract for our times all will read who have any concern for the future of democratic civilisation'—and added that 'the leading theme is a belief we have always maintained in these columns.' As these last remarks make clear, one of the reasons why Mayoism was so well received in Britain was that it seemed to provide a scientifically validated demonstration of the best ideas and practices already espoused the advanced guard of British management thinkers.[38] To the advanced guard Mayo's ideas were not new—they merely confirmed them in beliefs they had long held and gave them more confidence in espousing them.

The majority of British managers in the 1930s however, ignored the work of Mayo and his colleagues, just as they ignored the work of the British management thinkers. As John Child has pointed out, 'the attempts of many employers in this period to cut wage rates and lengthen hours of work in a desperate search for lower costs were completely at variance with those elementary lessons of industrial psychology which had long been absorbed by the management intellectuals.'[39] This cost consciousness, indeed, was responsible for the greater enthusiasm with which the Bedaux and similar systems were received. Although the Bedaux system was obviously crude, it continued to spread. In modified forms and often masquerading under other names it was to become, especially after 1945, the most commonly used system of work measurement in British industry.[40] As we have seen, F. B. Gilbreth had concentrated on motion study, while Charles Bedaux had concentrated on time study. After a period of terminological chaos ('time and motion study', 'movement study', 'motion study', 'time study',) the two specialisms tended to come together, and in Britain came to be known under the inclusive label of Work Study. This term was developed by R. M. Currie, who was responsible in Imperial Chemical Industries' plants after the war for taking forward and extending the applications of the Bedaux system that had been adopted in the 1920s.[41] The motion study strand of work study properly understood was also developed somewhat in British industry in the inter-war years, and again the links with American management practitioners were strong.

Anne G. Shaw, an English woman who had been trained in motion study by Frank Gilbreth's widow, Lillian, in America in the 1920s, returned to England in 1930 to take up a post in the women's employment department of Metropolitan-Vickers, at Trafford Park, Manchester. George Bailey, chairman of Associated Electrical Industries of which Metropolitan-Vickers was a part, already aware of the possibilities of motion study, decided to take advantage of Miss Shaw's training. He set her to work on attempting to improve by motion study a job which had already been recently re-planned, and on which little improvement was thought possible. Bailey felt that 'if motion study were successful here we should have less difficulty in convincing everyone of its value. The results obtained amazed most people and our faith was justified.'[42] From that point the work spread, with the company chairman cleverly involving the Works Committee and the Women's Works Committee from the start. The work developed throughout Metropolitan Vickers and later encompassed the whole of the A.E.I. group of companies with its 50,000 workers. On top of this, in Miss Shaw's own words, 'Training courses were organised for motion study engineers from each factory in the group and the type of motion study taught and developed was in the direct Gilbreth tradition since it had been derived at first hand from Mrs. Gilbreth herself.'[43] During the Second World War—when, to use Miss Shaw's own words again, 'maximum output was of primary importance'—Miss Shaw became a person of considerable importance in the British war effort. The A.E.I. chairman has recorded that the Minister of Aircraft Production, Sir Stafford Cripps, 'was so much impressed by what he saw at Trafford Park' that in 1942 he invited Miss Shaw to become a member of a select group of output experts assembled in the Production Efficiency Board of the Ministry of Aircraft Production.[44] Motion study was not, however, the only device summoned to the aid of the war economy's immense appetite for increased production and higher productivity. Some 'human relations' type ideas—harnessed to popular support for the Soviet Union—also flourished. Before we deal with the Second World War we must turn to an examination of the development of output raising techniques in the Soviet Union between the wars.

NOTES

1. R. M. Currie *Work Study* (London 1964 imp.) pp. 7-9.
2. R. M. Currie *Work Study* p. 9; K. G. J. C. Knowles *Strikes—A Study in Industrial Conflict* (Oxford 1952) p. 53 footnote 3.
3. N. Branson and M. Heinemann *Britain in the 1930s* p. 96.
4. R. M. Currie *Work Study* p. 9.
5. Report on Bedaux Survey of Messrs. Richard Johnson and Nephew Ltd., Strand Shop, Manchester, signed J. Leslie Orr, Chief Consulting Engineer, Chas. E. Bedaux Ltd., 6 July 1932, quoted in the fine pamphlet by Mick Jenkins *Time and Motion Strike—Manchester 1934-7: The Wiredrawers' Struggle against the Bedaux System at Richard Johnsons* (Our History Pamphlet No. 60. Autumn 1974) p. 5.
6. Ibid.

7. J. H. Richardson *An Introduction to the Study of Industrial Relations* (London 1965 imp.) pp. 80-81. See pp. 77-82 for a full description of Bedaux.

8. *The Bedaux Method of Wage Payment* (Chelmsford July 1928).

9. Philip Livingstone 'Stop the Stop Watch' in *New Society* 10th July 1969.

10. *Bedaux: the T.U.C. Examines the Bedaux System of Payment By Results*, pp. 9-10 and p. 14.

11. Quoted in Knowles *Strikes* p. 53, note 3.

12. Quoted in Knowles *Strikes* p. 184, see also p. 23.

13. Allen Hutt *The Post-War History of the British Working Class* (London 1937) p. 247, see also H. A. Marquand in *Organised Labour in Four Continents* (London 1939) p. 183.

14. Remarks made by Arthur Exell in paper on 'Morris Motors in the 1930s' given at History Workshop, Ruskin College, Oxford, May 1975.

15. N. Branson and M. Heinemann *Britain in the 1930s*, pages 86 and 127, and A. Hutt, op. cit., p. 247.

16. Mick Jenkins op. cit., p. 6.

17. Mick Jenkins op. cit., p. 9, from resolution passed at mass meeting of the men on 22 July 1933.

18. Mick Jenkins, op. cit., p. 29. W. F. Watson in his *The Worker and Wage Incentives* (London 1934) p. 39 gives another example of workers objecting to rate-fixers walking round the shop with stop watches. In that case it led to a strike in a Lewisham engineering firm.

19. Mick Jenkins op. cit., p. 14.

20. Mick Jenkins op. cit., p. 31.

21. Mick Jenkins op. cit., p. 14. My debt to Jenkins' pamphlet in writing this section is considerable.

22. N. Branson and M. Heinemann *Britain in the 1930s* p. 96.

23. Cited in R. Marriott *Incentive Payment Systems* (London 1957) pp. 116-117.

24. S. Wyatt, J. Langdon, and R. Marriott, 'The Bedaux System of Labour Measurement', unpublished report of the Industrial Health Research Board, 1938, quoted in R. Marriott *Incentive Payment Systems* p. 100.

25. C. A. Oakley *Men at Work* (London 1945) p. 176.

26. R. Bendix *Work and Authority in Industry* (New York 1963 edn.) p. 338. Bendix uses the term 'indifferent neutralism' to describe 'all activities which manifest the worker's desire for independence from managerial control.'

27. Patricia Hall and H. W. Locke *Incentives and Contentment* (London 1938) pp. 109-111.

28. Seebohm Rowntree, foreword to Hall and Locke, op. cit., pp. xi-xii.

29. Asa Briggs *Social Thought and Social Action*, p. 245. Rowntree had met Mayo and was interested in his research.

30. Quoted in David Ashton, 'Elton Mayo and the Empirical Study of Social Groups' in *Management Thinkers*, p. 296. I have relied a lot on this account because of its virtue of assembling concisely some of the central quotations from the investigators themselves.

31. The words are those of Mayo's associates, Roethlisberger, Dickson

and Wright, from their *Management and the Worker*, quoted in Ashton, op. cit., p. 297.

32. Quoted in Ashton, op. cit., pp. 298-299.
33. Quoted in John Child *British Management Thought* (London 1969) p. 95.
34. See, for instance, Paul Blumberg *Industrial Democracy: the Sociology of Participation* (London 1968); and for a brief but powerful demolition job see Alan Fox *Man Mismanagement* (London 1974) esp. pp. 74ff.
35. R. Bendix *Work and Authority in Industry* p. 313. Bendix's analysis of Mayo's work (pp. 308-340) is well worth reading.
36. The words of one of the Mayo school, T. N. Whitehead, in his *Leadership in a Free Society* (1936), quoted in Bendix, op. cit., p. 317.
37. John Child *British Management Thought*, p. 93.
38. J. Child, op. cit., p. 94 and p. 96. The chief ideologues of British management thought, Urwick and Brech, were extremely keen on Mayo's work and devoted a whole volume of their three volume *The Making of Scientific Management* to the Hawthorne investigations.
39. J. Child, op. cit., p. 103.
40. See, for example, Transport and General Workers' Union, *The Union, Its Work and Problems*, Pt. IV (London 1948) pp. 46-49, and R. Marriott *Incentive Payment Systems* p. 51.
41. See R. M. Currie *Work Study* pp. 8-9, Anne G. Shaw *The Purpose and Practice of Motion Study* p. 9, M. Avery *Time Study, Incentives and Budgetary Control* (London 1966 imp.) p. 169.
42. Sir George Bailey, 'Preface' to Anne G. Shaw *The Purpose and Practice of Motion Study*, p. vii. Bailey recommended the book to all industrialists who wanted 'a means of increasing production per man hour.'
43. Anne G. Shaw, op. cit., p. 7.
44. Bailey, preface to Anne G. Shaw, op. cit., p. vii.

XII

STAKHANOVISM OR SOCIALISM?

Before the Russian Revolution, Lenin had denounced Taylorism as 'the enslavement of man by the machine.'[1] Only months after the October Revolution, however, he saw the matter differently, and in an article in *Pravda* on April 2nd, 1918, where he was urging in no uncertain terms the need for higher productivity of labour, he wrote :

'We should immediately introduce piecework and try it out in practice. We should try out every scientific and progressive suggestion of the Taylor System. . . . The Russian is a poor worker in comparison with the advanced nations, and this could not be otherwise under the regime of the Czar and other remnants of feudalism. To learn how to work—this problem the Soviet authority should present to the people in all its comprehensiveness. The last word of capitalism in this respect, the Taylor System, as well as all progressive measures of capitalism, combined the refined cruelty of bourgeois exploitation and a number of most valuable scientific attainments in the analysis of mechanical motions during work, in dismissing superfluous and useless motions, in determining the most correct methods of work, the best systems of accounting and control, etc. The Soviet Republic must adopt valuable and scientific technical advance in this field. The possibility of Socialism will be determined by our success in combining the Soviet rule and Soviet organisation of management with the latest progressive measures of capitalism. We must introduce in Russia the study and teaching of the new Taylor System and its systematic trial and adaptation.'[2]

Circumstances clearly alter cases. But, nevertheless, it was still surprising that such an 'about-turn' could have occurred. The theme embodied in Lenin's article was raised with great urgency

at a congress of labour commissars in May 1918—in the context
of severe unemployment, inflation, acute shortages of food and
most manufactured goods, and a sharp fall in production. The
economy of the infant Soviet Republic was, in short, on the brink
of collapse. One of the three main questions discussed at the
conference was that of labour productivity, and its allied topic
of labour discipline. The discussion on this topic was opened by
Schmidt, of the All Russian Central Council of Trade Unions,
who set the background by pointing out that there had been a
fall in the productivity of labour of about 80 per cent since
February 1917, mainly brought about, he argued, through malnutrition. He had no doubt that the job in hand was to improve
the economic position of the workers while at the same time
raising output and improving labour discipline. The huge difficulty as far as he was concerned was that enforced labour
discipline was precisely one of the things that the Russian workers
thought they had seen the last of as a result of the Revolution.
Schmidt was sensitive enough to realise that any new work
discipline would have to be very different from the older forms
of compulsion—he therefore called for the generation of self-
discipline through comradely persuasion.[3] Lenin's speech to the
conference, on the other hand, was less enamoured of this sort
of approach. Instead he stressed the danger of economic collapse—and called for iron discipline. Before long this would
obviously mean the enforcement of labour discipline from above.

At another conference which followed shortly afterwards the
two views clashed quite sharply. Lenin's powerful advocacy of
the Taylor system now entered the arena. This idea was strongly
supported from the floor by a speaker who asserted that Taylorism was a necessity for any industrial country no matter what
kind of government it had, and he justified its introduction by
saying, according to Margaret Dewar, that 'there was sabotage
not alone by the bourgeoisie, but also by the workers, who were
resisting the introduction of fixed output norms.[4] Schmidt again
said that he did not share this view, and argued that it was
pointless to adopt piecework or aspects of the Taylor system
only as they applied to the intensification of labour since other
factors on which higher productivity depended—like machinery,
work organisation, supplies of materials etc.—were so unsatis-

factory that high productivity was impossible. Schmidt's views did not prevail. The whole tendency of the development of Soviet industry in the period after these conferences was away from workers' control at the point of production and towards Lenin's idea of one-man management. The debate in the early part of 1921 as to the respective merits of Lenin's view, as against Trotsky's call for the militarisation of labour, and as against the view of the Workers' Opposition under Kollantai and Shlyapnikov for speedy trade union and workers' control of the economy, was particularly intense and soon resolved itself in favour of Lenin's view. Lenin denounced the Workers' Opposition as 'the syndicalist deviation which will kill the Party if it is not completely cured of it.'[5] George Hardy, then the General Secretary/Treasurer of the I.W.W. and one of the many in the syndicalist movement internationally who at this time were a long way down the road from syndicalism to communism, was in Russia at the time of the debate.[6] Reporting back to the 13th Convention of the I.W.W in Chicago in May 1921 Hardy, perhaps regretfully, told his fellow workers that his opinion was that 'Schlapnikoff's scheme would not work in Russia now, and although I would like to see his plan go through I feel the Russian workers are not ready to control industry.' Hardy also gave his comrades in the I.W.W. a glimpse of the existence of a small degree of workers' participation in management—one which was soon to be severely reduced. Of a visit to a rubber factory he reported that :

'We met the management committee first. They told us they were out for efficiency and would introduce the Taylor system to get efficient production. Then came a man from the workers' committee. He listened to the management committee telling me what they wanted, then I asked the members of the management committee : "Do you propose to move a worker from one machine to another, when you think he will do better by changing him?" and he said, "Exactly. That is efficiency". That if the man would do more work at another machine, they wanted to move him. The old man who had come from the workers' committee spoke up and said, "No, no, we don't want that". He said that if a worker wanted to stay in one place and work he could stay there regardless of the management committee. I then asked him if he thought that was the system. He thought it was absolutely right. The factory committee sometimes reasons differently from the management committee.'[7]

As the industrialisation of the Soviet Union proceeded through the 1920s and 1930s, workers' committees became less and less powerful as labour discipline was increasingly imposed from above. Enthusiasm for American management methods continued to be a feature of Soviet industrialisation even after Lenin's death. Stalin in the 1930s talked of the need to combine the 'Russian revolutionary sweep with American efficiency.' Management methods were not the only contribution the Americans made—American capital equipment and personnel also played a considerably more important part in the Soviet industrialisation than most people would imagine to have been possible. In the 1940s Stalin admitted that two thirds of all the industrial enterprises in the U.S.S.R. had been built with American aid or technical assistance.[8] We have already noted Lenin's considerable enthusiasm way back in 1918 for 'every scientific and progressive suggestion of the Taylor System.' This adoption of American management methods gained momentum throughout the period of intense industrialisation which began in the 1920s. In the early 1920s small groups in the Red Army, in the offices and in the factories began to agitate for the 'proper use and economy of time.' Before long these groups were organised into the 'Time League'. The desire to emulate America and the ideas and objectives of the 'Time League' emerge quite clearly from a leaflet it issued at the time :

'Time! System! Energy!
What do these words mean?
Time :
      Measure your time, control it!
      Do everything on time! exactly on the minute!
      Save time, make time count, work fast!
      Divide your time correctly, time for work and time for leisure!
      Utilize your leisure so as to work better afterwards!
System :
      Everything according to plan, according to system!

A note book for the system. Order in your place of
work !
Each must work according to plan.

Energy :

Pursue your goal stubbornly !
Try hard. Don't retreat after failures !
Always finish what you have started !
Communist Americanism, realism and vigilance !'[9]

When Walter Citrine visited Russia in 1935, one of the first
factories he went round was the Skorokhod Shoe Factory, about
which he commented that : 'It seemed to me that they were
using a similar system to Taylor and Munsterburg with modern
adaptations.'[10] The Five Year Plans, setting as they did production targets which needed fulfilling, were, to some extent,
dependent on the improvement of management techniques. On
top of this a plethora of moral incentives and material inducements were trained onto the workers. Strictly speaking the moral
incentives were applied first and constantly : the end, the industrialisation of the Soviet Union, being, it was hoped, sufficient
inducement to spur workers on to prodigious feats of production.
It is no surprise to learn that this sort of thing was often not
enough, and workers had to be shamed or intimidated into
improving their output. Citrine recorded that 'Everyone there
were exhortations to increase output. Everywhere there were
complaints against workers of slowness and inefficiency. . . . There
is no question whatever in my mind that there is coercion for
the backward workers.'[11] One of the techniques for stimulating
production was 'socialist competition'—whereby contests were
held between works departments, or factories to see which could
fulfil its production targets first. Shock workers (udarniki)
sometimes organised into brigades, were set up at work places
where, according to one account, they 'worked harder, wasted
less time and set an example to their more indolent or less interested fellow workers.' Many shock workers were no doubt
dedicated to their cause, but there were substantial rewards in it
for them. They were given extra rations, put to the top of
housing lists, got holidays, their children were the first to get
milk or school places, and so on.[12] Differentials between shock
workers and their less conscientious fellow workers did not only

take the form of fringe benefits and higher status, but they also existed most notably in wage and earnings differences. This came about largely because of the extremely widespread use of piece-work and related payment systems. Citrine observed that workers could earn without limit under piecework. But, in practice, the earnings were limited not by rate cutting but rather by moving the 'norm' up as workers improved their production. This had the effect, of course, as far as the slower workers were concerned of making it more difficult for them to secure decent earnings without speeding up. 'For the run of the mill proletarian, the *udarnik* was frequently someone who curried favour with the administration and forced down wages per unit of production by setting new standards of speed.'[13]

Out of the shock workers' campaign there grew the Stakhanov Movement. Alexei Stakhanov was, in August 1935, a 29-year-old miner in the Donetz coalfield who was looking for a way to increase his output. He decided that he could cut more coal in his six hour shift if he concentrated on cutting coal with his pneumatic drill and if he could enlist some of his workmates to prepare the face and remove the cut coal on an ongoing basis as he worked. Previously he had to service his own coal cutting, thus interrupting it frequently. After some difficulty in getting permission for his new scheme of work, he and his workmates were allowed to start, Stakhanov doing continuous coal cutting and his workmates continuously servicing him. Instead of producing the 6 or 7 tons that was usual in Donetz, Stakhanov at first cut the astonishing amount of 102 tons a shift, and later improved it still further.[14] Stakhanov was immediately given massive publicity by the Communist Party, and 'Stakhanovism', as it came to be called, was assiduously fostered in all other sectors of the economy. Before the end of 1935, the plenum of the party's central committee had decided to urge managers and planners to raise work norms upwards,[15] to give the Stakhanovites a new carrot to reach for. At about the same time the 'First All-Union Conference of Stakhanovites' was held in Moscow. Stakhanov himself, and his female counterpart Evdokia Vinogradova (a cotton weaver who eventually could look after 220 Northrup looms) and a number of other coalminers, weavers, forgehammer men, machine knitters and so on who had also brought about prodigious improvements in labour productivity, spoke to the conference.[16]

The first phase of Stakhanovism was accompanied by much hostility by ordinary workers towards Stakhanovists. Stakhanovists were sometimes so unpopular that they risked being beaten up or even killed by fellow workers.[17] A considerable campaign was mounted by the Soviet bureaucracy, according to Trotsky, against this resistance to Stakhanovism. Accusations of resistance, sabotage and murder were common.[18] The organ of the trade unions stated that 'The wrecking and breaking of machines is the favourite method of struggle against the Stakhanov movement.'[19] Trotsky suggested in 1937 that it was the proliferation of piecework and its multiplier effects through Soviet society that was at the root of much of this hostility. He suggested that :

'In the chase after the rouble, which had now acquired a very real meaning, the workers began to concern themselves more about their machines, and make a more careful use of their working time. The Stakhanov movement to a great degree comes down to an intensification of labour, and even to a lengthening of the working day. During the so-called "non-working" time, the Stakhanovists put their benches and tools in order and sort their raw material, the brigadiers instruct their brigades, etc. Of the seven-hour working day there thus remains nothing but the name.'[20]

The observations on the same question of a British management expert are worth noting here. G. H. Miles in an article called 'Incentives in Russian Industry' in *The Human Factor* in August 1932 noted that the second Soviet Five Year Plan had been heralded in the *Moscow News* of February 12th of that year with the headline, 'Second plan brings in classless society.' But, Miles pointed out, two of the main features of the plan would probably work against the achievement of classlessness. These two features were the spread of piecework and the growth of trading and its associated ending of rationing. He argued that : 'The worker, for instance, is clamouring for differentiation in wages according to type of labour performed and this is recognised by Stalin as essential to supply sufficient incentive for effective work.' And of the growth of trading he wrote : 'This trading is intended as an incentive to stimulate initiative on the part of state and collective bodies. But since it involves buying by bodies of workers with differentiated wage payments, it will inevitably tend to develop class differences as it had done in the capitalistic countries. It will be interesting to see in the next five years how Russia will meet the effect of such incentives, which would appear to cut right across the ultimate communistic aim that man shall receive his share in the product of labour not in proportion to his own labour but according to his needs.'

Writing at the end of the second Five Year Plan, Trotsky had no doubt that these conflicting tendencies had not been reconciled. In some brilliantly scathing passages in *The Revolution Betrayed* Trotsky noted just how completely the Soviet bureaucracy had made piecework its own property, and how this conveniently involved their forgetting Marx's words as to it being a system of payment most suited to capitalist methods of production. A 'new myth of a "socialist" piecework payment' had been created, and Trotsky finds chapter and verse to this effect from the pen of the president of the State Planning Commission, Mezhlauk. The latter also asserted that 'The fundamental principle of socialism is that each one works according to his abilities and receives payment accordance to the labour performed by him.' Trotsky cannot resist the temptation to comment that 'These gentlemen are certainly not diffident in manipulating theories!' He also puts under scrutiny Stalin's notion that the Stakhanov movement was a 'preparation of the conditions for the transition from socialism to communism'—for this transition in Trotsky's opinion had to be accompanied by 'more human forms of control than those invented by the exploitative genius of capital'. Piecework was manifestly incompatible with this aspiration, and he points out that in the Soviet Union 'the classic methods of exploitation, such as piecework payment, are applied in such naked and crude forms as would not be permitted even by reformist trade unions in bourgeois countries.'[21] This intensification of labour might conceivably be acceptable if the workers were truly working 'for themselves' and not at the whim of 'an autocratic bureaucracy'. Trotsky explains :

259

'In any case, state ownership of the means of production does not turn manure into gold, and does not surround with a halo of sanctity the sweatshop system, which wears out the greatest of all productive forces : man. As to the preparation of a "transition from socialism to communism" that will begin at the exactly opposite end—not with the introduction of piece-work payment, but with its abolition as a relic of barbarism.'[22]

The Stakhanovists soon came to constitute a workers' aristoc-racy, based on high earnings—and, in spite of the fact that, as Trotsky himself acknowledges, some of them were 'genuine enthusiasts of socialism',[23] it is highly likely that many of the Stakhanovists were prompted to their great efforts by the finan-cial rewards they personally could secure. Molotov admitted as much when he stated that 'The immediate impulse to high productivity on the part of the Stakhanovists is a simple interest in increasing their earnings.'[24] Some Stakhanovists earned 1,000 roubles a month, and others 12,000 a month, as against the many Russian workers who got less than 100 a month. Not only did the Soviet bureaucracy reward the labour aristocracy with higher wages, but Trotsky argued 'They literally shower privileges upon the Stakhanovists.' These privileges included better housing, medical and rest treatment, free teachers and doctors, free cinema tickets—and, in some places, free haircuts and shaving and a place at the front of the queue. These 'fringe' benefits meant that the average real earnings of Stakhanovists often were twenty or thirty times greater than those of the 'lower categories of workers.' He concluded : 'In scope of inequality of payment of labour, the Soviet Union has not only caught up to, but far surpassed the capitalist countries !'[25]

As late as 1950 Stakhanovism was still assiduously preached. One example of this can be found in the social realist novel *Kuznetsk Land* (1950) by A. Voloshin.[26] The novel is full of such things as 'Emulation Agreements' (i.e. Output competitions) with neighbouring mines (p. 3); 'High Output Days' ('No end of pretexts for the H.O.D.'s were invented. Either it was a "flying start" that was needed at the beginning of the month, or else a "spurt" and a "gathering in of loose ends" at the close of each ten-day span.' p. 5); we read about the latest issue of *Battle for Coal* with its item under the headline 'Productivity has dropped in District Two' (p. 39); and about Stakhanovite meetings ('The spacious vestibule of the club was crowded with hundreds of Stakhanovites whose faces betrayed both a festive elation and sober efficiency.' p. 32). One of the main themes of the novel is the conflict between the old fashioned mine manager, Drobot, who reached his output targets by sending all his surface workers—'even the cooks' (p. 5)—underground and the new young mining engineer, Rogov, who felt that this was all wrong and that the problems of the pit 'essentially resolved themselves into one thing—increase of output. The remedy lay in a smooth operating production cycle.' (p. 5) At the Stakhanovite meeting where the mine was being presented with a challenge banner for its output achievements, Drobot made a speech of thanks 'compounded of the proper proportions of pride for the joint achievement, promises not to rest on the laurels won and reproaches levelled at the laggards.' Rogov found this unduly complacent and initially made himself very unpopular with Drobot and the Stakhanovites when he predicted that unless things changed radically the mine would lose the challenge banner within three months. He told the Stakhanovites the facts:

> 'You know the mine has 320 coal hewers, but only 221 of them are fulfilling their output quotas. Only 73 have a Stakhanovite output showing.'[27]

This was just not good enough. Rogov's tactics paid off—for later in the novel we read that 98 per cent of all the workers were fulfilling their quotas and that 63 per cent were Stakhanovites. Later still, Rogov pioneered the installation of a combination coal cutting machine and loader capable of prodigious performance.[28]

Sidney and Beatrice Webb had long been enthusiastic for 'scientific management' methods. Sidney had written enthusiastically about it in his little book *The Works Manager Today* back in 1918, and Beatrice (after some hesitations about it after reading Taylor's *Principles of Scientific Management* way back in 1911) had been extremely impressed by what Lenin's ambassador in London, Krasin, had told the Fabian Summer School in 1920 about the Soviet Union's plans to industrialise. She had written in her diary that:

'Every expedient of modern industrialism designed to increase the output of the individual worker, whether new mechanical inventions, new forms of power, new methods of remuneration, piece work, premium bonus, the concentration of business in the best equipped factories, were to be introduced into the new plan.'[29]

The Webbs were, therefore, entirely happy about the drive for increased production and for higher productivity of labour in the Soviet Union in the late 1930s. In their account of Stakhanovism there is scarcely a word of criticism, qualification or hesitation. What is more they are sure that Stakhanovism represented a step forward from Taylorism—a sort of Taylorism with workers' control—and that the two phenomena were not, as was so often said, the same or even a similar thing. They held that the Stakhanov Movement was

'the obverse of the American system of "scientific management" as devised by Taylor. He [Taylor] went on the plan of emptying out of the workman's job every factor of initiative, thought or mental effort, so as to get from the labourer almost exclusively physical effort, and so to arrange that physical effort, by motion-study and prescribed rest pauses in such a way as to increase its productivity to the utmost.[30]

That, doubtless, was so. They claim, however, that Stakhanovites in Russia 'devised and introduced' the system themselves, and that the workers re-arranged their own jobs, using their own mental and physical skills. They add, incredibly, that workers were not driven to greater production by having to keep pace with constantly speeded-up machinery, but instead that:

'The pace for each member of the team was set, not by any wheel that the management turned, but by the workers' team itself, which determined its own rate of working, and set its own rest pauses. Nor was it a case of the leading operator forcing greater speed on subordinate attendants.'

To compound their naivety they also claim that 'Worker after worker testified that he or she did not thereby suffer either increased physical exertion or mental strain.' Even their strong assurance ('It need hardly be said') that the piece rates weren't cut—a statement which bears a good deal more credibility than some of their earlier ones—was rather disingenuous; some piece rates *were* cut, and in 1936 there was a very sharp rise in work norms : by 30–40 per cent in engineering, by 51 per cent in electricity generation, by 26 per cent in coal mining, and so on. Work norms were geared up again, notably in 1938 and in 1939. Since Stakhanovism was seen as a blanket campaign for all Russian industry, there was no doubt that in situations where extra productivity was hard to get—i.e. where the design of jobs was good and where the most modern equipment was already installed—it became increasingly difficult for workers to reach the desired targets without subjecting themselves to considerable speed-up and intensification of labour.[31] There is little doubt that the essential function of Stakhanovism was, to use the words of Herbert Marcuse, the 'streamlining of alienated labour.'[32]

How much has changed? Twenty-five years after *Kuznetsk Land* was published things, in what are now the Comecon countries, seem little different. Exhortation, so called 'emulation agreements' and the like still seem common. Workers are still required merely to respond to managerial initiatives and to abate the appetites of the plans and output requirements of the command economy. There is little or no workers' control over the plan, either in terms of its grand design, or even in terms of the achievement of specific parts of it. The power of moral incentives seems to be exceptionally weak as is clear from the fact that in the Comecon countries the vast majority of industrial workers are on piece-work. Russia and the Eastern European countries are classified, along with the Scandinavian countries, as being heavy users of incentives—with between 50 and 70 per cent of workers on incentives—as against light users such as the United States with about 30 per cent.[33] So the trend that Trotsky complained of in the 1930s has not been reversed, and nor has the other tendency of which he complained—the accompaniment of privileges with high piecework earnings for certain favoured groups of workers. This combination of factors leading to increased inequalities now glories under the name, in the Polish coal industry at least, of 'social incentives'. Polish mineworkers are the best rewarded workers in that country, with faceworkers earning 60 per cent more than the industrial average. A recent delegation from the British coal industry to Poland observed that 'On top of their high pay, miners have a host of fringe benefits—better standards of housing at low rents, subsidised food, extra holidays with cheap or possibly free accommodation, a free uniform for ceremonial occasions, and free working clothes laundered without charge. Retirement age for a man who has worked a minimum of 25 years underground is 55.' These social incentives were not given away, and nor were they merely socially just rewards for the arduous and dangerous nature of the work; essentially they were rewards for high output, or, as First Secretary Gierek put it, 'The miners can have more money for more output.'[34] An exceptionally interesting document on piecework in another East European country, Hungary, in the early 1970s has recently been published in the West.[35] The author, Miklos Haraszti, had worked in the Red Star factory and had written a book about his experience. Haraszti was put on trial in October 1973 on the ground that his book was 'liable to provoke hatred of the State.' At his trial he stated : 'I certainly criticised piecework, but this is not a basic institution of socialism, it is not even a socialist institution at all, it is a capitalist institution.' He went on to say that 'The principal aim of socialist strategy in this area is to eliminate wages tied to performance.'[36] This, indeed, was rank heresy and subversion. In his book, Haraszti recalls some of the things which started off his interest in piecework. He recalls that in one newspaper : 'a Hungarian expert in "Management science" claimed that payment by results was the most perfect form of socialist remuneration, since it embodied the principle : "from each according to his abilities, to each according to his work." ' (!) This, of course, is a gross deformation of the traditional socialist proposition which ends with the word *needs*. Haraszti points out the irony in this revised version by noting that he had also read in another issue of the same newspaper a story of an old and prominent Communist who 'recalled in glowing terms a comrade who, before the war, had organised workers' demonstrations against the Bedaux system, the "scientific" method of payment by results of those days.'[37] This, of course, is exactly the same sort of double standard that we have seen from the British Communist Party—which in the 1930s was in the forefront of the struggle against the Bedaux system and yet, during the Second World War, became ardently enthusiastic for it and for other related aspects of 'management science.'

None of this should lead people to draw the conclusion that the nature of work and of the labour process is necessarily exploitative under socialism as well as under capitalism—or that in this respect there is a necessary 'convergence' between the nature of work in all conceivable advanced economies, on account of the fact that the nature of the technology appropriate to such economies makes it inevitable. The only thing that has been shown is that in the Soviet Union and East Europe the labour process is not fundamentally different from that in the capitalist countries. State ownership of the means of production has not, to borrow Trotsky's phrase, 'turned manure into gold.' Because the accumulation of capital was given the first priority in the Soviet Union this has meant, as one writer has argued, that it 'repeated the history of capitalism, at least as regards the relationship of men and women to their work. . . . The Soviets consciously and deliberately embraced the capitalist mode of production.'[38] The same writer goes on to suggest that the consequence of this means that it would take just as great an effort to transform work in the Soviet bloc as it would in the Western capitalist countries. This situation has its origins, not in any sort of technological determinism affecting all advanced industrialised countries, but in the marked absence of any determined attempt in the period of the industrialisation of the Soviet Union to do anything other than adopt capitalist ways of organising work. Harry Braverman puts it like this:

'Whatever view one takes of Soviet industrialization, one cannot conscientiously interpret its history, even in its earliest and most revolutionary period, as an attempt to organize labour processes in a way fundamentally different from those of capitalism.'[39]

Braverman, after noting Lenin's views on Taylorism, points out that Taylorism ceased to be a purely temporary expedient, but rather became a permanent and central feature of the Soviet organisation of work. The only thing that was temporary about Taylorism in the Soviet Union was the view that it was a temporary, short term measure which was to be replaced with a socialist alternative as soon as possible. He suggests that :

'In practice, Soviet industrialisation imitated the capitalist model; and as industrialisation advanced the structure lost its provisional character and the Soviet Union settled down to an organisation of labour differing only in details from that of the capitalist countries, so that the Soviet working population bears all the stigmata of the Western working classes.'[40]

NOTES

1. Quoted in M. Brinton *The Bolsheviks and Workers' Control 1917-1921* (London 1970) p. 40.
2. This was quoted with great enthusiasm by Taylor's official biographer, F. B. Copley in his *Frederick Winslow Taylor: Father of Scientific Management* (New York 1923) p. ii. Tomsky in an article called 'Labour Discipline and Piece work' written at about the same time was saying virtually the same thing: see M. Dewar *Labour Policy in the U.S.S.R.* 1917-1928 (London 1956) p. 39, footnote.
3. M. Dewar, *Labour Policy in the U.S.S.R.* 1917-1928 pp. 37-38.
4. M. Dewar, op. cit., p. 39.
5. Quoted in M. Brinton *The Bolsheviks and Workers Control* p. 76.
6. On Hardy see his autobiography *Those Stormy Years* (London 1956), and on the transition of many syndicalists to communism in this period see G. Brown 'Tom Mann and Jack Tanner and International Revolutionary Syndicalism, 1910-1922', abstract in *Bulletin of the Society for the Study of Labour History*, No. 27. Autumn 1973, pp. 19-21.
7. Report of George Hardy in *Proceedings of the 13th Convention of the I.W.W., 1921*, p. 66. The previous statement of Hardy's comes from the same source, p. 67.
8. W. H. G. Armytage, *The Rise of the Technocrats: a Social History* (London 1965) p. 223.
9. From Franziska Baumgarten, *Arbeitswissenschaft und Psychotechnik in Russland* (Munich 1924) pp. 111-112, quoted in Bendix, *Work and Authority*, pp. 208-209.
10. W. Citrine *I Search for Truth in Russia* (London 1938 Popular Edn.) p. 37.
11. W. Citrine, op. cit., p. 330.
12. Eugene Lyons *Assignment in Utopia* (London 1938 edn.) p. 208.
13. Eugene Lyons, op. cit., p. 209.
14. Sidney and Beatrice Webb *Soviet Communism: A New Civilization* (2nd edn. London 1937) pp. 1165-1166. Their account of the Stakhanov movement is incredibly enthusiastic.

15. Alec Nove *An Economic History of the U.S.S.R.* (Pelican edn. 1972) pp. 233-234, in mining for example by 26 per cent.
16. Sidney and Beatrice Webb, op. cit., p. 1167. The Webbs accept without question the claims for increases in output under Stakhanovism. For a more sceptical contemporary account see Citrine's *I Search for Truth in Russia* (pp. 401-404). Nove seems to have no doubt, however, that whatever the precise order of the increases in output that Stakhanovism was one of the reasons for the improvement in Soviet productivity in the late 1930s: Nove, op. cit., pp. 232-233.
17. J. P. Nettl *The Soviet Achievement* (London 1967) p. 129, and A. Nove op. cit., p. 233. W. Citrine, op. cit., p. 404 says that 'There have been reports in the Soviet Press of Stakhanovites being murdered by fellow-workers.'
18. Leon Trotsky *The Revolution Betrayed: What is the Soviet Union and Where is it going?* (first published 1937, New York 1974 imp.) p. 84.
19. Trotsky, op. cit., pp. 127-128.
20. Trotsky, op. cit., p. 80.
21. Trotsky, op. cit., p. 82.
22. Ibid., pp. 82-83.
23. Ibid., pp. 80-81 and p. 126 for similar remarks.
24. Quoted in ibid., p. 125.
25. Ibid., p. 125.
26. Published in *Soviet Literature*, 7. (Moscow 1950)
27. *Kuznetsk Land* p. 36.
28. Ibid., pp. 108 and 143.
29. Beatrice Webb, quoted in W. H. G. Armytage *The Rise of the Technocrats* p. 221. Armytage's chapter 14, 'Amerikanski Tempo', is a good account of the American influence on Soviet industrialisation.
30. Sidney and Beatrice Webb *Soviet Communism* p. 1168.
31. See Alec Nove *An Economic History of the U.S.S.R.* p. 233.
32. Herbert Marcuse *Soviet Marxism: A Critical Analysis* (Pelican 1971 edn.) p. 194, footnote.
33. Royal Commission of Trade Unions and Employers' Association, Research Paper 11, 'Two Studies in Industrial Relations': 2. 'Changing Wage Payment Systems' by Robert B. McKersie (London 1968) p. 35.
34. 'Lessons for Us from Poland's Coal Expansion' in *Management News*, published by the National Coal Board for their management staff, Vol. 11. No. 15, February 1976.
35. Miklos Haraszti *Stücklohn* (Berlin 1975), a section of it is translated by Stuart Hood in *New Left Review*, No. 91. May-June 1975, under the title 'I Have Heard the Iron Cry'.
36. Information from 'Introduction to Miklos Haraszti' in *New Left Review*, 91, pp. 5-8.
37. Haraszti 'I Have Heard the Iron Cry' in *New Left Review*, 91, p. 9.
38. Stephen A. Marglin, quoted in Harry Braverman *Labor and Monopoly Capital: the Degradation of Work in the Twentieth Century* (New York 1974) pp. 22-23.
39. Braverman, op. cit., p. 22.
40. Ibid., p. 12.

Part Six

1939–1976

XIII

The Second World War

During the Second World War British industry faced broadly similar problems to those it had faced in 1914–1918. In the first stages of the war it sought similar solutions to those adopted in the earlier crisis. Later on in the war one new development to solve the output problem, Joint Production Committees, came to prominence—and it is to these that most of the later parts of this chapter are devoted. But in the early phases of the war it was the old solutions that were being sought to the problem. According to the historians of scientific management in Britain :

> 'British industry faced in May and June 1940 a task of Herculean magnitude—to double, treble, quadruple, output of all warlike stores in the shortest possible time, and then over a long period to keep up the new high level unbroken and uninterrupted.'

Initially the most usual attempt at trying to solve this problem involved the lengthening of the working day—a policy which had been adopted in the First World War, but which then had soon been rejected because it did not take into account the problem of fatigue. The 'lessons of the last war' were forgotten and had to be rediscovered through trial and error.[1] The Mass-Observation study *People in Production* of 1942 commented that it had been proved 'over and over again that the extension of the usual hours of work does not for any length of time give a proportional increase of output. On the contrary, it causes the rate of output to decline with increasing rapidity. . . . Yet during the greater part of 1940, these lessons, mainly learned in the last war and statistically proven, were ignored. In many factories they are ignored now.'[2] Similarly in the early stages of the war immense reliance was put on exhortation—not least in the aircraft industry, the key industry in the war effort. Under Beaverbrook, the Ministry of Aircraft Production (until May 1941) depended heavily on a policy of *ad hoc* exhortation in an attempt to increase the output of aircraft. Beaverbrook, indeed, was responsible for the first great intervention in the field of production propaganda, often going straight to the workers themselves rather than through trade union officials or through managements. The official historian of the Munitions Industries records that : 'By radio, telegrams, posters, speeches and through the newspapers the Minister himself and specially appointed assistants appealed to and thanked the workers for extra efforts.'[3] These spectacular appeals, though they often had an immediate impact, tended, however, to ignore longer term needs for steady progress—something, in fact, which was often impeded by the short term gains. Mass-Observation commented of Beaverbrook's tenure of office both at the M.A.P. and later at the Ministry of Production that the weakness of this sort of approach by the 'Psychological Leader of Industry' was that it had been 'overwhelmingly *ad hoc*' and that 'Production is perhaps the least suitable subject for *ad hoc* propaganda, which is nearly always an inefficient way of developing a frame of mind valuable to *long-term* effort.'[4] The dramatic use of exhortation, although constantly used throughout the war, had built-in defects. The regular repetition of the same message, even in different words, of the sheer urgency of more production, inevitably wore a bit thin.

When Stafford Cripps took over as Minister of Aircraft Production in mid-1941 a new approach began to emerge. Efficient management was the core of the new strategy, and new techniques such as Motion Study replaced mere exhortation. Cripps quickly established a Production Efficiency Board in his Ministry, enlisting the services of such people as Miss Anne Shaw, the disciple of the Gilbreths, who, as we saw, had pioneered the introduction of Motion Study in the factories of Metropolitan Vickers in the 1930s. Under her guidance vast numbers of Motion Study experts were trained and subsequently deployed throughout the war industries.[5] The factories brought under the control of M.A.P. were veritable hot-beds of applied industrial psychology, of 'human factor' style management. One instance of this is afforded by the activities of C. A. Oakley, who was before and after the war a lecturer in Industrial Psychology at Glasgow University, Scottish Divisional Director of the National Institute of Industrial Psychology and chairman of a 'well-known Scottish foodstuffs canning company.' During the war Oakley was metamorphosed into Regional Controller for Scotland of M.A.P. In this post he was, in his own words,

'particularly concerned with getting as much production as possible out of five hundred factories while ensuring that the quality of their workmanship did not fall off materially.'[6]

In 1945 Oakley stated that 'Since 1939 really remarkable developments have been made in applying psychological ideas and methods in industry.' Hundreds of thousands of psychological tests had been given to people in the armed forces—but even more remarkable were the developments on the home front : 'Rest pauses', 'music while you work', 'rhythm at work' and the like all spread apace.[7] Welfare work, this time round under the label of 'personnel management', spread considerably. The Production Efficiency Board of M.A.P. saw to it that personnel managers were trained for the aircraft factories, and it forced the aircraft industry (an industry 'without a welfare or personnel management tradition'[8]) to appoint them. The reluctance of the aircraft industry to accept them often meant that little more than lip service was done to personnel management, and even where they were accepted with enthusiasm it seems that they brought about no significant decreases in absenteeism or in labour turnover—the 'accepted tests of good personnel management'.[9] Many workers found personnel management as intrusive as welfare work had been in the First World War. One worker, who deliberately left her employment in a Midlands factory 'famous for its Welfare', was presumably not alone when she complained that 'You couldn't call your soul your own, they *welfared you to death*.'[10]

It could be said, indeed, with a fair degree of accuracy that Stafford Cripps and the Ministry of Aircraft Production were to the Second World War what Lloyd George and the Ministry of Munitions had been to the First World War. Lloyd George, as we have seen, was peculiarly troubled by shop stewards in the munitions industries. Cripps had to deal with their less intransigent successors in the aircraft industry. The workers in the aircraft factories were, in fact, the key workers in the war effort. Prior to Cripps' appointment as Minister of Aircraft Production in the summer of 1941 there were some serious worries that the shop stewards of the Second World War would prove as troublesome to the then Government as the shop stewards of the First World War had been to Lloyd George and his colleagues. These worries were rooted not so much in any belief in the original sin of shop stewards but rather in the fact that the Communist Party had from the mid-1930s made a good deal of headway in the aircraft industry and in factories which were to switch to war production on the outbreak of war.[11] It had been the Communists, as we have seen, who had been in the thick of the fight against the Bedaux system, and generally active fighting the good fight against the forces of capital. The outbreak of war did nothing to slacken that fight. The fact was, that after some initial uncertainty (occasioning the resignation of Harry Pollitt as General Secretary of the Communist Party), the C.P. finally adopted the Communist International's line that the War was an Imperialist war, as the first world war had been. Consequently opposition to the war—on the party platforms, in the press and in the workshops and factories—was called for. By the end of 1940 an organisation had been created to convey and spread this message. This was the People's Convention, a 'Broad Left' movement, which urged, in sum, that the War was 'a rich man's war, and that the workers, the majority of the people, had no real interest in it.'[12] The propagation of such views led, in January 1941, to the banning of *The Daily Worker*, which in late 1940 its editor William Rust said had become 'the organising centre of working-class opposition to the war-spreaders and the enemies of the Soviet Union.'[13] The C.P. began to operate to some extent clandestinely, still opposing the war effort. In the workshops and factories a National Shop Stewards' Movement, dominated by C.P. members, was beginning to emerge.[14] The opposition to the war effort of this body can be seen by the fact that, at a National Shop Stewards' Conference in Birmingham in April 1940, a resolution was passed which affirmed the stewards' determination to continue the fight 'to defend and improve our wage-rates and working conditions built up through long years of trade union effort and sacrifice.' This involved, as before, opposing the employers, who, it was argued, were 'taking full advantage of the war, and the National Government propaganda for sacrifice, [and who] are intensifying their normal peacetime attacks upon our conditions and standards.' And in a key section of the resolution—which admirably epitomises Communist Party industrial policy and practice up until the middle of 1941—it was stated that:

'Taking our stand on the basis of working-class solidarity in wartime no less than in peacetime we proclaim our determination to resist all such attacks [from employers and Government] and to fight unreservedly for the interests of the working class in every field.'[15]

The Shop Stewards' Movement flourished throughout 1940 round a programme of that sort. There was a widely held belief amongst the shop stewards that the Government and the employers were alarmed at the strength of the stewards and that (in Wal Hannington's words):

'in an effort to smash the organised power of the workers at the point of production, they have embarked upon a campaign involving the victimisation of militant shop stewards and the replacing of factory committees by class collaboration "factory councils".'[16]

The Ministry of Labour was, indeed, beginning to sponsor the formation of factory councils and committees which—in good Elton Mayo fashion we may say—were intended to increase production by creating co-operative relationships between workers and management. These relationships were most unwelcome to the shop stewards movement: Hannington in February 1941, for instance, suggested that engineering workers would 'bitterly resist' the introduction of factory councils and that they would 'defend their right to independent trade-union shop stewards.'

Six months after these words were written the point of view of the shop stewards' movement on this question had changed totally. At a National Shop Stewards Conference held in London on October 19th, 1941, Walter Swanson, the convenor of Shop stewards at Napiers aircraft factory, told the audience that :

'We have now reached a position where every one of us has to approach the problem of production from a new angle, and we believe we will get the best results from our conference, not merely by discussing the waste, mismanagement and inefficiency of present methods of control and direction of production, but what we can do and will do to increase production from our side, and in so doing help to effect changes which will go right through industry even to the top. We cannot over-emphasise that once the political conviction of the workers has been won, they will display an initiative, drive and energy to increase production never witnessed in this country before.'[17]

Swanson was not howled down. On the contrary this statement and his further advocacy of the acceptance of dilution, and the relaxation of demarcation rules were thoroughly approved of by the 1,200 delegates, who proceeded to spend the next five and a half hours discussing ways of increasing production. Douglas Hyde, a young Communist journalist reporting the conference for *World News and Views* (the successor to the Comintern's *Inpreccor*), commented that 'Over and above everything was the need for co-operation through production committees by means of which, the discussion went to show, considerable progress has already been made.'

The extent of the progress already made was revealed in the reports from delegates from factories all over the country. One of the local reports was that made by Thomas Stewart of Clydebank who told how shop stewards in the shipyards there had already pushed forward with the new policy. The stewards 'were taking the lead in suggesting constantly new ways and means of saving time, and saving labour—regardless of traditionalism.' (A thirty per cent. increase in work done was his estimate of what could be achieved by some of the changes now being advocated in regard to riveting.) 'Stewart also reported that the stewards had got for the workers 'a really fine new canteen' seating over 1,000 and 'really first class heating arrangements in the shops.' Trevor Robinson of Sheffield reported in similar vein—efforts by

Joint Production Committees in Sheffield had already led to a 10 per cent increase in the production of certain guns in the previous ten days. In other places the burgeoning new spirit was leading to the formation of J.P.Cs, as this report from a de Havillands aircraft factory makes clear :

'We found a tradition of complete lack of interest. Nobody, either workers or management, seemed to be aware of what was being made in the works, namely airplanes, or to know or care what they were going to be used for. Now, as a result of the new drive, they both know and care. A Joint Production Meeting has been arranged. All questions affecting production are being taken up.'

There were, however, a few voices of dissent. Some people had obviously not yet 'adjusted' to the new situation. The *Workers' News*, a paper produced by the staff of the still banned *Daily Worker* (it did not resume publication until September 1942) commented of them, parenthetically, as follows :

'(Incidentally, the Conference made pretty short work of those few who tried to put forward the fantastic and suicidal suggestion that there is "no use" trying to produce arms for the Soviet fighters, arms for ourselves, arms for all the enemies of Fascism, unless and until the whole existing social system has been overthrown in Britain.)'[18]

Some of these dissident voices as we shall see were not, however, so easily silenced.

The explanation for the dramatic change of opinion in the shop stewards' movement from opposition to the war effort to powerful support for it is to be found in the fact that, for the Communist Party and its supporters, the war had been transformed in June 1941 from being an Imperialist War to being a war against Fascism. The Hitler-Stalin pact had been rudely shattered by the Nazi invasion of the Soviet Union in June 1941. The speed of the C.P.G.B.'s reaction to this can be seen from a small incident concerning Bob Cooney, former C.P.G.B. organiser in Aberdeen, who before the invasion of the Soviet Union had been standing as C.P.G.B. candidate in the Greenock by-election on an anti-war platform, and who after the invasion quickly withdrew his candidacy. At a public meeting in Greenock on July 6th Cooney issued the following statement to explain his action :

'In the struggle against the Nazi drive for world dominion, there must be the most resolute unity. There is no time for sectional strategy, for short-sighted chatter of a "breathing-space" being afforded this or that section of the people. . . . We require a mobilisation of the British people as enthusiastic, as disciplined and as resolute as that which is enabling the Soviet people to put up so magnificent a resistance. An end must be made to waste, mismanagement and corruption in industry. Every obstacle to the production of munitions must be removed, and those munitions must be used boldly and at once.'

The Communist Party, the statement continued, 'cannot but recognise that to continue in the by-election would lead to misunderstanding, which would delay the organisation of the mighty united effort which we wish to obtain.'[19] Harry Pollitt was quickly welcomed back into the fold as General Secretary of the C.P.; the People's Convention was wound down; and, cynics and anarchists had it, His Majesty's Communist Party came into being. Factory councils were no longer the subject of hostility, but rather now were enthusiastically supported and canvassed for by the C.P.G.B., being regarded now as indispensable vehicles for the increased production of aircraft and other war material. Factory councils, or to use the contemporary term, Joint Production Committees, were considered to be of key importance in the war effort. The Shop Stewards' movement could not have been more keen in agitating for their creation. Frequently where they were established a dramatic improvement came about in worker-management relations and considerable gains were made in production. As early as December 1941 workers at a Hertfordshire aircraft factory reported of the changes that had recently come about as follows :

'Relationship with management : since the attack upon the Soviet Union and signing of the Anglo-Soviet Pact, a complete change has taken place. Stewards have been given greater scope, and the management, after being approached, offered to meet six stewards regularly to discuss production.'[20]

The views of the Communist shop stewards and the Minister of Aircraft Production coincided to a remarkable degree. Cripps gave every encouragement to the formation and successful operation of J.P.Cs., and had by the autumn of 1943 visited the meetings of about 200 of them.[21] He was later to hold that J.P.Cs. had made 'a significant contribution to the war effort.'[22] By the end of 1943 about 4,500 of them existed in engineering and allied establishments with over 150 employees.[23] What, though, were the J.P.Cs. like? The Agreement of 1942 between the Engineering Employers and the Engineering unions which led to the establishment of them stated that their functions were to be : 'to consult and advise on matters relating to production and increased efficiency for this purpose, in order that maximum output may be obtained from the factory.'[24] Many managements, it should be noted, were extremely reluctant to establish J.P.Cs and it was only a result of considerable cajoling by the Government (this cajoling being in turn largely a product of trade union pressure) that so many of them came into being. Managerial caution expressed itself further through the insistence on two conditions for J.P.Cs. : first, that there should be no encroachment on managerial 'rights' and second, that there should be no discussion of topics usually regarded to be the subject of negotiation.[25] The Committees, then, did not come into existence as a deliberate stratagem by employers to incorporate and emasculate shop floor trade unionism. Having said this however, there is little doubt that the effect of J.P.Cs. once established often involved a move in this direction, and as one writer put it in 1948 that J.P.Cs. rested on 'participation of a limited nature, with the influence remaining in the hands of imposed management, the managed groups having the power to criticise and make suggestions in certain fields.'[26] But by no means all J.P.Cs. brought about a weakening of shop floor unionism and its replacement by a facade of participation. As Ken Coates and Tony Topham point out the effect of the Committees was an ambiguous one— for alongside the keeping of workers' aspirations 'within channels which did not fundamentally challenge management prerogatives', the establishment of J.P.Cs. also often brought about the considerable extension of shop steward representation.[27] It was often the case that in factories where trade unionism had been weak or non-existent before the war that the J.P.C. was 'the first body to secure a fair degree of collective negotiation and bargaining with the management. In such factories the proportion of shop stewards elected as workers' representatives would be high.'[28]

On the other hand, it is frequently possible to observe the incorporating and emasculating tendencies of J.P.Cs. For instance, one small employer, a firm advocate of joint consultation, in a publication in October 1943 called *Methods of Stimulating Interest in Production*, said of the committee in his factory that 'We do not even discuss things more than we can possibly help, because they contain a hint of antagonised viewpoints which is unpleasant.'[29] In some cases the Committees seem to have served primarily as devices to get workers' representatives to make vigorous criticism of absenteeism on the part of their fellow workers. The Pit Production Committees in the coal industry were notorious for this.[30] In 1942 the A.E.U. in a survey of the work of 550 J.P.Cs. complained that the 'bad' J.P.C. was :

'an Absenteeism Court, an occasion for management to harangue the workers' representatives on their obligations and duties, a secret cabal where mysteries are never reported outside the committee room, a conspiracy between foremen and managements to speed up production without interference from below, or a futile and highly infrequent gathering of workers' and management representatives at which suggestions are made and grievances aired merely to be ignored, while any actual increases in production represent an immediate cutting of rates and worsening of conditions for the workers.'[31]

But, just as often, if not more often, the tables could be turned, and participation on the Committees could involve the encroachment by workers into the managerial prerogatives, and the revelation and challenging of managerial inefficiency. The best J.P.Cs. acted in the spirit of the C.P.G.B.'s publication of March 1942 called *An Urgent Memorandum on Production* in which it was stated that :

'the traditional attitude of managements to allowing workers to "encroach on the management's preserve" needs to be broken down, in order to make possible the full collaboration and rapid development and improvement of technical methods, as well as incentive to greater output, which can be achieved by these means.'[32]

The A.E.U. survey in the autumn of 1942 suggested that about 1 J.P.C. in 5 was going beyond the formal terms of the agreement and was discussing such things as piece rates and output bonuses,[33] and many more than this number trespassed into the field of welfare matters. Sixty per cent of J.P.Cs. studied by the survey regularly included welfare matters on their agendas and another 12 per cent had Welfare Sub-committees. The report quoted with approval from one report to a welfare sub-committee :

'When or how welfare can be divorced from production questions I cannot see. Whether it be lack of ouput, absence from work, scrap work or anything else, welfare in shape of ventilation, sickness, unsuitability of labour, all enter into it.'[34]

In some cases the committees aroused 'real interest and enthusiasm' among workers and this seems to have been the case especially where there was 'a prospect of the workers' representatives attacking the management.'[35] The official historian of the munitions industries writes that :

'Everyone loves a fight : when there were prospects of the workers' representatives condemning the management roundly, but not necessarily soundly, interest and support on the workers' side ran high. With the growth of co-operation and the absence of fireworks, interest sometimes declined and counter criticism arose that the representatives had "sold out to the management".'[36]

Bert Williams of Birmingham recalled in 1953 that the recommendation of the Midland Regional Board of the Ministry of Production for the setting up of J.P.Cs. 'went right to the heart of "managerial functions" and threatened for the employers their right under Clause 1 of the 1922 agreement to the effect that the employers have the right to manage their own establishments.' He recalled that in many factories workers went ahead with arrangements for Committees without waiting for formal managerial agreement, and that fierce struggles ensued when employers tried to restrict the functions of them, in such a way as to head off any challenge to management's 'right to manage'. In Rovers' this attempt took the shape of the company's trying merely to turn the existing company dominated Works Councils into Joint Production Committees. The Shop Stewards' Committee vigorously and successfully combated this, and saw to it that a genuine J.P.C., dominated on the workers' side by the stewards, was established. Alongside this a system of independent shop steward activity and plant level wage militancy flourished.[87] In other factories, however, the changed situation after the Nazi invasion of the Soviet Union quite unambiguously led to the cessation of militant action on the part of C.P. shop stewards. This process has been documented in some detail for the Royal Ordnance Factory at Dalmuir—where, amongst other things, C.P. stewards acquiesced in an agreement which lost the workers their Saturday rest day, agreed to redundancies, and sabotaged growing combine activity with stewards from R.O.Fs. throughout Britain. According to the account of these developments, produced by the Anarchist Federation of Glasgow, 'the C.P. dream had come true, they were recognised consultants of the engineering management.'[88]

The source of that statement means that it is inevitably biased against the Communist Party. But there is, nevertheless, more than a grain of truth in it. In its almost obsessional enthusiasm for more production the Communist Party did sometimes take up postures which led it to advocate the acceptance in the factories of management methods which had previously been anathema to it in the 1920s and 1930s. An example of this can be found in the little book, *War in the Workshops*, which appeared in 1942. The book was written by the *Daily Worker* columnist Jack Owen. It is interesting to note, first of all, that in the early summer of 1920, in the wake of an overwhelming vote by A.S.E. members against the employers' proposals for payment by results, the very same Jack Owen (then the President of the London District Committee of the A.S.E.) had written a pamphlet, *To Engineers and Other Wage Slaves*, in which he

made his hostility to payment by results and other manifestations
of 'scientific management' crystal clear. But, 22 years later, Owen
had changed his mind. Basically *War in the Workshops* (with
its chapters headed 'Realising our Responsibility', and 'The Path
to Victory', and chapters in favour of 'Payment by Results',
'The Principles of Scientific Management', and 'Joint Production
Committees') was a manual for shop stewards and production
committees devoted to ways of stimulating production and creating ways in which workers could 'join a crusade' to that end.
That this was something new, and against the grain of generations of workshop struggles, is clear from Owen's wordy attempt
to reconcile the class struggle with the production drive. He
begins by stating that there had always been a struggle between
the boss and the trade unionist—'the one to lengthen the working
day the other to shorten it. This struggle has, of course, not
always shown itself in an open fashion. The boss, by the introduction of labour-saving devices, seeks to intensify the speed at
which labour produces, which is the equivalent of a lengthened
working day, and the worker resists with all his power, through
the medium of "ca'canny" and by opposing the introduction of
"cheap" labour and the manning of new types of machines by
the semi-skilled.' So far, so good. Next followed the first hesitation to the customary position :

> 'Lest some readers think this statement that the workers
> practise "ca'canny" is a shameless admission, they should
> understand, that, in relation to the methods operating under
> the capitalist system, it is a perfectly legitimate proceeding.'

The consequence of the realities of this daily struggle was that
the skilled worker had always 'kept a little up his sleeve.' 'But,'
Owen stressed, 'in the face of the danger threatening us, all this
manoeuvring and bargaining must go by the board.'[39] This point
that old workshop practices were legitimate in ordinary times,
but were not for the duration of the war, was made time after
time. For example, in normal circumstances, in a well organised
shop 'overbooking' (booking in all jobs finished even if this
produced more than the agreed rate of bonus in the shop thus
making rate-cutting a possibility) was 'a workshop crime'. Not
'overbooking' may have been a legitimate tactic in ordinary

times, but at present it was not. Owen, conscious of the difficulty
that shop stewards would have in persuading their members to
book jobs accurately, went on to say :

> 'Now let us view the matter as it will affect a production com-
> mittee asking the men in the shop to go all out. At first sight,
> it would appear that the fear built up over a generation of
> fighting would prevent the workers doing that dreaded of all
> things, "giving the show away" to the rate-fixer.'

Some rate-fixers, he thought, would probably relish the new
workshop honesty and take advantage of it—but he didn't
expect that this would lead to much trouble since the workers
were 'ready to recognise the danger we are in and to place that
consideration higher than a temporary price gain.'[40] To offset
the problem of smaller pay packets Owen recommended that
there should be the pooling of all earnings from all jobs. But
this sort of action went against the grain of many craftsmen. In
one factory where there had been a Joint Production Committee
early on, the convenor reported 'a strong tendency for workers
on high-priced jobs to work steadily until they have made what
they consider a good wage for the week, and then to slack off for
the rest of the week. It is not enough to say that this is indefensible at the present time; we should endeavour to win the workers
to a system which will prevent this tendency.'[41] This, of course,
could prove to be pretty difficult. After enlisting all the forces
of the previously detested scientific management, especially in
the Gilbrethian variety, to eliminate inefficiency and fatigue,
and to increase production, Owen praises American management methods with some generosity :

> 'Managers must spend most of their time in the works, where,
> on the job, they would see the actual difficulties and not be
> working from their ideals, up in the air. Right through Ameri-
> can efficiency practice, this principle is observed, and the sooner
> it operates in this country the better. When Stalin asked the
> Russians to combine "the Russian revolutionary sweep with
> American efficiency" he knew the full meaning of that term.'

A little later Owen is able to bring the example of the Soviet
Union into it,

'The Stakhanovite movement of Russia, of course, has learned much from these American methods, but the two systems differ greatly in the sense that one is animated by the desire for increased profits and the other for the good of the workers as a whole.'[42]

Jack Owen got his way. The National Council of Shop Stewards took up the Stakhanovite idea of socialist competition. At a meeting under its auspices in London in December 1942, trophies were presented to representatives of factories which had achieved the biggest increases in production during a week which had been labelled 'Soviet Anniversary Production Week'. The production banner was won by the workers of a Greater London gun factory who had increased their production for one product by 150 per cent and for another by 56 per cent. The assembled crowd was told that these new records were to be the basis for new production levels for the works who joined the next competition.[43]

But much of this sort of thing was difficult for many workers to stomach. That there were difficulties in persuading workers accustomed to the conflicts of industrial capitalism to drop their customary hostility to the achievement of managerial objectives is clear from some passages from a dinner hour talk given by the C.P. General Secretary, Harry Pollitt, to workers in a London engineering factory. For Pollitt there were two key, related, objectives: first, the opening up of a second front, and second, 'to utilise the productive resources of Britain to the uttermost'. He told his audience:

'I know it's easy in public meetings to get loud applause for the demand that a second front should be opened up in the West, but I notice that when I come on to deal with the need for more tanks, planes, guns, shells, ships and coal, another kind of atmosphere can be felt. This is easily understood . . .'

It was 'easily understood' because of the long history of appalling inefficiency, waste of materials and man power, the introduction of management 'experts', and the making of huge profits in British industry over the years. All this, Pollitt thought, could well explain why workers had 'become fed-up and cynical whenever the word "production" is mentioned.' Another legitimate fear was that the temporary suspension of hard won trade union conditions would mean that they would never be restored when the war was over. But Pollitt tried to allay the fears of his (obviously male) audience. He said :

'I know it can be done, and that if we stand together no power in Britain after the war can take advantage of anything we have done. I know we can prevent piece-rates being cut, or labourers permanently displacing skilled men, or woman labour displacing male labour, or refusals to restore Trade Union customs and practices, if we stood firmly together . . .'

and invoking the Russian example he continued :

'This is why I think we should all have now to set the personal example on the job. Yes, if you like, to adopt the same type of attitude as the Russian shock-brigades. To do this in regard to time-keeping, skill and speed on the job.'[44]

Groups of workers, like those at Dalmuir, who found such reassurances as these to go against the grain of their instincts were often labelled by the C.P. as 'Trotskyists'. This, of course, was meant as no flattery. In a C.P.G.B. pamphlet of August 1942 called *Clear Out Hitler's Agents! an exposure of Trotskyist disruption being organised in Britain* it was stated that :

'the Trotskyists try their hardest to hold up the production of arms. . . . They talk about the boss's profits. . . . They want you to go slow, not to give your best work, to be misled by their talk of strikes and the boss's profits into sabotaging our troops and the Red Army.'[45]

At first it was the Independent Labour Party which was on the receiving end of most of the criticisms like these. But later the groups which came together in March 1944 to form the Revolutionary Communist Party received the lion's share of the attacks. *Socialist Appeal*, the paper of one of the groups which was to merge into the R.C.P., was, for instance, subject to a strongly worded criticism in February 1943 from John Mahon in his C.P. pamphlet *Hitler's Agents Exposed!* The pamphlet contained sections headed as follows : 'Trotskyites Weaken Trade Unions to serve Hitler', 'Trotsky never the Colleague of Lenin', and 'Trotsky Became an Agent of Hitler.' *Socialist Appeal* was condemned for its advocacy of full-scale public ownership of industry. Mahon quoted with great disapproval from the December 1942 issue as follows :

'The nationalisation of the whole industry, without compensation and its operation under workers' control is the only foundation on which a truly great increase in production can take place . . .'

Mahon then subjected the paper to rigorous content-analysis, reaching the conclusion that it sought to promote strikes. *Socialist Appeal* had 28 columns 'of these it devoted to reports of strikes or the working up and exasperating of disputes which it hoped would result in strikes—in November 1942, 13 columns; in December, 12 columns; in January, 1943, 13 columns.'[46] In a Marx House/*Daily Worker* leaflet produced in 1944 at the height of the small R.C.P.'s notoriety (especially in connection with the apprentices' strikes on the Tyne and the Clyde),[47] in answer to the question 'How Do the Trotskyists Sabotage Production?', it was stated that recent strikes had not broken out because any large body of workers supported the Trotskyists, but rather because the latter latched on to the fact that 'certain sections of the employers pursue a policy in industry that provokes a justified sense of grievance among workers.'[48] This analysis is probably right. The R.C.P. probably had little real influence in promoting strikes—Marxists would presumably always argue that under capitalism strikes promote themselves because of the contradictions inherent in the system and that Communists, Trotskyists and others merely channel the fruits of the contradictions into constructive paths. If, then, the R.C.P. had little influence in causing strikes, the C.P.G.B. probably had very little influence in stopping them. In 1941 there were 1,251 disputes as against 922 in 1940, and the figures for 1942, 1943, and 1944 were respectively 1303, 1785, and 2194. Striker-days similarly went up in the same years—all this in spite of the fact that strikes had been made 'illegal' and in spite of the fact that the C.P. was committed to an anti-strike policy. Knowles, who has looked at this matter in some detail, suggests that, while the C.P. arguably contributed to a 'general steadying influence' after June 1941, 'there seems to be little trace of direct short-term Communist influence in restraint of strikes.'[49] Inman similarly concludes that at best the Communists had only 'a strong influence in preventing minor disagreements from leading to serious stoppages of work.'[50] Industrial conflict seems also to have expressed itself very dramatically through high levels of absenteeism, another thing which J.P.Cs. were concerned to root out.

In a cautious conclusion on the effectiveness of J.P.Cs., the official historian of labour in the munitions industries writes that :

> 'by 1945 worker-management co-operation was greater and more widespread, and there was greater understanding on the part of workers of the problems of management and by the management of the problems of the workers than had existed in the previous fifty years.'

But this new spirit did not last long after the war. Many J.P.Cs. quickly ceased to function after 1945, with the employers in the engineering industry, for instance, resisting union demands that the agreement which had established them should be continued after the war. Inman suggests that when war production 'which had given both sides of industry a common purpose' stopped 'some of the old fears, which were only just under surface during the war, reappeared.'[51] The long-term collapse of J.P.Cs. was accompanied by a steady rise in the number and activity of shop stewards in Engineering Employers' Federation establishments.[52] By 1961 less than 1 in 10 of federated establishments had a functioning Joint Production Committee.[53] There was, however, in the period of the immediate post-war Labour Governments an attempt to revive the Joint Consultation idea, not only in the newly nationalised industries, but also in private industry generally.

One of the strongest advocates of Joint Consultation was G. S. Walpole, the owner of a precision engineering works employing 700 workers. In a book published in 1944 Walpole made a determined plea for the spread of Joint Consultation precisely to perpetuate the wartime spirit. But Walpole was aware of the problems that would arise after the war. It is clear from the following statements that he felt that this spirit was extremely fragile and vulnerable to a resumption of open industrial conflict. He wrote :

'That Management-Labour relationships are reasonably satisfactory just now arises from the existence of a transcendent common interest in the winning of the war—which overrides sectional interests of every kind. But this particular common interest will no longer apply after the war is over.'[54]

It was essential, therefore, to get the 'right' relationship—'the policy of Common Interest'[55]—established before it was too late. This would be no easy task since :

'The suspicion and distrust generated in a century of industrialism, during most of which the employee was frankly and crudely exploited by his employer, will not be dissipated by the utterance of a few pious platitudes and the establishment of a Joint Production Committee.'[56]

But, after the war, in the absence of 'a transcendent common interest', what Walpole regarded as the right relationship frequently failed to emerge. The old, time-honoured relationship between employer and worker re-emerged. One striking instance of this revival of the class struggle (and also of the failure of Pollitt's prediction that wartime sacrifices would not be taken advantage of after the war) is revealed by the case of Bill, a worker in a Manchester engineering factory in the late 1950s who, in spite of his status as a 'Blue Eye', gave his support to the 'fiddle'. Bill traced the origins of his support for the 'fiddle' to the fact that during the war the firm he worked for (like many other firms), in the interests of increased production for the war effort, gave a solemn promise not to cut piece-rates—'the sky was the limit for earnings'. And that was how it worked out for the duration of the war, but when it ended, the management went back on its promise and according to Tom Lupton

'All the loose rates which had been exposed during the war years were cut, and the workers' capacity to earn, and their scope for control, were reduced. The lesson of all this for Bill was never to expose loose rates however good the management happened to be.'[57]

Joint Consultation in the industrial atmosphere of post-war Britain soon became discredited and irrelevant. There were, however, soon brave spirits who were prepared to try it. One shop steward recalled in 1965 that:

'We did originally have joint consultation after the war. It started off full of enthusiasm and ideas but, gradually, as we met, probably once a fortnight or once a month, the ideas that were brought forwards gradually petered out and simply came down in the end to the quality of the tea in the canteen or something of that trivial nature.'[58]

This tendency to triviality had sometimes been found in the war-time J.P.Cs. Some of those wartime Committees which were considered by C. A. Oakley of the Ministry of Aircraft Production to be 'unsuccessful' were partly so because of the reluctance of some managements to accept advice and because of their attempts 'to limit agenda to trivial or somewhat irrelevant points—in some factories agenda were devoted solely to such matters as absenteeism, A.R.P., and canteen management.' Others were 'unsuccessful' because the representatives of labour attempted to take things 'too far', by 'concerning themselves with personalities and with controversial questions outside the functions of the committees.'[59] The post-war tendency was entirely in the direction of the growth of independent shop steward representation, with the emphasis on shop floor bargaining. No new 'transcendent common interest' emerged in spite of numerous appeals by employers, governments and many trade union leaders for the need for industrial harmony. Not only was there a new 'War after the War' in British industry, there was also the 'Cold War', and, of course, connections between the two were frequently made in no uncertain terms. In 1949, however, it was still thinkable for two of the chief ideologues of British management to appeal for a renewal of the spirit which had animated so much Communist Party activity in the war. It is more than a little ironic that this involved an attempt to re-import Taylorism into one of the places of its infancy on the basis of its acceptance, in its Stakhanovist form, in the Soviet Union. In the final chapter of one of their books on scientific management, Lyndall Urwick and E. F. L. Brech argue that 'sound management is the only foundation on which any society can base a rising standard of living and a realisation of labour's legitimate aspirations.' They were somewhat worried, however, that the further progress of management ideas in Britain would be hampered by 'unenlightened opposition from vociferous elements among organised labour.' To reassure the labour movement they go on to argue that this was not an attempt to introduce larger than ever instalments of an unreconstructed Taylorism of early 20th century vintage. Things, they stated, had improved (become more subtle?) since then. The clinching argument, especially directed no doubt at the 'vociferous elements', then followed :

'If any worker doubts it, he should study what is happening in Russia today. Ever since the inauguration of the first five-year plan the drive for production has been speeded up— Stakhanovism, Shock Brigadiers, socialist competition, the strictest discipline, individual responsibility and leadership, all these are features of industrial life under the Soviets just as they are in capitalist countries.'[60]

NOTES

1. L. Urwick and E. F. L. Brech *The Making of Scientific Management*, Vol. 2, *Management in British Industry* (first pub. 1949, London 1964 imp.) p. 208.
2. Mass-Observation *People in Production* (London 1942) p. 189.
3. P. Inman *Labour in the Munitions Industries* (London 1957) p. 369.
4. *People in Production* p. 61.
5. Inman, op. cit., p. 430.
6. C. A. Oakley *Men at Work* (London 1945) p. viii.
7. Ibid., p. vi; for further details on these things see *People in Production* pp. 216-219.
8. Inman, op. cit., p. 269.
9. Inman, op. cit., p. 264. See also Urwick and Brech, op. cit., for a eulogy on the importance of personnel management during the 2nd World War: pp. 211-214.
10. *People in Production* p. 353. Emphasis in original.
11. For details on C.P. industrial policies and activities amongst aircraft and other engineering workers from the mid-1930s, see Ken Coates and Tony Topham eds. *Workers' Control* (London 1970 edn.) pp. 148-156.

12. Douglas Hyde *I Believed: the Autobiography of a Former British Communist* (London 1952 edn.) p. 93. This book, by a former Communist, who at this time was close to C.P.G.B. headquarters, contains a chapter 'Working for Defeat' which gives some information on this phase of the C.P.'s wartime policies. For a fuller account see Henry Pelling *The British Communist Party* (London 1958) Ch. VII, 'Imperialist War and Anti-Fascist War. 1939-1943'.

13. William Rust *It's Your Paper: the Story of the 11th Year of the Daily Worker* n.d., p. 10.

14. Inman, op. cit., pp. 400-401.

15. Extracts quoted in Coates and Topham, op. cit., pp. 157-160.

16. W. Hannington, 'The A.E.U. and the Stop Stewards' Movement' in *Labour Monthly* February 1941, quoted in Coates and Topham, op. cit., pp. 16off.

17. Speech by W. Swanson at National Conference of Shop Stewards, Stoll Theatre, London, October 19th, 1941, as reported in *World News and Views* October 25th, 1941 and quoted in Coates and Topham, op. cit., pp. 162-163.

18. All information on Stoll Theatre Conference from *Workers' News*, n.d., ? October 1941.

19. Leaflet inserted in *The Volunteer for Liberty* (International Brigade Association) No. 13, June 1941. Cooney had been a Battalion Commissar in the International Brigade.

20. 'Joint Production Committees' in *Labour Monthly* December 1941, quoted in Coates and Topham, op. cit., p. 169.

21. Inman, op. cit., p. 380.

22. Ibid., p. 388.

23. Angus Calder *The People's War* (London 1971 edn.) p. 460. See pp. 458-461 for an account of the establishment and progress of J.P.C.s.

24. Quoted in H. A. Clegg and T. E. Chester 'Joint Consultation' in *The System of Industrial Relations in Great Britain*, eds. A. Flanders and H. A. Clegg (Oxford 1964 imp., first published 1954) p. 323.

25. R. O. Clarke, D. J. Fatchett and B. C. Roberts *Workers' Participation in Management in Britain* (London 1972), p. 46.

26. J. J. Gillespie *Free Expression in Industry* (London 1948) p. 125.

27. Coates and Topham, op. cit., p. 143.

28. Inman, op. cit., p. 387.

29. Quoted in Clarke, Fatchett and Roberts, op. cit., p. 47, note 1.

30. See Calder, op. cit., pp. 507ff, and A. R. Griffin *Mining in the East Midlands, 1550-1947* (London 1971) p. 288.

31. Quoted in K. G. J. C. Knowles *Strikes* (Oxford 1952) p. 82.

32. C.P.G.B. *An Urgent Memorandum on Production*, March 1942, p. 23.

33. Calder, op. cit., p. 460.

34. Quoted in Gillespie, op. cit., p. 125.

35. Calder, op. cit., p. 461.

36. Inman, op. cit., pp. 386-387.

37. Bert Williams, 'The Transformation of Birmingham' in Coates and Topham, op. cit., pp. 188-190.

38. 'A Dissident Complaint' in Coates and Topham, op. cit., pp. 180-188.

39. Jack Owen *War in the Workshops* (London n.d., 1942) p. 13.

40. Ibid., p. 31. For a more recent account of 'fiddling' see Brian Jackson *Working Class Community* (Pelican edn. 1972) pp. 100-102, and for

much detail see Tom Lupton *On the Shop Floor* (Oxford 1963).
41. Owen, op. cit., p. 33.
42. Some telling extracts from this section are quoted in Coates and Topham, op. cit., p. 142, footnote.
43. Oakley, op. cit., pp. 169-170.
44. H. Pollitt *A Call to Arms*, n.d., pp. 11 and 13.
45. *Clear Out Hitler's Agents*, August 1942, p. 9.
46. J. Mahon *Hitler's Agents Exposed*, pp. 7-8. For similar views see J. R. Campbell *Trotskyist Saboteurs*, (1944).
47. See Calder, op. cit., pp. 509-510, and Inman, op. cit., p. 334.
48. Marx House/*Daily Worker* leaflet No. 3, 'Truth about Trotskyism'.
49. Knowles, op. cit., p. 56. See pp. 55-56 for full details. See also *People in Production*, pp. 334-337 for details on wartime strikes.
50. Inman, op. cit., p. 392.
51. Inman, op. cit., p. 389.
52. A. I. Marsh and E. Coker 'Shop Steward Organisation in Engineering' in *British Journal of Industrial Relations*, Vol. 1, No. 2, June 1967, quoted in Coates and Topham, op. cit., pp. 202ff.
53. See H. A. Clegg *The System of Industrial Relations in Great Britain* (Oxford 1970) p. 192.
54. G. S. Walpole *Management and Men* (London 1944) p. 28.
55. Walpole, op. cit., p. 62.
56. Ibid., pp. 26-27.
57. T. Lupton *On the Shop Floor* (Oxford 1963) pp. 179-180.
58. P.E.P. *Attitudes in British Management* (1965) quoted in Clarke, Fatchett and Roberts, p. 47.
59. Oakley, op. cit., pp. 51-52.
60. Urwick and Brech, op. cit., p. 224.

XIV

PRODUCTIVITY, 'RESTRICTIVE PRACTICES,' AND PIECEWORK IN THE 1950S AND 1960S

In 1948 James J. Gillespie (author of *Dynamic Motion and Time Study* and other works) wrote a pioneering book, *Free Expression in Industry*, in which he tried to apply social psychology to the situation in industry. Gillespie's book in many respects stood firmly in the British tradition of 'Human Relations' in industry, and as such was hostile to scientific management (. . . 'I fail to see why I should try to be nice about the way it totally ignores . . . the effect on the human being of its imposed disciplines.'[1]), and also advocated the abolition of piecework ('Individual piece work and bonus schemes . . . should be abolished, are productive of many group tensions and jealousies, and do not foster proper group relations, i.e. "the team spirit".'[2]). Gillespie sought to create a system of industrial organisation the aim of which was :

> 'To foster a socially effective work situation in which, as far as is possible, reasonable human interest is so expressed that personal aggressive and regressive trends are sublimated and personal growth is encouraged by the promotion of a cooperative, free work structure in which each participant contributes as a responsible person.'[3]

It is not, however, our intention here to dwell on the relatively unusual aspects of Gillespie's management thought, but rather to draw attention to Gillespie's starting point—a starting point which, in fact, was highly typical of British managers in the immediate post-war years. How were they to arrest the decline in productivity that had come about since the war had ended? How were they going to make workers work harder now that the moral incentive of the 'war effort' and to some extent popular support for the Soviet Union had disappeared? And, how were

managers to achieve their objectives now that the great goad
of the inter-war years, mass unemployment, was absent in the
full-employment economy of post-war Britain? In his first
chapter, called 'The Problem', Gillespie begins by recounting
that in a factory he had recently visited 'the output per operator
hour had dropped considerably in comparison with pre-war
output.' In a discussion with factory executives to try and work
out the reasons for this, the following points were amongst those
made : 'Managers have no control now that they cannot effectively use dismissal, and the threat of dismissal, to beget proper
discipline'; 'There is opposition among the workers to the
introduction of new organisational techniques that we need—
like motion and time study and planning'; 'All the workers want
is more money for less effort—in fact, laziness'; 'Some of the
working groups have an agreed standard of earning and will
produce no more than a certain amount'; 'The workers pay
much more attention to their shop stewards than to foremen and
managers; and the power of the shop stewards is gradually
increasing and the power of management decreasing'; 'People
are not now driven to effort by fear of the sack or by needing
money for sheer physical maintenance; the drive is now for
power and prestige and I don't know how we can meet it.' In
another meeting Gillespie recalls that he had the following
question put to him :

'What will be the effect on effort in industry, not only of full
employment and social security measures, but of better education? If people are no longer driven by fear of unemployment, if their primary wants for food, clothing and shelter of
an adequate kind are satisfied, who will want to work hard?
and who will choose to do the dirty, disagreeable work, the
heavy work, the monotonous work, the low status work?'[4]

These questions and these perspectives continued to haunt British
managers for years to come. Britain's low productivity problem
became a veritable obsession in the 1950s and 1960s.

In 1953, Graham Hutton, in the final chapter of his book *We
Too Can Prosper: the Promise of Productivity* (published for the
British Productivity Council) stated that :

'The social ferment of our times faces Britain with graver problems and greater challenges than any other land. Five years ago she took up, as the foremost challenge, and as her problem of No. 1 priority, the task of raising industrial productivity. She took it up under the economic leadership at that time of a great Englishman whose almost solitary voice before war ended warned the nation that its way after the war would be hard, and whose effort to bring the economic facts of life home to Britain's people achieved so much in preparing the ground for the raising of productivity. Sir Stafford Cripps sowed that others might reap.'[5]

Cripps earned this eulogy on account of the concern he had shown for 'productivity' at the Ministry of Aircraft Production during the war, and which he had taken with him into his post as President of the Board of Trade in Attlee's Government. From this office he had been largely responsible for the establishment of the National Production Advisory Council on Industry, a body which he chaired. Concerns of this sort were also carried with him into his next post in 1947 as Minister of Economic Affairs, and later as Chancellor of the Exchequer. In October 1948 Cripps and the American Administrator of the Marshall Plan, Paul G. Hoffman, created the Anglo-American Council on Productivity on which they secured the support both of the trade union movements and employers' organisations in their respective countries.[6] According to an American commentator, the goal of the Council was 'to increase productivity in Britain through study by various British industries of manufacturing methods in similar industries in the United States. Teams representing management, technicians and shop [-floor] workers went to the United States to study American methods. They returned to boost British productivity.'[7] Between 1949 and 1952, sixty-six A.A.C.P. teams left Britain for study tours in America. What they saw led them to the conclusion that, according to Graham Hutton, *British industrial productivity must be raised, and can be raised, comparatively quickly.*[8] The trade union members of the Productivity Teams were in broad agreement with the industrialists on the teams. Trade union leaders like Sir Lincoln Evans, and Tom Williamson—firmly in the saddle on the General Council of the T.U.C.—and their colleagues were all for exhorting their own members towards an acceptance of American management methods. A team of British trade union officials which visited the U.S.A. and published its report through the T.U.C. in 1950 argued that: 'Unions should seek to co-operate in the application of "scientific management" which, even if not an exact science, can make a valuable contribution to increasing productivity in industry.'[9] The same year also saw the establishment at the T.U.C. of the Production Department, a development called forth in the T.U.C.'s own words 'as a reflection of the growing importance placed by the General Council on the need for consistent and steady growth in industrial efficiency.'[10] This concern by the trade union leadership for increased efficiency cannot be explained merely by its desire to help the Labour Government to fulfil its economic objectives, for after the fall of the Labour Government these concerns still found expression. In 1952, indeed, the T.U.C., along with the main employers' organisations, helped to form (and thereafter actively participated in) the independent body, the British Productivity Council, which replaced the Anglo-American Productivity Council.[11] All this lent considerable weight to the growth of the general feeling that British labour was not pulling its weight— an ideological offensive that was to grow in the 1950s and to intensify in the 1960s.

In an enquiry into the trade unions published by the *Daily Mirror* in 1956, its authors Sydney Jacobson and William Connor ('Cassandra') made major allegations on this score which were highly typical of the contemporary mood. The 'restrictive' practices of British workers were, it was argued, a major source of Britain's relative economic backwardness. Having gone back to the Luddites they wrote:

'The suspicion towards new methods has never entirely died out in this country, and although sabotage of machinery is rare (but not unknown) the protests have taken a new direction—the slowing down of output by the men themselves and the development of a whole series of practices that cut down the production of goods and services.'[12]

Individual 'restrictive' practices in a host of industries were regularly written up by the press and by popular commentators.

The popular consciousness was supplied with countless examples of hostility by trade unionists to new labour saving machinery and processes; of demarcation disputes; of workers being 'sent to Coventry' and so on. The Rolls-Royce strike of 1955 in Scotland centring round Joseph McLernon, a connecting rod polisher, was a highly typical *cause célèbre* of the crusaders against 'restrictive' practices in the 1950s. In order to preserve overtime shop stewards in Rolls-Royce decided to organise a slow-down of work. McLernon took no notice of this instruction and continued to polish his rods at the normal speed. McLernon's union disciplined him, and eventually expelled him, after he again refused to reduce his output. Since the firm's agreed policy was only to employ union labour, the stewards urged that the firm should sack McLernon. When it refused to do this, the workers at the Scottish plants ordered a strike, but this was soon defeated since the English plants refused to follow the Scottish lead. McLernon, of course, was regarded as a great hero by the newspapers, not least because of his militant anti-Communism.[13]

The 'quality' papers came to similar conclusions. In March 1956 the *Manchester Guardian* in a Survey of Industry, Trade and Finance claimed that

'In most places it is taken for granted that the workers tend to "go a bit slow" whenever the pace is not set by the machines. "The men admit that they could do 20 per cent more by pulling their weight; their shop stewards do not allow them to earn more than a certain amount" was a typical remark. . . . That work restriction exists is not worth arguing about.'[14]

Even if particular 'restrictive' practices were hard to identify, then what Ferdinand Zweig in 1951 had called the 'restrictive spirit' (which he felt was far more of a problem than 'restrictive' practices) was not.[15] In the 1950s sedulous attempts were made, it being after all the height of the 'Cold War', to foster an image of the developing shop floor unionism as a hotbed of communist and militant socialist activity and the very seat of the 'restrictive spirit.' A *locus classicus* of this view was the best-selling comic novel (soon transformed into a highly successful film—and since given numerous repeat showings on television) by Alan Hackney, *I'm All Right Jack* of 1958. The hapless Stanley Windrush, ex-

Oxford University and Foreign Office throw-out, takes a job as an 'ordinary worker' (because of the high wages) in a missiles factory. He is instantly forced to enrol in the General and Electrical United Projectile Workers and Operatives Alliance (G.E.E.U.P.W.O.A.). Having after his first day as a fork-lift truck driver forgotten to plug his truck in to the battery re-charging machine, he asked a workmate :

' "Why couldn't the mechanic have plugged my truck in if he saw the plug was out?" "I told you," said Knowlesy. "It's not his job. It's a question of demarcation. He doesn't touch it." "But I thought we workers were all solid together?" "'Aven't you 'ad no education? He's in a different union, the Amal-gamated, so we can go and take a running jump as far as he's concerned, and so can he take a running jump as far as we're concerned in the General. Otherwise someone might be out of a job and it might be me".'

Stanley's shop steward is the Communist Party member, William Kite, who shows an alarming proclivity for the most arid trade union jargon and who is the proud owner of such books as *Collective Childhood and Factory Manhood* ('very descriptive. Tells you about factory life, what it's like in a socialist country. . . . It's different in the Soviet Union.') Another archetypal figure is the young Time and Motion man who said of the objects of his observations : 'If only they *realised*, . . . the way to a higher standard of living depends on higher output, and casting aside all the old prejudices . . .' His more experienced, and, therefore, cynical colleague, having talked of the workers' 'natural rhythm' added :

'You probably don't know it yet, but there's chaps here can break out in a muck sweat merely by standing still. It's abso-lutely astonishing. And they can hear a stop watch ticking with compressed air and road drills going full belt.'

Not dismayed by these revelations, the young Time and Motion man waxed lyrical :

'I have a sort of vision of management and unions sinking all differences and working harmoniously side by side to double and treble our national production and give us living standards that will, er—astonish us today.'

The workers' views on these questions, and especially on the instrument for its achievement, Time and Motion Study, were rather different. Time study was a constant threat. For instance, when a party of visitors was taken round the factory by the management 'the whole tempo' of work in the lathe shop suddenly slackened in case the workers were thus being secretly timed : 'The high hum of the machines climbed down almost at once to a lower, slower tone and the practised movements of the operators became instantly more careful and studied.' The key incident in the novel is, in fact, the timing of the naïve Stanley, who fails to recognise a Time and Motion man. The new, reduced piece-rates produced on the basis of his times led to a full scale strike, with Stanley at first being sent to Coventry, and being lionised in the Press as a hero in the Battle for Productivity.

Small wonder, then, that by 1959 the incoming General Secretary of the T.U.C., George Woodcock, could admit that the trade union movement was more unpopular with the general public than it had been for many years, and that it had a very poor public image.[16] So strong was the barrage of criticism that a case was even made out, by the Inns of Court Conservative and Unionist Society in its pamphlet of 1958 called *A Giant's Strength*, for the use of Restrictive Practices legislation to eradicate workers' 'restrictive' practices using the test of whether or not any practice was justified in 'the public interest'. The Government in circumstances like these could not keep out of the debate. In 1959 a White Paper called *Practices Impeding the Full and Efficient Use of Manpower* was published. But, interestingly, it rejected this legislative approach, even though it estimated that 57 per cent of the working population were employed in industries which had to contend with 'restrictive practices.'[17] The White Paper not only rejected a legalistic attack on 'restrictive' practices, but also felt that exhortation was likely to be unsuccessful. Instead it recommended that managements and unions in specific industries should attempt to take joint action to eliminate 'restrictions.' This approach was to be taken one stage further in the 1960s through what might be called the 'company specific' approach embodied in productivity bargaining. But, in the early 1960s, there were still plenty of generalised attacks on 'restrictive practices' and on the 'restrictive spirit.' A notable one was the persuasively argued and superficially well-documented best-seller by Michael Shanks, *The Stagnant Society*, of 1961. In a typical passage, Shanks talks of 'the restrictive practices of which we hear so much in British industry today.' He goes on to state that 'These restrictive practices, by which a man deliberately limits his output below what he could perform' were 'especially prevalent' amongst craftsmen such as print and shipbuilding workers. But they were also to be found among 'unskilled' workers—the reluctance of dockers, for instance, to use fork lift trucks was given as 'a well-known but by no means unique example of modern Luddism.' Shanks continued by asserting that 'the biggest single restrictive practice in Britain today is almost certainly the tea-break, and the general reluctance of workers to speed up the pace of work. The slow traditional pace of work in British industry is a far bigger problem than any specific craft restriction of effort.'[18]

An important landmark in the attack on 'restrictive' practices was the publication on March 1st, 1964, of an article in *The Sunday Times* called 'Half time Britain on half pay'. Its author was the American management consultant William Allen, who had been involved in the pioneering Fawley Productivity Agreement of 1960 (which we shall discuss shortly).[19] Allen's article set in train a whole series of newspaper articles, television programmes and even academic statements which sought to make the same general point. One television programme, indeed, under the title 'Half-Time Britain' was expanded in 1967 to a full length book called *Britain on Borrowed Time* which contained such chapters and sections as 'Wasting Time Pays', 'The Great Docks Scandal' and 'Underwork, A National Pastime'. The book's argument hinged round the assertion that 'the wholesale waste of manpower is one of the roots of our industrial crisis.'[20] The industrial relations academics were not going to be left out of the act. In December 1964, the journal of the Labour Party revisionists, *Socialist Commentary*, carried an article by H. A. Clegg which was considered sufficiently authoritative to be quoted in one of the Research Papers of the Royal Commission on Trade Unions and Employers' Associations in 1967. Clegg was quoted as having said :

'Under-employment of labour is one of the major scandals of the British economy. There may be few workers—outside the newspaper industry—who are paid to do nothing at all, but throughout British industry there must be hundreds of thousands of workers who are paid to do nothing for a considerable part of their working time. . . . Then there are the new machines and changes in technology—many of them in use in other countries—which would be introduced here but for limits placed by workers on their output, or "manning" rules governing the number of men to be employed on a given process. Restrictive practices are popularly associated with craft trades, especially in shipbuilding and printing, but in fact they are by no means confined to craftsmen . . . restrictions on output are to be found almost everywhere that workers are paid by results, and elsewhere as well; and manning rules are also widespread.'[21]

The right wing Institute of Economic Affairs, which had been founded in 1957, was exceptionally vigilant in rooting out examples of 'restrictive' practices. In November 1964 it established an 'Industrial Practices Inquiry' supervised by Graham Hutton under the eagle eye of a group of assessors which included many former members of the Anglo-American and British Productivity Councils (including Sir Lincoln Evans and Lord Williamson). The Inquiry used a wide-ranging definition of 'restrictive' practices, stating that :

'Our society is riddled with practices which cause enormous wastes of our scarce economic resources. From this viewpoint, a restrictive practice is any action or inaction which intentionally or otherwise results in using up more scarce human and other economic resources than would be otherwise necessary to produce any good or service of specified quality, having regard to the agreed limitations required for safety and health. From tariffs to apprenticeship limitations or professional recruitment, from "ca'canny" to work-sharing and unjustified absenteeism, there are almost infinite variations on the theme of restrictive practices.'[22]

The I.E.A. publication from which this quotation comes contains in its Part Two ('Sources and Examples of Restrictive Practices') a sample of about sixty cases from newspaper articles, speeches, and Government enquiries which gave details on 'restrictive' practices, between William Allen's article in March 1964 and the end of 1966. An exceptionally interesting enquiry was that carried out by Hutton himself in 1965 and 1966, during which he paid a number of visits to English and Scottish enterprises in various industries which used 'American machinery or methods, or non-American machines with the same capacity and performance as American machines.'[23] This investigation was regarded as being particularly important because, if it showed that productivity was lower in these British enterprises than in their American equivalents, there could be no possibility of that part of the trade union movement which was not completely browbeaten by the welter of bad publicity, arguing that Britain's poor productivity performance was due to inadequate capital investment and outdated machinery. The American contrast which, as we have seen, had often been made in the past was being made much of in the 1960s. William Allen himself had made the point quite clearly in his March 1964 article when he stated (on the basis of his first hand experience as a consultant to the Steel Company of Wales) that for every person required to produce a ton of steel in the U.S.A. it required three men in Britain. In the case of the steel industry, however, that could be explained by the higher capital/labour ratio in the U.S.A.— though one account of productivity bargaining in the steel industry stated that there was still 'some validity' in the attack on labour.[24] But the investigations by Hutton in 1965 and 1966 led to quite definite conclusions. Hutton summed up his findings as follows :

'Both in plants where the same (American) machines or equipment were used, and where similar but not identical equipment was used, the number of British operatives required for the same output over the same working-time (quality disregarded) ranged from 25% more (only rarely) to 3 and 4 times the number needed in America. . . . Throughout such visits the comparative absence, or diminished use, of multiple shift working was notable : clearly because the available work-force was too much crowded into single-shifts or, if not by nature continuous processing, at most double-day shifts; and the fixed capital was thereby under-utilised, well-treated, never being worn out, and consequently out-of-date.'[25]

The 'Source Book' edited by Hutton was only one of the products of the I.E.A.'s 'Industrial Practices Inquiry'. Two similar interim papers were produced on *Restrictive Practices in the Building Industry* and on the *Economic Consequences of the Professions*, and in 1967 a book called *The Restrictive Society: a Report on Restrictive Practices* was published. Its author, John A. Lincoln, explicitly acknowledges his debt to William Allen 'for a long and frank exchange of views',[26] and at great length argues his basic thesis that 'restrictive' practices of all sorts were largely responsible because they interfered with the benevolent invisible hand of the market economy, for Britain's economic crisis. Lord Shawcross, who in a speech to the Institute of Directors in November 1965, had spoken of 'a barely concealed unemployment of several million' workers who were 'paid for by industry, and a charge upon production'[27] contributed a foreword to Lincoln's book. But even he, enthusiastic as he was in the battle against workers' 'restrictive practices' could not see his way clear to agreeing with Lincoln's 'central purpose' which was the 'restoration of the common law doctrine against restraint of trade'.[28]

By the time Lincoln and the I.E.A. were making their unsuccessful bid for legal action against 'restrictive' practices, the owners and controllers of British industry were already engaged in a far-reaching attempt to attack the 'problem' on another front. Between January 1967 and the end of 1969 about 4,000 productivity agreements covering several million workers were registered with the Department of Employment and Productivity. This period represented the high point of a process that had begun in the earliest years of the 1960s.[29] Throughout the sixties the British working class was subjected with monotonous regularity and great persistence to the dubious appeals of productivity bargaining, with increase in productivity being a leading criterion for pay increases under the terms of the various versions of Incomes Policy in the same period. The report of the Royal

Commission on Trade Unions and Employers' Associations (Donovan Report 1968), as well as one of its Research Papers (No. 4, 1967), and three Prices and Incomes Board Reports gave productivity bargaining the official stamp of approval as the salvation of the British economy.[30] The Productivity Agreements negotiated in 1960 at the Fawley Refinery of Esso Petroleum—and especially the comprehensive account of them written by the leading industrial relations academic and stalwart of the *Socialist Commentary* group, Alan Flanders, and published in 1964—were in many respects the starting point of much of this. In his book Flanders made large claims for the 'elaborate set of agreements' concluded at Fawley (William Allen had played an important part in this during his consultancy there), asserting that they were 'without precedent or even proximate parallel in the history of collective bargaining in Great Britain.'[31] There were, he felt, two remarkable features of the 1960 agreements. The first was that 'they embodied in a practical form what might be called a "productivity package deal." ' Under this deal the company provided large increases in pay 'in return for the unions' consent to certain defined changes in working practices that were hampering a more efficient utilisation of labour.' The second feature was the considerable reduction of the systematic overtime (about 18 per cent of the total hours worked in 1959) that had grown up over the years. The two features were, of course, quite closely connected at a number of points—for example, the reduction of overtime was accompanied by a considerable extension of shift working. (We shall deal with the growth of shift working in a later section.) It was, indeed, this overtime reducing feature which seems, in the long run to have been the most significant achievement of the Fawley Agreements. Amongst the large claims that Flanders made for the impact of the agreements was one with a revealing qualification attached to it. Set alongside such unqualified statements as 'the withdrawal of craftsmen's mates' and 'greater freedom for management in its use of supervision', there was the qualified phrase '*some* relaxation of job demarcations' (my emphasis). By the time the Prices and Incomes Board produced its second Report on productivity bargaining in 1969 it asserted the view, after a careful analysis, that productivity bargaining did not have an inflationary effect in the local labour market. The Prices and Incomes Board also rejected the charge that it involved the buying out of restrictive practices in a way that would set a premium on them, and thereby make them more difficult to remove. But this was basically argued through the use of persuasive definition—if a deal involved the crude buying out of restrictive practices it was not a 'true' productivity deal. Added to this the P.I.B. suggested that the wrong view also involved fundamental misunderstanding of the nature and origins of restrictive practices. The wrong view conceived of a restrictive practice as 'a commodity that can be manufactured, bought and sold at will.' To quote W. W. Daniel's excellent summary of the P.I.B.'s attitude : 'Restrictive practices are not manufactured out of thin air. They are patterns of attitude and behaviour that grow and develop over time, out of custom and practice, without conscious intent on the part of workers and in the absence of conscious remedial action on the part of management. They are the consequence of a set of circumstances, historical, social, technical and economic, born essentially out of workers' needs to establish control over their own situations.'[32] This admirable definition of 'restrictive practices', of course, goes a long way towards explaining why many trade unionists in fact reject the term 'restrictive practices' completely and prefer to speak of *protective* practices—things done by workers to provide some protection against the insecurity inherent in the employment relationship under industrial capitalism.

As Daniel adds, it is highly likely that too many people did have the 'wrong' idea about productivity bargaining and 'restrictive' practices—and, therefore, the 'buying out' charge, whilst not true of the 'pure concept of productivity bargaining or its ideal practice', may well be 'all too true of many deals in practice. Particularly where they are instituted by unsophisticated managements concerned only to buy out restrictive practices and impose greater crude unilateral control over workers rather than accepting the principle of joint regulation and moving towards more effective machinery for joint regulation.'[33] The 'right' idea is, clearly, rooted in the ideology of contemporary academic industrial relations—with its emphasis on joint regulation, and on 'pluralism'. This view, summarised crudely, held basically that there could be no possibility under modern circumstances of managements' holding a divine right to manage, and in fact where this right was claimed it was likely that there were significant areas at the workplace where workers were exercising de facto unilateral controls. The ideal to strive for was joint regulation—and this could only be done by a managerial acceptance of 'pluralism' and the seeking of ways to incorporate work-making managerial control more likely at the same time as seeming to give greater participation to workers. Alan Flanders, in an article in the July 1966 *Steel Review*, explicitly linked the 'restrictive' practices and managerial control issues. He wrote :

'It's very unfortunate that productivity bargaining has been saddled with this "buying off" tag. You can't possibly conduct productivity bargaining on a completely fragmented basis, paying "the economic price" for each particular restrictive practice. . . . Any fragmented approach would be entirely incompatible with the modern view of the employment relationship, which sees the output of the plant stemming from a network of co-operative relationships between all the groups concerned. Productivity bargaining should certainly not be seen as the payment of bribes . . . more and more managements seem to me to be becoming aware that the labour situation has drifted dangerously far and that they are faced with the need to re-establish control over their workers. And since in the modern world they can't re-establish control uni-laterally, the plant productivity bargain seems to them a logical first step towards a modern viable system of managerial control over pay and effort.'[34]

This 'modern view of the employment relationship' is obviously shot through with paradoxes and contradictions. The paradox of simultaneously re-establishing control over workers and at the same time giving workers greater participation over their own destinies was one which many managements (not to mention workers) found difficult to grasp, and Flanders himself conceded this difficulty when he wrote in 1967 that 'The paradox whose truth managements have found it so difficult to accept, is that they can only regain control by sharing it.' There is, then, little doubt that, whether managements engaged in productivity bargaining for the 'right' or the 'wrong' reasons, they were usually motivated by a desire to push the balance of power between management and labour further in their favour, and to attempt to wrest from workers even the small degree of power they were able to exercise informally and unilaterally at the point of production.[35] But by the 1970s it was clear that productivity bargaining had 'lost its momentum', and even Flanders in 1972 acknowledged that many people might well ask if the subject had 'anything more than an historical interest.'[36] Perhaps the final irony is that in 1975 the Fawley refinery remains one of the least efficient of a dozen comparable refineries owned by the Exxon group, and that the latest agreement at the refinery has had the word 'productivity' dropped from its title—with the more humble 'efficiency' taking its place.[37]

It is abundantly clear that, in practice, the productivity bargaining boom of the 1960s represented a major and concerted attempt by employers to eradicate 'restrictive practices'. It was no accident, for instance, that the Royal Commission on Trade Unions and Employers' Association published in 1967, under one cover, two research papers : one on 'Productivity Bargaining' and the other on 'Restrictive Labour Practices'. The two topics went together because the latter was one of the 'problems' that it was hoped the former would cure. Indeed, the introduction to the paper on Productivity Bargaining revealed that the Commission had decided to seek evidence on productivity bargaining 'with the object of learning more about restrictive labour practices and methods of securing more efficient use of manpower.'[38] In an appendix to the paper on 'Restrictive Labour Practices' a number of 'Examples illustrating the problem' were given from printing, the docks, shipbuilding, road haulage, heavy electrical engineering, and oil refining. But what is a 'restrictive labour practice'? What to an employer is a 'restrictive labour practice' may well be a 'protective practice' to a worker. This point was conceded by Lord Devlin in his report on the Dock Industry in 1965. Devlin, indeed, preferred to talk in general of 'time-wasting practices' (things such as the continuity rule, bad timekeeping and excessive manning) and from there attempted to break them down into 'restrictive practices' and 'protective practices'. 'Protective practices' were those practices which were regarded as justifiable under casualism and by which work groups sought to protect 'the less efficient or less favoured workers from constant under-employment.' But, for Delvin, 'time-wasting practices' would become 'restrictive' under a system of regular employment. The analysis, therefore, is not taken far enough—for are not all groups of workers subject, albeit in usually less direct forms, to basically the same sort of insecurity under capitalism as the dockers were under the casual system? And nor, indeed, is protection all that is involved in what Tony Topham has called 'unilateral workers' regulation'.[89] Topham notes that Clarke, Fatchett and Roberts in their book on *Workers' Participation in Management in Britain* of 1972 classify 'unilateral workers' regulation' as a 'negative form of participation'. Topham, however, suggests that unilateral workers' regulation has positive aggressive advantages for workers and that 'Enforcing work standards not only protects people from excessive workloads, and makes work itself more tolerable, but is also a sanction against the employer.' Clarke, Fatchett and Roberts asked a sample of managers in both the private and public sectors of industry which 'restrictive practices' bothered them. In the private sector refusal to work overtime when desired by management was experienced and found 'fairly significant' by 9 per cent of managers, and found 'very significant' by 2 per cent of managers. Limitation of speed of work or volume of output was the other bane of managers in this sector, with 9 per cent finding it fairly significant and 2 per cent finding it very significant. In the public sector refusal to work overtime was a fairly significant problem for 6 per cent of managers, and very significant for 6 per cent. 10 per cent of public sector managers had fairly significant demarcation problems and 3 per cent found them very significant. Opposition to the introduction of new machinery and techniques was a fairly significant problem for 7 per cent of them, and very significant for 5 per cent. 12 per cent found limitation of speed of work or volume of output fairly significant and 13 per cent found it very significant.

Although Clarke and his colleagues found the incidence of these expressions of unilateral workers' regulation less common than had been widely suggested—for instance by the Confedera-

tion of British Industry in its evidence to the Royal Commission
—they comment on the two 'restrictions' most widespread in
private industry that they 'emphasised the workers' desire for
job control and autonomy, and also served to illustrate the nature
of the sanctions that workers can impose upon management,'[40]
and that they can be interpreted (as for instance they were by
Tom Lupton in his book *On the Shop Floor*) 'as attempts to
maintain control over the job in the interests of employment
and the exercise of market pressures.' This analysis seems to be
the right one—though we must join Tony Topham and question
the finding that these practices were relatively uncommon, and
with him suggest that 'Perhaps those who answered did not
know very much about what was going on on the shop floor,
or were reluctant to admit how much they were being affected.'[41]

Shipbuilding was one of the industries which came under
most fierce attack for its 'restrictionism'. On one occasion, in
1965, the Shipbuilding Employers' Federation compiled a
dossier on workers' restrictive practices and presented it to the
Confederation of Shipbuilding and Engineering Unions. The
'restrictive practices' mentioned included : overmanning, restrictions on overtime, rotas, restrictions on transferability of labour,
restriction on work by ships' crews and generally rigid demarcation rules.[42] An academic study of the economics of the shipbuilding industry in 1960 played down the harmful impact of
demarcation and sought instead to give 'pride of place' to 'bad-
time keeping; excessive tea-breaks; late starting and early stopping; faulty organisation of work and labour.'[43] This last point
(ignored by the Shipbuilding Employers) is of considerable
importance, for it seems to be the case that to a great extent the
actual production system itself in the shipbuilding industry of
the 1960s was itself the factor that enabled shipbuilding workers
to carve out so much leisure at work for themselves, and gave
them a considerable degree of control over the work process. It
was an appreciation of these facts which led the management of
the re-vamped Fairfields shipyard on the Clyde in the 1960s to
attempt to make serious inroads on this leisure at work and on
this degree of workers' control, by significantly altering the production process. On top of this the new management also
introduced a modified system of Measured Day Work into the

yard. This new payment system met with a surprisingly favourable response from the workers. As the authors of a study of Fairfields pointed out, the changes 'did not induce either resistance or an attempt to substitute alternative controls to those which work-people would lose as a result of the new methods.'[44] The reasons they put forward for this acceptance of change were, firstly, that an 'atmosphere of trust' had been generated between workers and managers at the yard; and, secondly, that the stewards had been trained in work study methods. But, in the opinion of Robin Murray, the basic reason was that this particular pill had been sugared with higher wages.[45] The company's managing director, Sir Iain Stewart, estimated that before the changes 'the men were not really doing two hours work a day . . .'[46]

Alexander and Jenkins paint a similar picture, stating that 60 per cent of work-time was non-productive and that a further 10 to 20 per cent was 'abortive' (work involving modification and rectification, and involving no adding of value to work done). But, as Murray points out, this position was soon transformed: 'The two hours work a day which the men were effectively limited to at the beginning of Fairfields, became five hours in the space of two years.'[47]

The case of Fairfields illustrates quite clearly how, in shipbuilding at least, 'leisure at work' was an important and large scale phenomenon. Although shipbuilding may well be something of a 'special case', it is quite clear that the taking of leisure at work is a similarly important area of worker-resistance to managerial objectives, and that, even if the system of production in an industry makes it difficult to take quite so much leisure at work in this way, it is nonetheless a widespread aspiration of workers. Workers on assembly lines, to give an obvious example, will naturally find it difficult to do as little as five hours, let alone two hours, work in a shift: but, as we shall see later, they (and other workers in less unfavourable situations) can still find effective ways of producing a good deal less output than their managers would like. In a study of the 'occupational culture' of shipbuilding workers in the North East of England, it is stated that, as far as these workers are concerned, leisure is by no means totally encompassed by specific activities, hobbies, or pastimes engaged in outside the workplace and in non-work time. Instead, the opportunity for leisure, often of a non-'classifiable' sort, is also 'inherent in the work process of the shipyard.' The major feature of the production process which makes this possible is the 'difficulty of close managerial control of work.' Nearly three quarters of the sample of shipbuilding workers spoken to, said that they had never had the time they took on a job checked. Nearly eight out of ten of the workers said that they suffered hold-ups due to other workers. The authors of the study argue :

> 'Workers can legitimately move about to seek information from other workers before they can start their job, to seek tools or equipment that may be required, to obtain access to a job or the removal of obstructions, or to seek any servicing their job may require such as drilling, burning or welding . . . a shipyard worker is constantly on the move, and the layout of shipyards and ships ensures that quiet corners out of the eye of authority abound. Many opportunities exist for the making or taking of leisure at work.'[48]

In the period of the productivity bargaining boom, piecework was frequently singled out for attack. The late 1960s saw a strong turn against payment by results systems and a move towards Measured Day Work. In a contribution to a Royal Commission Research Paper of 1968, Professor R. B. McKersie talked of there being a 'crisis' in wage payment systems in British industry, suggesting, rightly, that 'The age-old question of how to elicit and reward worker effort has been receiving increasing attention in Britain in recent years.'[49] He noted that there was 'some evidence that systems based on output incentives have not been increasing in coverage in recent years and may even be declining' and that a number of major enterprises had replaced piecework with some form of time work. This trend was a reversal of the long term towards piecework in British industry. In a typical management primer published in 1946 (which, interestingly, it was hoped would be 'of assistance to members of Joint Production Committees, both from the staff and the workers' side.'), a chapter on 'The Payment of Labour' pointed out, quite correctly, that basically there were two ways of rewarding labour—'either by payment for the amount of time spent at work, or by payment for the amount of work performed.' The author went on :

'The modern tendency is more and more towards a basis of payment by results rather than for time put in, and it is generally agreed that the adoption of such a method can be a valuable means of increasing output, reducing costs, and, at the same time, increasing the earnings of the efficient worker.'[50]

As long as piece rates were not cut, and as long as they were in the first place based on 'scientific' work study (which did indeed spread rapidly in this period), the argument for the greater extension of piecework seemed incontrovertible. Left to his own initiative, it was argued, the industrial worker was 'frankly inefficient.' Worker efficiency was most likely to be forthcoming if there was 'a financial incentive for increased effort.' Even with 'proper management and good supervision', efficiency under day work was, he estimated, likely to be only $62\frac{1}{2}$ per cent as against 100 per cent on incentive or piece work.

To an important extent this reliance on financial incentives went against the grain of academic enquiries into ways of raising productivity. Professor P. Sargant Florence and his colleagues, who produced their book *Productivity and Economic Incentives* in 1958 openly acknowledged this fact, pointing out that the dominant academic emphasis was on psychology, sociology and anthropology especially in the wake of Elton Mayo's work. They pointed out that not since the First World War had prime attention been given to the 'actual effect on productivity of schemes of economic incentives', and although they felt that much of this emphasis had been well-directed, they felt that the time had come to see if in fact the tide had turned too far. It was argued that 'fashion may have swung too far and the element of the Economic Man among industrial workers requires rediscovering as a complement to the Sociological Man who looms so large in the literature of today.' This 'common-sense' view—that workers might give more output if they were rewarded with more money—seemed in fact to fit well with the growing 'money-mindedness' and 'instrumentalism' of British industrial workers in a period of rapidly rising consumption by working-class families. Many managers shared this perspective too, as Florence and his associates made clear in the summary to their work, where they pointed out that the neglect of economic incentives by writers was 'not shared by the employer and the trade union organiser or the rank and file worker on the spot, who regardless of theory, continue to be immersed in such money-matters as disputes on wages, economic security, cost of living and earnings differentials.'[51] For a growing number of managers piecework seemed to be, by and large, the best way of achieving their fundamental objectives of maximising output and minimising unit labour costs.

Consequently the Ministry of Labour in 1961 could report that about 43 per cent of wage earners in manufacturing and 33 per cent of all wage earners were on some sort of payment by results system.[52] For many workers piecework was an unpopular system, associated with greater work intensity and increased exploitation. This was certainly the case in the engineering industries, where piecework seems to have made its biggest strides. But in recent years there has been a fundamental change of attitude—piecework has become popular with many workers and unpopular with many managers—because, as Cliff has put it, piecework has 'turned on its maker.'[53] Hugh Scanlon, the President of the Amalgamated Union of Engineering Workers, put it this way in 1967 : 'I've attributed most of the ills of the engineering industry to an iniquitous piece-work system. Yet . . . we fight . . . to retain it, and correctly so. Because with piecework you have the man on the shop floor determining how much effort he will give for a given amount of money.'[54] It was in the years of 'affluence'—the late 1950s and early 1960s—that piecework seems to have been 'captured' by the workers. In years of economic boom, with tight labour and product markets, many managers were willing to pay fairly generously for labour and for extra output—and the growing army of shop stewards located much of their power in their ability to force the pace through aggressive piecework bargaining. The conditions were such that, in the engineering industry for instance, the agreement which allowed for alterations in rates if the job or materials were altered, was transformed from being something which frequently in the past had allowed employers to cut rates to being something which enabled workers to jack up the rates—and this process could in itself set off a chain reaction of claims through-out a factory.[55] In similar fashion the size and number of rate-compensation allowances could also be vastly increased. In the mid-1960s Dr. Dennis Pym of Birkbeck College in the University of London claimed to have discovered 'a network of rates and rate-compensation allowances which apparently make it more profitable for workers to manufacture breakdowns rather than the product.' Pym told the authors of *Britain on Borrowed Time* that :

'Technological advances bring greater complexities in the form of special allowances, including compensating allowances for machine breakdowns. I have seen a scheme in which the operators have discovered ways of earning more money through frequent machine stoppages than they could get through production work. Some wage incentive schemes have literally dozens of pages of clauses and sub-clauses regulating their operation.'[56]

Phil Higgs, the Convenor in a Coventry aircraft factory, has superbly illustrated the generation of shop floor power through piecework bargaining. Having pointed out that, when piecework was introduced into the engineering trades, 'it was a method of intensive exploitation and often of self-exploitation by the individual', he adds that in a highly organised factory piecework had come to have some positive advantages :

'It is direct, it can lead to higher earnings, and it gives the workers a measure of control over their production. The continued battle over rates makes the workers very militant, for when the rate-fixer comes out to argue with you, you're immediately faced with the basic element of the class struggle : exploitation, potential or actual.'

The actual process of bargaining with the rate fixer is described as having the following crucial features :

'In disputes over prices there is one thing that is never discussed : the speed at which the job is done. We will discuss basic engineering problems such as maintaining certain finishes and dimensions, but not those of feeds and speeds. The reason is simple : the company must not be allowed to assert direct control over the speed at which a worker does his job. He must remain sole arbiter of that. It is part of his control over his working environment. The firm doesn't like this, of course, and would prefer so-called scientific methods such as time and motion studies etc. to determine rates, rather than what comes down fundamentally to a clash of individual strengths.'[57]

In less well organised plants this amount of workers' control over the piecework system was absent, but even here worker control over work speed and restriction of output (the very thing that it was felt piecework would eradicate) was common. This is illustrated in the account, based on personal experience, of the battle with the rate fixer in a Nottingham cycle factory by Alan Sillitoe in his novel of 1958, *Saturday and Sunday Morning*. Sillitoe's Arthur Seaton put it like this :

'At a piecework rate of four-and-six a hundred you could make your money if you knocked-up fourteen hundred a day—possible without grabbing too much—and if you went out for a thousand in the morning you could dawdle through the afternoon and lark about with the women and talk to your mates now and again.'

The fear of the rate-checker, and possible rate-cutting if 'too much' was earned, was ever present :

'Though you couldn't grumble at four-and-six a hundred the rate-checker sometimes came round and watched you at work, so that if he saw you knock up a hundred in less than an hour Robboe would come and tell you one fine morning that your rate had been dropped by sixpence or a bob. So when you felt the shadow of the rate-checker breathing down your neck you knew what to do if you had any brains at all : make everything more sophisticated, though not slow because that was cutting your own throat, and do everything deliberately yet with a crafty show of speed.'

In theory, piecework offered a worker the opportunity to maximise his earnings, but this rarely happened because of the danger of rate cutting. On one occasion Seaton works out, 'for fun', how high his wage would be if he worked all week at his top speed of 400 an hour. The answer was £36, a wage which he thought would leave him in the next week 'grabbing at the same flat-out lick for next to nowt. So he settled for a comfortable wage of fourteen pounds.'

Even where cutting of piece rates did not appear as an immediate threat London dockers would, for instance, settle on an output for a day's work before they started. Colonel R. B. Oram, who worked on the management side for the Port of London Authority from 1912, and who in the 1950s was Superintendent of the Surrey Commercial Docks, recalls an incident where he, in his early years, had hoped for an average of 400 tons discharge in a day by his gangs. When the noon average reached 250 tons Oram was greatly pleased and congratulated his foreman shipworkers on an output that would by the end of the day easily top 400 tons. The foreman told Oram that he was wrong and that he could not be more ignorant of the docker and his methods. 'Don't you know, guv'nor, that the men settle what they are going to do before they start work? Today they have settled for 350 tons.'[58] The foreman, according to Oram, went on to explain 'that the men had no intention of going home with a wet shirt. A man had promised his wife to take her to the Poplar Hippodrome that evening. It was only common sense that he shouldn't tire himself out when the morning was the right time to work hard.' But although Oram himself learnt this fundamental lesson early on in his career, it was not something that was realised by successive waves of management consultants with their productivity plans for the docks. Oram comments : 'As applied to the portworker they seemed to be based on an erroneous assumption that a docker comes to work to see how hard he can work and how much money he can earn. Nothing could be further from the truth. In the mind of every docker is the fixed sum he will be satisfied to earn and below which his domestic commitments will not permit his take-home money to fall.'[59] The opportunity which these dockers had to maximise their earnings was stoutly resisted. What they were looking for was a predictable, stable wage on the basis of a level of effort which made work as comfortable as possible, and which left them in decent shape to enjoy their non-work time. A vast amount of academic literature, both American and British, was in fact available, which confirmed the wrongness of the 'economic man' argument which lay behind much of the 'common sense' managerial thinking on this question.[60] But the belief in the output maximising effects of incentive schemes, much evidence notwithstanding, remained powerful with such people as R. M. Currie, the author of the standard book on Work Study, lending his support to it, for instance in his pamphlet for the British Institute of Management in 1963, *Financial Incentives.*

But how did this 'commonsense' view square itself with the reality observed by many managers of the existence of 'ca'canny' under payment by results? Wilfred Brown of the Glacier Metal Company realised the inconsistency here and in the late 1950s and early 1960s began to point it out to groups of managers. In 1962 he wrote that:

> 'In as far as the practice of "ca'canny" exists, it is the negation of the ostensible aim of W.I. (Wage Incentive) schemes which is to maximise output. On two occasions at conferences of managers I have pointed out to them the inconsistency between the two views held and expressed by the entire group present:
> (a) that wage incentive schemes are essential to high output, and
> (b) that "ca'canny" practices are widespread wherever wage incentive schemes operate.'[61]

Brown believed that ca'canny was practised in many workshops. By it he meant the fixing by a work group of maximum rates of output, with the use of group pressures to force transgressors into line. But he could find no workers ready to admit that they themselves practised it, though most of them would readily justify it on the following grounds:

> 'If a particularly adept or fast operator . . . produced a job at a rate well above the norm, he thereby set up the situation in which management could claim that the time allowance was too generous and demand a re-timing; thus, by his act, the operator might bring about a situation where the time was reduced and everybody must work at a more than reasonable speed to earn a reasonable wage. They claimed that such a practice as "ca'canny" protected slower operators from low wages by preventing the setting of time allowances, based on super-speed performances of abnormal operators, which would be unfair to them.'[62]

A practice related to this was that of 'banking of work' or what others called 'cross booking'. Under this system an operator in a week where, say, the rates on the jobs he had been allocated were 'loose', and therefore above average earnings could be made, would fail to return all the job tickets for jobs completed in that week, but rather would save some of them for the following week. This had two functions, first, to hide his high bonus, and secondly to carry over some of his earnings into the following week when jobs might be such that it was difficult to achieve the desired wage.

Tom Lupton in his study *On the Shop Floor* found this system operating in an extremely well-developed form in one of the workplaces he studied. The workers at 'Jays' themselves described what Lupton has called 'their systematic manipulation of the incentive scheme' as the 'fiddle'. The workers claimed the following advantages for the fiddle : a) to provide a defence against rate-cutting, b) to stabilise earnings, c) to protect themselves against the effects of management shortcomings, d) to give a measure of control over the relationship between effort and reward.[63] In the work group there were two persistent 'rate-busters' or 'job spoilers'. But these two were in fact tolerated by the others on the grounds that they did not pose a threat to the rest of the work group, since the two had become known as speedy workers and therefore were regarded as exceptions around whom the rates could not be legitimately altered. But the actual earnings difference between one of the job spoilers and one of the 'strict conformers' was very small indeed—almost a case of the hare and the tortoise, with the hare coming home only a short neck in front of the tortoise after some energetic sprints, in contrast with the tortoise's steady pace. The difference in earnings was only 2/9d. a week. Lupton observes that the 'tortoise' 'bought a lot of leisure at work for his 2/9d. per week, if one may put it thus crudely.' In general, Lupton concludes that the 'fiddle' did do most of the things that the workers felt it did— in short, it worked, and also it was an entirely rational stratagem from their point of view. It brought the earnings stability that was desired to facilitate family budgeting. It was also an important protection against rate-cutting, and it had obvious advantages from the point of view of providing 'some sort of compensation for dislocation of the planned work flow.'[64] In view of the fact that there was no adequate managerial estimate of what the output of the shop could be, as against the actual output, no adequate calculation of 'restriction of output' could be made. But management did make such charges against workers—though Lupton argues that such a charge of restriction of output could only be a 'general one stating that the workers could work harder than they were doing.'[65] This charge, of course, has been a common and persistent one—and Lupton is right to draw attention to the fact that much restriction of output has to be blamed on managerial failings in the organisation of production.

Labour quite obviously has a different view of what constitutes a fair day's work—and what level of pay should be forthcoming for the degree of effort involved—than does Capital.[66] Lupton's general conclusion confirms this. The 'fiddle' is 'an effective form of worker control over the job environment. The strength and solidarity of the workers, and the flexibility of the management system of control, made a form of adjustment possible in which different values about a fair day's work, and "proper" worker behaviour, could exist side by side.'[67] It has often been observed that there is great scope for such 'effort bargaining'.[68] As Lupton has suggested elsewhere 'These *effort bargains* for each job might take the form of tacit limitation of effort for a fixed wage, or active bargaining about a piecework price or time allowed to complete a job under P.B.R.' In a situation of labour scarcity or a tight product market workers' scope for the achievement of a favourable effort bargain is enhanced. And in any situation where the manager insisted on his prerogatives to make changes in job or method, 'the scope for detailed effort bargaining within the collective agreement' was increased.[69] This situation becomes an important factor in leading to a payment system 'getting out of control' as far as managers are concerned. Lupton and Gowler give a striking illustration of this process of loss of control, using an incentive bonus scheme of the kind common in the engineering industry as their example :

'Such a scheme probably rests on some formula that pays bonus for time saved on an agreed allowed time for the job. If there are a lot of changes of job, and method, if there are problems that come up unpredictably about shortage of work, or poor materials, or absence of parts, and labour is short and shop stewards powerful, there will surely be pressure from the men to slacken the allowed times and an inclination on the part of management to give way. There will also be a tendency for special allowances for one thing and another to be asked for and granted. We heard recently of a "frustration allowance"! It is also common for the effort side of the equation to be adjusted by the emergence of work group output norms—which are not the norms of management.'[70]

Wilfred Brown, whose work we quoted above, had long realised the fact that piecework bargaining in all its aspects could seriously undermine managerial control. It is no accident that the subtitle of his book of 1962 *Piecework Abandoned* was *the effect of Wage Incentive Systems on managerial authority*. Brown's perspective was that, due to piecework, managerial authority had diminished, was diminishing and should be increased. Brown's own firm, Glacier Metal, had taken its first move away from wage incentives to a flat rate system in the foundry of its London factory in June 1949.[71] The rest of the firm's plants followed suit shortly afterwards. In this, of course, Brown and Glacier Metal were swimming against the tide of the spread of payment by results and accompanying work study. Brown argued that the benefits claimed for Wage Incentive systems were greatly exaggerated and that, indeed, they created serious problems—of the sort outlined above. Brown was greatly concerned to illustrate that it was not only possible to run a successful enterprise without wage incentive systems, but also that their absence was central and indispensable to that success. He argued, for instance, that there were 'many inconsistences between W.I. systems and managerial control of work'; that W.I. systems, as well as making supervision of work less necessary, also made it 'less possible.' 'These systems,' he argued, 'thus tend to stimulate abdication of necessary decisions on the part of supervisors and foremen.' This theme recurs throughout the book. Wage Incentive systems deprived managers of even their 'minimal authority' which Brown argued ought to involve the acceptance of 'full responsibility for the manner in which his subordinates discharge the work he has delegated to them. . . . Wage incentive systems, however, tend to set up circumstances which are inconsistent with managerial-subordinate relations because they have concealed within them the more independent entrepreneur—sub-contractor relationship.'[72] The bargaining situation under piece-work lessened managerial authority—Brown complained :

'The sequence in which jobs are performed ceases to be wholly at the dictate of what is optimum for the company's manu-facturing programme; new methods are delayed; the distribu-tion of work between subordinates ceases to be based entirely on who is available or who can best do it; assessment of progress by operators in a holistic sense is substituted by a consideration of his record of bonus earnings; subordinates are not criticized for unnecessary loss of output because, in one sense, they are "paying" for such loss themselves. This abdica-tion of the full management-subordinate relationship seems to me to stem partly from wage incentive schemes.'[73]

The flat-rate wage system avoided all these pitfalls—put 'sub-ordinates' firmly in their subordinate roles—and allowed the setting up of 'full managerial roles'.

Brown's words tended to fall on deaf ears for a long time. But, given the erosion of much managerial control on account of vigorous shop floor bargaining over piece-rates, wage drift, strikes and the rest in the 1960s, the views put forward by Brown became increasingly heeded. In many productivity package deals the payment system was changed from piecework to measured day work. As MacKersie suggested in 1968 it was realised that many payment by results systems had lost their original 'pull' and managements were 'searching for new methods that will "freshen up" the works atmosphere.'[74] In the next sections we shall look at the nature of this 'freshening up' process, and its implications for the workers concerned.

NOTES

Many of the themes in this chapter were first developed by Tony Topham in an article in the International Socialist Journal, *Sept.-Dec. 1964 and reworked in his article 'New Types of Bargaining' in* The Incompatibles, *editors R. Blackburn and A. Cockburn (Pelican 1967)— my debt is considerable.*

1. J. J. Gillespie *Free Expression in Industry* (London 1948) p. 147
2. Ibid., p. 113.
3. Ibid., p. 107.
4. Ibid., pp. 16-17.
5. Graham Hutton *We Too Can Prosper* (London 1953) p. 233.
6. John Lovell and B. C. Roberts *A Short History of the T.U.C.* (London 1968) p. 158.
7. Drew Middleton *The British* (first pub. 1957, London 1958 edn.) p. 194.
8. Hutton, op. cit., p. 8.
9. T.U.C. *Trade Unions and Productivity* (1950), quoted in Hutton, op. cit., p. 49.
10. T.U.C. *Trade Unionism* (Jan 1967 edn.) p. 16.
11. Middleton, op. cit., p. 195, and Alan Flanders *The Fawley Productivity Agreements* (London 1964) p. 239.
12. Quoted in Middleton, op. cit., p. 201.
13. See Michael Shanks *The Stagnant Society* (Pelican 1964) p. 66, and Middleton op. cit., pp. 207-208.
14. Quoted in R. Marriott *Incentive Payment Systems* (London 1957) pp. 152-153.
15. F. Zweig *Productivity and Trade Unions* (Oxford 1951) p. 24.
16. Woodcock in *The Listener* 23 July 1959, quoted in Shanks, op. cit., p. 70.
17. See John A. Lincoln *The Restrictive Society. A Report on Restrictive Practices* (London 1967) p. 79.
18. Michael Shanks *The Stagnant Society* (first pub. as Pelican Special, 1964 imp.) pp. 63-64. It would be nice to have £5 for every time the British working class has been accused of 'luddism' in recent years.
19. The *Sunday Times* has returned to this theme on many occasions since 1964, and in an article in its issue of January 2, 1972, called it 'one of the most controversial and widely-read articles the *Sunday Times* has ever carried.'
20. Glyn Jones and Michael Barnes *Britain on Borrowed Time* (Pelican 1967) p. 15.
21. H. A. Clegg, quoted in Royal Commission on T.U.s and E.A.s, *Research Papers*, 4, (London 1967) pp. 56-57.
22. Institute of Economic Affairs *Source-book on Restrictive Practices in Britain* edited by Graham Hutton (London 1966) p. 4.
23. Ibid., p. 24.
24. E. Owen Smith *Productivity Bargaining: a case study in the steel industry* (London 1971) p. 3.
25. G. Hutton ed., op. cit., pp. 24-25.
26. Lincoln, op. cit., p. 14.
27. G. Hutton, ed., op. cit., p. 25.
28. Lord Shawcross, 'Foreword' to Lincoln, op. cit., p. 11.
29. R. B. McKersie and L. B. Hunter *Pay, Productivity and Collective Bargaining* (London 1973) p. 1. Perhaps the most valuable survey of the economic and industrial relations background to productivity bargaining is Lloyd Ulman, 'Collective Bargaining and Industrial Efficiency' in R. E. Caves (ed.) *Britain's Economic Prospects* (London and Washington 1968).
30. W. W. Daniel *Beyond the Wage-Work Bargain* (London 1970) p. 1.

31. A. Flanders *The Fawley Productivity Agreements* (London 1964) p. 13.
32. Daniel, op. cit., p. 18.
33. Daniel, op. cit., p. 18.
34. Quoted in Royal Commission, *Research Papers*, 4, p. 41.
35. See Daniel, op. cit., pp. 34-35 and T. Topham 'Productivity Bargaining' in *Trade Union Register 1969* (London 1969).
36. Alan Flanders, preface to B. Towers, T. G. Whittingham, and A. W. Gottschalk (eds.) *Bargaining for Change* (London 1972) p. 11.
37. Eric Jacobs in *Sunday Times* July 20, 1975.
38. Royal Commission, *Research Papers*, 4, p. 1.
39. T. Topham *The Organised Worker* (London 1975) p. 43.
40. R. O. Clarke, D. J. Fatchett, and B. C. Roberts *Workers' Participation in Management* (London 1972) pp. 104-105.
41. Topham, *Organised Worker*, p. 43.
42. See Royal Commission, *Research Paper*, 4, 'Restrictive Labour Practices', pp. 60-61.
43. Quoted in ibid., p. 61.
44. K. J. W. Alexander and C. L. Jenkins *Fairfields: a study in industrial change* (London 1970) p. 213.
45. Robin Murray *U.C.S. The Anatomy of Bankruptcy* (Nottingham 1972) p. 71.
46. Quoted in Murray, op. cit., p. 65.
47. Murray, op. cit., p. 71.
48. R. Brown, P. Brannen, J. Cousins, M. Samphries 'Leisure in Work: the "occupational culture" of shipbuilding workers' in *Leisure and Society in Britain* eds. M. Smith, S. Parker and C. Smith (London 1973) p. 103. They also suggest (p. 109) that leisure-taking at work will become less and less regarded as 'illicit or improper.'
49. R. B. McKersie, 'Changing Wage Payment Systems', Royal Commission on Trade Unions and Employers' Associations, Research Paper No. 11, p. 31.
50. A. W. Willsmore *Modern Production Control* (London 1946) p. 134. The hope that the book would be of use to both sides on Joint Production Committees appears on p. vi.
51. J. P. Davison, P. Sargant Florence, Barbara Gray, and N. S. Ross *Productivity and Economic Incentives* (London 1958), pp. 17, 19, 24, and 262.
52. McKersie, op. cit., p. 35. It is further estimated that before the Second World War the percentage of all wage earners on P.B.R. was about 25 per cent, and in 1957 about 31 per cent.
53. Tony Cliff *The Employers' Offensive* (London 1970) pp. 46ff.
54. Scanlon, interview in *New Left Review*, No. 46, Nov-Dec 1967.
55. See A. I. Marsh, *Industrial Relations in Engineering* (Oxford 1965) pp. 170-171. The recent study *Piecework Bargaining* (London 1973) by William Brown has shown that, in fact, wage drift is greatest where steward organisation is weakest.
56. Glyn Jones and Michael Barnes *Britain on Borrowed Time* (Harmondsworth 1967) p. 122.
57. Phil Higgs 'The Convenor' in R. Fraser (ed.) *Work*, Vol. 2 (Harmondsworth 1969).
58. Colonel R. B. Oram *The Dockers' Tragedy* (London 1970) p. 113.

It is highly interesting to note that in 1970, when the payment system on London docks was being changed from piecework to a day work system, an observer recorded that 'I am told that dockers have currently worked out how much work they propose to do when piece rates are abolished; this has been explained to me with a wealth of figures by a docker. Put crudely, this means that if the new time rate gives the docker, say, £10 for his day's work, then he proposes to do a tonnage equivalent to £10 at present piece rates. To exceed this tonnage would be to give the employer the excess.' Letter from G. Pattison in *Bulletin of the Society for the Study of Labour History*, Autumn 1970, p. 16. Not very long ago, because of output problems under day work, there was a return to a financial incentive scheme on the docks.

59. Ibid., p. 113.

60. See for example William F. Whyte and others *Money and Motivation* (New York 1955) and, also, the selections from the work of Whyte, Leonard Sayles, Donald Roy, Melville Dalton in *Payment Systems* ed. T. Lupton (Harmondsworth 1972). Lupton in his introduction to R. G. Searle-Barnes *Pay and Productivity Bargaining* (Manchester 1969, p. xii), puts the position as follows: 'Much research throws doubt on the widely held opinion that, given a choice between expending more physical or mental effort, taking more care etc., in order to increase income, and withholding effort at the risk or certainty of decreasing income, operatives will *in all circumstances* necessarily make the first choice. There is an extensive scientific and popular literature on 'limitation of output' (ca'canny in pit parlance), and the clear inference that can be drawn from it is that there are some circumstances where, beyond a point well short of the onset of fatigue, the lure of extra money does *not* call forth extra effort.'

61. Wilfred Brown *Piecework Abandoned: the effect of wage incentive systems on managerial authority* (London 1962) p. 22.

62. Brown, op. cit., pp. 21-22.

63. T. Lupton *On the Shop Floor* (Oxford 1963) p. 170.

64. Ibid., p. 181.

65. Ibid., p. 182.

66. For much stimulating discussion on this point see Richard Hyman and Ian Brough *Social Values and Industrial Relations* (Oxford 1975) esp. Ch. 2 'A Fair Day's Work', and pp. 64-74.

67. Lupton *On the Shop Floor* pp. 182-183.

68. H. Behrend 'The Effort Bargain' in *Industrial and Labour Relations Review*, July 1957, W. Baldamus *Efficiency and Effort* (London 1961), Hyman and Brough, op. cit., esp. pp. 64-74.

69. Lupton, introduction to Searle-Barnes, op. cit., pp. xiii-xiv.

70. T. Lupton and D. Gowler 'Selecting a Wage Payment Scheme', 1969, in *Payment Systems* ed. T. Lupton (1972) p. 245.

71. Wilfred Brown *Piecework Abandoned* p. 43, and generally Chapter 4 'Dropping Wage Incentives'.

72. Ibid., p. 70.

73. Ibid., p. 71.

74. McKersie, op. cit., p. 31.

XV

The Coal Industry and the National Power Loading Agreement

One of the major industries to make the changeover from piecework to a system of Measured Day Work in the 1960s was the British coal industry.[1] It is worth recounting this transition in some detail since it raises a number of important points about restriction of output and about the effect of changes in payment systems on managerial control. The miner had traditionally enjoyed a good deal of independence from close managerial control, and had exercised a good deal of control over his own work. The advent since 1966 of the National Power Loading Agreement has, in the words of a group of Yorkshire miners, considerably altered this and the 'old work-group self-management' has been replaced by 'new managerial supervision.'[2] The old work-group self-management had been noted by Carter Goodrich in 1918. Discussing the contemporary 'control demand' he noted that:

'I heard a group of Derbyshire miners thrashing out the problem. "Supervision is nauseous". On that they heartily agreed. "But supervision is necessary". Yes, if only for safety. Then one of them men suggested that there might be another sort of supervision—"amicable discipline" he called it—in which the supervisors should be elected by and responsible to the workers.'[3]

Recounting a story told to him by a former miner's agent in Lanarkshire, Goodrich made an even more telling point on how in practice miners effectively rejected any externally imposed supervision. Detailing a case in which an overman was called, under the Minimum Wage Act, to give evidence as to whether or not a certain workman did his job properly, the overman said:

'I never saw him work.'

'Magistrate : "But isn't it your duty under the Mines Act to visit each workting place twice a day?"

' "Yes."

' "Don't you do it?"

' "Yes."

' "Then why didn't you ever see him work?"

' "They always stop work when they see an overman coming, and sit down and wait till he's gone—even take out their pipes if it's a mine free from gas. They won't let anybody watch them".'[4]

It was not, of course, merely a matter of miners' resentment of supervision which led to this sort of thing. The other important factor was that managerial supervision of the sort common in above ground employments was difficult to translate into practice underground. Colliery managers had to rely on other managerial stratagems than supervision to attain their goal of seeking constantly to reduce the labour cost per unit of output—which in its turn would lead to the margin between costs and proceeds being increased and profit margins maximised. Many mine managers relied on their choice of payment system to do this. In practice this amounted to the use of piecework. The situation in South Wales, for example, just before the First World War was put in the following way by a writer sympathetic to the coal owners :

'In a coal mine such supervision as is possible and is generally practised in surface employments is impracticable. The piece rate may not be a perfect method of wage remuneration; but while it automatically punishes the lazy and the indifferent workman it at the same time automatically rewards the capable and industrious workman. Both get the wages they have earned, but in the one case they are low and in the other high; and as the labour of the man who earns the higher wage yields the larger return of marketable commodity for the capital and managerial energy expended on the undertaking he is the better servant of the two.'[5]

So, in short, notwithstanding the remarks above about the expenditure of managerial energy, piecework was partly a substitute for supervision, adopted in the hope that workers would drive themselves towards high earnings via high output. The manager, however, with his ever-present preoccupation with the productivity of labour, as opposed to mere production, had to pay attention to the problem of what each unit of production, in this case ton of coal, would cost to produce. The crucial question, therefore—having dispensed with the supervision problem through the adoption of piecework instead—was the initial establishment of the piece rate for a particular face at a particular time. This was no easy or uncontentious matter. It was precisely at this time of the establishment of the rates that capital and labour fought tooth and nail in pursuance of their divergent objectives—the one to minimise labour costs per unit of production and thereby to increase profit margins, the other to establish rates of pay per unit of production which would maximise earnings without undue expenditure of effort. The power that management had to manage by virtue merely of their ownership and control of the means of production was, at this stage of the proceedings, used to considerable advantage. This is made abundantly clear in some remarks made not long ago by the late Dai Dan Evans, former General Secretary of the South Wales Miners :

'These negotiations were conducted wherever a new seam was being developed. These were very important days, weeks or months of negotiation for both parties. The main item of contention was the price to be paid per ton of coal produced by the collier. . . . The haggling would go on for weeks or months. Here again the employers were at an advantage inasmuch as they managed the pit and would develop the seam on a day-wage basis until such time as agreement was arrived at on the terms of the Price List. Later they would employ the "Ianto Full Pelts" in the seam, i.e., those men who were overblessed with brawn . . . the pace setters . . . men of no scruples. The employers' representative at the pit or boss would pay these men wages much in excess of the daywage. This was a private arrangement and would by this method measure the productive capacity of the workmen working in the new seam. This did not deter the men's representatives; they held out as long as possible and later would be obliged to settle the price much to their disadvantage because of the indiscretions committed by the Iantos who were members of their ranks.'[6]

This victory for the employers was often only temporary. The Price List established often failed to provide men with the earnings they wanted, and this produced much discontent, and continuous haggling. Dai Dan Evans said that 'Disputes arose and strikes and go slow tactics were adopted in an effort to secure redress. At first the boss remained absolutely rigid and paid the men strictly in accordance with the agreed Price List. . . . The relationship between men and management became exceedingly strained.' In the end it was sometimes found that a Price List was subsidised, or that a compromise was arranged at rates somewhere between the men's demand and the employers' original offer.[7]

This picture of highly localised piecewage bargaining—which produced great variations in earnings not only within coalfields and between different groups of workers but also between coalfields—was the situation the National Coal Board inherited on its establishment in 1947. South Wales, for instance, because of substantial geological difficulties in many pits and also because of an extremely powerful and real tradition of hostility, if not warfare, between Capital and Labour, was at Vesting Date at around the bottom of the table of relative earnings in the coal industry. It continued to stay there through the first two decades of the nationalised industry's existence. Nottinghamshire, on the other hand, to give a contrasting example, had relatively favourable geological conditions, a high degree of mechanisation and many modern pits, and Nottinghamshire miners (along with their colleagues in Kent) were usually at the top of the earnings table. On top of this relations between Capital and Labour in the Notts coalfield were in sharp contrast to those in South Wales. The Notts coalfield in the inter-war years had been dominated by the activities and philosophy of trade unionism of George Spencer, which involved striving to combine high earnings for the Notts mineworkers with high profits for the employers (the two being regarded as dependent on each other), all carried out because of and through a high degree of co-operation between Capital and Labour. In 1948, three years after his retirement as General Secretary of the Notts miners, and three years after the formation of the National Union of Mineworkers (something which he opposed) and one year after nationalisation of the industry, Spencer reviewed his own beliefs as follows :

'I have always made it a cardinal point of policy to show that by joint effort with the Management material benefits will result to the worker. It is no exaggeration to say that in Nottinghamshire the employees fully accept this thesis and the consistent and good labour record exemplified as it is by the increasing output per man shift over the years, shows that the theories which I propounded in 1926 and which I acted upon, when put into practice with a co-operative management produces the best possible kind of results, both from a managerial and labour point of view.'[8]

In the 1926 lockout, with many Notts miners returning to work unofficially, Spencer had decided that further resistance to the owners was likely to be ineffective and therefore he attempted to negotiate a return to work in Nottinghamshire. This led to his expulsion from the Miners' Federation of Great Britain, and before long Spencer was at the head of a breakaway union supported by most of the owners. The Spencer Union stood for, amongst other things, district agreements whereas the Miners' Federation of Great Britain, and especially the South Wales Miners, were striving for a national wages structure. The eventual 'defeat' of the Spencer Union in the late 1930s was followed by the amalgamation of the two rival Notts miners' unions, with Spencer at its head. The new union was admitted to the Miners' Federation of Great Britain. Even then, Spencer resisted attempts to take away autonomy from its component unions. He was not in favour of the formation of the National Union of Mineworkers, though he was powerless to stop its formation in 1945. The rules of the new union meant that Spencer had to retire. But this did not quite silence him and he continued to criticise what he regarded as Nottingham's subsidisation of 'less efficient or less fortunate' coal fields.[9] But Spencer was swimming against the tide.

On its formation in 1945 the N.U.M. issued a Miners' Charter in which, amongst other things, a call was made for the general application of the day wage system, and for the abolition of piecework. In the twenty years after Vesting Date little progress was made. The abolition of piecework, however, soon became an objective of the National Coal Board as well as of the N.U.M. The reason for this was that piecework was the major source of stoppages. An American academic in 1955 put the situation like this :

'The conclusion is clear : the great majority of unofficial strikes begin with the coal-face grades, particularly the "direct labour" groups (colliers and fitters) although stoppages among rippers, packers, wastemen, pan-turners (conveyor shifters) are not uncommon. It is the highest wage groups (those paid under incentive contracts) which produce most stoppages and the lowest wage groups (those paid by time) which provide the fewest; it would appear the prevailing method of incentive payment underlies the great majority of stoppages.'[10]

Six years after the end of piecework the Board, in its evidence in 1972 to the Wilberforce Commission, still spoke out strongly against piecework : 'It was an extremely complicated system which militated against the efficiency of the industry. It contained many marked differences in wage rates for the same job, which were often indefensible and which the men felt to be unjust.'[11] What progress was made in the early years of nationalisation did, to some extent, telescope differentials between jobs, and more especially between Wages Districts. The upshot of this was that the Notts coalfield tended to lose some of the earnings advantage it had previously had over other districts.[12] In April 1955 a national day wage structure was established. This covered virtually all surface jobs and most underground jobs which were away from the coal face. On the coal face, however, 84 per cent of the total labour force was on piecework—and so thorny were the problems involved in the attempt to establish a national piecework structure that during the mid-1950s it seemed that further progress in rationalising the industry's wage structure would not be forthcoming. In 1958 however, the Coal Board and the N.U.M. agreed that piecework should be tackled bit by bit, with power loader men as the first bite of the cherry.[13] Power loading men were, in fact, becoming increasingly more numerous in the industry both in relative and absolute terms.

331

From the 1950s a spectacular range of new machinery was introduced into the mines. The number of power loading machines employed on longwall faces increased from 280 in 1954 to 1,052 in 1957.[14] By 1963 61.2 per cent of deepmined output came from mechanised faces. Throughout this period of increasing mechanisation mineworkers were subjected to barrages of exhortation from the Board to 'use machines more fully.' In a N.C.B. Public Relations Department pamphlet, *Coal-recipe for success*, published about 1964, it was pointed out that machine operating times on most mechanised faces averaged just over two and a half hours per shift. The pamphlet commented : 'Surely we can do better than this.' The N.C.B. certainly felt that 'we' could— 'This has been proved by method study.' It went on to say :

> 'Greater use of manriding will get the men to the coalface more quickly, leaving more time for production on each shift. Each coalface must be considered individually. Method study will show where performance can be improved. There are many possibilities. Some delays are due to human failings; unskilled or careless operation of the machine; poor time-keeping; poor organisation of the face team; substandard work in the clearance of service systems outbye resulting in hold-ups on the face. Such failings call for better organisation and teamwork.'[15]

By 1971 92.2 per cent of deepmined output came from mechanised faces. Over the period output per manshift at the face increased dramatically : from 92.9 cwt. in 1963 to 143.5 cwt. in 1971.[16] The spread of mechanisation at the coalface was indeed one of the main justifications adopted by both the N.U.M. and the N.C.B. for moving away from piecework towards a fixed day rate. In 1966 when this finally happened and the National Power Loading Agreement was adopted, the N.C.B. and the N.U.M. in a joint statement pointed out that coalface mechanisation had reached a point where 'it is the machine . . . in the main that determines the amount of production that comes from a coal face.'[17] The object of N.P.L.A. was, according to the preface to the 1966 agreement, to ensure that 'a man's wages will be determined not by the part of the country in which he works, but by the job he does.'[18]

The N.P.L.A. of 1966 did not immediately create one standard national rate of pay for each job. Rather it carried a commitment to bring about a uniform national rate by 31 December 1971, taking the Nottinghamshire rate as the rate at which uniformity would be established. In 1966 the Nottinghamshire N.P.L.A. shift rate was 86/9d., second highest to Kent at 89/5d. Six other coalfields (Yorkshire, Lancashire, North Derbyshire, South Derbyshire, Northumberland, and Warwickshire) were on rates in the 81 to 84 shilling range. There were six coalfields at the lowest rate of 75 shillings, including Scotland, Cumberland, Durham and South Wales. By January 1972 shiftrates were £5 in all coalfields.[19] Maintaining our South Wales-Nottinghamshire comparison, it will come as no surprise to learn that South Wales was happy with this equalisation of earnings between areas (though by no means happy, of course, with the level of the earnings), whereas Nottinghamshire was hesitant. It is perhaps exceptionally surprising that Nottinghamshire, in view of its Spencerist past, in the end acquiesced in an arrangement which deliberately depressed its increase in earnings. At a Special Conference of the N.U.M. held in April 1966 to discuss the N.P.L.A., Will Paynter, the then General Secretary of the N.U.M. and a former South Wales miner himself, commended the proposed Agreement to his members saying amongst other things that it represented a move 'in relation to face workers towards the realisation of a national uniform rate for the job.' An echo of one aspect of Spencerism then emerged, when Joe Whelan of Nottinghamshire delivered the main speech in opposition to the Agreement, pointing out that many Notts miners would lose money, and adding that whilst he supported the principle of a standard rate he felt that there were 'justifiable reasons to feel that it is at the expense of our pieceworkers in the Notts. coalfield.'[20] In the event, however, the Notts miners selflessly acquiesced in the arrangement—though the argument, as we shall see later, was not quite over.

The National Power Loading Agreement came into effect from 6th June, 1966. Under the agreement men on powerloaded coalfaces (i.e. over 90 per cent of all faces) were to be paid on 'standard shift payments' rather than on piecework. Levels of manning on jobs and workloads were to be established by method study. Wage negotiations were transferred from local level to national level.[21] Bob Heath has extracted from the N.C.B.'s Report and Accounts for 1966–67 the reasons which the Board itself gave for wanting to move away from piecework. They are as follows :

1. 'Piecework was becoming increasingly inappropriate as a means of payment for men on mechanized faces where productivity depends less on physical effort than on the utilization of machines.'
2. 'Agreements based on piecework needed constant revision and re-negotiation and they were the source of many stoppages and disputes in the industry.'
3. 'Deployment of men can be more flexible than when earnings varied from face to face and with a standard shift wages can be more effectively controlled.'
4. 'The agreement considerably changed long-standing practices and habits.'[22]

Amongst the implications of N.P.L.A. which Heath foresaw were the following : a much greater degree of supervision; a transfer of job control and job discretion away from the individual worker and his work group and towards the management and the immediate supervisors; and also because of the transfer of negotiations from local to national level 'a diminishing effectiveness of local power.'[23] Heath was not just making inspired guesses when he wrote his article in 1969. Already at that time there was a good deal of evidence of the growth of management and supervision in many respects. Production plans were drawn up for each face unit in each pit, and they were accompanied by notes which stated that the objectives of the Face Manager should include the following things : 'Check the *exact* time the men arrive at and leave the face.' 'Check the *actual speed* of the machines against planned speeds.' 'Attaining shift objectives.' 'The Face Manager will ensure efficient and economical working of his face with maximum machines utilisation time.'[24] By 1969 also there was abundant evidence not only of 'faster and more continuous working within the shift' but also of a significant increase in multi-shift working. Citing the N.C.B. *Report and Accounts*, Heath reports that in the first year of the operation of N.P.L.A. the number of longwall faces working three or four shifts increased by about 33 per cent.[25] An example of this growth of shift work appears in a rank and file miners' paper, *The Mineworker*, in 1969. Dave Douglass, a spare collier at Hatfield Main Colliery, near Doncaster, in an article called 'Events at Hatfield' was writing of the militant feeling that was at that time present in Branch meetings over the 'issue of 4 shifts rearing its ugly head again.' The Hatfield men were at that stage managing to fight off the introduction of four shifts, but Douglass expected the issue to re-emerge before long. A number of other pits in the Doncaster coalfield had already had four shifts forced on them. In an appeal for solidarity with Hatfield when the issue came up again Douglass wrote : 'You may already be on 4 shifts but remember how hard you fought against them and all the cunning, clever or dastardly means which were concocted to break your fight. STAND WITH HATFIELD. The issue goes further—Silverwood struck recently, the first pit in Doncaster fighting off continental shifts (no weekends).'

It is worth looking at the growth of shiftwork in the coal industry—using Nottinghamshire as an example—in some detail. But it should be remembered first of all that the growth of shiftwork was not only taking place in the coal industry—but in many other sectors too. Shiftwork had long been regarded as a potential productivity raising technique. An extension of shiftwork had been recommended by several of the Anglo-American productivity teams; perhaps the most successful change at Fawley brought about by the productivity deal was the eradication of systematic overtime and its replacement by an extension of shiftworking. In 1971 the acknowledged expert on the economics of shiftwork, Robin Marris, in a National Economic Development Office monograph on *Multiple Shiftwork* suggested that a substantial contribution to economic growth could be made by productivity agreements consisting of the following basic package : 'shorter hours (less overtime) with higher hourly earnings; shiftwork with higher output per man hour.' By 1968 it was estimated that about two million workers were on shifts—and that the proportion of the working population on shifts would grow at about one per cent per year.[26] In spite of a good deal of medical evidence about the physiological and psychological problems caused by working unusual hours, shiftwork has proliferated precisely because it is an important way in which the capitalist can secure an adequate return on his capital outlay over a short enough period and before obsolescence sets in. One medical authority on shiftwork has explained the great growth of shiftworking in the 1950s and 1960s in the following terms : 'The sophisticated nature of much modern plant and equipment has meant that continuous operation, and continuous manning, has been increasingly necessary on technical grounds.' And further that even where these technical necessities have not applied that 'the high cost of such plant has usually been economically justifiable only if intensive use has been intended. The speed of technological development, and the consequent need for early replacement, has also placed a premium upon intensive use.'[27] In recent years not only has shiftwork become more widespread, but it has also become more structurally elaborate. In the past the most common forms of shiftwork were the double-day shift system (two eight hour shifts starting at 6.00 a.m. and 2.00 p.m.) and the day shift and night shift systems, and a variety of other discontinuous shift systems. In recent years the numbers of workers being expected to work on continuous shift systems (where work never stops even at weekends) has increased markedly. The so-called 'Continental' shift system of four teams operating three eight hour shifts in rotation has found increasing favour with employers, but is widely disliked by workers, especially since so much of society's 'normal' leisure activities are a reflection of the leisure patterns of those who work from 9.00 a.m. to 5.00 p.m., Monday to Friday.[28] Trade unionists who did not relish the thought of the spread of shiftwork were, however, in the period of the great productivity drive, accused of being guilty of heinous crimes against the British economy. Their accusers, it is important to note, were predominantly drawn from those occupations which were singularly unaffected by shift work. These people in fact often enjoyed what Marris has called 'one of the most valued middle-class privileges' that of 'getting out of bed an hour later than the rest of the population.'[29]

Two television journalists bemoaned the fact that Nottinghamshire mineworkers were unwilling in the mid-1960s to relinquish their traditional work and leisure patterns to service the National

Coal Board's '21st Century Mine' at Bevercotes, where £18 million of new capital investment, if the Board's capital utilisation objectives were to be fulfilled, required servicing by men 24 hours a day, seven days a week.[30] The National Coal Board had not counted on the opposition of the Notts miners to the venture. In the Notts coalfield, as in other coalfields, long-established patterns of shift work had elevated the weekends to a place of singular importance as, by and large, the only regular guaranteed leisure time. Consequently the N.C.B.'s proposals for weekend working at Bevercotes were rejected by the Nottingham Area of the N.U.M. The National officials of the N.U.M. were clearly not prepared to accept this and—in the summer of 1966—they secured new terms for the Bevercotes workers and strongly urged the Notts Area to accept them. At a Special Executive Committee meeting of the Notts Area in August 1966 it was decided to recommend that the Notts miners should accept the new terms, but a rider was added to this that an assurance should be sought from national level in the N.U.M. that acceptance of the proposed Bevercotes agreement 'will not prejudice the operation of the Five Day Week Agreement at all other collieries in the Notts Coalfield.'[31] Shortly afterwards, Will Paynter, the then General Secretary of the N.U.M., was able to reassure the Notts area that the withdrawal of the Five Day Week agreement at Bevercotes would have no influence on other collieries. The proposed Bevercotes agreement, however, still had to be put to a ballot of the members of the Notts area. In the event they voted to reject the agreement. Not to be out-manouevred by mere rank and file democracy, the N.U.M. national headquarters spent much of the autumn of 1966 seeking ways of getting Bevercotes working on terms acceptable to the N.C.B. One reason for this was undoubtedly the barrage of hostile criticism in the newspapers and elsewhere, on account of the rejection of the deal. After a meeting of the N.E.C. on 13 October 1966 the N.U.M. National President, Sidney Ford, said about the rejection by the Notts area members of the proposed Bevercotes agreement that :

'It has been suggested in certain press reports that the attitude of the National Union and/or some of its members is preventing this colliery (in which the industry has invested over £18m) from commencing production. Let me make it quite clear that there is no question of Luddism, nor any question of the N.U.M. or its members preventing Bevercotes from commencing production.'

He went on to do the N.C.B.'s job for it, by pointing out that the Board could in fact, run the pit on existing agreements— although the National Executive Committee still favoured the new agreement.

No attempt was made to run Bevercotes on existing agreements : to have done so would perhaps have made it plain that all pits could lose their Five Day Week agreement. Instead the two Notts members of the N.E.C. found themselves confronted at that body's next meeting with a new, unannounced discussion on Bevercotes—with firm suggestions being put forward by the National Officers for a compromise agreement. The N.E.C. tack was now that the Bevercotes Agreement was a 'National Matter' 'which could not be over-ruled by an area'—and that a compromise agreement had to be reached or else the N.C.B. would unilaterally decide to work Bevercotes under existing national agreements.[32] At this point the N.E.C. by 'an overwhelming majority' agreed that National Officials should approach the N.C.B. 'with a view to Bevercotes Colliery starting production under the special agreement for an experimental period of three years, with three shift coal turning per day and eighteen coal turning shifts per week, and the decision as to which three remaining shifts at the weekend should be non-productive should be taken at the pit.' At the Notts Area E.C. meeting on 14 November, where all this was reported and debated upon, a strong protest was made about the N.E.C's action.[33] This protest, however, had relatively little effect. A letter from the General Secretary pointed out that the N.E.C. had always hoped that the Bevercotes agreement would have been accepted by the Notts Area, 'but', he added, 'at no time has the N.E.C. been prepared to abrogate its authority in this matter. Following the last vote of your Area, and the report that the opposition centred around weekend working, we had further discussions with the Board and obtained a modification as to the number of coal winding shifts which should be worked. . . .' To drive his point home Paynter again stated that the principles concerned were of a national, and not of a local, character. These 'national principles', drafted at the safe distance of the Euston Road in London, were decidedly unpopular when they became 'local practice' at Bevercotes in North Nottinghamshire. It was no surprise, therefore, that as the three years of the Bevercotes Agreement were coming to an end the 625 Bevercotes mineworkers voted in November 1969 not to continue the seven day working week, 20 shift rota system, when the agreement expired in January 1970.[34] The reasons for the rejection of the continuation of the Bevercotes agreement were twofold. Firstly, that the Bevercotes workers were sick of working weekends because it interfered with 'their weekend social life, particularly Saturday afternoon football,'[35] and secondly, some Bevercotes workers argued that, although they were not entirely opposed to weekend working, they would only do it if the Board offered them a good deal more money.[36] At the time of writing Bevercotes is losing money—over £2 on each ton produced—and there is evidence that the '21st Century' mine has already in its short life had an extremely large labour turnover.[37]

Worker resistance to management was also forthcoming at around the same time over what miners were calling 'rough-shock treatment by management'—for instance, at Bentley Colliery, Doncaster in August 1968. The increase in supervision was real enough—the ratio of officials to workers in North Derbyshire increased from approximately 1 to 12 in June 1967, to 1 to 9.5 in July 1968.[38] 'Pent-up frustration resulting from the new system of management' was, according to a powerful document issued by leaders of the Yorkshire miners' strike in October 1969, a factor behind the strong unofficial action that was taking place. The document contrasted the new managers unfavourably even with the hated buttyman when it came to the question of job allocation (over which, under N.P.L.A., the management had much greater control): 'the buttyman boss could be relied on to be off at Doncaster Races or elsewhere, while the management is on your back and breathing down your neck all the time. . . . The result of these efforts at managerial control over our working lives has been to create a mixture of flaming anger and dull despair.'[39] In Yorkshire, at least, if one National Association of Colliery Overmen, Deputies and Shotfirers branch secretary is to be believed, this anti-management feeling was by 1975 widespread. P. Morris, a N.A.C.O.D.S. branch secretary from Maltby, wrote to *The Observer* in October 1975 to comment on a long interview with the Yorkshire Area N.U.M. Secretary, Arthur Scargill, that had been published in the paper a few weeks before. Morris wanted to raise the issue of 'discipline in the pits' which he felt had rapidly deteriorated and was affecting safety. 'Since 1972,' he commented, 'the philosophy emanating from Barnsley has created a climate of opinion amongst members of the N.U.M. which questions the value of colliery management.'[40] There is, in fact, little doubt that anti-supervision sentiment had manifested itself strongly in the 1972 and 1974 miners' strikes—with N.A.C.O.D.S. members complaining that they were being harassed and abused in various ways by N.U.M. members. These strikes were, of course, in themselves also largely products of the new situation in the mining industry that had been brought about as a result of changing from local piecework bargaining to national day wage bargaining.

In an academic article written not long after the 1972 strike, Dr. A. R. Griffin, Area Industrial Relations Officer for the North Notts Area of the N.C.B., makes a number of interesting points about output under N.P.L.A. and the attendant intensification of management. Griffin makes it clear that, under N.P.L.A., the prime managerial problem is that of low productivity. He controverts the view of a writer in the *Financial Times* in March 1969 who sought to attribute the improvement of productivity in the coal industry in the late 1960s to N.P.L.A. The *Financial Times* writer had said that:

'Productivity growth over the past year also owes much to the introduction of a new wages agreement which gives the coal face worker guaranteed earnings unrelated to output or variations in mining conditions.

'Contrary to the gloomy predictions of those who believe in the piecework system the new agreement has been followed by increased productivity.'

But Griffin pointed out that N.P.L.A. coincided with the introduction of improved machinery, powered supports systems *and* supervision and added that 'there is no evidence that the N.P.L.A. generated increased productivity. On the contrary,' he continued, 'on the one coal face job where no change other than the N.P.L.A. has taken place (namely hand ripping) performances have dropped in some cases alarmingly.' He also believed that there had probably been 'a similar, though probably smaller, reduction in effort by men employed on other face jobs which was for a time masked by the other changes.'[41] Griffin concludes that by 1970 productivity increases were slowing down in spite of big injections of capital, and that by 1972 when he was writing productivity was 'at best, standing still.' He had no doubt that the N.P.L.A. had a clear disincentive effect. He specifies the disincentive effect as follows :

'For example, one effect of the absence of an incentive is to walk more slowly to the face at the beginning of the shift and to leave as early as possible at its end : improved and extended man-riding facilities can offset the first and improved supervision can hold the second tendency in check. Again with the absence of an incentive, where a machine breaks down during a shift, the face team have no interest in making good the lost time subsequently : this can be offset by buying more robust machinery and maintaining it better so as to reduce the number and duration of breakdowns.'[42]

But, as Griffin rightly points out, there are obvious limits to what can be done to improve productivity in these ways. Believing that improved productivity could only be substantially improved with 'the conscious co-operation of the men', he goes on to explore ways of involving the men in the decision-making process. Besides looking at the existing arrangements for consultation and conciliation in the industry, he also looks at the possibilities of 'direct participation at the place of work', at job enrichment, self-regulating work groups, and productivity bargaining. Writing only six years after the introduction of the N.P.L.A., Griffin not surprisingly dismissed the idea of using financial incentive schemes. 'Wage rates are now determined at national level and they are unrelated, except in the most general way, to productivity. It is therefore no use looking in our case to a productivity deal to help to produce shared objectives.'[43]

It is a rather large surprise that those words were rendered less than accurate, at least temporarily, within two years of their being written. In 1974, only eight years after the introduction of the N.P.L.A., but two national strikes later, the N.C.B. was, after all, talking 'productivity' with a suggestion for a partial return to a payment system based on a direct financial incentive. In the context of an energy crisis brought about through massive increases in the price of oil, and in the context of the return of a Labour Government to office committed strategically to a *quid pro quo* arrangement with the trade unions, the Secretary of State for Energy, the former Derbyshire mineworker Eric Varley, established a tripartite examination of the coal industry. In June 1974 the Interim Report of the Coal Industry Examination appeared. The Working Group of the Examination on Industrial Relations (made up like the Examination as a whole of representatives of Government, the N.C.B., and the trade unions) put the problem like this :

'The Working Group is examining the factors which tend to limit output and productivity. Outstanding amongst them is the urgent need for a new attitude and spirit in the industry.' (para. 27)

The Working Group felt the prospects for this were good, and in their Final Report published in early November 1974, they welcomed a resolution passed at the N.U.M. Executive urging members of the union to give full co-operation to the N.C.B.'s agreed output targets. But, the Final Report went on, this was not good enough. The Working Group believed that existing pits had the capacity to produce 'perhaps eight or nine million tons more than the present deepmined output target of 120 million tons a year.' Paragraph 29 on 'Use of machinery' is of considerable interest for it stated that on mechanised faces 'the level of output achieved depends on the proportion of time during which the cutting machinery is working and this remains disappointingly low.' An improvement in this direction was, of course, a long-standing aspiration. The Final Report, however, was not content to rely on such hopes—instead it re-iterated the suggestion for a return to an incentive scheme which had been outlined in the Interim Report a few months earlier. Paragraph 28 of the Interim Report was reproduced :

'A sound and effective incentive scheme could make a major contribution in raising the efficiency of production and matching performance to the industry's true potential. We hope that negotiations for such a scheme will be resumed as soon as possible and be pursued with the greatest vigour and determination.'[44]

In the period between June and October 1974 the N.C.B. had indeed made a feverish attempt to produce an incentive scheme which was acceptable to the N.U.M. The first suggestion for such a scheme revolved round having bonuses based on the output of each face and development. A norm was to be established, by method study, for each face. This norm was to make allowances for geological and physical difficulties. Non-face workers were to be rewarded by a bonus based on the achievement of the pit. It was intended that they would earn 50p in bonus for every £1 earned by face workers. Criticisms were soon forthcoming from the N.U.M. The substance of these were incorporated in a second version of the scheme under which bonuses were now to be based on the performances of each pit. All the face and development workers in a pit were to have an equal bonus based on the extra yardage cut in the whole pit. Other miners would receive bonus at half this rate. This scheme was still regarded as being potentially divisive of the miners by the strong left wing contingent on the N.U.M. Executive, which preferred a nationally ascertained bonus arrangement under which increased output in the industry as a whole would be totalled up, and then shared out among all workers. The N.C.B., whilst resisting this suggestion, which they felt, did not provide enough of an incentive, were eventually encouraged to believe that they had produced a scheme which would secure acceptance—since it embodied the principle that bonuses should be based on the performance of each pit and that all face workers and development workers should have an equal bonus. To make it more attractive the bonus gap between these workers and non-face workers was narrowed. Non-face workers were, however, to have their bonus calculated on the national increase in output with the improved offer of earning 65p for every £1 earned by the face workers.[45] The opening paragraph of the N.C.B.'s final proposal read as follows :

'The scheme provides the opportunity to increase earnings by improved performance (in some cases present performance will already qualify for incentive pay). In any case no one will be paid less than his establishment under existing wages agreements and the national standard grade rates will still be the principal feature of the industry's wages structure.'[46]

In the revised version it was proposed that extra pay should accumulate after a pit reached its basic output. This basic output was estimated at 25 per cent less than the standard output which it was felt could be achieved when there were no delays or breakdowns in production. This standard output was to be determined by work study, which would make allowance for (and so hopefully neutralise through extra pay) local conditions. The N.U.M. had been successful in resisting the N.C.B.'s original proposal to make the incentive apply to individual coalfaces, changing it instead to a system where bonuses were to be based on each pit's performance with the proceeds being divided equally among all workers in the pit. The N.C.B. clearly felt that this was a sufficient change to persuade the N.U.M. to forget its fears about the re-establishment of wage inequalities from pit to pit or from coalfield to coalfield. Nevertheless, great division occurred on the N.U.M. Executive over this proposal—with the eventual result that the Executive voted narrowly in favour of rejecting even the N.C.B.'s new offer.[47]

The nature of the N.U.M.'s structure, giving as it does considerable independence and autonomy to the union's areas, led in particular to an extremely bitter debate over the merits of the scheme in Nottinghamshire. The Executive of the Notts Area of the N.U.M. had voted in favour of the deal, and recommended that Notts N.U.M. members should vote in favour of it in the national ballot which was to take place in mid-November. Nottinghamshire was, of course, the major coalfield which was mostly likely to benefit from the deal, and significantly it was the area which had suffered most (along with the very small Kent area) under the wage equalisation that had been brought about in the wake of the N.P.L.A. Joe Whelan, the Notts Area Financial Secretary, and one of the representatives of the Notts N.U.M. on the National Executive, had been one of those members of the N.E. who had voted for the rejection of the Board's offer. He therefore came into severe conflict with the other full time officials in Notts, who favoured the scheme.[48] This conflict became more acrimonious still after it emerged that Whelan's voting behaviour on the National Executive had tipped the balance towards recommending rejection of the deal. Whelan defended himself by saying that he had never been mandated by the Notts Area, and by arguing that acceptance of the deal would 'breed an atmosphere of greed, which means the survival of the strongest and the weakest going to the wall. It will bring out the worst in human nature. . . . I'm in favour of a productivity agreement, but one that doesn't set men against one another in this way. As we increase output per man shift, a percentage of the value should be divided nationally among all the miners. Of course, if I were a manager, I'd be saying what they're saying : that if the miner doesn't see the immediate result of his extra effort, the incentive becomes remote. I accept their point of view, but the evils of what they wish to introduce are greater than the advantages.'[49] Len Clarke, the President of the Notts Area, continued to press for acceptance of the N.C.B. scheme. Arthur Scargill, his opposite number in Yorkshire, crossed swords with Clarke in no uncertain fashion—and both Scargill and Whelan criticised (sometimes implicitly, sometimes explicitly) the Notts Area for resurrecting the spectre of Spencerism. 'Stop acting on behalf of the Coal Board,' Scargill told Clarke, 'Follow the line of the national executive and support the union's policy.'[50] Clarke replied by saying that talk of Spencerism was an insult to the Notts miners, the men that Whelan had been elected to represent. The Notts miners had shown immense loyalty to the N.U.M., he argued. In defending his position he revealed why he felt the feeling in Notts was in favour of the deal :

'With the National Power Loader Agreement Notts miners lost pounds and then again in 1971 with the parity deal every area received increases of from 5p to over £2.75 but the Notts miner did not get a penny. These were far more divisive than anything in the proposed incentive deal, and despite this we have never faltered in our loyalty to the N.U.M.'[51]

Before the ballot in mid-November 1974 the Yorkshire and Notts Area of the N.U.M. were at daggers drawn over this issue. According to one local paper in the Notts coalfield, 'Carloads of men from the Yorkshire coalfield carrying the message of their outspoken union president Mr. Arthur Scargill brought their campaign to local pits where they handed out leaflets calling for support.' Sutton Colliery, for instance, received a deputation from Hickleton Main Pit near Doncaster. One of the Yorkshire men is reported as having said that 'The productivity deal is designed to be divisive by creating anomalies in the wage structure. We do not want this form of pressure in our industry.'[52] Even the *Daily Mirror*, which gave massive prominence to the ballot and strongly urged the miners to vote for the deal under the headline 'Give Britain A Break', admitted that there was some substance in the claim that 'it will set pit against pit, coalfield against coalfield.' But it added that 'Any genuine incentive scheme is bound to produce varying rewards. It happens in Communist countries. There it is called "socialist competition" and—unlike in Britain—cannot be improved upon by free negotiation.'[53] This clever reasoning, however, seems to have had relatively little effect on the outcome of the ballot. The miners eventually voted 61.5 per cent against the deal and 39.5 per cent for it (123,345 against 77,119). Nottinghamshire was the only major coalfield to show a vote in favour—but then only by a narrow margin, with 53.5 per cent in favour. The Yorkshire coalfield produced a result of 83.5 per cent against the scheme, and South Wales showed 82 per cent against.[54] The results of the ballot produced a good deal of acrimony with accusations of ballot rigging, intimidation, and other irregularities, particularly in South Wales and Yorkshire. The N.U.M. Vice-President, Michael McGahey, interpreted the result as a signal for a demand for a £30 a week over-all wage increase; whereas Len Clarke declared that the rejection of the deal had produced a situation which 'may well turn into a test case as far as the social contract is concerned.'[55] A National Coal Board spokesman, although expressing disappointment over the result of the ballot, stressed that 'The one thing that is essential is that the unions and the board together still need to maintain and increase output to meet our joint commitments to the nation.'[56] The coal board's productivity problem remains as an issue. The attempt to solve the problem by a partial return to a payment system based on piecework met with failure, as it was perhaps bound to do given the long striving of the N.U.M. to establish national standard rates for mineworkers. The struggle against piecework and district bargaining had been so long, and success so recent, that the 1974 incentive scheme was probably doomed to failure from the start. But for the Coal Board the productivity 'problem' remains to be dealt with. The N.C.B. will clearly be to some extent looking again at suggestions of the sort raised by Griffin in his 1972 article. One possible approach will involve closer managerial control and supervision at the point of production—though this is not likely to be widely used since it may prove counter-productive. If, however, it is employed and if it is not to mean the intensification of labour, then the N.U.M.'s strategy of advance will probably have to be of the sort suggested by Bob Heath in his 1969 article on the N.P.L.A. Mere wage militancy of the sort so vigorously promoted by the left in the leadership of the N.U.M. will not be adequate. In the end money is no compensation for the intensification of labour and further managerial encroachments on job control. Heath in 1969 suggested that the N.U.M. had to have twin policy objectives. 'The union,' he wrote, 'will be forced to recognise that national *wage increases* must be pursued at *national* level and at the same time more control gained over the *system of production* at *pit level*.'[57] Vigorous national wage bargaining is now firmly established—1972 and 1974 bear adequate witness to that. Extremely little attention, however, seems so far to have been given to the other suggested policy objective. Yet there is clearly great scope for progress here. As Heath points out it is precisely the absence of piecework bargaining (which was previously a source of some degree of workers' control of production at pit level) which at one and the same time creates a new urgency about and new possibilities for the intensification of efforts to force management 'to transfer to the miners more job control.' According to Heath 'it need not take the form of pit stoppages but rather of "go slows", "ca'canny" and "work to rule". It is the day-wage structure which allows these more subtle forms of pressure to be successfully supported and used. Their obvious attraction lies in the fact that they can be pursued without necessarily having an adverse effect on earnings.'[58]

One imagines that many miners habitually engage in 'ca'canny' and other output restricting activities be it under piecework or under day work. The National Coal Board certainly exhorts them as if that is the case. Exhortation is, in the present situation, one of the major stratagems available to the N.C.B. Home-spun 'Stakhanovism' is rife in the coalfields at present. Local newspapers, in Nottinghamshire at least, regularly contain news items giving details of new tunnelling records and so on, and many photographs have been published of groups of miners jubilant at having surpassed their output targets. But even in Nottinghamshire, one of the high productivity areas, it is becoming increasingly clear that miners are not, after a certain point, spurred on to even greater efforts merely for the greater glory of their colliery's output record. It is no consolation to face workers at big-producing pits, especially when they are often finding themselves earning less than other underground workers. In Nottinghamshire miners seem to be saying 'if we can't have more money, then we'll go for shorter hours.' The practice seems to be emerging that managers, in order to keep up morale and avoid disputes, are being forced to be indulgent in this respect and to allow men to go to the surface early if output targets have been achieved before a shift finishes. Where they are unwilling or unable to do this trouble emerges. In October 1975, for instance, miners at the record-breaking Pye Hill Colliery tried formally to establish an hour shorter afternoon shift as a reward for their achievements. The N.C.B. were clearly unhappy about formalising such a concession, in spite of the fact that it was informally being allowed. A Coal Board spokesman said 'they recognised Pye Hill's achievement but to alter working hours there would be to break the national agreement.'[59] The Pye Hill miners replied by going on strike.

If it is 'Stakhanovism without financial incentives' that is being used in Nottinghamshire, then it might be said that the South Wales coalfield is the scene of 'shock-brigadism' through the re-vamping of the largely discredited and ineffectual consultative machinery. The N.C.B.'s *Management News* in January 1976 gave great prominence to a 'production case study' showing 'how consultation is helping the output drive in South Wales.' A joint team of top management and union officials were reported as visiting all the 43 collieries in the South Wales coalfield (where losses in 1975 were running at more than £1m. a week) 'to investigate reasons for the general shortfall in face performances and, more importantly, to take bilateral action to bring about improvements.' The N.U.M. leadership in South Wales is keen on the idea because of the 'danger to job security if the Area continues to incur heavy losses,' and it wants to overcome the difficulty in motivating N.U.M. members to greater levels of productivity at a time when coal is being stocked. On top of this 'there is the need to combat the negative approach among mineworkers which has inevitably built up over 30 years of contraction—when the number of South Wales collieries has fallen from 214 to 43.' A number of problems have been identified so far—it being up to the N.C.B. to ensure that action is taken on them : inadequate coal clearance, lack of investment in previous years, poor supplies routes, and excessive walking to districts. Then, according to the N.C.B., 'Industrial democracy was taken a stage further by asking every face team to set their own achievable targets.' Only six pits refused to do this—on the grounds that this was management's job. The total output objective suggested by the face teams turned out to be about 5 per cent higher than management's estimate. A joint production drive then followed.

But stratagems of this sort notwithstanding, it is quite clear that the N.C.B. pins it long term hopes for its drive for improved efficiency essentially on a return to a payment system at least partly based on financial incentives. The irony here is, not just that it is only ten years since piecework was replaced by the National Power Loading Agreement, but also that the N.C.B. is casting envious eyes towards Eastern Europe. There 'socialist emulation' and shock-brigadism are old hat—piecework is the thing. The N.C.B.'s *Management News* in February 1976 (the month after the report on South Wales) carried a leading article under the headline, 'Key objective is to minimise costs', and then gave a summary—headed 'Lessons for us from Poland's coal expansion'—of the report of the joint management and union study visit of the Polish coal industry. The report placed great emphasis on the contribution of financial incentives in Poland. First Secretary Gierek was quoted as having said that : 'The miners can have more money for more output', and considerable detail was provided about the 'social incentives' received by mineworkers : better than average housing, lower rents, subsidised food, extra holidays, and cheap or free holiday accommodation, even free uniforms for ceremonial occasions. The British delegation was told that 'face workers quite frequently earned bonuses equal to more than 100 per cent of their basic wage : indeed, in some cases, 60 per cent of their wages comes from these incentive payments.'[60] In the summary and conclusions to the report, in a section on 'Wages and Conditions', the enthusiasm for a return to financial incentives in British coal is made abundantly clear :

'When the N.C.B. and the N.U.M. agreed to end payment by results some years ago the decision seemed correct at that time. Completion of the mechanisation process meant that a man's output bore little relation to his physical effort. Some workers were getting better wages than others without working any harder.

'Since then, more efficient and powerful machines have been introduced but they are not always used to their capacity. The Poles, who are almost as highly-mechanised at the face as we are, have shown that bonus systems can produce extra output and extra wages.'[61]

NOTES

1. For an account of the general background to the industry in the period see M. P. Jackson *The Price of Coal* (London 1974).
2. 'A Future for British Miners?' by J. Oldham, R. Rigby, R. Walton, S. Crawshaw, in *Trade Union Register 1970* (London 1970) eds. K. Coates, T. Topham and M. Barratt Brown, p. 133.
3. Carter Goodrich *The Frontier of Control* p. 35.
4. Ibid., pp. 137-138.

5. David Evans *Labour Strife in the South Wales Coalfield, 1910-1911* (Cardiff 1911) p. 219.
6. Interview with D. D. Evans, 1973, quoted in David Ingli Gidwell 'Philosophy and Geology in Conflict. The Evolution of Wages Structures in the South Wales Coalfield, 1926-1974' in *Llafur: the Journal of the Society for the Study of Welsh Labour History*, Vol. 1, No. 4, Summer 1975, p. 46.
7. D. I. Gidwell, op. cit., p. 46.
8. Quoted in A. R. Griffin *Mining in the East Midlands, 1550-1947* (London 1971) p. 302; and see Griffin's account of 'Spencerism', pp. 302-318 for more detail.
9. Ibid., p. 312.
10. G. B. Baldwin *Beyond Nationalization—the Labour Problems of British Coal* (Harvard 1955) pp. 86-87.
11. Quoted in Gidwell, op. cit., p. 49.
12. R. G. Searle-Barnes *Pay and Productivity Bargaining; a Study of the Effect of National Wage Agreements in the Nottinghamshire Coalfield* (Manchester 1969) p. 5.
13. Ibid., pp. 7-12.
14. Ibid., p. 12.
15. National Coal Board *Coal—Recipe for Success* (London n.d. ? 1964) pp. 10-11. I wish to thank Keith Bradshaw for this reference, and for other help on matters relating to this section.
16. J. Hughes and R. Moore (eds.) *A Special Case? Social Justice and the Miners* (Penguin 1972) p. 73, and see their section, 'Mechanization and the coal-face worker', generally.
17. Quoted in A. R. Griffin, op. cit., p. 314.
18. Preface to the 1966 Agreement, quoted in Gidwell, op. cit., p. 57.
19. Hughes and Moore, op. cit., p. 16.
20. These extracts from speeches by Paynter and Whelan come from Griffin, op. cit., pp. 314-315.
21. R. H. Heath 'The National Power-Loading Agreement in the Coal Industry and Some Aspects of Workers' Control' in *Trade Union Register* (London 1969) eds. K. Coates, T. Topham, and M. Barratt Brown, p. 185. I have relied heavily for what follows on Heath's excellent article.
22. Ibid., p. 186.
23. Ibid., pp. 186-187.
24. Ibid., p. 189.
25. Ibid., pp. 189-190.
26. Quoted in John Gretton 'The Hours We Work' in *New Society* January 7, 1971. Marris is also the author of the standard work on this subject, *The Economics of Capital Utilization* (1964).
27. Robert Sergean *Managing Shiftwork* (London 1971).
28. For an excellent account of shift work and its relationship to family life and leisure patterns see Michael Young and Peter Willmott *The Symmetrical Family* (Harmondsworth 1975) Ch. VII, 'Shiftwork'.
29. Marris, quoted in Sergean, op. cit., p. 165.
30. Glyn Jones and Michael Barnes *Britain on Borrowed Time* (Pelican 1967) pp. 33-34.
31. Special E.C. Meeting, Notts Area N.U.M., 17 August 1966.
32. The Five-Day Week Agreement does not, in fact, specify Monday to

Friday working.
33. Notts Area N.U.M., E.C. Meeting, 14 November 1966.
34. *Financial Times* December 1, 1969.
35. *Financial Times* December 15, 1969.
36. R. Kershaw 'Waiting for Coal from the £18m Showpit' in *The Times* January 9, 1970. I wish to thank Ken Coates for providing me with these last three references.
37. *Mansfield and North Notts Chronicle Advertiser* February 19, 1976, and oral information from Notts miners—who also state that Bevercotes has had a total of 20,000 workers on its books, though never more than 700 at any one time.
38. Heath, op. cit., p. 190.
39. 'A Future for British Miners?' in *Trade Union Register 1970* pp. 132-133.
40. Letter in *The Observer* October 12, 1975.
41. A. R. Griffin 'Consultation and conciliation in the mining industry: the need for a new approach' in *Industrial Relations Journal* Vol. 3, No. 3, 1972, pp. 31-32.
42. Ibid., p. 32.
43. Ibid., p. 44.
44. Coal Industry Examination *Final Report 1974* (Dept. of Energy 1974) p. 18.
45. Details from John Fryer 'Coal: the undermining of a compromise' in *The Sunday Times*, November 3, 1974.
46. Quoted in *Mansfield and North Notts Chronicle Advertiser* November 7, 1974.
47. *The Times* October 31st, 1974.
48. See, for instance, Whelan's letter replying to criticism from his colleague George Cheshire, the Notts Area N.U.M. Agent, in *Notts Free Press* October 18, 1974.
49. *The Observer* November 3, 1974.
50. *The Times* November 8, 1974.
51. *Mansfield and North Notts Chronicle Advertiser* November 7, 1974.
52. *Notts Free Press* November 15, 1974.
53. *Daily Mirror* November 11, 1974.
54. Full results with breakdown of voting by area are in *The Times* November 18, 1974.
55. *Mansfield and North Notts Chronicle Advertiser* November 21, 1974.
56. Ibid.
57. Heath, op. cit., p. 192.
58. Heath, op. cit., p. 197. Since this was written the N.U.M.'s national executive committee has adopted a revolutionary five-point plan to change the consultative set-up at pit and area level—replacing it with a system of colliery management teams (elected by the workers by secret ballot) made up of 12 members with responsibilities for output, financial targets, budgeting, marketing, and the appointment of colliery managers and experts: see *The Miner* April-May 1976.
59. *Daily Telegraph* October 20, 1975—and information from Notts and Derbyshire miners.
60. *The Polish Coal Industry. Report of the British Mining Delegation* January 12-16, 1976, pp. 13-14.
61. Ibid., p. 16.

XVI

THE CAR INDUSTRY AND MEASURED-DAY WORK

The motor industry is the other major British industry that has over the past few years brought to a conclusion the long process of changing from piecework payment systems to Measured Day Work. Unlike the transition in the coal industry (which was described above) the changeover in the car industry was not an agreed objective of both management and unions—rather it was a source of bitter conflict. In the early 1970s the British Leyland Motor Company, which had been established in 1968 and was by then the only remaining British owned car company, moved over totally from piecework to M.D.W. In this respect Leyland only brought itself into line with the other three major car firms operating in Britain:—Vauxhall (General Motors), Rootes (Chrysler), and Ford. Vauxhall Motors had made the change in 1956.[1] Ford had never been on piecework. Henry Ford the First felt way back before 1914 that piece rates 'would have meant endless bother', and consequently he preferred to use tight supervision and strict labour discipline to get control over the work produced on his lines.[2] Ford's instinct about the 'endless bother' deriving from piecework was prophetic. In 1967 Fords in Britain completely restructured its payment system via job evaluation and Measured Day Work. In the other British car plants piecework bargaining was one of the main cornerstones of shop floor strength and organisation throughout the 1950s and 1960s. By the late 1960s and early 1970s the managements at Rootes and British Leyland were determined to change from piecework to M.D.W., and thus to reassert managerial control over the rate of increase of wages and to undermine the basis of shop floor strength. Rootes introduced M.D.W. in phases. Their new plant in Scotland, Linwood, was put straight onto M.D.W. It took longer to make the changeover in the older Coventry plants where piecework was traditional—but even here the change was more or less complete by the beginning of the 1970s. It is interesting to note that during the period in which Linwood alone was on M.D.W., the ratio of supervisors to operatives there was three times greater than it was in the Coventry plants.[3] The Coventry 'Blue Book' made it quite clear that this problem was very much in the forefront of management thinking when the process of going over to M.D.W. was under urgent consideration :

'Rootes Group has, over the past year, been considering the implications in regard to supervision, of a move from piecework to a fixed day-rate. They concluded that the supervisor has a more direct responsibility for production in that he must ensure that each operator does, in fact, perform the operations, as specified, at the required rate and for the set period.'

The ratio of men to supervisors, if low output per worker was to be avoided, would, it was thought, have to be about 25 or 30 to 1 rather than 50 to 1 that was the case under piecework. Not only would the amount of supervision have to increase under M.D.W., it would also have to be of a different type. The Coventry Blue Book suggested that M.D.W. would bring about the 're-establishment of the supervisor as a leader and manager of his section. He will be expected to take more decisions and exercise much closer control over his operators. . . . He will be required to criticise subordinates when work or conduct fall below set standards.'[4] This analysis turned out to be quite correct as will be seen shortly when we discuss the process of change in Leyland.

After the formation of British Leyland in 1968 one of the main managerial objectives was to introduce M.D.W. in all the company's many plants. Patrick Lowry left his job as head of the Engineering Employers' Federation to become Leyland's director of Industrial Relations and to master-mind the whole process. Piecework had, in the inter-war years, been a good servant of managerial objectives in the British motor firms. It was exceptionally unpopular with workers and their unions— but little could be done about it because of low levels of organisation in the industry and high levels of unemployment outside it. In that sort of situation the car workers had little option but to work under a system of managerially defined piece rates. The only way that higher wages could be achieved was through producing more at the given price—in that way piecework was clearly a means of increasing the rate of exploitation of workers. The post-war boom in car manufacture however soon brought about a radically different situation. Full employment brought with it a massive increase in shop floor bargaining power based on intense competition between firms for labour and for markets. High levels of trade union organisation were achieved, and with this development came the creation of strong shop steward organisation in the plants. Piecework itself was now one of the factors which encouraged this development. Employers began to use piecework as a way of topping up wage rates agreed at national level between trade unions and employers' organisations. Shop stewards became wage bargainers at the plant level—and there was plenty of scope for them to exercise their talents in this direction. The piecework agreement that had been signed in the aftermath of the 1922 Engineering industry lockout had included a clause which laid down that piecework prices must be agreed with the operator and that no change in price could take place unless there was a change in the means, method or material used on the job. The severe competition between car firms for an increased share of the buoyant and growing market for cars, for instance, led to the frequent introduction of new models or other market expanding differentiations of product. At this point stewards could, and usually did, demand higher piecework rates. More often than not employers had to concede the demands if they wanted to keep, let alone increase, their share of the market.[5] Piecework, then, led to 'wage drift' which managements could not contain. The creation of wide piece rate differences between jobs, plants and companies introduced a dynamic element into the bargaining process—with the worst paid groups of workers seeking parity with the best paid. The constant haggling over piece rates meant that companies lost a lot of control over their labour costs—and also lost much direct control over the management of workers in relation to effort.[6]

British Leyland began to realise by the late 1960s that the sort of thing that Alan Flanders had talked about applied to them. Flanders said : 'More and more managements seem to me to be becoming increasingly aware that the labour situation has drifted dangerously far and that they are faced with the need to re-establish control over their workers.'[7] Measured Day Work was to be introduced to re-assert managerial control. The growing difficulties of the car industry, and British Leyland in particular, made this imperative. Labour costs had to be reduced both in aggregate and per unit of output. In Leyland the first step down this road was taken with the 1968 Productivity Agreement. In the agreement the principles of work study, job evaluation and the rest were conceded by the unions alongside a general agreement that the unions should 'undertake to co-operate fully on the elimination of impediments to efficient utilisation of labour which cause unit costs to be higher than they should be.' The agreement also stated that pay increases 'may be made provided there is a measurable increase in labour productivity or efficiency to which the efforts of the workers concerned have contributed.'[8] But the major attempt by management to reach its new objectives was via M.D.W. The Cowley plant was the scene of the first battle. Leyland management had decided that the new Morris Marina model, regarded as the great salvation of this part of the Leyland empire, would not be produced on piecework. As production was about to begin on the new model, according to a well-informed account :

'The company played their first card. Normally in the pre-production stage of a new car, when piecework prices are still under negotiation, workers begin production on the "piecework average"—the average of the rates throughout the factory. Leyland refused to follow this practice. They offered to pay a rate higher than the piecework average—but it was a fixed rate, unconnected with the piecework system and, therefore, a crucial step towards measured day work.'[9]

A six week strike followed. The senior stewards issued several leaflets warning workers of the dangers of M.D.W. One of them contained the words : 'always remember that once you give up piecework you can never get it back. Measured Day Work is like concrete—it is easy to get into when soft, but impossible to get out of once it sets.' Eventually a return to work was negotiated, in October 1970, on the basis of an agreement under which the company said it would continue to observe the piecework agreement, but that in effect it would seek to change over to M.D.W. by using the agreed procedure. By January 1971 the procedure had been exhausted with a 'failure to agree'. The company was now in a position to take up the initiative again. This it did in a letter that month from the Cowley plant manager to the workers producing the Marina stating again that the company had 'no intention of producing the new model with a piecework system', but at the same time offering the reassurance that 'We will not try to impose work standards arbitrarily. On the other hand we are not prepared to enter a Dutch Auction over operational times in the way that was customary under the old piecework system.'[10] The shop stewards now changed their tack. Although they remained opposed in principle to M.D.W. they decided to go for a M.D.W. *with* a Mutuality Agreement, in order to get some protection for workers on M.D.W.

This agreement by workers and stewards to accept M.D.W. in practice did not mean that the management's problems were over. Levels of output under M.D.W. were considerably below what the management required. A typical communication urging the Marina workers to step up their output is that from the South Works production manager on March 30, 1971. 'It is vitally important,' he wrote, 'that the production of the A.D.O. 28 (the Marina) is rapidly increased if we are to capitalise on the favourable initial reaction to the model. . . . Plans for increasing production therefore must be implemented.'[11] This speed-up could only be achieved by the plant-wide application of work study. The resistance by the workers to speed-up coincided with the stewards' campaign for mutuality, with the result that in December 1971 a Factory Agreement dealing with the Application of Industrial Engineering (Work Study) Techniques was signed. This contained important mutuality provisions. Basically it said that changes in work effort could only be introduced after prior agreement with the stewards.[12] The company had made a major concession in return for considerable progress towards M.D.W. But later events were to show that they were far from happy with the progress of M.D.W. in Cowley. The initial move towards M.D.W. involved only the workers on the Marina. But in the next twelve months it spread to other sections

357

at Cowley. At the same time the Leyland management attempted to make the same changeover in the company's other plants. In May 1972 the changeover was attempted at the Coventry plants of Triumph Motors—and in this case even involved a drop in wages of £4 a week for some men.[13] November 1972 saw the beginning of the end of piecework at the Longbridge Austin plant, 'the most militant piecework stronghold' of all. Just as at Cowley the Leyland management decided that the production of a new model would be carried out under M.D.W., rather than on piecework. Eighteen months of protracted and bitter argument with the stewards gave the Leyland management the change it wanted. Leyland's chief at Longbridge, George Turnbull, a man according to *The Times* who was 'not given to making headline comments', forsook his customary silence to make the following revealing observations on the day after the 'breakthrough'. Turnbull had been looking forward to and planning for that day ever since he had arrived at Longbridge four years earlier :

'I felt immediately that because of the vast scale of the operation at Austin Morris—and, quite frankly to preserve the future of the company—we had to get on to day work. The frequent small disputes arising from piecework had a much more damaging effect on profitability in a high volume plant than in a low volume operation.'

Turnbull's piecework problem was evidently a real one. In the first ten months of 1972, 84 per cent of all disputes at Longbridge had been caused by piecework problems. But, he went on to admit a flat-rate system would not of itself solve 'all our problems'. 'There are obviously,' he conceded, 'some industrial relations problems with flat-rate systems.' The main one of these was clearly the question of output under a payment system that offered no direct financial incentive for extra production. A changed role for the foremen and supervisors was to be the key here. *The Times* journalist interviewing Turnbull indicated that one of the latter's 'most pressing needs will be the re-education of supervisory staff. Under piecework foremen had to tread so warily that their activity on the shop floor passed to shop stewards.' The journalist went on to quote a Cowley foreman (who by then would have had nearly two years experience of M.D.W.) as saying:

> 'We had to learn how to give orders, and if you think that's easy try talking sharply to an assembly line worker who will yell, "Steward" if you wish him good morning and he doesn't agree.'[14]

British Leyland had, indeed, at the expense of relatively little outlay and trouble, undermined the considerable degree of shop floor power that had been established, with greater expense of effort and struggle, by workers over many years. There was, therefore, a great deal of truth in the words of an Austin worker in the immediate aftermath of the M.D.W. deal. He wrote:

> 'Measured Day Work is to be brought in with all its implications for loss of job control and, eventually, more work for less money . . . British Leyland has in fact bought its increase in control over the shop floor with very little outlay. The struggle to preserve shop floor organisation against the implications of this deal will be an uphill one but the fight must go on.'[15]

But in the first year or so of M.D.W. in the various Leyland plants this sort of view seemed almost alarmist and exaggerated. In Cowley, for instance, nearly two years after the introduction of M.D.W. on the Marina lines, stewards and workers could, with considerable justification, talk about how they had got M.D.W. under control, and how it amounted, not to speed up, but to 'leisured day-work.' The real crunch had yet to come. This can be seen quite clearly from the remarks of four Cowley stewards on the subject of M.D.W. in June 1973. But although some of the remarks made below indicate that workers were doing better out of M.D.W. than were the Leyland management, there is also a strong sense that things might soon alter and that the sources of the former strength of the stewards had evaporated. One steward, Andrew, noted that under M.D.W. 'some of the familiar problems' were disappearing—the former central core of a steward's activities, the bargaining over rates, had gone and was now replaced by what might often be minor problems. Another steward, Mark, said:

'Now we have accepted Measured Day Work we are in a position where once a year the wage problem comes round. Before that we had that question constantly before us. If they wanted to change the speed of a line, you could always associate it with cash.'

Mark thought that a gradual speed-up would take place which would eventually build up to 'an intolerable situation. At the moment things look all right, but the Industrial Engineers have only just gone in. The members let them in out of a naïve misunderstanding that they weren't so different from the old rate-fixers : they came along, measured a job and worked out a rate on the spot. You could argue with them and usually get an extra half-penny an hour or whatever it was. Now you can't do that. People don't yet understand that the I.Es. are different. But I do believe the I.Es. will have difficulty in explaining to members why the Company wants them to work harder for the same money they were getting before.' At that time Leyland was still trying to install M.D.W. *in toto* throughout its operations and so, the stewards argued, M.D.W. seemed more like 'leisured day work' than anything else in order to secure workers' acquiescence in it. Similarly, *pour encourager les autres*, M.D.W. was usually accompanied by a straight increase in real wages—the £1 an hour flat rate in Cowley produced a weekly wage of £42, 'a rise for most people.' But, it was felt, this was a passing phase. M.D.W. had been introduced to bring about in the long run the restoration of the company's profitability and as such it would eventually involve not just speed-up but also redundancy. Pete, another steward, put the whole thing into perspective when he said that :

'The introduction of Measured Day Work should be seen as part of a concerted plan by the capitalist class to restore the rate of profit . . . they want to break down the traditional strength of trade union organisation at the point of production by introducing Measured Day Work, getting more work out of us for the same pay and preparing the ground for redundancies.'[16]

The conflict at Cowley began barely six months after those words were spoken. Early in 1974, during the Three Day Working week (when, nationally, interestingly enough, output was not much below that achieved in a five day working week) imposed by the Heath Government, the company began its offensive. According to one account :

'On February 5 it told foremen that production would be cut and the "model mix" changed on the Marina lines. Mutual agreement on the changes would not be observed; instead re-manning for the lines would work to new schedules according to man-assignment sheets based on work study. This was an open challenge to the mutuality agrement.'

The deputy senior shop steward, around whom the dispute came to personalise itself, Alan Thornett, had been one of the key architects of the mutuality agreement. In the T.G.W.U. 5/55 *Branch News* he stated that the company was challenging the agreement and was attempting to impose speed-up and increased effort on the Marina workers. Under the guise of reducing the amount of effort involved in production by 14 per cent (by reducing track speed from 35 to 30 cars per hour) the company was in fact increasing the amount of effort demanded by reducing manning levels by $17\frac{1}{2}$ per cent. But, Thornett went on, the amount of speed up involved was not merely the amount indi-cated by the difference between 14 per cent and $17\frac{1}{2}$ per cent, for the company at the same time proposed to double the number of cars that were intended for the North American market. These cars required a good deal more work on them to meet the strin-gent U.S. safety regulations.[17] Thornett's analysis was compelling enough to bring about a full-scale stoppage in April 1974. But the support for the strike was less than firm—the assembly workers concerned, within days of being threatened with the choice be-tween the sack and giving their assignments 'a fair effort at a line speed of 30 per hour' (the plant director's words), went back to work without union approval under the new manning assign-ments. The mutuality principle had been well and truly breached. Thornett's determined fight against the company and for the mutuality principle was the underlying cause which soon led to his being refused facilities as a shop steward by the company.

What normally would have been a minor dispute which would have been sorted out very quickly (involving Thornett's own section, the transport drivers) was magnified into a major issue around which the company hoped to remove Thornett from his leadership in the plant. Even the business journalists of the 'quality press' (not normally the best friends of trade unionism) openly stated that the transport drivers' issue was merely a subterfuge by which the management hoped to remove Thornett from his position of influence, and thereby remove one of the main impediments to the fulfilment of their objective. The Thornett case became one of the *causes célèbres* of trade unionism in the early 1970s, raising as it did the question of whether management had the right to say who it would or would not accept as a shop steward.

One important point needs to be made about this episode at Cowley. It concerns the question of mutuality. As we saw, the Cowley stewards secured what most people regarded as a major safeguard against speed up when they negotiated the Factory Agreement on the Application of Industrial Engineering Techniques, in December 1971. The terms of that agreement in relation to mutuality fulfilled amply the criteria laid down as being necessary for the protection and promotion of workers' interests in two important pamphlets published by the T.G.W.U. in 1970—Harry Urwin's *Plant and Productivity Bargaining* and the Education and Research pamphlet, *Plant Level Bargaining*. Urwin, for instance, pointed out that the reason why managements were proposing to change over from piecework to M.D.W. was to try to impose 'stronger managerial control', and he drew his members' attention to the fact that the American car workers union, the U.A.W., in a M.D.W. situation automatically negotiated mutuality of control over performance standards and manning assignments. Ken Coates and Tony Topham made the following comments about the Cowley situation in the light of this : 'Mr. Urwin's advice on this point has been triumphantly applied by his union in the making of an agreement to introduce day-work wages in place of piece-work at the Cowley Body Plant of Austin-Morris, a section of the British Leyland Motor Company. This 1971 agreement is a model of simplicity and precision in the establishment of all the union's principles contained in the Urwin pamphlet.'[18] This, of course, is quite right. But as we have just seen the company broke the mutuality agreement in the spring of 1974, and were able to do so given the massive insecurity generated in the ranks of the car workers as a result of the intensification of the economic crisis. M.D.W. *without* the mutuality principle clearly represents a very sharp defeat for the unions at shop floor level. But it must be added that mutuality does not always provide a defence against managerial encroachments on such things as work intensity. On top of this, under M.D.W. even with an impregnable mutuality agreement, the initiative for changing the effort-reward relationship lies first and foremost with management : under M.D.W. the role of the steward becomes more and more that of resisting managerially desired and initiated change, rather than, as often happened under piecework, initiating changes desired by the work group. Tony Topham had given eloquent expression to this point of view a few years earlier in his excellent article on 'Productivity Bargaining' in *The Trade Union Register* of 1969, where he pointed out that M.D.W. was one of the more important 'managerial devices in their attempt to weaken shop steward controls and sanctions on the jobs.' Topham had quoted with approval some of the remarks made on this question in 1968 by the then Education Secretary of the T.G.W.U., who had stated that it was essential that stewards appreciated that going over to M.D.W. was not just a question of earning capacity but that 'The change may involve a loss of workshop participation and control over the payments system.'[19]

This perspective of Topham's was later challenged by two industrial relations academics, one British the other American, in a joint work in 1973. Professors McKersie and Hunter suggested that Topham's concern about the impact of M.D.W. on the control question may well be ill-founded. They suggested that any such setback on the workers' part would probably be a short lived phenomenon, and that they would soon learn the new rules of the game and re-establish some shop floor control under M.D.W. They wrote that 'if American experience is any guide (where measured day work has been used for several decades), workers will develop their own devices for controlling the effort bargain involved in measured day work to the same extent as they have for the wage bargain involved in traditional payment-by-results systems.'[20] There is, of course, some substance in this optimistic view that, given time and experience, workers will salvage something from difficult situations. However, many defeats can take place before that process of learning and mastering the new situation has taken place. There is clearly no room for complacency here. It is not inevitable that workers will re-assert their control over a new payment system : though having said this one must acknowledge that the sheer belief that it can be done is in itself of great importance. One of the Cowley stewards had no doubts on this point :

'I know the ingenuity of the working class. When piece work came in it was strongly opposed, and the Transport and General Union said under no circumstances would they accept it. But eventually they did and they found the loopholes in it. They found ways of using it and turning it to their advantage. And I see no reason why we can't do the same where Measured Day Work is concerned.'[21]

It is important to remember here that there is nothing intrinsically good or bad as far as workers are concerned about a particular payment system. Neither piecework nor measured day work is inherently in the best interests of the workers. A payment system does not exist in a vacuum—rather it exists in a situation where other factors (such as levels of organisation, the relative strengths of capital and labour) interact with it. As far as employers are concerned, however, it might well be true that the sheer process of changing from one payment system to another invariably operates in their interest since the very process of change restores managerial initiative and gives management an important breathing space while workers go through the learning process.[22]

The collapse of British Leyland in 1974 and its subsequent 'nationalisation' only postponed the crisis over M.D.W. Leyland's new managers were still committed to trying to make M.D.W. work. The issue surfaced amid a glare of publicity in the newspapers and on radio and television in November 1975. Six hundred assembly line workers in the North Works at Cowley were confronted on the weekend of November 22nd–23rd with an ultimatum from the plant director that 28½ cars (Maxis and Princesses) had to be produced every hour, starting on the first shift from 7.30 a.m. the following Monday morning, November 24th. The plant director further stipulated that each car had to be ready for the showrooms if it was to be counted towards the required output, which itself would be monitored hour by hour. Workers who failed to reach the target would be sent home. A management report a month earlier had revealed that at certain times in a shift as few as 11 cars an hour were being produced and that 7 of these were rejected by inspectors. This nadir of output seems to have occurred at the end of a working week, when absenteeism was widespread. One management official said that :

'When the men are paid on Thursday they clear off or don't come back after lunch, and they stay out on Friday as well. On the night shift as soon as some men get their pay they leave the factory, even in the middle of a shift. The single men or the young marrieds without children feel that the last three-tenths of their working week nearly all goes in tax. So it's not worth their while staying on at the factories once their pay is in their pockets.'[23]

Cowley workers interviewed by *Daily Mirror* reporters had a different point of view, blaming inadequate supplies of materials and parts and out of date equipment, rather than lack of effort by workers, for the shortfall in production (the $28\frac{1}{2}$ cars an hour target had been incorporated in an agreement signed earlier between management and unions). One worker of fifteen years standing at Cowley, Joe, said that 'there is no way that $28\frac{1}{2}$ cars an hour can come off the production line and management know it.' A worker on the Maxi trim line said that 'Men cannot make cars if the components are not there. We just haven't got the materials." Joe felt that M.D.W. was largely responsible for lack of components and said : 'What the management expects is a fantasy. It would be better if piece-work and bonuses were re-introduced. . . . Now we are on measured day work and the trouble has started. These days we are told that our cars are wanted by the public so our production lines should never stop— but we are not given the components and the company loses money. . . . If the bonuses were re-introduced the workers would make damn sure that the components were available, and such

mix-ups wouldn't happen. If the work is there we will do it.'
Another Cowley worker also singled out M.D.W. : 'Ask the
bosses why in the Sixties 33½ 1100s could be made an hour on
one line. The answer is : Piecework.'[24] How, then, will Leyland
get the output per worker it wants without piecework? Exhortation, threats, speed-up—all will play their part. How might
Leyland workers respond to this? The experience of workers at
Fords in Britain and of workers in other measured-day work
car plants in America may provide some of the answers.

Between the end of January and the beginning of April, 1971,
one of the biggest post-war strikes was raging amongst the workers
at the various Ford plants in Britain. Over two million striker-
days were involved; £2 million in dispute benefits were paid
out by the T.G.W.U. and the A.U.E.W.; and the Ford Company claimed to have lost production worth £100 million.[25] The
Ford plant at Halewood, near Liverpool was one of those
affected—and the Liverpool papers, like most of the national
papers, were full of stories about the strike. The usual process of
claim and counter-claim was reported, accusation and denial
chronicled. On March 10th, 1971, however, in the sixth week of
the strike the Liverpool papers carried, under banner headlines,
reports of a totally unexpected intervention. The person who
made the intervention was Mr. Tim Fortescue, Conservative
M.P. for Garston and a junior member of the Heath Government, which at that time was having a particularly rough ride
from the trade union movement over the Industrial Relations
Bill. In a speech in the House of Commons on March 9th,
Fortescue not only made the customary appeal to the strikers
(some of them his own constituents) to return to work, but he
also made some startling accusations. His intervention was head-
lined in one of the Liverpool papers as follows : 'Anarchy at
Ford, Strikers Tell M.P.'[26] Fortescue had said that he had been
approached by three Ford workers, 'middle-aged, apparently
responsible men, who declared themselves opposed to the current
strike.' Fortescue told the Liverpool papers :

'They told me of anarchy at Halewood; lack of discipline
because power is in the hands of the shop stewards, numbers
of men who never work but, with the compliance of the

stewards, spend their time playing football and drinking tea; incidents when men, wishing to leave early deliberately sabotaged machines.'

This last accusation was the most controversial. It was immediately denied by the trade union leaders in Halewood. Les Moore, the convenor of the stamping and body shop, replied to Fortescue's statement as follows :

'I think it is quite ridiculous for these men to come forward and start saying things like this. If any of their allegations were true the management would soon know about them. Men could not play football inside the works because they would soon be spotted. They do play outside—but in their lunch break. We don't have any set tea-break times so a worker could be having a cup of tea any time between 9 a.m. and 11.20 a.m. because he has been relieved by another man.'

Specifically on the machine-breaking charges, Moore said :

'It is true that in the past we have had a couple of cases of men breaking tools on machines on purpose. But on all occasions they have been sacked. We frown on this as much as management. We have a very good relationship with the local management and it is a fact that most of the strikes at Halewood are disputes over things which the local management have no control.'[27]

Another convenor, Bill Maguire of the assembly plant, also denied the charges and accused Fortescue of poisoning labour relations at the plant. Ford management also refuted Fortescue's suggestions—to have accepted them indeed would have been to have admitted that managerial control was not all it might have been. Merseyside Labour M.Ps. similarly resented what they regarded as the slur on members of the local working class, and they tabled a Commons motion of censure against Fortescue. The motion noted that the 'allegations of sabotage and the intriguing suggestion of football being played whilst the assembly line is running' had been refuted by the Halewod management.[28] The management spokesman in his statement of denial made it quite clear that the sort of work discipline in operation at Halewood was, in fact, thoroughly incompatible with (and therefore we might add, highly likely to produce) the sort of behaviour Fortescue talked of. The spokesman said:

'The whole of our industrial system is geared to every employee working conscientiously and every failure by an individual or a group of employees to do this would have an effect on other areas and other employees. We really cannot believe that anyone could spend their time drinking tea and playing football without action being taken by supervisors and certainly other employees would not stand for this sort of activity. We have strict disciplinary procedures laid down in co-ordination with the trade unions and supervisors would take action. It must be common knowledge that we run a very efficient operation. Management are undoubtedly in control of the situation.

This picture of the repressive work situation in a car factory is, of course, well known—a worker on a car assembly line cannot even go to the toilet or go for a drink of water, let alone play football, unless he can find someone to take his place on the line. Machine-breaking, however, is a different matter. On the machine breaking issue Halewood management admitted that it had happened in the past—though of course it was no longer a problem, since (the implication is clear) the 'deviants' responsible had been weeded out from the labour force in the same way, indeed, that Fortescue and many others wanted to weed out the group of 'some 30 known agitators' who were currently responsible for bad industrial relations at Fords. The management spokesman said of machine breaking: 'There have been a few cases of this and disciplinary action has been taken in these cases and the unions have co-operated with us on this.'[29] A few days later, again in Parliament, Arthur Lewis, Labour M.P. for West Ham North was asking, no doubt in an attempt to ascertain the details of Fortescue's case, the Attorney-General if he would prosecute workers at Halewood 'who have been sabotaging machinery.'[30] The written reply he was given stated that the police had received no such complaints.[31]

How much sabotage of the machine breaking sort was there in Fords? The short answer is quite a lot. And why does it seem to have been much more common in Fords than in other car plants using basically the same production techniques? No accusations of sabotage have to the writer's knowledge been levelled at British Leyland workers; whereas a considerable number of cases have arisen from Ford plants in Britain. In 1962, a member of the *Solidarity* group working at Ford's Dagenham plant was fined £100 for writing a pamphlet advocating sabotage as a legitimate weapon in the class struggle in the factory. Apparently an 'experimental speed-up' at Dagenham on the day of the trial led to production losses on account of 'accidental mechanical breakdowns.'[32] And, according to a *Solidarity* pamphlet : 'At one time in the early sixties, on the firm's own admission, damage to the track was costing thousands of pounds per year.'[33] D. G. Rhys, in an excellent article on the British motor industry has, correctly to my mind, located the reason why Fords have been 'sabotage prone' whereas Leyland and other car firms have not. He states that : 'The assembly track and its speed is regarded as less of an ogre in piece-rate factories or where generous bonuses are tied to time rates, but the Ford track had led to tremendous animosity.' Of Ford he adds, 'Not only are cars produced at a faster rate of one a minute along each line, Ford workers, unlike their Midland colleagues, had no control over the pace of their work.'[34] In Leyland, for instance, the ability in the past to bargain about effort through piecework negotiations was crucially important in enabling workers to control work intensity or at least to trade off extra effort for more money. This explains why writers about the Midland car firms, in sharp contrast to writers about Fords, do not make much of the 'tedium of the track' as a source of grievance amongst car workers.[35] Also the very nature of the way in which disputes can be handled in piecework plants means that pieceworking car workers are much less likely to take direct and immediate action (such as stopping the line by sabotage or by walking out) than their counterparts in day work plants. McKersie has suggested that :

> 'Other things being equal there is a tendency for the daywork dispute to come to the crisis stage very quickly, if only because the workers have no other redress than to have the condition eliminated. By contrast, in incentive plants, workers can agree to allow work to continue on the conditions desired by manage-

ment while a dispute over the rate to be paid is processed, if they know that they should establish a case for higher pay they will obtain retroactive compensation under a revised rate.'[36]

In day work plants, like Beynon's Halewood, on the other hand, there is clear evidence of massive worker-hostility to management's unilateral control of the speed of the track. McKersie points out that Fords have used 'suspensions and discharges' for people 'not performing up to standards,' and that Fords take 'a fairly direct approach to eliciting acceptable performance. Production standards are established by management and in most cases released to the workers.'[37] It was a point of managerial principle in Fords that the speed of the track was not negotiable. In other words, there was no possibility of any worker control over the intensity of work. The development of shop floor organisation in the Halewood plant in the late 1960s and early 1970s hinged to a great extent around the shop floor struggle to wrest some control of work intensity away from management. This involved a struggle against speed-up whether it was brought about by increasing the speed of the line or by reducing manning levels on the line. Beynon makes this abundantly clear. He writes : 'One of the most firmly held policies of the Ford Motor Company has been its opposition both to piece rates and to negotiations of job manning and individual workloads.'[38]

It is no surprise, therefore, to learn that 'mutuality' agreements between unions and management in Fords over such things as timing of jobs, work organisation and line speeds were anathema to the Ford management. A senior labour relations executive that Beynon spoke to in 1969 made this quite clear, arguing indeed that the work standards, set unilaterally by management, were reasonable and that there was no necessary conflict between management's 'right to manage' and the effects on workers of the pursuit of efficiency. Ford workers, needless to say, frequently felt differently—and at the Halewood assembly plant in the 1960s there was acute conflict precisely over the issues of job timings and job control. Work study was, to say the least, unpopular, and those on the receiving end of it were quite certain that its claims to scientific accuracy were sham.[39] Even when work speeds had been thus determined they were often, in the early years of Halewood, subsequently increased. In short speed-up was common. Beynon writes that the history of the assembly line is 'a history of conflict over speed-up—the process whereby the pace of work demanded of the operator is systematically increased.' One of the most common ways in which this speed-up took place was by the secret speeding-up of the line during a shift. The resultant increase in work intensity soon became obvious to the assembly line workers. A frequent reaction on their part was quite simply to walk out. This was effective enough for the forcing of an agreement with management that the stewards should have the right to hold a key to lock the assembly line. Some work groups also secured a right to check line speeds and to stop the line if they exceeded laid down levels.

Acts of sabotage by individuals, such as pulling the safety wire to stop the line, were another reaction to speed up and as such constituted an effective means of job control.[40] Beynon goes on to give a striking example of collective, organised sabotage in the Paint Trim and Assembly Plant in the late 1960s. In the Wet Deck of the Paint Shop—where cars are sanded while being sprayed with water—sabotage was used collectively in order to secure redress of grievances. He writes:

'If there was a problem on the Wet Deck, a manning problem, speed-up, if the foreman stepped out of line, they always had a comeback. They could sand the paint off the style lines— the fine edges of the body that give it its distinctive shape. And nobody could know. The water streaming down, the whirlies [sanders] flailing about, the lads on either side of the car, some of them moving off to change their soaking clothes. The foreman could stand over them and he couldn't spot it happening. Three hours later the finished body shell would emerge with bare metal along the style lines. They *knew* it was happening.'[41]

In the end the foreman was usually forced to concede the men's demands in order to prevent this damaging of the product from taking place.

Some remarkable tape-recordings made in September 1974 of conversations between former Halewood press shop workers are at hand. These recordings make it quite clear that the cases that Beynon unearthed were by no means unique. One of the press operators says that the 250 or so press operators were divided into work groups of between 18 and 30 people—and that in each of these groups there were those who committed acts of sabotage. In one conversation one of the workers recalls two mates on the trim lines who located the place on the line where if something was done to the cars it was not detected for about twenty minutes—the cars went through a small tunnel. On one occasion the two mates slashed every seat of 27 or 28 cars with razor blades and squirted brake fluid on to the paint work—thus ruining the paint. Another example was given about the production of police cars, obvious by their special livery and also (and this was a point of some importance) the extra attention to quality that management gave these cars. Milk bottles, often with some milk left in them, just fitted into the small space behind the dash panel. Police cars, as well as other cars, commonly had a couple of nuts and bolts left in the tank and in the door panels. One worker known to the interviewees knew enough about a car's electrics to be able to produce a situation where before a car had been on the road very long a complete rewiring would be needed. This sort of production of deliberately shoddy work seems to be a common tactic of car workers : note, for instance the Ryton workers' denigration of the quality of Chrysler cars during the 'shoddy work' strike of 1973.

The interviewees recalled that in the press shop itself they found that if the panel had the slightest bit of 'shit' on it, the panel would split. The same thing would happen if a 'slug' (dirty grease with bits of metal in it) was on the panel. On occasions these things went unattended to. In another case a round disc of metal was put on to the die—with the result that a sheet of flame leapt up from the panel which then ripped and split. Another interviewee also recalled similar acts which were carried out to get temporary relief from the pressures of the job—'put a slug or something on to a die . . . it wouldn't damage the die . . . the machine would cut out . . . put it down to a crack on the panel.' What was undoubtedly sabotage had, of necessity, to be disguised or explained away in this fashion. The worker quoted above in collaboration with a workmate, instead of put-

372

ting one panel either side of the press, put two, with the result that the panels scored badly and an overload was produced. He was accused by the supervisor of having done it deliberately. He denied this vehemently and in the end 'carelessness' was put down on the report of the incident, but the worker said 'we knew what we'd done. We accepted responsibility for carelessness as opposed to sabotage.'

It emerges quite clearly from the interviews that the amount of scrap generated in a plant may well be an important, but frequently unacknowledged, indicator of industrial conflict. The deliberate generation of scrap was in these cases a tactic to earn respite from the demands of externally imposed work loads. When asked whether he had ever seen good panels thrown down the scrap shute when an operator couldn't keep up with the flow of production, this worker replied :

'Yes, yes. Yeah, but on those occasions it was a question that the . . . it generally came in the last hour and a half of a shift, and one tended to find that the operator on the front of a job could go faster than the guy on the trim . . . so there would be a build up of stock coming from the first person and then you'd generally find that the guy on the trim . . . he'd tend to throw panels, good panels, down the scrap shute.'

Another version of sabotage practised by these workers was what could be called sabotage by default. Here defective jobs not deliberately caused by workers were allowed to go unreported to the supervision. Two of the interviewees said that on many occasions they let the job go on when they knew things were going wrong. One of them ignored a succession of split panels for about an hour—even though he was meant to tell the foreman. Another interviewee gives impressive testimony to the fact that on some occasions the supervision and even higher management failed to take action against poor quality work even though they knew of its existence. When asked whether he knew of cases of workers carrying on working when something was wrong, he said that when he was working on the quarter panels for the Capri, quality control was stopping the job 'every five minutes'. He estimated that in 24 hours 'over 2,000 had gone through defective. . . . It was a die fault, you know. Not an operator's fault. It had nothing to do with the operator. The operator could see the fault in the panel, the quality control could see the fault in the panel. They had the general foreman of the quality control down, and the person who had the last word at all levels was either the production supervisor or the general foreman of production, and he allowed it to be passed. It went over to the assembly. The assembly kicked up about it, and again it was management who turned round and said 'let it go through.' So, O.K., we were aware panels were going through defective . . . I mean, y'know, the big laugh—was the sign "Quality Depends on You"—when in point of fact it didn't. It depended on the people in top management—they defined what was quality and what wasn't.'

Another version of sabotage, again carried out to get some respite from the job—under M.D.W. you have a standard output to reach in a day—was for an operator to 'fiddle' the number of panels or whatever was being produced. The number of items produced were recorded by a clock. When asked whether he had been involved in fiddling the clocks the reply of the worker quoted above was 'Yeah, oh Christ, yeah' and he proceeded to list the ways of doing it. The other two workers quoted above were equally forthcoming with details on this point. It was also pointed out that fiddling was so widespread that in one Ford Bulletin to supervisors it was stated that although stock figures (calculated by adding up what was on the clocks) stated that there was £½ million worth of panels in stock, in reality there was next to nothing.

What were the underlying causes of and motives behind these acts of sabotage? Two of those interviewed said that 'they can be defined in one word—monotony.' One of them held that it was basically a spontaneous and individual response to that monotony. But the other felt that although sabotage was usually not premeditated there was often a good deal of interaction between workers about it, with exchange of opinion about the best way of doing particular things, or suggestions for new forms of sabotage. The third interviewee, who had worked for Ford for four and a half years and who had been a shop steward for part of this time, was of the opinion that sabotage in his experience was :

'basically a secretive, small-scale operation. It wasn't sort of a planned operation, as such. We weren't even going into work with the idea or the intention of cutting down the line you know.'

When asked whether only small numbers of workers committed acts of sabotage he said :

'In that way, yeah, y'know, on purpose, I mean obviously, I honestly believe it was the spontaneous guys y'know—the guys that take part in everything—and who sort of do their own thing in respect of the job . . .'

He went on to talk about the crucial question of whether those who committed acts of industrial sabotage had to keep what they were doing secret from their workmates. He took a specific example of a worker in the press shop who deliberately pulled an electrical lead out of the press—an action which to his surprise produced massive sparks and sheets of flame : 'in that particular instance that particular person could have killed himself' and 'the actual gains in that case were minimal.' Pulling that lead was, he felt, a reaction to the frustration of the job and as such 'It was a reflection of something we all felt . . . he made a stand.' Asked specifically whether a worker who commits an act of sabotage will keep it secret from his workmates he commented :

'I think it's like a criminal code. Y'know. You know what goes on but you don't say nothing. Actually in this particular instance we knew what he was going to do—because he'd discussed it with about three or four of us, and possibly seven or eight . . . and we didn't give a fuck . . . no one was going to stop him. The only way we would have to stop would have been if we realised what was going to happen. . . . In this case it wasn't a spontaneous sort of reaction. It had developed over a few hours. In this few hours he'd sort of planned . . . and what of course he wasn't to know was the actual reaction due to that sabotage.'

Asked if workers *ever* objected to acts of sabotage carried out by others he replied : 'No, no. If they do they don't talk about it. . . . Again this is what I was saying before about the criminal code. You know what goes on, but you don't say nothing. The only time you would have got a reaction would have been if it was going to go against them. If it was not going to be beneficial.' For him industrial sabotage was an entirely rational response in the context of that particular working environment:

'These are sensible and mature sort of people—in their own outside environment these sorts of acts of vandalism and sabotage would never be tolerated. But in the workplace it was a different kettle of fish. . . . Fords never tended to sort of inspire loyalty. You just don't give a fuck. . . . You weren't interested in the job you were actually performing. You were never made to feel responsible in any manner—so consequently, I think that some people tended to think that if we're going to be treated like children we'll fucking act like children. You know, they tended to talk in terms of ignorance is bliss and y'know you just thought fuck it . . . and at times sensible intelligent people became totally ignorant of the situation and consequently reacted in that manner. I imagine, I can only imagine that Fords were responsible. Fords probably killed, mentally, more people in their time than any fucking company. So consequently whatever action was ever taken against them I can feel very humane in favour of the people who performed that action.'

This sort of careful appraisal of the rationality of industrial sabotage as far as the 'saboteurs' themselves are concerned is in sharp contrast, not surprisingly, to managerial responses to sabotage and similar acts. For the managers of car factories, sabotage is no doubt a 'social problem'; for the 'saboteurs' the work itself is the problem. Sabotage is one of the solutions. The managers of car factories can, it seems, see no rationality in sabotage and similar things. Rather they see in it nothing but irrationality, irresponsibility and even lunacy. Some documents from the Ellesmere Port plant of Vauxhall Motors make this quite clear. A notice, for instance, headed 'Waste Bin Fires' which was sent to all Hard Trim Personnel at the plant on January 17, 1975 by the Assistant Production Manager, Car Assembly, contained the following words:

376

'Over the years there have been many fires in the waste bins on the area, a further two last Wednesday night shift. I do not believe that these are accidental, through thoughtlessness or careless behaviour but rather that they are deliberate acts of lunacy, designed to disrupt production.'

This was just one of Vauxhall's 'discipline' problems at the time. A works notice headed 'The Disgrace of Christmas 1974' had been issued by the Plant Manager and Director on January 2nd, 1975. This talked of 'exceptional losses in production and many flagrant abuses of Works Rules during this period. Examples included people arriving late and, in many instances, being drunk, both to the danger of themselves and their fellow workers.' On the nightshift of December 23, 1974 one of the canteens was 'invaded before the lunch break and a large amount of food stolen from the counter.' On Christmas Eve there was 'a lack of willingness to work'—by mid-afternoon the plant was 'virtually empty'. The Plant Manager then spelt out seven points to the miscreants : they had let themselves down, they had let the Company down, they had let their fellow workers down, they had let the unions down, they had 'further reduced the Company's ability' to meet the future, they had let the North West down, and finally 'Those of you who were involved should be ashamed.'

In similar vein, in November 1974, after a former Halewood employee had been fined in court for an act of sabotage, a Ford spokesman said : 'I don't know if this man was frustrated by his job, but this was an act of vandalism.' He added, interestingly, that 'We have had a few isolated incidents similar to this, but when you consider there are 14,000 people working here it isn't a major problem.' The 'act of vandalism' in question was described as follows in the *Daily Express* :

'Production belt boredom got too much for car worker Eric Lawson. So he decided to break the monotony. It cost Fords 50 cars and £6,000 in lost profits and left 2,000 men idle for an hour while engineers carried out repairs. For the 22-year-old operative took his unofficial break by jamming an 18-inch strip of metal into the assembly line gears. Yesterday Lawson paid the price of bringing the wheels of industry to a halt. He

377

was fined £30 with £21 compensation and ordered to pay £10 costs at Huyton, Lancs. Lawson of Downing Street, Bootle, pleaded guilty of causing £21 worth of damage to the production line at Fords Halewood plant.'

Lawson's act had been a dramatic parting shot. He was leaving the employment of the company that day. He told the court, no doubt with an eye on the size of the fine that the judge was about to give him, that 'The job just got on top of me and I did it on the spur of the moment. I am very sorry.'[42]

Professor Hans Eysenck, of the Institute of Psychiatry at the University of London, was asked to comment on Lawson's case. He said that he thought Lawson's act was 'an understandable reaction from a man chained to a production line and it is a very serious problem for British industry. It was rather a drastic step to take, but I can understand a person becoming so frustrated by a boring job like this that he resorts to vandalism.' He went on to recommend that car firms considered the introduction of the autonomous assembly group approach to car production, as already used by Swedish firms such as Saab and Volvo. 'This,' he observed, 'has certainly helped to combat production line boredom and has actually increased efficiency.'[43] The changes at Saab and Volvo have certainly attracted a good deal of attention but much of it has been superficial. Volvo, for instance, introduced its particular job enrichment scheme in 1970 in a context of labour turnover on its final assembly lines of 55 per cent per year. With the cost of training each worker standing at £40 this meant that the former production methods in Volvo were highly expensive even before any other production costs were incurred. Although Volvo was not troubled by strikes, it felt that the labour turnover problem was sufficiently important to merit making the changes. It was felt that the increased production costs under the new methods (estimated at increasing unit car costs by 10 per cent) could be offset by the savings made on the reduction of labour turnover. But it must be remembered that the previous form of assembly in Volvo was very different from, and not comparable to, that in the mass production British plants, which are geared to high-speed output and low unit costs. The time taken to produce each Volvo car under the old method was already a good deal longer—9 hours—than the less than $2\frac{1}{2}$ hours in the most modern mass production plants. If the Volvo scheme does reduce absenteeism and labour turnover and there are no strikes it might just bring about savings per car. But it is highly doubtful that autonomous assembly groups would save money in British Leyland or in Ford, the possible savings in unit costs through the absence of strikes and sabotage notwithstanding.

D. G. Rhys has pointed out that costly 'workshop' methods such as Volvo may mean that 'the only efficient locations for motor manufacture will be where the need to escape from poverty is enough to compensate for assembly line tedium, areas such as Spain, South America, or Japan.'[44] This stricture did not, however, prevent Mr. Graham Edwards of the University of Manchester Institute of Science and Technology from warning the British car industry in 1972 that it would continue to suffer from serious strikes unless it replaced 'the mindless drudgery of the assembly line with team production.' He then gave the British car firms about one year's grace to follow the Swedish example. 'They are lucky in that they have been granted this time by the present unemployment situation which has taken some of the steam out of their labour relations situation.'[45] Since 1972 things have got considerably worse as far as the bargaining strength of British car workers is concerned, and consequently, British car firms have had their period of grace considerably extended. Commenting in June 1975 on the effects of the changed market situation Huw Beynon quite correctly pointed out that in the motor industry :

'The air is full of talk of "rationalisation", and our attention is no longer drawn towards the tedium of assembly-line work. John Clare, writing on the Chrysler strike in the *Observer*, could say that it is "not news that the work [there] is hot, noisy and boring," that there is nothing unusual about dropping 72 axles an hour off a moving belt. (18 May). And he is right. Of course, it's not unusual; certainly it's no longer news, because the problem now is inflation and depression. That's the news. Save the ship before we all sink. The car worker will have to wait : let's get the economy straight, and we can begin to talk about "monotony" again.'[46]

N*

All this of course makes the likelihood of the British car firms following the Swedish example less and less probable. Changes will only be made if they can be made to pay, and if the social forces demanding change are silenced change becomes unnecessary as far as the car firms are concerned. Much more likely than any reversion to production methods of the pre-assembly line car industry is the further automation of some aspects of car production. This, of course, will be costly in terms of capital equipment, but it should enable the firms to reduce costs per car since, for one thing, it will be labour saving. A number of Japanese firms have taken this path, and as such have followed the example of General Motors' allegedly 'fully automated' plant at Lordstown. Sabotage has been carried out and job enrichment talked about here too.

The most highly automated car plant in the world is the General Motors plant at Lordstown, Ohio. In spite of the fact that '26 bellows-like armed robots that can bend around corners and that make some 520 welds in each car' were installed in the plant, human beings were by no means dispensed with. Several thousand, mainly young (average age 24–25) workers were employed in the plant, and many of them were employed on the plant's assembly lines. The lines were the fastest in the United States, capable of turning out up to 100 cars an hour. The partly automated line began operation in 1970 at what turned out to be less than full capacity. After about a year's 'running-in' period some of the plant's original labour force was laid off, and the remaining labour force had now to contend with increased workloads and general speed-up. According to *Time* magazine:

'The grievances got little response from G.M., but as they grew, so did the number of damaged cars.'

The plant's repair lot which could hold 2,000 cars often became full—and workers were sent home. In October 1971 an assembly line control box shed was set on fire—thus stopping the line. To quote *Time* again: 'Autos regularly roll off the line with slit upholstery, scratched paint, dented bodies, bent gear-shift levers, cut ignition wires, and loose or missing bolts. In some cars, the trunk key is broken off right in the lock, thereby jamming it.'[47] Shortly afterwards, Albin B. Anderson, the general manager of the Lordstown plant added to this list : 'caving-in of radios, scratching of instruments in the instrument panels . . . tearing glove-box doors, etc.'[48] To intensify their campaign the Lordstown workers, through their U.A.W. Local, leaked a story to the press charging that General Motors was sending defective Vegas to its dealers. The president of the union local made it clear that this leak was a part of their campaign to get concessions from the company. Money was not an issue. What the workers wanted was the revision of the work rules, which would involve increasing the labour force and eliminating some small jobs extra to their main one. The workers claimed that these 'chores' 'rush them as the autos move by at an average of one every 36 seconds.' General Motors had, apparently, added these chores 'partly in the hope of alleviating the mind-numbing boredom of endlessly doing just one task.' (!) The comments of a *Time* journalist who had talked to both sides on this issue are worth repeating :

'There has been much talk of "job enrichment", assigning a worker more tasks in order to give him a sense of fulfilment. But some union leaders charge that "enriching" a worker's job by making him do two jobs each 30 times an hour is a "con". At Lordstown the workers want more time to do their single, simple job—and that is certainly the opposite of what many outsiders think they want. Many workers complain that they do not want to work as hard as they are being asked to do. It may well be that what were considered ordinary norms in the past are no longer acceptable.'[49]

In February 1972 the Lordstown workers voted almost unanimously for a strike—which in the event lasted for three weeks. The strike attracted a great deal of attention—not least because of the fact that General Motors was the world's largest corporation. It had been built up under the direction of Alfred P. Sloan Jr., who in his own way, made a contribution to the car industry and to the techniques of industrial capitalism as great as that of his great competitor Henry Ford. Sloan had pioneered and developed to a high pitch the archetypal techniques of market expansion adopted by giant capitalist firms. Right from the early days of G.M., Sloan had developed the practice of the annual model change, and had realised that if more cars were to be sold (and more money to be made) then G.M. had to create its own vast consumer credit system. Sloan had once said, entirely correctly from his point of view, that 'The primary object of the corporation was to make money, not just to make motor cars.'[50] One writer, who has written a detailed account of the Lordstown story in order to highlight what she calls 'the decline of the auto-industrial age', has suggested that G.M. at Lordstown on its Vega project for all its appearance of having made a revolutionary departure from the usual methods of car production, had in fact merely refined and intensified the use of the combination of 'Fordism' (the extreme division of labour on the production process) and 'Sloanism' (the hard-nosed process of expanding the markets for the product). Lordstown's robot welders were not new : Henry Ford had developed them in 1931 (it should also be noted that the Lordstown robots took the more interesting jobs away from people); and the second alleged innovation was factory planning, but this too was entirely 'Fordist'. Emma Rothschild has written that 'The major principle of Lordstown production is the speed-up, as developed in the 1910s.'[51] If in reality the Lordstown production process was merely the old system writ large, then it is perhaps appropriate too that George Morris, G.M.'s vice-president at the time of the strike, six months after the strike (which was widely interpreted in the American press as being a revolt of youth against work and work discipline) said that the strike and its prelude of sabotage and the rest was basically not due to anything new. It was due rather to what he regarded, quite rightly, as a common feature of industrial capitalism in the 20th century; the 'consolidation of operations'. This consolidation of operations at Lordstown involved three things which in the circumstances were bound to lead to trouble : 1) manpower reductions, 2) disciplinary actions, and 3) negotiation of new local agreements. Each of these led to responses from the workers which were, in Morris's words, 'expected', 'typical' and 'old hat'. Strikes over working conditions were, then, a normal consequence of inevitable corporate reorganisation, and were not 'really related' to 'boredom on the assembly line' or 'the age of the workers'. George Morris could document this from the history of the firm itself—looking at the historical record of G.M. he found evidence that strikes were especially frequent after consolidation and reorganisation of operations. In all in General Motors, 'ten consolidations have produced eight strikes. It should be apparent, to employ an understatement, that these consolidations are difficult to accomplish without conflict.'[52]

Sabotage is neither new to American industry, nor unique to Lordstown. It seems to have been a long-time accompaniment of assembly line production. In 1948 one writer recalled how American workers 'used to fight the speed-up. When it got over sixty say, someone would just accidentally drop a bolt in the line and as soon as it worked its way round to the end, bang, the line would stop. Then there'd be a delay and everyone would take his break.'[53] But it seems to have been the case that the use of sabotage increased from the late 1960s, especially in car plants. In July 1970 *Fortune* magazine said of the American motor industry that :

'in some plants worker discontent has reached such a degree that there has been overt sabotage. Screws have been left in brake drums, tool handles have been welded into fender compartments (to cause mysterious, unfindable and eternal rattles), paint scratched, and upholstery cut.'

Tom Cagle, a worker at the General Motors Fremont, California plant, in his *Life in an Auto Plant* provides vivid documentation of worker resistance to the inevitable speed-up during the model changes. Cuts in manning levels and lay offs were common, and it was up to the foremen to impose speed-up on those workers who remained. Repair work mounts up : 'When the foreman then angrily tries to bring pressure on the workers, he often gets only broken tools, grievances, and more repair work.' But still the pace mounts :

'During the second week after model changeover, management becomes impatient to knock the stops out of the line and let her roll. This produces some interesting results. A flood of "cripples" comes rolling off the end of the assembly line, loose fans fly off through the radiator and hood, electrical harness shorts and burns, gas lines leak and produce fires. Roll test inspectors become nervous as these cars literally fall apart and blow up on the roll test. Cars have fenders, hoods, bumpers, doors, and hard trim missing. Operators have put two gallons of gas into a car only to discover that the gas tank was missing. Oil leaks are common . . .'[54]

Similarly, Bill Watson in his pamphlet *Counter-Planning on the Shop Floor*, gives examples, from his own experience in a Detroit car plant in the late 1960s, of organised sabotage which was carried out as a protest against a managerial decision to produce what the workers regarded as an ill-designed new six cylinder model. After numerous suggestions made by workers as to how the car should have been improved, all were rejected and a campaign of systematic and organised sabotage was embarked upon. Watson records that the initial acts were mainly the misassembling or even omitting of parts 'on a larger-than-normal scale' so that the cars would not pass inspection. Deals were struck between inspection and assembly and trim workers. Unmachined spots on motor heads were not welded; gaskets were left out; faulty or wrong size sparking plugs were fitted; bolts were left loose in the motor assembly; plug wires were assembled in the wrong firing order. These and other things, not surprisingly, led to a sharp rise in the number of cars which failed to pass inspection. Sabotage tactics were also applied to V-8 models. The number of motors awaiting repairs increased to such an extent that the plant had to be closed.

Watson is of the opinion that in the case of both models the workers had engaged in 'an organised struggle for control over the planning of the product of labour; its manifestation through sabotage was only secondarily important.' Having given those examples above illustrating the use of sabotage as a 'means of reaching out for more control over one's work' he goes on next to detail the use of sabotage 'as a means of controlling one's working "time"'. This sort of 'sabotage of the rationalisation of time', the 'shutdown of production', is in his opinion not, as popularly thought, 'a rare conflict'. Rather it happens regularly and at some times of the year, for instance in the summer months, hourly. He writes:

'The shutdown is nothing more than a device for controlling the rationalization of time by curtailing overtime planned by management. . . . Sabotage is also exerted to shut down the process to gain extra time before lunch and, in some areas, to lengthen group breaks or allow friends to break at the same time. In the especially hot months of June and July, when the temperature rises to 115 degrees in the plant and remains there for hours, such sabotage is used to gain free time to sit with friends in front of a fan or simply away from the machinery.'

To do these things Watson says that 'a plant-wide rotating sabotage programme' was planned by groups of workers with each worker in a group of 50 being allocated a period of 20 minutes at some time in a two week period. When an individual's allocated time came along 'he did something to sabotage the production process in his area, hopefully shutting down the entire line. No sooner would the management wheel in a crew to repair or correct the problem area than it would go off in another key area.' In this way the entire plant could usually sit it out for from 5 to 20 minutes of each hour for a number of weeks on account of a stopped line, or a line going past with no units on it. This sort of sabotage—a resistance to the managerially desired rationalisation of a worker's time—has, clearly, as its object the creation of more free time at work. This sort of common activity is one which 'counteracts capital's prerogative of ordering labour's time' and as such

'it is a profound organized effort by labour to undermine its own existence as "abstract labour power". The seizing of quantities of time for getting together with friends and the amusement of activities ranging from card games to reading and walking around the plant to see what other areas are doing is an important achievement for labourers. Not only does it demonstrate the feeling that much of the time should be organized by the workers themselves, but it also demonstrates an existing animosity toward the practice of constantly postponing all of one's desires and inclinations so the rational process of production can go on uninterrupted. The frequency of planned shutdowns in production increases as more opposition exists toward such rationalization of the workers' time.'[55]

It must be remembered that the nature of the technology and the production process in a car factory, involving as it does virtually continuous production externally determined by the speed of the assembly line, means that if workers are to resist the full brunt of the nature of their work they must either slow down the belt or they must stop it completely. The Halewood workers mentioned above eventually managed to get themselves in a situation where they could ensure that agreed line speeds were maintained. British Leyland workers under piecework were, through their bargaining over piece rates, engaged in fixing the intensity of work at a temporarily acceptable, optimum level. The Detroit workers were stopping the line by causing 'shut-downs'. All these workers were basically seeking to do the same thing through different means. In other jobs, where work speeds or work intensity are not so tightly determined by the technology of the job, workers need not destroy or disable machinery in order to assert some control over their own work intensity—they can, as has been shown on countless occasions in this study, sabotage the job merely by restricting their output or by 'ca'canny.' These forms of sabotage are as radical and as effective in diminishing the level and the rate of surplus value expropriated from the worker as the superficially more dramatic form of machine-breaking. This, as we saw at the beginning, is precisely what Emile Pouget said. It is with another passage from Pouget's classic *Le Sabotage* that we shall conclude :

'. . . sabotage is in the social war what guerrilla warfare is in national wars : it flows from the same feelings, responds to the same necessities and has identical consequences in workers' minds.

'We know to what extent guerrilla warfare develops individual courage, daring and decisiveness—the same can be said for sabotage : it keeps the workers going, it prevents them from getting bogged down in a pernicious flabbiness, and as it necessitates permanent and ceaseless action, it has the happy result of developing the spirit of initiative, of accustoming the working class to self-activity, and of stimulating combativity.'[56]

NOTES

1. See R. B. McKersie *Changing Wage Payment Systems*, Royal Commission on Trade Unions and Employers Associations, *Research Paper 11*, London 1968, pp. 49-50, and H. A. Turner, G. Clack and G. Roberts *Labour Relations in the Motor Industry* (London 1967) pp. 98-99.
2. Huw Beynon *Working For Ford* (Pelican 1973) p. 20.
3. Turner, Clack and Roberts, op. cit., p. 100.
4. Quoted in T. Cliff *The Employers' Offensive: productivity deals and how to fight them* (London 1970) pp. 52-53.
5. See T. Cliff, op. cit., esp. the section 'Piecework turns on its maker' pp. 46-48 and Stephen Johns *Victimisation at Cowley* (London ? 1974) pp. 24-25.
6. For a good summary of such managerial objections to piecework see D. T. B. North and G. L. Buckingham *Productivity Agreements and Wage Systems* (London 1969) p. 74.
7. Flanders, quoted in Royal Commission on T.U.s and E.A.s, *Research Paper 4*, p. 41.
8. Quoted in S. Johns, op. cit., p. 26.
9. S. Johns, op. cit., pp. 28-29.
10. Ibid., pp. 31-32.
11. Quoted by S. Johns, op. cit., p. 38.
12. See S. Johns, op. cit., Appendix I for the full text of the Agreement.
13. *The Times*, May 15, 1972.
14. Clifford Webb. 'Exit the Villain of the Piecework' in *The Times* November 7, 1972.
15. 'Danger Strings in M.D.W. Deal' in *Socialist Worker* November 18, 1972.
16. All these remarks by Cowley stewards come from 'Politics and the Shop-floor', interview with four Cowley Shop stewards, June 1973, in *New Left Review*, 80, July-August 1973, pp. 32-35.
17. The full text of Thornett's article appears in S. Johns, op. cit., pp. 97-100.
18. K. Coates and T. Topham *The New Unionism* (Pelican 1974 edn.) p. 84.
19. Quoted in Topham 'Productivity Bargaining' in *Trade Union Register* (London 1969) p. 86. Topham has slightly modified his views on the merits of P.B.R. versus M.D.W.—see the table of advantages and disadvantages of either system given in his *The Organised Worker*, pp. 68-69. For a more detailed treatment of the merits of the respective systems—coming down strongly in favour of M.D.W.—see Bill Conboy *Pay at Work* (Society of Industrial Tutors, London 1976).
20. R. B. McKersie and L. C. Hunter *Pay, Productivity and Collective*

Bargaining (London 1973), p. 289. A similar point is made by T. Lupton, cited in D. T. B. North and G. L. Buckingham, op. cit., p. 78.
21. 'Politics and the Shop-floor' in *N.L.R.*, 80, p. 33.
22. See R. B. McKersie *Changing Wage Payment Systems*.
23. Quoted in Edward Laxton and Philip Mellor 'Mission Impossible, Say Men' in *Daily Mirror* November 24, 1975. The same issue of the Mirror also carried the Cowley story on its front page under the headline 'Not So Fast!'
24. *Daily Mirror* November 24, 1975.
25. Richard Hyman *Strikes* (London 1972) p. 13.
26. *Liverpool Daily Post*, March 10, 1971.
27. *Liverpool Daily Post*, March 10, 1971.
28. *Liverpool Echo*, March 10, 1971.
29. *Liverpool Echo*, March 10, 1971.
30. *Liverpool Echo*, March 13, 1971.
31. *Liverpool Echo*, March 17, 1971.
32. See Laurie Taylor and Paul Walton 'Industrial Sabotage: Motives and Meanings' in S. Cohen ed. *Images of Deviance* (Pelican 1971) pp. 238-239.
33. Mark Fore *Strategy for Industrial Struggle* (London n.d.) p. 5.
34. D. G. Rhys 'Employment, efficiency and labour relations in the motor industry' in *Industrial Relations Journal*, Vol. 5, No. 2, Summer 1974, pp. 11 and 18.
35. See, for instance, G. Clack *Industrial Relations in a British Car Factory*, p. 90, Turner, Clack and Roberts *Labour Relations in the Motor Industry*, esp. the section on 'Production stresses, Effort Bargaining, and Management', pp. 88ff, and Graham Turner *The Car Makers* (Pelican 1964). The work of Beynon on Ford clearly illustrates worker-hostility to management's unilateral control of the speed of the track.
36. R. B. McKersie, op. cit., p. 52.
37. R. B. McKersie, op. cit., p. 51.
38. H. Beynon *Working for Ford*, p. 134.
39. Ibid., pp. 136-137.
40. Ibid., p. 139.
41. Ibid., p. 141.
42. 'Spanner in a Car Works' in *Daily Express* November 15, 1974.
43. Ibid.
44. D. G. Rhys, op. cit., p. 16. I have drawn heavily here on Rhys's section 'Job Enrichment: a current fad or a real issue?', pp. 15-17. For another account, reaching broadly similar conclusions, see Robert Taylor, 'The Volvo Way of Work' in *New Society* April 15, 1976.
45. Quoted in A. F. L. Deeson, 'Autonomous Assembly Groups'.
46. Huw Beynon, 'Car Making: an industry at war with its workers' in *New Society* June 12, 1975. In this article Beynon also criticises the car workers' unions for their failure to attend to the real problems faced by car workers. Jack Jones's reply, a defence of the unions' activities, can be found in the letter columns of *New Society*, June 26, 1975.
47. 'Sabotage at Lordstown?' in *Time* February 7, 1972.
48. *The Times* March 16, 1972, quoted in Ken Weller *The Lordstown Struggle, Solidarity* pamphlet No. 45. Similar things have been hap-

pening in Australia. In 1973 at Ford's Broadmeadows plant over 10,000 dollars worth of damage was caused. In 1971 the Australian R.A.C. tested 672 new cars and found nearly 3,000 faults: see 'Explosion in Australia' in *Solidarity* pamphlet *Motor Bulletin No. 1, Ford Struggle 1973.*

49. *Time* February 7, 1972.
50. Emma Rothschild *Paradise Lost: the Decline of the Auto-industrial Age* (London 1974 edn.) pp. 38-39. See also Alfred P. Sloan *My Years With General Motors* (first pub. 1963, London 1967 edn.) esp. Ch. 13 'The Annual Model Change', and Ch. 17 'G.M.A.C.'—General Motors Acceptance Corporation. Sloan points out (p. 326) that G.M.A.C. extended between 16 and 18 per cent of all credit in connection with car sales in the U.S.A., and that G.M.'s incursion into consumer credit began in 1919 when the banks were reluctant to help customers buy cars—'so some other means had to be found if the auto industry was to sell cars in large numbers.'
51. Rothschild, op. cit., p. 107.
52. Rothschild, op. cit., pp. 121-122.
53. K. G. J. C. Knowles *Strikes,* p. 15, quoting Wahl in *Modern Review,* 1948.
54. Tom Cagle *Life in an Auto Plant* (New York 1970) pp. 5 and 8.
55. Bill Watson *Counter-Planning on the Shop Floor,* originally published by *Radical America,* reprinted by Anarchist-Syndicalist Alliance, London, c. 1971.
56. Emile Pouget *Le Sabotage* (Paris, n.d., ? 1909) pp. 32-33. My translation.

Index

Other Spokesman Titles on Labour History

BRITISH LABOUR AND THE RUSSIAN REVOLUTION
Ed. Ken Coates

This book is a complete reproduction of the *Daily Herald's* report on the 1917 Leeds Convention, as it was reprinted by the Pelican Press. There are illustrations and a full explanatory introduction by Ken Coates.

"you should get this well-produced and well-bound pamphlet."
        - AUEW Journal

Cloth £1.10   Paper £0.40

THE INDUSTRIAL SYNDICALIST

During the years of 1910/11 when the syndicalist upheaval, which transformed whole sections of the British Trade Union Movement, was being seeded, *The Industrial Syndicalist* brought together some of the most effective labour organisers of the time and had an immediate and electric impact. Its republication is a milestone in the re-discovery of the roots of the modern workers' control movement and casts a vivid light on some of the key episodes in labour history.

The Industrial Syndicalist was edited by Tom Mann whose name is a by-word in the British Labour Movement; this collection has an authoritative introduction by Geoff Brown, who admirably explores the context in which Mann was operating.

Cloth £4.00   Paper £1.75

THE SYNDICALIST

This facsimile edition makes available again some of the epic pages in British Labour History.

Tom Mann and Guy Bowman (the first editor of the paper) had worked their way into the production of a regular newspaper by issuing a monthly series of pamphlets (see *The Industrial Syndicalist*) which grouped together spokesmen of the labour unrest in several industries and key industrial areas. In its pages were to be found contributions from the authors of *The Miners' Next Step*, expositions of syndicalist doctrine by Mann himself, and news of the early conferences of the Industrial Syndicalist Educational League.

In January 1912 the new journal came out with a version of the famous "Don't Shoot!" open letter to British soldiers. Bowman was arrested, and so, shortly after, was Tom Mann. Their trials were major events, and both men received stiff sentences. The early issues of the paper were thus compelled to preoccupy themselves with reports and agitational articles about the imprisonment of its founders, including the text of a fascinating letter to *The Times*, signed, and judging by its style, at least partly written, by Bertrand Russell.

The subsequent convulsive development of the syndicalist movement, revealed in part in the evolution of this newspaper, is carefully explained and analysed in a scholarly introduction by Geoff Brown. With the republication of this vital source material, the record will be at least partly set straight. British Syndicalism still awaits its definitive historian, but *The Syndicalist* will reveal something of the importance of the movement for which it spoke.

Limited edition   Cloth £12.00

DEMOCRACY IN THE MINES
Ed. Ken Coates

The miners of Great Britain started the historic debate on industrial democracy with these firecracker pamphlets, first circulated in the heroic age of Tom Mann and Noah Ablett. They are highly relevant to the current debate on the key political issue of the 1970s.

"The sheer vitality shines through" – *Tribune*

Cloth £3.00   Paper £0.75

Some Other Spokesman Titles

THE NEW WORKER CO-OPERATIVES

Ed. Ken Coates

The work-in at Upper Clyde Shipbuilders in 1971 stimulated a whole series of factory occupations where redundancies and closures had been declared. Some groups of workers involved in these struggles conceived the notion of re-activating their enterprises as workers' co-operatives.

The book tells the story of three of the best-known of these ventures: Triumph Meriden, Kirkby Manufacturing and Engineering and the *Scottish Daily News*. It portrays the obstacles with which the workers were faced and the extent to which they were able to overcome them. Developments in these enterprises since they became operational are carefully examined.

Tony Benn explains the thinking behind his encouragement of these new co-ops which leads him to much more optimistic conclusions than the Webbs on the capacity of worker co-ops to survive. Richard Fletcher points the way forward for workers' co-operatives while Ken Coates relates co-operatives to the wider aspirations of the trade union and labour movement.

There is a useful bibliography and an Index.

Cloth £5.50   Paper £2.25

INEQUALITY

The Complete Evidence of the Transport and General Workers' Union to the Royal Commission on the Distribution of Income and Wealth which was researched with great thoroughness and ingenuity by John Hughes at the Ruskin Trade Union Research Unit. It represents a powerful indictment of the great inequalities that continue to exist in Britain today and in particular of the privileges enjoyed by wealthy shareholders and company directors.

Cloth £5.50   Paper £2.50

A SHOP STEWARD'S GUIDE TO WORKPLACE HEALTH AND SAFETY
by Denis Gregory and Joe McCarty

A wealth of factual and statistical data make the book indispensable for reference as well as compelling reading.

"A useful and stimulating booklet. Most of its judgements seem to be eminently sensible and right."
– *Labour Research*

"We can highly recommend . . . full of interesting and useful facts and figures."
– *AUEW Journal*

Paper £0.60

Practical Guide to Industrial Relations No. 1

A WORKER'S GUIDE TO THE EMPLOYMENT PROTECTION ACT
by Ivor Clemitson MP

A comprehensive and invaluable handbook for trade unionists, shop stewards and industrial relations practitioners composed by the parliamentary private secretary to the Minister of Employment.

Paper £0.95

Practical Guide to Industrial Relations No. 2

All the titles listed in these pages are available from
**SPOKESMAN BOOKS BERTRAND RUSSELL HOUSE
GAMBLE STREET NOTTINGHAM NG7 4ET**
from whom a complete list together with details of carriage charges etc., can be obtained.